Christian Beginnings

Edinburgh Studies in Religion in Antiquity

Series editors: Matthew V. Novenson, James B. Rives, Paula Fredriksen
Edinburgh Studies in Religion in Antiquity publishes cutting-edge research in religion in the ancient world. It provides a platform for creative studies spanning time periods (classical antiquity and late antiquity), geographical regions (the Mediterranean and West Asia), religious traditions (Greek, Roman, Jewish, Christian and more), disciplines (comparative literature, archaeology, anthropology, and more) and theoretical questions (historical, philological, comparative, redescriptive, and more). Deconstructing literary canons and confessional boundaries, the series considers and questions what we moderns call "religion" as a prominent feature of the human past and a worthy object of historical enquiry.

Advisory Board
Helen Bond, University of Edinburgh
Kimberley Czajkowski, University of Edinburgh
Benedikt Eckhardt, University of Edinburgh
Martin Goodman, University of Oxford
Oded Irshai, Hebrew University of Jerusalem
Timothy Lim, University of Edinburgh
Yii-Jan Lin, Yale University
Candida Moss, University of Birmingham
Paul Parvis, University of Edinburgh
Matthew Thiessen, McMaster University
Philippa Townsend, University of Edinburgh
Greg Woolf, University of California-Los Angeles

Books published in the series
Stanley K. Stowers, *Christian Beginnings: A Study in Ancient Mediterranean Religion*
Elena L. Dugan, *The Apocalypse of the Birds: 1 Enoch and the Jewish Revolt against Rome*
Megan S. Nutzman, *Contested Cures: Identity and Ritual Healing in Roman and Late Antique Palestine*
Matthew T. Sharp, *Divination and Philosophy in the Letters of Paul*

Visit the series webpage: https://edinburghuniversitypress.com/series-edinburgh-studies-in-religion-in-antiquity

Christian Beginnings
A Study in Ancient Mediterranean Religion

Stanley Stowers

EDINBURGH
University Press

Edinburgh University Press is one of the leading university presses in the UK. We publish academic books and journals in our selected subject areas across the humanities and social sciences, combining cutting-edge scholarship with high editorial and production values to produce academic works of lasting importance. For more information visit our website: edinburghuniversitypress.com

© Stanley Stowers, 2024, 2025

Edinburgh University Press Ltd
13 Infirmary Street
Edinburgh EH1 1LT

First published in hardback by Edinburgh University Press 2024

Typeset in 11/13 Bembo Std by
IDSUK (DataConnection) Ltd

A CIP record for this book is available from the British Library

ISBN 978 1 3995 1006 6 (hardback)
ISBN 978 1 3995 1007 3 (paperback)
ISBN 978 1 3995 1009 7 (webready PDF)
ISBN 978 1 3995 1008 0 (epub)

The right of Stanley Stowers to be identified as the author of this work has been asserted in accordance with the Copyright, Designs and Patents Act 1988, and the Copyright and Related Rights Regulations 2003 (SI No. 2498).

Contents

Acknowledgments	vi
Introduction	1

Part I: Everyday Religion and Its Alternatives

1. The Religion of Plant and Animal Offerings Versus the Religion of Meanings, Essences and Textual Mysteries	33
2. Locating the Religion of Associations	57
3. Why "Common Judaism" Does Not Look Like Mediterranean Religion	80

Part II: Paul as Freelance Expert

4. Kinds of Myth, Meals and Power: Paul and the Corinthians	101
5. The Social Formations of Paul and His Romans: Synagogues, Churches and Occam's Razor	142

Part III: Paul's Message and Objectives

6. The Dilemma of Paul's Physics: Features Stoic-Platonist or Platonist-Stoic	159
7. What is Pauline Participation in Christ?	181
8. Paul's Four Discourses about Sin	195
9. Are Paul's Moral Teachings Designed for Ordinary Humans?	217

Part IV: Historians and Critical Historiography

10. The Concept of Community and the History of Early Christianity	233
11. Jesus the Teacher and Stoic Ethics in the Gospel of Matthew	250
12. The Secrets of the Gods and the End of Interpretation	267

Bibliography	278
Ancient Sources Index	300
Subject Index	306

Acknowledgments

The basis for this book lies in articles written over many years for whom I owe thanks to numerous individuals who cannot be named here due to their sheer number. My first thanks goes to the editorial board of the Edinburgh Studies in Religion in Antiquity: Paula Fredriksen, Matthew Novenson and James Rives. Without their encouragement I would not have published this volume. These three also stand as pioneering and exemplary models of scholarly excellence. I am extremely grateful to Matt Novenson, who drew on funds available to him to make possible bringing the styles of the several articles into uniformity. Without that work I would not have published this book. And I thank Ryan Collman for his expert work on this task. Finally, I thank the two anonymous reviewers who encouraged publication, and Rachel Bridgewater, Senior Commissioning editor for Classics and Ancient History and Isobel Birks, Assistant Editor in those areas, for their efficient and expert work.

* * *

The chapters in this volume have been reprinted with varying degrees of revision from the following publications and copyright holders.

Chapter Two reprints "Locating the Religion of Associations" from *Re-Making the World: Christianity and Categories: Essays in Honor of Karen L. King*, (2019) ed. Taylor G. Petrey used with the permission of Mohr Siebeck.

Chapter Three reprints from "Why 'Common Judaism' Does not Look like Mediterranean Religion," from *Strength to Strength: Essays in Honor of Shaye J. D. Cohen* (2018) ed. Michael L. Satlow, BJS 363, 235–55, with permission from Brown Judaic Studies.

Chapter Four reprints "Kinds of Myth, Meals and Power: Paul and the Corinthians," from *Redescribing Paul and the Corinthians* (2011), 105–49, ed. Ron Cameron and Merrill P. Miller, with permission of the Society of Biblical Literature.

Chapter Five reprints "The Social Formations of Paul and His Romans," from *A Most Reliable Witness: Essays in Honor of Ross Shepard Kraemer* (2015), 77–87, ed. Susan A. Harvey, Nathaniel DesRosiers, et al., BJS 358, with Permission from Brown Judaic Studies.

Chapter Six reprints "The Dilemma of Paul's Physics: Features Stoic-Platonist or Platonist-Stoic?" from *Stoicism to Platonism: The Development of Philosophy 100 BCE-100 CE* (2017) ed. Troels Engberg Pederson. Copyright is held by Cambridge University Press; reprinted with permission.

Chapter Seven reprints "What is Pauline Participation in Christ," from *New Views of Jewish and Christian Self-Definition: Essays in Honor of E. P. Sanders* (2008), 352–71, © 2023 by the University of Notre Dame. Reprinted by permission of the publisher.

Chapter Eight reprints "Paul's Four Discourses About Sin," from *Celebrating Paul: Essays in Honor of Jerome Murphy O'Connor, O.P., and Joseph Fitzmyer, S.J.*, ed. Peter Spitaler (Catholic Biblical Quarterly Monograph Series 48; Washington, DC: Catholic Biblical Association of America, 2011), 100–27. Reprinted with permission.

Chapter Nine reprints "Are Paul's Moral Teachings Designed for Ordinary Humans?" from *The Social Worlds of Early Christians: Essays in Honor of L. Michael White* (Brill, 2022). Reprinted with the permission of Brill.

Chapter Ten reprints "The Concept of Community and the History of Early Christianity," *Method and Theory in the Study of Religion* 23 (2011), 238–56. Reprinted with the permission of Brill.

Chapter Eleven reprints "Jesus as Teacher and Stoic Ethics in the Gospel of Matthew," from *Stoicism in Early Christianity*, eds. Tuomus Rasmus, Troels Engberg-Pedersen, and Ismo Dunderberg, copyright © 2010. Used by permission of Baker Academic, a division of Baker Publishing Group.

Chapter Twelve reprints "The Secrets of the Gods and the End of Interpretation," from *Tra pratiche e credenze. Traiettorie antropologiche e storiche. Un omaggio ad Adriana Destro*, ed. C. Gianotto and F. Sbardella, (Morcelliana, 2017), 335–46. Reprinted with the permission of Editrice Morcelliana.

INTRODUCTION

Gifts Received:
An Autobiographical Introduction

I beg the pardon of my readers for indulging in some autobiographical reflection. I justify the endeavor because I am often asked how I came to the approaches that I use and why they have made sense to me. Hopefully, this narrative of a few salient episodes can serve as an orientation to the chapters here that originally spanned many years of my career and varied interests. Looking back, and I realize the ever-present risks of corrupt and selective memory, the questions that have animated me already started taking form in graduate school so that I must credit professors, fellow students and the stirrings of the field at the time for the options available and directions taken.[1] I cannot claim originality.

It was an exciting time when several developments were beginning to shake up the staid areas of New Testament Studies and Patristics. For one, as Abe Malherbe explained to us, some generations of brilliant continental scholarship by individuals steeped in a knowledge of the Greek and Latin texts and cultures had been made to all but disappear with the rise of dialectical theology and the Biblical theology movement from the late 1920s through the 1950s and beyond. The pure Old Testament/Jewish origins of Christianity had only later been corrupted when enveloped by Hellenism. But worse than the ideology was the loss of scholars who had a deep knowledge of the ancient world. As I struggled through my studies at Yale, issue after issue vindicating Malherbe's judgment came to light, even though it was a place that strongly emphasized the "Jewish background" of the New Testament, and Malherbe did not disagree. The Dead Sea Scrolls were much at the center of attention with Nils Dahl and Wayne Meeks among those who taught us that literature. In slightly different ways, all three of our professors taught us to resist the ideologically driven oppositions between Judaism and Hellenism. The message was

---

[1] I should add that the account hits a few key spots and is quite incomplete.

only reinforced by the young Carl Holladay who taught us the importance of Hellenistic Judaism.

The Department of Religious Studies at Yale had only recently separated from the Divinity School, with varied reactions of happiness and unhappiness among faculty.[2] Because of this divorce the question of the place of the study of religion in the non-sectarian university was constantly in the background and often explicit. Before coming to Yale, I already knew that my interests were not in the two dominant approaches to New Testament Studies and early Christianity. Studying with the generous and charismatic Chris Beker made this particularly clear to me. Beneath all of the scientific apparatus of textual historical study was a highly normative enterprise of producing Christian theology. On my view, this came in two major forms. The first explicitly located itself as work from inside the church, either some particular tradition or The Church. The second, especially a European phenomenon, took theology or New Testament Studies to be a kind of disciplinary area like philosophy. It seemed to me that it was more like the production of normative thought for something like Christian civilization. The relatively new phenomenon of religious studies departments was located somewhere among the arts and sciences, the humanities and social sciences, but where exactly should they be conceptually in relation to other areas, methodologically and so on? All of these areas, of course, centrally involve normative commitments, but in quite different ways.

My decision of where to go for doctoral work came down to either the University of Chicago or Yale. A young Jonathan Z. Smith was starting to make a name as a scholar of early Christianity who brought the area into contact with something called the history of religions and the generic study of religion. His article, "The Wobbling Pivot," had made a great impression on me, and Smith's notions of locative and utopian religion stuck with me and have contributed to my work on religion as a social kind and my idea of ancient Mediterranean religion.[3] I also liked that Smith's work was informed by philosophy and considered issues about language and knowledge. In my MA work, D. Campbell Wyckoff had us read and discuss Thomas Kuhn's *The Structure of Scientific Revolutions*. I tried to follow the controversy about the book and the encounter convinced me that all areas of knowledge and of the academy needed to justify themselves.

When the chips were down, I did not have the courage to study with Smith. Trained as I was in conventional Biblical Studies, I wanted to enter into that academic world with new approaches, but Smith's work seemed like a different world. At the national meeting of the Society of Biblical Literature

---

[2] In 1963 I believe.
[3] "The Wobbling Pivot," *Journal of Religion* 52 (1972): 134–49; Reprinted in Jonathan Z. Smith, *Map Is Not Territory: Studies in the History of Religions* (Leiden: E. J. Brill, 1978), 88–103.

in 1973, I attended the organizing session for a new group, "The Social World of Early Christianity," co-chaired by Wayne Meeks. The programmatic paper, "The Social Description of Early Christianity," was presented by Jonathan Smith. I then learned about the exciting work that Meeks was doing and his ambitions for social description. Throughout my career, I think that I have been torn between the caution of Meeks and the boldness of Smith, not that I could begin to compare myself to either. I decided that I would go to Yale and seek to write a dissertation with Meeks. In Wayne's seminars we read a great deal of theory from Clifford Geertz and Mary Douglas to Peter Berger. Afterwards I would constantly read widely in social and literary theory. But most of the actual publications of Meeks and the students looked more like conventional social history not unlike that of Ramsay MacMullen's in Classics who was taking in us students in early Christianity and teaching us how to use epigraphical and archeological sources.

Plans changed, however, when I discovered the diatribe in the Malherbe seminar, "The Hellenistic Moralists and the New Testament." The number of books, articles and careers that have found their beginnings in the years of that seminar is astounding. Malherbe seemed to us to be opening up an unexplored continent that often brought the passages in and issues of the early Christian writings to life in striking ways. My dissertation, though heavily philological, argued the case for the social setting of the literature known as "exhibiting the style of the diatribe." I developed an interest in the ancient rhetoric, but what has continued until the present to be most productive for me has been Malherbe's approach to ancient philosophy as a social phenomenon, and not just its usual treatment within the history of ideas. In the 1990s I discovered a perfect fit here with the sociological category of "the intellectual" developed most famously by Max Weber and Pierre Bourdieu.

With my chastened approach and dissertation topic on Romans, I did much course work on Paul. At that time New Testament Studies was dominated by the Bultmann School and by German scholarship. Malherbe, Meeks, Dahl, Holladay and the newly arrived Bentley Layton all looked to other models of scholarship. But Dahl brought something special that would shape my thinking. He introduced us to Scandinavian scholarship that was engaged with the great tradition of German scholarship, but different especially in the way that it treated Judaism and read the New Testament writings without an anti-Jewish straitjacket. I discovered scholars like Johannes Munck, Krister Stendahl, Jacob Jervell and Nils Dahl's own long oeuvre.[4] By the time that I completed the dissertation, I had decided that another book on Romans was needed that would somehow avoid the historically unjustifiable anti-Judaism that was a constant in the scholarship.

---

[4] Jervell was a visiting professor at Yale in 1970.

The Yale years were at the height of the "linguistic turn" that deeply affected all but the most hidebound areas of the humanities and social sciences. Malherbe told me that the faculty liked that I had mentioned my interest in the Russian Formalists in my application. An amazing scene was going on at Yale in French Studies and Comparative Literature. A friend who was a graduate student in Spanish talked me into reading Jacques Derrida's *Of Grammatology*. I found it interesting and had done enough reading in philosophy to be skeptical, but then I did not understand all of it. That encounter and my friend made me into somewhat of a voyeur of the scene with Derrida coming for several months of each year to give seminars with lectures he read that more than challenged my French. Paul de Man, Hillis Miller and other soon-to-be doyens of deconstruction would hold forth and debate. Although deeply excited by the evolving approaches that I only partly understood at the time, I did not take that direction. But one thing that stuck with me from the prevailing literary theory showed up in *Rereading of Romans*.[5] That was the conviction that even the historian needed to read the literature in terms of kinds of imagined readers and consider even the author as a kind of reader.

The dominant models of disciplinarity that enticed involved accepting a literary approach as the queen of the sciences – everything was about text and language – or alternatively social history informed by cultural anthropology (favored by Meeks). I decided that the role of the historian informed by a critical filtering of the literary was the way to go and tried my hand with *Rereading of Romans*. I was still left with a big question that sat in the shadows at Yale, but that burst into the open when I arrived at Brown. What about the study of religion? Was it not a bizarre situation for academics who constantly studied what everyone admitted centrally involved religion to not have thematized and theorized it? Jonathan Z. Smith thought that it was bizarre. Who, for instance, would accept literary studies without thematized and theorized notions of literature and language? The issue was brought home to me when in my last coursework at Yale, the faculty decided that it was somewhat of a scandal for the Department of Religious Studies to not have a course or seminar on the study of religion or on theory of religion. No one came up with a course, so they arranged for a different member of the faculty to meet with the graduate students each week and hold forth on how each person's area reflected the study of religion. The experience was eye-opening to say the least. The struggles of these brilliant scholars to say something coherent was often embarrassing.

Charting some ways that my thought has developed can perhaps best be done by briefly noting the effects of going to Brown, of two Society of Biblical Literature (SBL) units, the topics of sacrifice and the letters of Paul.

---

[5] *A Rereading of Romans: Justice, Jews and Gentiles* (New Haven, CT: Yale University Press, 1994).

Brown in religious studies and in the study of western antiquity was an exceedingly lively place in the 1980s. If Yale at the time did not know how to talk about the study of religion and theory of religion, Brown was the opposite: those were the hot topics. Jacob Neusner at that time wrote persuasively that Judaism should be studied alongside other religions *as religion* and not set apart. John Reeder, Sumner Twiss and others taught and wrote about ways to theorize religion, and worked partly from the philosophy of religion. Nearly every year the department would sponsor a major conference on some topic such as magic and religion and ritual and religion. Professors even in historical areas were expected to relate their particularities to the larger study of religion. I came with a steep learning curve challenging me. The combination was no easy matter in the study of the New Testament and early Christianity where in the larger academy away from Brown I quickly encountered a strong allergic reaction to the combination of theory and conventional historical critical study.

I also had amazing colleagues in the study of Greco-Roman and West Asian antiquity throughout my career at Brown. The colleagues and Brown's emphasis on inter and cross-disciplinary exchange nourished my work, but not much in the direction of theory. After Neusner left, Shaye Cohen, then Saul Olyan and Michael Satlow became valued colleagues in the study of ancient Judaism and the Hebrew Bible following a Brown tradition that went back at least to Horatio Hackett in the 1830s, and J. R. Jewett and David Blaustein teaching Aramaic, Akkadian, Hebrew and Syriac in the 1890s. I formed an especially close working bond with Olyan and we constantly shared graduate students and dissertation advising. The riches were equally abundant from Classics, Egyptology, Old World Archeology and Art and other related areas stimulated by the ongoing Seminar for the Culture and Religion of the Ancient Mediterranean. At the risk of leaving names out, the long-term relations with David Konstan and John Bodel in Classics must be mentioned. The vigorous area of ancient philosophy revolved around Martha Nussbaum and Konstan. Soon after I arrived, Horst Moehring, the senor person in ancient Christianity, died and Stephen Gero had just moved to Tübingen. I was suddenly the senor person and we hired Susan Ashbrook Harvey to focus on later antiquity and then Ross Kraemer to create a strong new graduate program.

None of these great colleagues had a marked interest in theory of religion until Kraemer arrived and my thinking probably would not have flourished had it not happened that no one was available to teach either the undergraduate or the graduate level seminars on theory of religion. I jumped at the opportunity. This seems a good point to interject that I have learned more and received more from the decades of amazing graduate students than any other source. By the early 1990s, I had concluded (along with the students) that none of the reigning theories such as the culture-as-text theory of Clifford Geertz were without serious problems. As the academy gradually moved away from structuralism/post-structuralism, social theory of practice arose as an attempt to solve some of the problems. I became mostly convinced and started thinking of how it might work with religion. The graduate students caught on and organized a symposium with Theodore Schatzki as the main attraction. One of the issues that continually arose was how to individuate religion as a social practice. Later, when I saw the newly established field of cognitive science of religion as providing resources for individuation, the students organized a splendid international conference with Edward Slingerland as the featured speaker.[6]

Several things important to me happened in the first half of the 1990s. I published *Rereading of Romans*, based on a decade or so of thinking about Paul; joined the consultation of two new SBL units; and discovered both practice theory and the cognitive science of religion. One measure of how my thinking has changed comes in the topic of sacrifice that I latched onto in the late 1980s as a cross-disciplinary topic prominent in ethnography, but also in the study of the ancient world including Judaism and Christianity. Such a central religious practice seemed perfect for developing a comparative and theoretical approach to early Christianity situated in its milieu. One result was "Greeks Who Sacrifice and Those Who Do Not," one of my most widely read and cited articles.[7] My current views seen in "The Religion of Plant and Animal Offerings Versus the Religion of Meanings, Essences and Textual Mysteries" (Chapter One in this volume) illustrate how I have changed. My general inspirations for "Greeks Who Sacrifice" were especially cultural anthropology of the era, Jonathan Z. Smith's work, Pierre Bourdieu and Michel Foucault. All were deeply indebted to structuralism and so-called post-structuralism in different ways that I came to see as problematic even while acknowledging their significant contributions. Such things as "schemes of oppositions in the body" and strong semantic holism will not work. I still see powerful relations of animal sacrifice to gender, descent and orders of power, but would now emphasize social indexing and the exploitation of evolved cognitive biases. But I was wrong to pick out animal sacrifice from the larger context of all types of offerings to the gods, and I underemphasized the role of the human imagination about exchange with the gods and similar beings. My recent effort adds minds to human practices and agency, which the earlier theoretical inspirations lacked or thought of in structuralist ways. The earlier piece on sacrifice also lacked a viable theory of religion.

---

[6] "Secrecy and Social Practice from Antiquity to the Present," February 2008. Chapter Fifteen below, "The Secrets of the Gods and the End of Interpretation," was first presented at that conference.

[7] "Greeks Who Sacrifice and Those Who Do Not: Toward an Anthropology of Greek Religion," *The Social World of the First Christians: Essays in Honor of Wayne A. Meeks* ed. L. Michael White and O. Larry Yarbrough (Philadelphia: Fortress, 1995), 293–333.

I had been involved in several SBL groups including "The Social History of Early Christianity," (later ". . . of Formative Christianity and Judaism") but by the early 90s I was disillusioned with what seemed to me either superficial nods to social theory or reiterations of conventional New Testament Studies by tacking on old fashioned social history that changed nothing. Two new units came to my rescue, the first inspired by Abe Malherbe, "Hellenistic Moral Philosophy and Early Christianity."[8] Leaders of the unit included John Fitzgerald, L. Michael White, David Runia, David Konstan and Troels Engberg-Pederson. The tremendously productive group that published several volumes was stimulating partly because it drew in the participation of very many of the greatest scholars in ancient philosophy from Europe and North America. These were sophisticated thinkers who often were also highly knowledgeable in modern philosophy. Without the unit I probably would have allowed my work in the area to have lapsed. My recent "The Dilemma of Paul's Physics: Features Stoic-Platonist or Platonist-Stoic?" (Chapter Six in this volume) shows the continuing fruit of that stimulation.

I began my participation in the second SBL unit with the consultation at the New Orleans meeting of 1996 when I presented a paper for the proposed "Ancient Myths and Modern Theories of Christian Origins." The brilliant idea for the unit thought up by Burton Mack and Jonathan Z. Smith was a kind of major experiment for which theory of religion and wider social theory inspired by Smith's work would be brought together with detailed reconsideration of conventional approaches to Christian texts and notions of beginnings. Although the first years were devoted to gospel's sources and issues where I was less comfortable, I found the debate and discussion about various theoretical approaches tremendously productive for my own thinking and as a place to air that thought. The paper I presented in 1996, since much revised and augmented, became the first of my publications to put together the basic elements of my current theoretical and historical approach (Chapter Four in this volume).

I have continued to use and to be inspired by Smith's scholarship. One area where I went my own way has been in leaving behind the exclusively Neo-Kantian social mind of the structuralist legacy and instead appropriating the evolved mind of the biological sciences seen in the cognitive sciences and mainstream linguistics. I also could not follow the parts of his thought that were too close to Neo-Kantianism in what I considered Smith's inconsistent flirtation with anti-realism. In 1999, a cognitive science of religion conference was held at the University of Vermont.[9] With hosting by Luther Martin, some of us from the Ancient Myths Seminar, including Smith, attended and

---

[8] I believe that the consultation launching the unit was in 1990.
[9] For realist elements in Smith's work see the perceptive article by Kevin Schilbrach, "A Realist Social Ontology of Religion," *Religion* 47 (2017): 161–78.

met to assess where we were in our discussions about theory. At one point a few of us met with the groundbreaking French cognitive anthropologist and linguist Dan Sperber, who had recently published his celebrated *Explaining Culture*.[10] He presented his ideas to our small group with a talk. With Sperber, a former student of Claude Lévi-Strauss who had moved on, and with Lévi-Strauss a central Smith inspiration, the Sperber/Smith encounter was most interesting. At the end of it, I think that only I and Luther Martin were convinced by Sperber. Later Smith, Burton Mack, Ron Cameron, Merrill Miller and I met over amazing locally discovered bargain bottles of the monumental 1989 Produttori Barbaresco that lubricated a long discussion with Smith about everything from Sperber to his relations with Mircea Eliade. Smith was quite open and interested, but extremely cautious about the cognitive psychology. I knew that being persuaded by it meant big changes in my own thinking about theory. For one thing, it meant that the humanist's seat-of-the-pants intuitive thinking could not be the sole arbiter of social theory or historical research.

All along I maintained my interests in the New Testament and especially the letters of Paul, but as time went on Paul more and more came to serve as an exemplar of broader social tendencies and I discovered that because of that framing his thought and social matrix made increasingly better sense. But even by more traditional standards my mind has changed in various ways. Perhaps the biggest flaw in *Rereading of Romans* comes in a central element of Paul's thought that is mostly missing, participation in and assimilation to Christ. I am still convinced of the basic argument of the book and my take on the rhetoric of the letter with tweaks here and there as well as Paul's relations within Judean religion. I think of two reasons for participation missing at that time – what I now consider to be absolutely central to Paul's thought. First, the scholarship dominating then, with the exception of E. P. Sanders's *Paul and Palestinian Judaism,* simply occluded the evidence in the way that it read justification by faith alone as Paul's totalizing obsession. Those you argue against always shape your argument. I later had the opportunity to write "What is Pauline Participation in Christ" for the volume in honor of Ed Sanders (Chapter Eight in this volume).[11]

Second, although I had worked out Paul's notion of Gentile descent from Abraham through participating in Christ by way of God's pneuma in the book, I made only minor use of those ideas, and had not figured out how to account for the wealth of language that suggested both assimilation and a richer

---

[10] *Explaining Culture: A Naturalistic Approach* (Oxford: Blackwell, 1966).
[11] "What is Pauline Participation in Christ," in *New Views of Jewish and Christian Self-Definition: Essays in Honor of E. P. Sanders* (Notre Dame, IN: Notre Dame University Press, 2008), 352–71. Reprinted in *The Holy Spirit: Classic and Contemporary Readings* ed. Eugene Rogers (Hoboken, NJ: Wiley-Blackwell, 2009), 91–105. The article was based on a conference in Sanders's honor that took place in 2003.

participation.¹² I had long noted the scholarly idiom of pointing out that Paul was using Platonic language here and there and been convinced that Romans 7 was explainable with clarity using a Platonic moral psychology as argued in the book. What I probably would not have seen if I had not stuck with the Hellenistic Moral Philosophy and the New Testament unit was that the Platonic language really was Platonic as later Christian intellectuals recognized and not a bizarre cover for supposedly uniquely Jewish or "Old Testament" ideas. Like Philo, Paul uses these conceptions newly prominent in his time. But he used them to explain how the baptized become assimilated to the archetype, Christ, and share his mind and pneuma.

To a large extent, due to certain invitations to present papers, my thought coalesced in two areas that changed all my work. Thinking came together on theory of religion and around the idea of there being something coherent that we could call "ancient Mediterranean religion." It included and helped to explain both Judean religion and the emergence of Christianity. In 2004 I was asked to present a paper for a conference on National Socialism (the NSDAP) and religion. Due to the prevalent idea of Nazism being a "secular religion" based on the then popular idea of political religion, I found deep and hopeless confusion among historians of modern Europe about what religion is and how to treat it historically. Yes, certain religious traditions such as Christianity, Islam and so on teach that the true religion is the most important thing in any human life, but religion cannot be delimited by what is important to people or what they feel most strongly about. That approach ends up making such things as one's politics or football or golfing religion. You cannot use secondary properties that just some expressions of religion have for defining it. It happens to be a historical fact that most religion of most people across the globe and across time has not featured "the most important." There had to be a better way to individuate religion as a human social phenomenon and such individuation of the kind had to feature the tendencies for human cognition to imagine interaction with a class of beings featuring gods and related non-evident beings.¹³ I think that my first published piece where I appealed to cognitive psychology in making that case was the article in the *Journal of Contemporary History* based on that paper from the conference.¹⁴

But, of course, the true challenge was to work out how to theorize the social in religion as a human phenomenon. One way to chart changes on that project would come from trying to explain how I got from "The Ontology of

---

[12] *Rereading of Romans*, 246.
[13] I am not suggesting that there was anything new about making gods, ancestors and so on central to religion, but rather developing their role in theorizing a social kind was what was of significance.
[14] "The Concepts of 'Religion,' and 'Political Religion' in the Study of Nazism," *Journal of Contemporary History* 42.1 (2007), 9–24.

Religion" in a 2008 volume in honor of Jonathan Smith to my recent writings about religion as a social kind.[15] The former approach featured social theory based on theory of social practices. I have not renounced that theory, but now find it too partial and unable to deal with the complexity needed for understanding the social – when treated as a comprehensive theory of the social. The approach via practice theory now fits into a much larger picture.

In the last twenty years, I have often felt like I was running up against a brick wall in trying to work with the way that social theory is used in the humanities and especially religious studies, for instance, getting turned into methods for reading texts, or into ideas or purported identities or notional communities. It took me a long time to diagnose the heart of the problem as legacies from idealism and other anti-realisms that most of the university had long ago left behind. So, I went to mainstream thought and brought back social kinds. The world is lumpy, dividing up into entities. How does one know what these are, including in the social world, their causes, their building blocks and means of stability and instability? Following the development of philosophy, the philosophy of sciences, and social scientific theory to recent times, religion looked like a perfect candidate for being explained as a social kind.

Religion as a Social Kind: Christianity within Ancient Mediterranean Religion

The chapters of this book illustrate principles or display historical examples of an approach to religion. The approach as suggested above affirms the existence of something real that we call "religion" and that makes it sensible to speak of ancient Mediterranean religion and to hold that ancient Christianity emerged from that Mediterranean religion. Because much of my work has been on Paul, and several of the chapters focus upon him and his letters, I will use what we know historically of him in order to illustrate the theory. I will then carry on the illustration with Christian literature from the late first and early second centuries and suggest how the Christian "movement" emerged from broader Mediterranean religion even as it centrally involved Judean religion.

Theorizing Historical Moments of Religion: Paul and His Followers

Fortunately, most of the affected areas in the academy have moved past the dark days of domination by doctrines reputedly from poststructuralism and postmodernism, but actually having their roots in German Idealism and

---

[15] "The Ontology of Religion," *Introducing Religion: Essays in Honor of Jonathan Z. Smith*, ed. Willi Braun and Russell T. McCutcheon (London: Equinox, 2008), 434–49.

Neo-Kantianism. Along with some areas of literary studies, the study of religion in the academy has been slower than the rest of the university to repudiate those doctrines. I agree with those who think that these postisms once had a salutary effect on awakening hidebound and uncritical areas of the academy, including the study of religion, but that they did not have the intellectual resources to underwrite positive work. In my estimation, two states of affairs now prevail. Persuasive arguments have been made against the claims that "religion" is only ideological, that it only has utility as a modern western notion, that it is only a feature of our linguistic usages, and that it cannot refer to anything that is real or outside of our minds and language.[16] Almost every area in the natural sciences, the social sciences and many areas of the humanities have decisively renounced these sad legacies of idealism and antirealism. I have argued that like racism, economic recession, feudalism, language (*la langue*), oligarchy and so on, religion is a real social kind. Like them it is theorized in modern attempts at knowledge that typically do not need to be named or recognized by the societies in question to exist. Such discovered – not invented – kinds are the very basis for the modern sciences, social sciences and humanities.

I have further argued that religion forms a robust social kind. "Social kind" refers to a way of theorizing social entities in the mainstream philosophy of the sciences, the social sciences and other areas. Two complimentary approaches to social kinds have dominated: epistemic and ontological or constitutive. I will not elaborate on these here, but only note that I presuppose that religion can be justified and theorized as a real entity in the world with both. In my own theorization of these as applied to ancient Mediterranean religion, I have argued that four interactive sub-kinds existed.[17]

On this view, religion consists of patterns of imagined human exchange with gods and non-evident beings given relative stability by human cognitive propensities and other physical conditions. Historically, the most important material condition has seen cognition situated in an agricultural environment. The first question I raise here asks how the instances of religiosity evidenced in the letters of Paul can be theorized. Can study of the letters constitute a contribution to the study of religion? I can only outline an answer in the briefest way here with selected aspects of the theory and limited discussion of some evidence.

---

[16] Kevin Schilbrack, *Philosophy and the Study of Religions: A Manifesto* (Oxford: Wiley Blackwell, 2014); See Chapters 2–4 of my forthcoming *History and the Study of Religion: The Ancient Mediterranean as a Test Case* (New York, Oxford University Press).

[17] See my *History and the Study of Religion* and the first three Chapters in this volume and "Why Expert Versus Non-Expert is Not Elite Versus Popular Religion: The Case of the Third Century," *Religious Competition in Late Antiquity*, ed. Nathaniel DesRosiers and Lilly C. Vuong (Atlanta, GA: Society of Biblical Literature, 2016), 139–53.

The types result from three basic inquiries. One charts the way that human cognitive propensities promote the imagination of gods and non-evident beings.[18] A second asks of the environments that shape those propensities. The last asks how social practices connected to religion cluster and form networks of practices and larger social formations. The definition and ontology of religion emerges from these inquiries. The types are not mutually exclusive and individuals and social formations can exhibit more than one mode at one time. Indeed, they are usually interactive, but still tend to maintain some integrity. The cognitively and socially most basic of the types upon which the second and third types depend is the religion of everyday social exchange (RESE). The second I call for convenience civic religion, the religion of cities, kingdoms, empires, priestly aristocracies and similar formations controlled by elites who shape religion according to their interests as the self-proclaimed guardians of the religion of the whole population in question. The third mode arises from competitive and highly interactive fields of semi-independent literate religious experts who write, interpret and teach complex texts, such as argumentative treatises, narratives and law.

The religion of everyday social exchange features approachable deities and similar non-evident beings such as local gods, the beloved dead, the familiar heavenly bodies, angels, demons, ghosts, divinized humans, spirits, vaguely identified agents, "high gods" imagined as local and many others. Participants believe that these beings affect their lives in personally relevant and tangible ways such as giving humans the offspring of animals and plants, children, weather, health and illness, help and hindrance with the contingencies of life and so on. Humans in turn want to build and maintain positive long-term relations with the beings most relevant to their lives. Humans intuitively feel that many of these normally unseen beings that are most relevant to their lives are open to alliances and even to entering into complex practices of human-like social exchange, but with key differences from humans in that these beings can see what people are doing but humans normally do not see them. Many of these have very great powers and abilities. Such beings who inhabit the world of cause and effect behind the scenes of everyday life normally do not need the gifts that people offer to them, but they take pleasure in these and in sharing human pleasures, in acts and relationships of honor, in acts of gratitude and recognition. Some ancients thought of these beings as serving under a high ruling god, but this did not eliminate the everyday and local qualities intrinsic to this religiosity. Any approach that treats the ancients as if they lived in our disenchanted world with a distant theoretical god rather than in a day-to-day environment filled with palpably present, but normally unseen beings, is, I would argue, a massive distortion. This religiosity does not

---

[18] A useful introduction to the cognitive science is Todd Tremlin, *Minds and Gods: The Cognitive Foundations of Religion* (New York: Oxford University Press, 2006).

require cities, temples, priests, books or literacy, but can exist in and alongside these formations.

Three sorts of practices are central to the religion of everyday social exchange: divinatory, prayer, and kinds of exchange ideally based on gift-giving. We moderns can scarcely imagine the importance of divinatory practices and their constant role in everyday life.[19] In the second mode, civic religion, divinatory practices were also important and deemed essential for the life of cities. However in contrast to the mundane religion, these usually occurred in highly controlled contexts belonging to aristocrats and elites such as in public animal sacrifice, established oracles and specialist diviners or prophets. Unlike the certain pronouncements and clear messages of the literate experts with their world of texts, these divinatory messages usually came in modest signs and traces or in dreams and visions. Also, unlike the experts, the mundane religiosity treated knowledge about the moods and intentions of gods as usually limited and often, but not always, difficult to determine for the conduct of everyday coping, an epistemological modesty. Households, farms, workshops, neighborhoods and the activities of daily coping and common life-courses were the premier sites. The ubiquitous and most well-known way of communicating with gods was prayer, and prayer often accompanied the giving of gifts to gods that was the center of the imagined social relation of reciprocity between unequals.

The central sites of religious production in civic religion were temples and similar "sacred" spaces with associated practices related to calendars of festivals, processions, spectacles and entertainments for the gods and so on. This religion entailed the sacralization of time that punctuated lives with special religious days. Temples collected, redistributed and consumed mostly agricultural goods produced on land centered on households. Civic religion thus tied itself structurally to the agricultural economy and the religion of everyday social exchange (RESE). It also enforced a structural opposition in that temples and sacred spaces had to be free from the pollution of childbirth, death and other pollutions intrinsic to the lives of households and families. When someone prayed a votive in a civic temple – "If my crops flourish, I will give you a sheep" – this religion connected with civic religion. If the god fulfilled the request, the person would offer the animal at an altar with a civic priest perhaps getting the animal's hide and some meat. Of course, the farmer did not have to go to a civic temple in order to carry out a votive exchange and civic temples were often not open to the general public.

The production of the semi-autonomous literate religious experts consisted of intellectual practices related to literate forms of cultural production. The expert's products were writings, textual techniques, learned interpretations; position-takings about what is true, just and good, narratives, forms of teaching

---

[19] Jennifer Eyl, *Signs, Wonders, and Gifts: Divination in the Letters of Paul*, (New York: Oxford University Press, 2019), 46–85.

and of transmitting knowledge, all taking form from existing literary and literate traditions. Such production in contrast to that of civic religion and everyday religion was separate from the agricultural economy and its products. The writer's study could be anywhere, and writings could circulate anywhere. A kind of *atopia* characterized the dynamics of the mode together with a complex cultural economy. Experts accrued social capital rewarded in various often non-obvious ways. While mundane religiosity sprang from intuitive cognition as extensively studied in the cognitive sciences, as did much of civic religion, the literary experts depended heavily upon reflective and rationalizing thought that was not intuitive and difficult to acquire and hold without the technical and social machinery of high literacy.[20] The relative stability of the social kind, religion, only happens when the imagination of exchange relations such as reciprocal gift-giving and obedience/reward with gods comes about partly due to the shaping of a particular environment.

Most scholarship on Paul's letters seeks to describe his thought or theology. Some approaches emphasize his biography with admittedly limited evidence. Much of this writing seeks to detail precursors, influences and social or cultural contexts for his thought and biography. The individuals and assemblies addressed in the letters also receive analysis, usually in terms of how well Paul's gospel took on them or as bits of social history. None of these standard approaches can add much if anything to our understanding of what religion is and how it works in particular historical moments. Toward these latter aims, I propose beginning instead with the environments for the religiosities of Paul and his addresses. If we can find a particular pattern of exchange with gods significantly shaped by an environment, we will have brought to light a historical instance of religion. My thesis holds that just as the environment that sustained the religion of everyday social exchange and civic religion was the ancient agricultural economy, so too was the sustaining environment for the formation of Christianity the field of literate and intellectualist cultural production where "mind goods" replaced agricultural goods in patterns of reciprocity and other exchange with the gods.

I have elsewhere discussed a field of literate intellectualist activity for the early Roman Empire.[21] Kendra Eshleman provides a rich trove of detail about that field with insightful analysis of its dynamics in *The Social World of Intellectuals in the Roman Empire: Sophists, Philosophers and Christians*.[22] She writes about how these categories were highly contested forms of claimed identity

---

[20] David Slone, *Theological Incorrectness: Why Religious People Believe What They Shouldn't* (New York: Oxford University Press, 2004).

[21] See the Introduction and first three Chapters in this volume and Heidi Wendt, *At the Temple Gates: The Religion of Freelance Experts in the Roman Empire* (New York: Oxford University Press, 2016).

[22] (Cambridge: Cambridge University Press, 2012).

by those competing in the same world of intellectual production. That field's approach

> to identity formation equates group membership with attendance and full participation in the group's defining activities. As a result, each group's boundaries were continuously reasserted and renegotiated through decisions about which persons to admit and which to exclude. The implicit notion that the "circle of sophists" or the worldwide church was coterminous with those participating in classrooms, declamations, or worship services around the empire is obviously fantastic. Attendance at those activities was not and could not be restricted to group members, however defined, nor for the most part would our subjects have wanted it to be, especially on the narrower conceptions of expert status.

The animating structure of the field consisted of the expert in some area of knowledge that for convenience I will call "the teacher," surrounded by a circle of those who were or who aspired to be experts. The circle ranged from "students" to peers of the teacher. A more variable and shifting number of consumers of the discourses, writings, discussions, performances and rites of the teacher and circle consisted of individuals who did not aspire to become experts but were attracted to the teacher's products. Whereas associations typically had a relatively fixed number of members seen in the many surviving lists, social formations in the field formed variably around the leadership and "performances" of teachers. The teacher, circle and non-expert insiders partly defined themselves by patterns of recognition. What other teachers did X teacher and circle recognize as legitimate? This question was the basis for networks of communication, the exchange of writings and other products. These dynamics also make sense of why sophists, philosophers and Christian experts attempted to contest and control the organization of their field niches by constructing lines of succession back to founding teachers.[23] The whole structure was obviously unstable and driven by a competition for prestige that gave social and even economic capital to the experts.

Our sources for the field from the Hellenistic age and the early Empire have come down to us in a highly distorted way as the literature preserved and transmitted by literate Christians and the classicizing movement ("Second Sophistic"): those who won. Most of the "lower literature," "unorthodox," and writings from ethnic sub-fields (such as Lydian, Judean) has been lost. But we have enough evidence to envision a large complex field with a variety of interacting

---

[23] Eshleman, *Social World*, 179–87, 191–210, 243–57.

subfields. Sophists, philosophers and Christian experts (eventually mostly clergy and bishops) differed from other areas of expertise (such as astrology, "magic" and medicine) in that the areas of knowledge to which they aspired were broad, even aiming at comprehensive, (history, cosmology, the nature of the gods, rites for the gods, literature, classical Greek culture, traditional Judean writings, morality, ideal sociality, futurism). Experts, for instance, did not treat "the Greek Bible" as narrowly about something called religion, but as a divinely produced compendium of knowledge about the world.

Perhaps the most important large-scale dynamic of the field was its tension between actors on the one side who were largely independent from institutional location and legitimacy and those on the other side who were well established in those ties, a semi-autonomous and a less autonomous pole that varied by degree on various scales. The poles shaped the field in that the sides party defined themselves one against each other. The most autonomous would be like the Cynic philosopher who had no possessions and rejected marriage, traditional religion, conventional social roles and obligations much like Jesus in the Synoptic Gospels and Q.[24] The Cynic life aimed to swing free of social positions of the household and city, including the religion of everyday social exchange and civic religion with their inherent norms and obligations.[25] The Cynic was only to be guided by knowledge regarding the true nature of God who was demeaned with gift-giving, statues and temples. Zeno the Stoic had none of those rites and objects in his ideal city (Diogenes Laertius 7.33).[26] Later Stoics said that the true beliefs about the divine were to guide the wise, but traditional rites could be understood as symbols of those truths. Most Judeans who wrote in Greek adopted a philosophical god that they read into their holy writings, and like the philosophers made connections with morality and immorality.[27]

Christians adopted this semi-autonomous-pole stance against the traditional norms already cultivated by the Judean writers, and philosophical notions about gods with the concepts of idolatry, the moral depravity of society, and anti-superstition, that is, opposition to civic religion and the practices of everyday religiosity. Sophists, as in Philostratus's "Second Sophistic," celebrated and defended the traditional religion of cities and Greek ethnicity, attacking the more independent philosophers as charlatans and radicals. Those on the

---

[24] John L. Moles, "Cynic Influence Upon First-Century Judaism and Early Christianity?," in *The Limits of Biography*. ed. B. McGing and J. Mossman (Swansea: Classical Press of Wales, 2006), 89–116.

[25] William Desmond, *The Greek Praise of Poverty: Origins of Ancient Cynicism* (Notre Dame, IN: University of Notre Dame, 2006).

[26] P. R. Bosman, "Traces of Cynic Monotheism in the Early Roman Empire," *Acta Classica* 51 (2008): 1–20.

[27] Emma Wasserman, "Philosophical Cosmology and Religious Polemic: The 'Worship of Creation' in the writings of Philo of Alexandria and the Wisdom of Solomon," *Journal for the Study of the Pseudepigrapha* 31 (2021): 6–28.

opposite pole said that thinkers like the sophists had sold out to power, vanity, wealth and convention. Still a Philostratus, like his fellow sophist, Lucian, could also idealize autonomous pole philosophers. In the former's case, by telling the story of Paul's itinerant contemporary, Apollonius of Tyana.

If the patterns of exchange with gods and non-evident beings conceived in intuitive ways central to the existence of the RESE and civic religion involved reciprocal gift-giving with goods from farm and field, what kind of exchange characterized the literate experts? The distance from conventional religion that literate experts promoted was often great, but several positions are illustrative. There can only be one god in charge of the universe, the top and final power and organizing principle or being. Immortal gods do not need or find pleasure in petty human gifts such as food, drink, entertainment and even praise. Cultic acts are kinds of bribery that only dishonor gods/God. God's nature is to be invisible and physical representations degrade the respect due to him (philosophical aniconism).[28] God isn't in a particular physical place. God's true nature is distorted by treating him as human-like with a body, emotions, the need to travel and on and on. God has ordered the universe to favor the good, the true and the just. Humans can only respect this God and his nature by being morally good and seeking truth. Proper exchange with God only involves the mind goods which were created to foster these principles. God rewards those whose entire lives follow what is good.

Intellectuals developed such ideas in numerous ways and to various degrees made accommodations with traditional conceptions. The field debated such ideas through writings and speeches. Even sophists sometimes resorted to allegorizing traditional views and valorized more conservative philosophers as products of Hellenic civilization.[29] Paul, I believe, like many Judean intellectuals, struggled to balance the views above that he found compelling or confirmed by holy writings such as idolatry, aniconism and God's moral order with the highly anthropomorphic and morally questionable depictions in much traditional scriptural and Judean writing.

With this breezy sketch of the field as the environment shaping a religiosity distinct from but interacting with the mundane religiosity and civic religion, we can ask whether the letters of Paul bear evidence of those field dynamics. First Thessalonians chapter 2 makes a good place to begin. In a celebrated, but greatly understated article, Abraham Malherbe showed how Paul positioned himself among others as a teacher in that chapter.[30] I will go over some of his striking

---

[28] So, Antisthenes (SSR 7 Fr.VA 181 G): "God is not known with an image, is not seen with the eyes, resembles no one." Translations are my own.

[29] Lucian excoriates most Cynics and other philosophers, but holds up Nigrinus the Platonist and Demonax the Cynic as ideal philosophers.

[30] Abraham J. Malherbe, "'Gentle as a Nurse': The Cynic Background of 1 Thess ii." *Novum Testamentum* 12 (1970):203–17.

evidence in order to show that it cannot simply be coincidental. Highlighting details also makes the standard approach to verses 1–12 look absurd. Although the letter trumpets Paul's highly positive relation to the Thessalonians who had turned from idols to the true God to await Christ's return (1:9–10), the verses supposedly show that these people had accused him of being "useless," afraid to enter "the struggle" like a serious teacher, only willing to speak with those who already agreed with him; having the goal of deceiving them to receive money, fame and sexual gratification by using flattery; lacking courage and boldness in speaking so that his teaching work was in vain. This is mirror reading gone wild.

Malherbe focuses on Dio Chrysostom's (40-ca.120 CE) 32 oration at Alexandria, but points out that the literary versions we now have of speeches given at Tarsus (33), Olympia (12), and Celaenae (35) also have him attempting to define himself in their *proemia* as a certain type of speaker or philosopher over against others. Dio should be of great interest for a number of reasons. He was a famous sophist, but claimed that exile had awakened him to the life of an itinerant Cynic philosopher. Thus, he represents the interaction of the two opposing poles of the field. His life also crosses the boundary of the mythic and magical age of the New Testament into the second century, a boundary that historians must seek to treat critically.[31]

For the sake of efficiency and clarity, I will simply italicize the English translation of the striking number of key Greek words and concepts that Dio and Paul share, and do so making the same points. Readers can find the Greek terms in Malherbe's article. In an antithetical style (32.11–18), Dio enumerates several types of philosophers, especially Cynics, to whom he contrasts his own approach. First, he is not like resident philosophers who served select patrons and households (32.8) instead of teaching more broadly. They are *useless* like athletes who will not *join in the contest*. Secondly, there are lecture hall philosophers only teaching selected students who already agree to accept the message. Eshleman shows how teachers in the field worried over these issues.[32] Again, Dio thought that such teachers had opted out of the *contest* to help humanity. Third, is the type of Cynic satirized by Lucian. They *flatter* people in order to collect money instead of speaking with the *frankness* that people need. Their motivations are *money, fame* and *sensual pleasure*. Fourth, are the would-be philosophers who are hard to distinguish from sophistic-like orators. Their entertainment speeches are *empty* and *vain*, having no substance. They do not *benefit* their audiences. The fifth type is the famously harsh Cynic who confuses true *frankness* with railing against humanity's sinfulness. Elsewhere (Or. 77/78.42)

---

[31] William Arnal, "The Collection and Synthesis of 'Tradition' and the Second Century Invention of Christianity," *Method and Theory in the Study of Religion*. 23 (2011):193–215.
[32] *World of Intellectuals*, esp. 21–66.

Dio expands his criticism of this harsh type of teacher and contrasts blanket castigation of human evil with *admonition* that involves *frank criticism* and *gentleness*. In the latter combination, the teacher adapts his methods to individual needs and conditions. Malherbe then shows that various types of philosophers and sophists discussed these issues, and some used the image of the *gentle nurse*.

Paul did not fear the *violence* of the audience; his teaching was not *in vain*, but he spoke with *frankness* (1 Thess 1:2). He is engaged in a great *contest*, here using a favorite Cynic term. Paul does not teach to *deceive* or out of *error* (vss. 2–3). He was not motivated by *impurity* or *guile*. He did not act from *greed*, or seek human *reputation* or to *flatter* his audiences (vss. 5–6). Both Dio and Paul claim that their teaching is divinely directed (vs. 4). Dio says that the teacher should not be only *harsh*, but adapt to *the condition of each individual*, and be *gentle as a nurse*. Paul writes that he worked with each person individually (vs 10) and was *gentle as a nurse* not *harsh* (vs. 7).

Chapter One does not find Paul defending himself against a long list of charges against him by the Thessalonians, but shows him describing the teaching ideal that he claims characterized his preaching to those people. He draws this sketch in a way that shows his embeddedness in the field of intellectualist and moralistic expertise. The large number of substantive, linguistic and rhetorical similarities that Malherbe demonstrated with Dio and other figures in the field cannot be accidental. Paul and his audience were highly conscious of the field of literate experts. Placing Paul in the field of contestation undermines our intuitive but anachronistic categories of Judaism, Christianity and Paganism that we habitually use exclusively to make sense of Paul and his letters. Recognition of Paul's high level of self-consciousness expressed rhetorically about his manner and method as a teacher and his expectation that those he is addressing would share the concerns opens the theological blinds covering his cultural location and the primary mode of his religiosity.

The Letters and Features of the Field

In the briefest way, I will reinforce my claims by noting some features of the letters that reflect the field. When Celsus looks at the Christian movement later in the second century, he perceives numerous contending schools of thought with circles of teachers, students and non-expert followers. He describes these self-proclaimed experts and their followers as would-be but woefully inept philosophers whom he compares to low class and poorly educated Cynics (e.g., Origen, *Cels.* 3.12). Celsus was a Platonist philosopher partly shaped by the Second Sophistic. The very fact that he spent so much time learning about Christian groups and considered the movement worthy of refutation shows that he saw the movement as attempting to contend in the field of intellectualist expertise. Otherwise, he would have had no reason to write a major work against it. I enumerate key field features such as suggested by Celsus.

(1.) The driving force of the field and of the formation of Christianity were experts in areas of knowledge (scripture, God's plans, desired behavior, Christ's effects and plans, evil), usually with circles of disciples, and other followers consuming the teachings and practices of the experts without wanting to become experts themselves. Paul's companions and fellow workers such as Barnabas, Silvanus, Prisca, Apollos, Timothy and Titus were peers in Paul's circle. Paul's so-called churches or Christ-gatherings consisted of non-expert consumers of Paul's goods.

(2.) The goods of these circles were cast in terms of true knowledge. Knowledge about the gods, their roles in human life and how to act toward them were central truths among philosophers, sophists and the Christ movement. By way of contrast, truth and the explicit formulation of true knowledge was not important in everyday and civic Mediterranean religiosity. The wife, son, master and slaves of a Roman household did not focus on discussion of the true nature of the house's Lares or an ancient book that authorized their rites or what might have been the real underlining meaning of those mundane practices. Their religiosity was not characterized by the messages of contending teachers who had broken into sects each arguing a different truth about the Lares. The same goes for the religion of most Judeans (Chapter Three in this volume).

(3.) The social processes of seeking knowledge and truth, including of the good, the just and sometimes the beautiful, entailed the social dynamics of competition. Teachers with circles and non-expert followers constantly fractured, formed and reformed around claims of possessing the genuine truth. All of the letters except Philemon contain attacks on or criticisms of teachers and/or teachings that Paul views as competing with his teachings.

(4.) A high degree of self-authorization characterized the field. The authorizing practices and institutions for becoming a modern professional – teacher, doctor, lawyer – begin in first grade and end in advanced professional education, and with various accrediting and disciplining organizations. But in antiquity, one might appeal to one's teacher or a lineage of teachers, but there were no certifying institutions until the late antique consolidation of the Church hierarchy. The teacher had to argue for her or his own credentials. Such rhetoric characterizes speeches and writings from the field. First Thes 2:1–12 finds Paul in one of his many arguments about his credentials. He is somewhat odd in that given the chance to establish a succession from Jesus through apostles to himself, he refuses. Rather, God was his teacher (1 Cor 1:18–2:16; Gal 1:11–2:10; Chapter Six in this volume). His message and his knowledge come directly from God. Figures in civic religion such as a Judean priest in the Jerusalem temple or a priestess of Artemis, or a mother in everyday religion who tended household Lares, did not need self-authorization.

(5.) The stance of the intellectualist experts entailed a critique of traditional religion. Because the field traded in truth claims rather than simply involving what one's ethnicity, city or family did to achieve their practical and local goals such as good crops, health and prosperity, truth about the gods was typically contrasted with falsehood about them. While sophists on the more conservative pole of the field held up the ideal of a classical Greek or Roman past as the measuring stick, philosophers tended to argue that the religion of everyday social exchange and of the city was fundamentally wrong.[33]

(6.) Philosophical critique of the religion of everyday social exchange has come down to us moderns distortedly packaged as the critique of superstition and critique of civic religion as the criticism of the poets (myth) and of anthropomorphizing the divine. Judean intellectuals writing in Greek claimed to have found these critiques in their traditional writings and developed versions that scholars have long seen echoed in the letters of Paul and other Christian writings.[34]

(7.) Social kinds endure through time and get socially reproduced because they possess relatively stable clusters of cognitive, social and environmental features. At the center of the cluster for religion one finds some sort of imagined exchange with gods and other non-evident beings. In the ancient Mediterranean, goods from the fields and animals seen as given by the gods were the most important gifts offered back as food offerings. The field with its urban practices broke from the agricultural environment for imagining exchange with the divine. In the religiosity of the literate experts, especially on the less conservative pole, true exchange required different conceptions of the gods that entailed offering mind goods instead of agricultural and other mundane goods. Paul, for instance, after excoriating the non-Judean peoples for false iconic worship, supposedly of the creation instead of the creator, and for their ensuing moral depravity (Rom 1:18–32), caps off the worship theme in 12:1–3. The gifts that God wants are cognitive and moral: "Offer your bodies as a living animal offering (*thusia*), holy and well-pleasing to God which is your rational worship. And do not be structured by this age, but be transformed by the renewal of your mind so that you

---

[33] Harold Attridge, "The Philosophical Critique of Religion under the Early Empire," *ANRW* 2.16.1 (1978): 45–78.
[34] Emma Wasserman, "Philosophical Cosmology and Religious Polemic: The 'Worship of Creation' in the Writings of Philo of Alexandria and the Wisdom of Solomon," *Journal for the Study of the Pseudepigrapha* 31 (2021): 6–28.

might test for what is the will of God. . . ." "Mind goods" have replaced agricultural goods.

(8.) The field and the Christ movement took a social form that possessed a division between experts (later the clergy) and insider non-experts (the laity), each with differing relations to the religion of everyday social exchange and its intuitive religiosity.

(9.) The experts typically write about the non-expert Christ followers (our only sources for them) in this way: They are God's people and are to live lives totally dedicated to the truth, but many are false followers, defectors and fail to live up to that total commitment. Critical scholarly reading of this rhetoric shows that non-experts often did not accept the totalizing message and adapted many practices advocated by the experts to their own local and intuitive religion of everyday social exchange.[35] The Corinthian acceptance of the man in 1 Cor 5:1–5, and the practices of baptism for the dead (1 Cor 15:29), and speaking in tongues may possibly have been their own practices interpreted according to their own religiosity. And as Paul seems to indicate (e.g., 1 Cor 5:1, 6), they probably did not feel like they had to follow Paul's strictures or interpretations.

I will end by saying a bit more about three areas of evidence for the field dynamics in the letters: competition, self-authorization and Paul's non-expert followers. Several books have been written about the opponents mentioned and implied in Paul's letters.[36] Eshleman, for instance, handily shows that the same dynamic of splintering into competing groups, circles and networks also characterized philosophers and sophists. I will limit myself to two points: The opponents given some substantive description in the letters are Judean, from a Judean sub-field, but Paul's writing also possesses a more general ethos of field-like competition. Phil 1:14–18 presents a good example of this last point: "Some proclaim Christ from envy and strife, but others from goodwill . . . some out of selfish ambition, not from pure motives, but thinking to increase my suffering in prison." Paul thinks of competition as the context of his work. And the competitors or at least the main ones relevant to the letters are other Judeans who are fellow experts in the knowledge and truth of the Christ movement. He expects that other literate experts will have different views that might well be convincing to his non-expert followers: "If someone comes preaching another Jesus different from the Jesus we preached, or you receive a

---

[35] See Chapter Four in this volume; Éric Rebillard, *Christians and Their Many Identities in Late Antiquity* (Ithaca, NY: Cornell University Press, 2012); Caroline Johnson Hodge, '*My God and the God of This House': Christian Household Cult Before Constantine* (University Park, PA: Pennsylvania State University Press, forthcoming).

[36] Heidi Wendt, *At the Temple Gates: The Religion of Freelance Experts in the Roman Empire* (New York: Oxford University Press, 2016), 168–74.

different *pneuma* (spirit) from what you received, or another good message to which you did not assent, you accede all too well."

As we have seen, matters of teaching methods and motives loom large. The major issue among philosophers and sometimes sophists of how teachers should finance themselves haunts many pages of the letters.[37] Paul defends his receipt of money and support and calls certain opponents "peddlers of God's word" (2 Cor 2:17). Skill in speaking ability relative to competitors also looms large, and is sometimes connected with educational credentials.[38] 1 Corinthians 1:10–17 begins with Paul bemoaning how affiliations with various teachers, including Cephas and Apollos, causes divisions among the non-expert followers. Everyone should just be loyal to Christ, which seems to mean being loyal to Paul's teaching and leadership. Paul contrasts himself as a purveyor of God's wisdom to human wisdom and eloquent oration (1:18–2:5). The highly allusive rhetoric makes concrete identification of the teachers that Paul is opposing impossible, but he makes them sound like practitioners of philosophy and sophistic rhetoric. Some commentators have thought that Apollos is the target.[39]

Paul begins his self-authorization as a teacher in 1 Thessalonians 2 by noting the suffering and mistreatment that he had endured (vs. 2). Nevertheless, he and his fellow workers taught with boldness using frank speech and they consider their enterprise to be "a great competitive contest" (vs. 2). He then continues: "For our appeal does not come from impure motives or deceit . . ." (vs. 3). Paul is here claiming that his willingness to endure suffering proves his motives as a teacher and legitimizes his activity and character. This appeal to sufferings and the endurance of hardships forms a major characteristic of philosophical discourse in Paul's era, and the use of hardship lists is an important rhetorical feature. Paul's letters abound with such rhetoric, the lists and appeal to his sufferings. I cannot here get into this large topic, but refer interested readers to the work of John T. Fitzgerald.[40] Reading only the list wielded against super-apostles in 2 Cor 11:22–29 provides a rich and detailed picture of life in a most competitive niche of the field.

Learning from the Approach

The way that we moderns think about religion with doctrines, educated professional clergy, long term plans of salvation, official moral teachings, true religion of the heart and mind and so on, should not be generalized. Such

---

[37] Eshleman, *World of Intellectuals*, 48, 51, 81, 83, 117-18, 122; Wendt, *Temple Gates*, 179–89; E. P. Sanders, *The Apostle's Life, Letters, and Thought*, (Minneapolis, MN: Fortress, 2015), 140–44, 183–84.
[38] Sanders, *Apostle's Life*, 246.
[39] Ibid., 240-49.
[40] *Cracks in an Earthen Vessel: An Examination of Catalogues of Hardships in the Corinthian Correspondence*, (Atlanta, GA: Scholars Press, 1988).

assumptions about religion have a history, and that kind of religion had beginnings. But the beginnings in the ancient Mediterranean did not result from an injection of the simply new and unique. That religiosity was the result of social and cultural dynamics with long histories in the Mediterranean and West Asia. Such religion gradually formed in a major way with Christianity, but similarly also in China and South Asia. In these cases, the religiosity developed by freelance literate experts eventually acquired an institutional power that limited the autonomy of the experts and gave institutionally empowered experts the rule of entire populations of non-expert insiders. The pattern in the west eventually took the familiar form of clergy claiming orthodoxy and the laity.

The letters of Paul display the earliest evidence for followers of Christ with social characteristics in that freelance mold. But again, they are not as detached or novel. The field of intense competition about truth and knowledge crossed the boundaries that we now designate as Greek, Judean, Roman or Christian. One might say that the freelance field dynamics ran wild in the Christian case. The movement was also thoroughly embedded in cultures inhabited by everyday religiosity and the religion of cities and peoples in two major ways, the first of which was negative. For the Christ movement with its organization around intellectualistic practices developed from the Judean sub-field and the more autonomous pole of philosophy, truth and knowledge took a form antithetical to the everyday religiosity and civic religion of the ancient Mediterranean. The Christian movement declared a culture war on the religious heart of ancient Mediterranean society.

Second, the central structure of the movement maintaining a boundary between expert and non-expert members produced a dynamic of tension, sometimes an instability, a two-level ethos, and constant accommodation to aspects of the non-expert's intuitive religiosity by the experts. These dynamics arose largely from the difference between the difficult doctrinal religiosity taught by the experts and the intuitive religiosity. The letters of Paul already bear witness to the social dynamics of a distinctive but not unique religiosity, featuring the exchange of mind goods that would characterize Christianity, but with an evident resistance from the everyday religion of the non-expert followers.

Discontinuity Then Continuity After Paul

Ludwig Wittgenstein wrote, "A picture held us captive. And we could not get outside it, for it lay in our language and language seemed to repeat it to us inexorably."[41] At least the first clause of Wittgenstein's aphorism ("A picture

---

[41] *Philosophical Investigations*, # 115.

held us captive. And we could not get outside of it,") well characterizes those of us who work in early Christianity. This, I would argue, prevails even though we should have known better since the work of Albert Schweitzer, Johannes Weiss and others. I am talking about the way that, as professional scholars, we have created an historical continuity when the evidence seems otherwise and discontinuity when the evidence abounds. These judgements, that I shall presently make less abstract, grow partly from the evidence that Christian teachers of various sorts only emerged as a critical mass in my theorized field of literate production at the end of the first century and beginning of the second. That was the beginning of a socially continuous movement.[42]

But let us go back to the picture of continuity that has captured us (Chapters Six in this volume). At the beginnings of the Church, after two sermons, more than eight thousand converted and formed an amazing community. It kept on growing until it burst out of Jerusalem with apostles going everywhere and Paul triumphantly from the holy city to Rome winning large numbers everywhere. Although we know that this picture, largely from Acts, dates to the end of the first century at earliest, and most likely to about 115–120 CE, this picture sits in the back of our head as we read Paul's letters and construct a history of the first century. We should also know that at best we have no way to confirm the reliability of Acts and that even the lightest critical reading shows it to be more of an imaginative foundation myth than a reliable history. From Eusebius and others, we get a continuity of Christianity from the first century, now in the form of the age of the apostles with successions of bishops and completely implausible dating of writings so they fall into that magical first century, the age of the New Testament, and create lines of succession.

But Paul tells us in Romans that his mission has been successfully completed across the Empire and that he just needs to pass through Rome and get to Spain to finish. Never mind the many millions that have not been converted. Clearly Paul did not have our modern or Acts' or Eusebius's idea of converting the world in order to save as many souls as possible. Paul expected Christ to return while he was alive. As I argue in Chapter Six, Paul was a Judean devoted to his people whose God-given task was to transform a cohort of gentiles to serve Christ when he returned to rectify the world's unfaithfulness and the cosmic situation. His gentiles transformed according to the archetype of Christ were probably meant to fulfill prophesies about gentiles bringing offerings to Jerusalem at the time of renewal. This did not happen, and Paul left no plan for a new religion to take form after his death. What did survive to bear fruit were collections of his letters studied over and reinterpreted by those from the field with the right education and talent.

---

[42] For groundbreaking thinking on this issue, see Arnal, "The Collection and Synthesis of 'Tradition' and the Second Century," (see n. 31 above).

Between Paul's death, likely in the late fifties, and a mass of writings dating to the end of the first and the new decades of the second century we know almost nothing. And while there may have been some small groups that somehow adapted and survived, scholars should stop treating Paul's letters as if they had laid out a plan for ongoing institutions. Controversial evidence for a few prominent places like Rome and Antioch having some kinds of continuity make claims that we should take seriously, but we should be cautious about how substantial such populations and the nature of their social formations were (Chapters Five and Ten herein). With the rise of critical scholarship in the nineteenth century, researchers realized that the age of the apostles was a fiction. Then there was the discovery of Judean apocalyptic thought. The New Testament writings were not the writings of apostles and their sidekicks. But scholars in the twentieth century created a way to posit a continuity again while seemingly affirming these critical findings. Instead of the apostles setting up and organizing churches everywhere, you would just talk about vague communities behind the writings from the first century (Chapter Ten in this volume). Communities would be the agents that drove the history of the church and could be imagined to somehow go back to the very beginnings. A few individuals or small groups that carried their oral traditions produced theologies finally deposited in the documents of the New Testament.

What about the discontinuity that seals off the magical New Testament age of the first century from the later church history, or in one version, "early Catholicism"? The very concepts of the age of the apostles, the first century, and the New Testament Age, of course, have that effect, but there is also a more subtle discourse. I refer to the powerful myth of original purity and intellectual corruption. A central notion from the Protestant Reformation, built partly upon earlier Christian traditions (such as Jerusalem versus Athens), held that Christianity's downfall from the purity of the apostolic first century was a form of corruption by philosophy in the second and third centuries.[43]

This myth of origins rules so powerfully that its nature needs a bit of elaboration. Henry Chadwick, one of the greats in treating Greek philosophical influence in the second and third centuries, wrote that the idea that New Testament writers did not use philosophy is "of providential importance since in consequence the gospel is not inextricably associated with a first century metaphysical structure."[44] For a non-Christian or non-Jewish writing, *pneuma* (spirit), God's presence in the temple, angelic messengers, purity and pollution, miracles and so forth would be counted as metaphysics. But early modern interpreters long ago proclaimed these symbolic when encountered

---

[43] Jonathan Z. Smith, *Drudgery Divine: On the Comparison of Early Christianities and the Religions of Late Antiquity* (Chicago: Chicago University Press, 1990), 7–22.

[44] *Early Christian Thought and the Classical Tradition* (Oxford: Oxford University Press, 1966) 4-5.

in scripture, though also real, without explaining how that combination for reading only Christian texts worked.

Discussing Greek writers who described Christianity as a "philosophy," Robert Wilken writes,

> Only a few enterprising intellectuals, and only after more than one hundred years of Christian history, had begun to take the risk of expressing Christian beliefs within the philosophical ideas current in the Greco-Roman world. Most Christians were opposed to such attempts. As late as the third century, after the apologetic movement had introduced Greek ideas into Christian thinking, Christian preachers complained that the rank-and-file opposed such ideas.[45]

Instead of an ordinary human social formation composed of the kinds of elements and principles seen in the theory of social kinds, Christianity already existed with Jesus and his disciples, and the earliest followers as depicted in Acts and the Gospels. Christianity was not organized like every other social formation out of causes, conditions and grounds that were already present, except vaguely out of the Old Testament and a Judaism that also in this way of thinking seem to float free of the world.

For Wilken, one could "express" Christian beliefs with philosophical ideas, and put an alien cloak on them, but he does not entertain the possibility that philosophical ideas were intrinsically part of and aided in the creation of thinking from an early point by Christians, or like Paul, by Judeans who were later baptized as part of the emerging movement. Christianity was instead already formed when it met philosophy. Nor does Wilken envision the notion stressed here that the struggle of Christian literate experts as intellectuals in a social field of other formations including philosophy was intrinsic – not incidental – to its formation, including its thought.

He also cites no evidence at all for his claims. The assertion about philosophy only touching the Christian movement with the second century apologists deserves at least a brief refutation. Wilken mentions Justin (mid 2nd c.) and Athenagoras (writing ca. 176 CE) as beginnings of intellectualizing the faith. In the first two decades we find Basilides and Isadore as Christian teachers in Alexandria. Valentinus and his followers were first in Alexandria, and he then worked in Rome from 136 CE. His known students famously include Ptolemy and Heracleon. I begin with these well-known examples to raise the question of whether, when Wilken writes about Christianity untouched by philosophical ideas, he means historical figures later declared orthodox by

---

[45] Robert L. Wilken, *The Christians as the Romans Saw Them*, 2nd ed. (New Haven, CT: Yale University Press, 1984, 2003), 78–79.

those who eventually won the competition to define? If so, then Wilken's is a normative Christian project of creating pure pedigrees.

He also does not mention Quadratus and Aristides. If Eusebius (*EH* 4.3.1–3) can be trusted, they both addressed defenses of their movement under Hadrian (117-38), the first's likely in 124–25 CE. Aristides clearly uses philosophy and probably also Quadratus, but we know too little to be certain. Surely the two did not suddenly acquire a religiosity informed by philosophy on the day that they wrote their defenses. Decades of formation are more likely. Marcion of Sinope was likely born about 75 CE and went to Rome about 130 CE.[46] The development of his thought and his teaching activity had to have begun sometime in the preceding decades. His central idea was to argue for a philosophical conception of God and then read parts of the Judean Greek holy writings through that premise. In another sort of example from the most semi-autonomous region of the field, Peregrinus of Parium, the Cynic who in an act of self-martyrdom burned himself on a pyre in 165 CE at the Olympic Games, was also a member of a Christian group ca. 120–134 CE and seems to have continued his relation to the Christians for several years thereafter as he travelled.[47] Among other locations we find these figures in Palestine, Athens, Alexandria, Asia Minor, Rome and on the Black Sea in the beginning of the second century and before. Like most experts in the field, they moved around a great deal, wrote and read writings that circulated widely and quickly. Much more could be said, but this much shows that both the supposed novelty of the mid-century "apologetic movement" and the idea of some major boundary at the beginning of the second century between the "primitive Church" unaffected by Greco-Roman intellectual life and the Hellenization of an already formed Christianity are illusions.

Claiming a Significant Foothold in the Field

In place of the standard temporal scheme, I want to advance the following historical hypothesis: After a quiet period from roughly the middles of the first century, where those connected with the Christ movement did not quite know how to go on, numerous teachers and their followers emerged in the nourishing environment of the Empire's field of literate production at the end of the century and beginning of the next. The canonical gospels make sense in this historical moment. I agree with Merrill Miller that someone wrote Mark about 80 CE.[48]

---

[46] For Marcion placed in the field, see Heidi Wendt, "Marcion the Shipmaster: Unlikely Religious Experts of the Roman World," *Studia Patristica* 99 (2018): 55–74.

[47] Gilbert Bagnani, "Peregrinus Proteus and the Christians," *Historia: Zeitschrift für Alte Geschichte*, 4 (1955): 107–112.

[48] "The Social Logic of the Gospel of Mark: Cultural Persistence and Social Escape in a Postwar Time," *Redescribing the Gospel of Mark* ed. Barry S. Crawford and Merrill P. Miller (Atlanta, GA: Society of Biblical Literature, 2017), 207–399.

The other gospels followed, probably over the next three decades. We can easily get caught up in the romance and similitude of the literary world portrayed in the Gospels, but as Robyn Walsh and others have shown, they are products of a sophisticated literary sub-culture in the Roman world.[49]

The Gospels reflect an intense interest from their own era in Jesus as a certain sort of model. They present him as a perfect model of the ideal teacher with virtues of the semi-autonomous pole of the field.[50] He has no place to lay his head, and wanders the towns and countryside with his circle of students amazing hearers and viewers of his teachings and powers. The model has a perfect fit with much of what Eshleman details about sophists, philosophers and second century Christian teachers. This applies especially to those on the more autonomous pole of the field, like the Cynics, who carried strong critiques of society and displayed that distance in their manner of life. Those like the Cynics and Jesus of the Synoptic Gospels partly defined themselves over against the institutional pole that they taught had sold out to power, wealth and opinion. Jesus opposes himself to the wealthy, Sadducees, Pharisees and legal experts. To be his disciple, one must leave behind one's mother, father, family, possessions and devote oneself fully to following him. Both the writing of the Gospels themselves and the model of teachers and students that they project provide evidence of Christian teachers and their followers having found a fertile niche in the field at the end of the first and beginnings of the second century.[51] In Chapter Eleven, I argue that the Gospel of Matthew uses elements from Stoic thought, and in Chapter Five that Christians came to consciousness as a movement for Roman elites only in the early second century.

Part One of this book develops the theory of four sub-kinds of religion in the ancient Mediterranean with considerations of sacrificial offerings and their meaning, the religion of associations, and the notion of common Judaism. Part Two treats various aspects of Paul as a historical figure and the interpretation of his letters in light of the theory and the historical hypotheses put forward in the introduction. Part Four uses instances especially from the Synoptic Gospels to raise some methodological and theoretical issues important for historical work such as the concept of early Christian communities as agents, getting beyond the Judaism/Hellenism dualism and the idea of special privilege for the study of religion.

---

[49] Robyn Faith Walsh, *The Origins of Early Christian Literature: Contextualizing the New Testament Within Graeco-Roman Literary Culture* (Cambridge: Cambridge University Press, 2021), esp. 42–49.
[50] I am certainly not claiming that this interest excludes other literary themes such as Jesus as messiah and a son of God.
[51] Runar Thorsteinsson's *Jesus as Philosopher: The Moral Sage in the Synoptic Gospels*, admirably fills a void and demonstrates the debt to philosophy. (Oxford: Oxford University Press, 2018).

PART I

Everyday Religion and Its Alternatives

CHAPTER ONE

The Religion of Plant and Animal Offerings Versus the Religion of Meanings, Essences and Textual Mysteries*

This chapter advances a thesis about how to make progress on "the problem of sacrifice." What is the problem of sacrifice? Emerging from a long history of learned discussion, the problem of sacrifice centers on the notion that sacrifice in its many refractions carries some deep and perhaps universal power. The problem for the researcher comes in attempting to evaluate and to explain this notion. Paradigmatically, the question would take the following form: How does the seemingly straightforward and even mundane act of killing an animal in a religious context exhibit this power? Even though grain and plant offerings were much more common than animal offerings, and one did not kill the cakes or grain, the question has typically focused on animals, and thus often death. Thinkers have proposed many explanations for its power. Is it a deep meaning, a symbol, a psychological transformation, a power of social cohesion and social transformation or one of many other proposals?

Any critical interrogation of this "problem" must involve noticing that that the idea seems to have arisen in the ancient Mediterranean. This discussion will find its examples there, especially with the abundant Greek examples.[1] Central facts must include that sacrifice was the focus of the Judean temple and that Christians came eventually to describe Jesus' death as a sacrifice, and in the Medieval West also the Mass. But sacrificial practices were ubiquitous across the Mediterranean and West Asia. And there was mutual recognition. Judeans, for instance, readily identified what Romans, Syrians, Lydians, Romans and Libyans did with plants and animals in relation to gods as in the same category

---

* Chapter One reprints "The Religion of Plant and Animal Offerings Versus the Religion of Meanings, Essences and Textual Mysteries," in *Ancient Mediterranean Sacrifice: Images, Acts, Meanings*, 35–56, with copyright by Oxford University Press, reprinted with permission.
[1] The major work on Greek sacrifice is now, F. S. Naiden, *Smoke Signals for the Gods: Ancient Greek Sacrifice from the Archaic through Roman Periods* (New York: Oxford University Press, 2013).

as what they did in their Judean temple. Romans and the others also recognized the Jews as sacrificers.

When the study of religion as part of the study of other cultures developed, missionaries and anthropologists found that numerous cultures around the globe had sacrificial practices, offerings to gods and ancestors. Some of these Europeans saw the ubiquity of the practices as the proof of an original true monotheistic religion recorded in the Bible that had degenerated into polytheism.[2] Others interpreted the ubiquity as the sign that a kernel of an innate religiosity implanted by God in human nature had survived. How did the sacrificial practices relate to the kernel of truth?

With the emergence of modern historiography and the social sciences, sacrifice became a central problem. How could one explain the ubiquity of the practices in terms that did not simply reiterate Christian theology and Christian myths of origins? These pioneers usually saw the challenge as calling for social or psychological explanation. But especially for historians and theologians, a question stood out: Can we use the ancient written authorities closer to sacrifice's origins to discover its essence? Others thought the researcher should rather investigate primitive societies that they assumed stood closer to human origins. One might list numerous names of those interested in sacrifice such as Tylor, Frazer, Robertson-Smith, Durkheim, Hubert, Mauss, Freud, Evans-Pritchard and Girard.[3]

Against many in recent years, I have argued that religion is a real social kind, and not just an arbitrary construction of the West. My answer to the supposed problem of sacrifice is in some ways deflationary, but in other ways not so. As I will argue, the scholar best understands sacrifices as gifts and offerings to deities and similar beings, but these practices lie at the heart of what makes religion a social kind with a relatively stable cluster of properties. As discussed in the Introduction, the difficulty of interpreting and explaining the enormous variety in the practices and where to find some coherence, can best come from viewing religion as having a common pattern of exchange but with four interacting sub-types. Those sub-kinds must be seen as often in dynamic and complex relations as I try to illustrate in this chapter. One of these relations is historical with some sub-kinds depending on the existence of other kinds for their own historical emergence and constitution.

I want to stress the analytically crucial distinction between religion, and "a religion" as in "Christianity and Buddhism are religions." I am interested in

---

[2] Peter Harrison, 'Religion' and the Religions in the English Enlightenment (Cambridge: Cambridge University Press, 1990); Stanley Stowers, "Gods, Monotheism and Ancient Mediterranean Religion," unpublished paper read at several venues.

[3] For a handy selection from this discussion, see Jeffrey Carter, ed., *Understanding Religious Sacrifice: A Reader* (New York: Continuum, 2003).

all activities connected with beliefs about gods, ancestors, and so on and not just those that can be thought of as belonging to activities sanctioned by the kinds of usually large and complex social formations and claimed populations that we call religions. Religion is simply a class of human activity that scholars can theorize as an epistemic object, but "a religion" is typically a set of social formations in which some elite group, their institutions, their writings, iconic art, and so on claims that a certain population forms some kind of social unity. Among other problems, the failure to distinguish between religion as a human cognitive-practical phenomenon and a critical category of the researcher, and "religions," has led to the minimization or exclusion by scholars of family and household religion, the religion of women, children, slaves, so-called magic, sorcery and any religious behavior that did not fit the legitimized descriptions and prescriptions of social formations called religions.[4] In particular historical contexts and for individuals living the complex interactions of their lives, various combinations of the types of religion that I propose might meld seamlessly together for an individual, family or household and might only be theoretically and hypothetically analyzed. But at other times and places an individual might experience them as distinct, even in opposition. Both sides must be given their due in order to understand religion.

Taking a closer look at the sub-kinds we can ask how sacrifice fits into each of those complexes. Recalling from the Introduction, the first type is the religion of everyday social exchange (RESE) and the second, civic religion, although examples range from larger towns to cities, empires and domains ruled by kings and priests. The religious practices of the family and household are central to the first sub-kind, but are by no means the only practices that characterize it.[5] Without individual actors with individual interests, the analysis bleads into "social" mysticism.[6] Particular women, men, female juvenile women, male juveniles, apprentices and household servants/slaves all had

---

[4] For classical Athens, one might add to this list many sorts of intellectuals, much practice in connection with the dead and heroes, many local and *ad hoc* rites of individuals and groups (e.g., Plato, *Resp.* 909e–910b), and foreign and mixed practices, all often marginalized or excluded in the polis-religion model.

[5] My sub-kinds are extremely relational and interactive when they exist together, and the latter is on a continuum of more and less. See my Introduction here and the essays in *Household and Family Religion in Antiquity*, John Bodel and Saul Olyan (Oxford: Blackwell, 2008). The chapters by Faraone and Boedeker join a mounting chorus of protest against the claim that all religion in the classical Greek city was "polis religion" as in Sourvinou-Inwood: "What is Polis Religion?" in *The Greek City from Homer to Alexander*, ed. Oswyn Murray and S. R. F. Price (Oxford: Clarendon Press, 1990), 295–322; "Further Aspects of Polis Religion," *Annali Instituto Orientale di Napoli: Archaeologia e Storia* 10 (1988): 259–274.

[6] Jörg Rüpke has pioneered in making the category of the individual important in the study of ancient religion, e.g., "Theorizing Religion for the Individual," in *The Greco-Roman Cults of Isis: Agents, Images and Practices*, ed.Valentino Gasparini and RichardVeymiers (Leiden: Brill, 2016), 61–73.

religious interests partly by dint of their social roles and partly due to their individual history and interests. Participants in this religiosity understood gods and similar beings as agents who impinge upon and participate in quite specific and local ways in their activities of everyday life. People everywhere in the various cultural areas of the Mediterranean and West Asia practiced this kind of religion. It was in some sense, as I shall argue, basic. Animal and plant offerings have a central place here, but only make sense as activities linked to certain other practices that involve inferences about a host of beings that share certain characteristics: gods, heroes and heroines, ancestors, the beloved dead, ghosts, spirits, demons, unknown or unidentified agents of this class, and many others. Now it would be a complete misunderstanding of these practices to construe these inferences as theologies, or as rationalized systematic thought, which were supposed to provide the meaning for the practices. Greeks normally did not, for instance, rationalize and theorize the relations of the supremely local Zeus of the Possessions, sometimes translated Zeus of the Pantry, or Zeus of the Household Fence and the cosmic Olympian Zeus.[7] They did not need to because they knew what to do in contexts relevant to each of these in order to achieve their goals. All Greeks seem to have known that Zeus was responsible for the weather. If rain was needed, an appeal to the heavenly or cosmic Zeus was in order. Zeus of the Possessions was represented by a jar, perhaps placed in a storeroom. Presumably one would appeal to him in order to protect the grain from mice. Scholars cannot agree on whether Greeks thought of these and numerous other Zeuses as manifestations of the same god or different gods.[8] This disagreement has arisen because Greeks normally related to their deities in locally particular ways organized by what I am calling "everyday social exchange." Few Greeks cared about the theoretical question regarding the nature of Zeus. We have no good scholarly reason to believe that it was any different for Judeans. As strange as it might seem to us academics, especially after centuries of Christianity, Judaism, Islam and Buddhism, there are social conditions necessary for having an interest in such questions.

---

[7] By my count, in classical Athens, Zeus went by at least twenty-eight different names or titles. On Zeus, see Hans Schwabl and Erika Simon, "Zeus," PW 2/19:253–376; with PWSup 15:993–1481; Karim Arafat, *Classical Zeus: A Study in Art and Literature* (Oxford: Oxford University Press, 1990).

[8] The two sides can be represented by Jon D. Mikalson, *Honor thy Gods: Popular Religion in Greek Tragedy* (Chapel Hill: University of North Carolina Press, 1991) and Christine Sourvinou-Inwood, "Tragedy and Religion: Constructs and Readings" in *Greek Tragedy and the Historian*, ed. Christopher Pelling (Oxford: Clarendon Press, 1997), 161–185; eadem, *Tragedy and Athenian Religion* (Lanham, MD: Lexington Books, 2003). Mikalson argues that Athenians did not have one unified Zeus in all of their cults, and also emphasizes the distance between the gods of everyday cult and of the poets. My approach undermines the idea of a totalizing official religion of the Greek city that formed a kind of systemic symbolic order.

Rather than imagining people carrying around highly organized systems of belief that then generate actions, we should imagine that religious inferences and beliefs were evoked as aspects of their practical skills for living life day to day and were dispersed in their practices. Thus thinkings, believings, and inferrings about the gods are to be themselves understood as aspects of human activities that make sense in the context of the locally specific unfolding practices of which they are a part. Practices take place at specific places in time and space. As I will suggest below, one important set of practices characteristic of the religion of literate experts (third sub-kind), reading and writing practices, by contrast tend to hide their location in time and place.

In this religion of mundane social exchange, gods and similar beings were conceived not primarily as relating to humans as dedicated patrons such as Athena to Athens and Yahweh to Judeans, legislators, or moral exemplars, but as interested parties.[9] They are inhabitants of the environment. Thus, a deity might be willing to guarantee an oath when two people called upon it. But the same god would have no interest in controlling and regulating human lives as its central goal. A goddess might champion a heroic warrior. A daemon might lend the power to cast a spell. Four characteristics of conceiving gods and similar beings in this mode of religiosity standout: People interact with them as if they were persons; they are local in ways that are significant for humans; one maintains a relationship to them with practices of generalized reciprocity, a kind of social exchange; and humans have a particular epistemological stance toward them. Religions with gods who are legislators or who are moral exemplars, I would argue, require an institutionalized literate elite. The default position found very widely around the globe is types of religiosity featuring gods and similar beings conceived as interested parties with whom people carry on mundane social exchange.

The practices that involve inferences about and representations of gods, ancestors, unknown beings and so on construe them as like persons, but persons who usually possess some very special and powerful abilities.[10] These beings have human-like minds in that they think, believe, have desires, emotions, personalities and preferences of various sorts. In the ancient Mediterranean and West Asia, they were often conceived as immortal, although this might not be the case also for ghosts or the most local of beings. Even with all of their often great and diverse powers, these beings are not unlimited. Indeed, they are limited by space and time. They, for example, are conceived as being in

---

[9] For a summary account of three of these models, see Pascal Boyer, "Why Do Gods and Spirits Matter at All?" in *Current Approaches in the Cognitive Science of Religion*, ed. Ilkka Pyysiänen and Veikko Anttonen (London: Contiuum, 2002), 81–82.

[10] A useful introduction the cognitive science approach is Todd Tremlin, *Minds and Gods: The Cognitive Foundations of Religion* (Oxford: Oxford University Press, 2006).

specific places (a mountain, a temple in Jerusalem or Rome) and as sometimes needing to use messengers for communication. Now we might be tempted to say that I am making these ancient beliefs literal when they are actually only symbolic and metaphorical.[11] But while symbol and metaphor are certainly sometimes involved in this kind of religiosity, I want to argue that this global move of claiming that these beliefs are essentially symbolic and metaphorical is precisely a move that belongs to the third kind of religiosity (literate experts) and to modernist thought.

These practices that involve contact with the gods, heroes, and ancestors typically take place at sites with special significance. This is partly related to the idea that these beings have a history, even before human history, connected to the land and the landscape.[12] Ancestors and the beloved dead had known human life in particular places and the very people who now talk to them and ask for help. Moreover, some of these beings are responsible for the plant and animal life and offspring that belongs to the land. When Greeks laid out new cities, they first decided which deities belonged to the area and set off places for temples.[13] The Greek household also had its yet more local sites for Zeus of the Possessions, Zeus of the Fence, Apollo, Hecate, Hestia, and Hermes. For all of their difference from mortal humans and their powers, such beings were natural inhabitants of the environment just as much as were eagles, olive trees and butterflies.

The persistent central practices in the religion of everyday social exchange follow from the very particular assumptions about the class of gods and related beings. Animal and plant offerings make sense in this context. Three families of practices have their sense in light of these assumptions: divinatory practices; speaking practices, including prayer, promising and other social transactions; and practices of social reciprocity more narrowly, including sacrificial gifts. These are not the only practices in this mode of religiosity, but they are the most important.

What knowledge was most important to this kind of religion? The answer, I believe, is not myth or theological concepts – these were often sketchy at best and usually did not align with the intuitive practical sense of interacting with a person-like being. Rather, it was a matching-up of the how-to knowledge of

---

[11] The groundbreaking book that definitively undermined symbolic interpretation is Dan Sperber, *Rethinking Symbolism* (Cambridge: Cambridge University Press, 1975).

[12] The best discussion of the locative nature of Greek religion is Susan Guettel Cole, *Landscapes, Gender, and Ritual Space: The Ancient Greek Experience* (Berkeley: University of California Press, 2004); eadem, *Placing the Gods: Sanctuaries and Sacred Space in Ancient Greece* (Oxford: Clarendon, 1994).

[13] A decree of fourth century BCE Colophon gives a plan to restore the neglected or abandoned old city and speaks of the gods and heroes "who occupy our city and territory" in Franz G. Maier, *Griechische Mauerbauinschriften* (Heidelberg: Quelle & Meyer, 1959), no. 69, lines 9–21.

common social practices with lore and intuitive inferences about how gods and such beings would behave as kinds of persons. Cognitive psychologists have produced impressive work on the way this kind of intuitive thinking works. Who in the ancient Mediterranean did not know how to give gifts, prepare food for others, share in celebratory meals, clean up a place for others, talk to others, request from others, ask for help, get someone powerful to help you, appease the hostile, make promises, honor and praise, sing for someone, seek information about another's disposition, whether kindly or hostile, and seek expert or insider advice? Simply add the idea that the other person involved was a god, a beloved dead one, ancestor, hero or another such being who might be a willing participant, and one has a list of the religious practices of this mundane religiosity. Modifications of everyday practices were the most important religious practices. Of course, such beings had special qualities and so there was a certain logic to the way that everyday practices of social exchange got modified. Gods, for instance, did not often directly show themselves or talk back directly like humans or consume food like humans did and so on. They had their own ways to participate, communicate and appear, even if they were ordinarily excellent partners in generalized reciprocity. An adequate theory of sacrifice requires an account of common human practices and the kinds of basic beliefs and inferences about gods and similar beings that provided the practical logic and skills for the religious modifications of the common practices.

The dominant epistemological mood in the religion of everyday social exchange was uncertainty; not uncertainty about the existence of the gods and similar beings or the gods as the source of goods from the land and aid for human activities, but uncertainty about how and when the gods act, as well as their moods and desires. Humans know very little about how the gods are feeling and what they are doing, but that the gods know much of or all of what humans think, feel and do.[14] This epistemological imbalance produces a situation for humans that is similar to being in a many-windowed house with curtains up after dark. Those inside have a feeling that they are being watched, and this may be likely in the busy neighborhood, but they do not know who, or when or with what intentions the watchers are observing them. The situation makes the gods excellent guarantors of human social transactions, for example, of oaths and vows. The gods can also be a uniquely valuable source for information about what humans are doing, whether it be the machinations of an enemy or the true feelings of a love interest. Thus, the enormous importance of divinatory practices for both this sort of information and for detecting the dispositions of the gods and the things that the gods can

---

[14] E.g., Boyer, "Why Do Gods Matter," 76–81 with what the best scholarship on these cultures has concluded such as Robert Parker, *Polytheism and Society at Athens* (Oxford: Oxford University Press, 2005), 105, 140.

foresee.[15] The dispositions and advice of the gods was seen primarily in signs and traces, and frequently took the form of yes or no, well-disposed or not. Pindar expresses the typical epistemological uncertainty that should be contrasted with the certainty in the second mode of religiosity: "Never yet has anyone who walks upon the earth found a reliable symbol from the gods concerning a future matter" (*Ol.* 12.7–12). Xenophon can both write, "The gods know everything and in sacrifices, omens, voices, and dreams they give forewarnings to whomever they want" (*Eq. mag.* 9.7–9) and point out that people were also skeptical of divine omniscience (*Symp.* 4.47–49; *Mem.* 1.1.19).[16] The gods at least knew a great deal, perhaps everything.

There is one activity of the gods that humans in this mode of religiosity know most clearly and feel as imminent. The gods regularly give the fruit of the land – the grain, the oil, the offspring of animals and the children of humans. These new products mysteriously come from somewhere. Why not from someone? This assumption, together with the default intuition that the gods are persons, forms the context for practices of social reciprocity with the gods. Market exchange creates a relationship between commodities by way of money and price equivalences.[17] Such an exchange comes to an end with the end of the transaction. Reciprocity is exactly the opposite. Exchanged commodities have no exact equivalence or exact value. Rather, exchange furthers an, in principle, unending relationship between persons. Mutual gift-giving across time maintains the relationship because there is always something left over that calls for another exchange. One never achieves a balance, an equivalence that would call for the end of gift-giving. These practices worked well even for quite unequal relationships, say between the wealthy or powerful and the poor, because their point is not the value of the gifts, but the relationship based in honor and mutual respect, at least in theory.

Greek and ancient Mediterranean religious practices acted out such reciprocity with the gods. At their center were gifts of food from plants and animals in return for the gift of those very goods from the gods. The overwhelmingly dominant forms of sacrifice were ritualized versions of festive food preparation and eating practices with very special guests. How did the death of the animal fit these activities? If you have ever tried to eat a live unbutchered

---

[15] See especially, Jennifer Eyl, *Signs, Wonders, and Gifts: Divination in the Letters of Paul* (New York: Oxford University Press, 2019), esp. 46–85.

[16] My translations.

[17] See the excellent discussion of reciprocity with bibliography in Daniel Ullucci, *The Christian Rejection of Animal Sacrifice* (New York: Oxford University Press, 2012), 24–30; Hans van Wees, "The Law of Gratitude: Reciprocity in Anthropological Theory" in *Reciprocity in Ancient Greece*, eds. Christopher Gill, Norman Postlethwaite, and Richard Seaford (New York: Oxford University Press, 1998), 13–50. For ancient Israel, the Hebrew Bible and ancient Judaism, see Glaim, n. 45 below.

and uncooked animal, then you know the answer. Were it not for the later Christian theologizing of Christ's death as a sacrifice we would not even be asking this question.

Because of Christian theology, scholarly attention has focused on so-called expiatory sacrifices, what the Greeks often called *enagismos*.[18] It is important to understand how these sorts of practices do not negate the generalizations about gift-giving and reciprocity. Although I have focused upon "the gods," these cultures contained both a range of non-evident beings and a range of personality among and with particular gods. "The gods" were the public, most powerful, and well-disposed of these beings with whom the various ethnic populations had had long and regular relations. But there were also other sorts of beings. Beings that we call spirits, demons, the restless dead, the beloved dead, angels, ancestors, daemons, nymphs and satyrs, and shading off into anthropomorphisms such as the evil eye, are typically found in very specific local contexts where they have a variety of temperaments. One might encounter these beings in specific contexts, or seek them out for specific purposes, but not do much – if anything – to maintain a steady reciprocal relationship with them. Even the Olympian deities have differing moods and contextual manifestations. As in reciprocity among humans, relations of reciprocity with non-evident beings are complex and may become strained or broken or difficult. A gift/sacrifice can even be rejected.[19] As personalities vary, such relations are more difficult with some than with others. Sometimes normal gift-giving is the wrong thing to do, and gifts that represent appeasement, conciliation, or caution about the relationship make sense. Thus, a whole range of incense, plant, drink and animal offerings gave people options for special occasions or difficult gods and daemons that did not show the presumption that festive *thusia* might indicate in such situations. But cleaning up, honoring, praising, lamp lighting, entertaining and so forth could also be creatively employed as gifts. So-called "magical practices" were important in the religion of everyday social exchange and made sense there, but often ran against the larger communitarian norms of civic religion. The more than three hundred curse tablets from Attica alone show us that the same people who were paragons of civic religion also secretly employed the curses aimed at people in civic contexts such as court cases.[20] The RESE often supported civic religion, but was also often at

---

[18] The old distinction between Olympian and Chthonian rites should be completely abandoned. See Maria-Zoe Petropoulou, *Animal Sacrifice in Ancient, Greek Religion, Judaism and Christianity, 100 BC–AD 200* (Oxford: Oxford University Press, 2008), 34–37 and Ullucci, *Christian Rejection*, 129-32, for important corrections of Petropoulou.

[19] F. S. Naiden, "Rejected Sacrifice in Greek and Hebrew Religion," *JANER* 6 (2006): 186–223.

[20] Fritz Graf, *Magic in the Ancient World* (Cambridge: Harvard University Press, 1997); (especially the chapter by Faraone in) Christopher A. Faraone and Dirk Obbink, eds., *Magika Hiera: Ancient Greek Magic and Religion* (New York: Oxford University Press, 1991); John Gager, *Curse Tablets and Binding Spells from the Ancient World* (New York: Oxford University Press, 1992).

cross-purposes with it. Interests of individuals, families and households might not be the same as those promoted by the city.

We can think about the religion of everyday social exchange more clearly if we talk of gifts and offerings rather than of sacrifice, and thereby avoid reading into these practices connotations related to theologies of Christ's death. These ancients imagined life lived among these beings who gave goods to them. Gifts and offerings made intuitive sense to people who sought exchange relations, often long term, with such beings. Cognitive psychologists have shown that humans generally have cognitive tendencies that make it easy to entertain thought about the existence of god-like beings and to intuitively feel that gifts and offerings represent the appropriate fairness and sense of gratitude toward them.[21] If such an explanation is approximately correct, the problem of sacrifice vanishes for the religion of everyday social exchange.

The third sub-kind is the religion of the literate cultural producer, together with people who clustered around more entrepreneurial versions of this expert.[22] These people were in various ways experts by virtue of the skills, prestige and legitimacy they derived from their belonging to the perhaps two percent or probably less of people who were literate enough to produce and authoritatively interpret complex written texts.[23] Although small in number in any one location, they formed a large network due to their mobility and the endurance of written texts across time and place. These networks or fields, to vary the metaphor, were united by a set of common literate practices that allowed skills, writings, ideas, motifs, and so on to cross ethnic, linguistic and status boundaries. The point-of-view of these literate religious experts has dominated scholarship on animal sacrifice. It has been difficult for scholars to notice that writing a text or taking an interpretive position as a literate specialist are different practices with other socio-cultural locations than killing, cutting up or cooking an animal to honor a god. This, I believe, is because scholars on religion have continued to use modernist forms to reproduce the discourse and to inhabit the practices of the ancient experts. It is a case of being able to see around oneself, but not oneself. I suspect that the scholar wants to reply to my claims that, "the sacrificer may not have been literate, but it is all about meaning; one writes it down and finds it in a writing, but the other possesses the meanings in his head. What is the difference?" It is however precisely this move of assimilation, which denies different modes of religiosity, that gives the specialist his or her unacknowledged assumption of an Archimedean point-of-view and God's eye vantage. It also allows both the ancient expert and the modern scholar to pose sacrifice as a universal problem.

---

[21] I work out in some detail an argument about the cognition in Chapter Four of my *History and The Study of Religion*.

[22] See above all Heidi Wendt, *At the Temple Gates: The Religion of Freelance Experts in the Roman Empire* (New York: Oxford University Press, 2016).

[23] See Chapter Four in this volume.

The person who offered a sacrificial animal did not need to be literate and the practice did not depend upon writings and their interpretation. Any Greek, Italian, Judean, or other culturally similar illiterate farmer could offer grain, cakes, or an animal. And while the religion of the literate expert might include the practices of the RESE, or even be parasitic upon them, the religion of the specialist could not exist without writings, high literacy, networks of literate exchange and various textually-oriented interpretive practices. It is important to stress that I am not here drawing a contrast between intelligent, knowledgeable people with skilled interpretive practices and those who did not possess these qualities. The illiterate farmer might be highly intelligent and a skillful interpreter of a vast amount of religious knowledge and be a skilled interpreter of the relevant signs, but his offerings and knowledge do not make him part of a distinctive arena of competing producers of writings and interpretive practices based upon the trans-local circulation of these products.

Two things must be kept in mind in order to understand the effects of literate experts on religion. First, any literate textual practice, including writing, reading, and interpretive practices, introduces modifications into, or over against, the religion of everyday social exchange and civic religion. Second, the kinds of novelty and degrees of difference from the RESE and civic religion varied greatly among different kinds of experts in the field. This field of literate exchange had many sub-fields along the lines of ethnicity, social rank and educational opportunity.[24] As already noted, it also had two poles that were in creative tension.[25] On the one end of the spectrum, literate experts were not very entrepreneurial and depended upon kings, patrons, the scribal needs of aristocrats and even public patronage. Although literate specialists on this pole tended to intellectualize and textualize sacrifice, they took a much less radical position than those on the other pole. By the second century CE, for instance, the dominant Greek and Latin rhetorical education and the orators and writers of the so-called Second Sophistic and certain kinds of philosophers represented the dominant pole of the field. But there was an opposing pole made up of certain sorts of philosophers, Christian teachers and many sorts of independent operators who defined themselves in opposition to the dominant

---

[24] On fields, see Robyn Faith Walsh, *The Origins of Early Christian Literature: Contextualizing the New Testament within Greco-Roman Literary Culture* (Cambridge: Cambridge University Press, 2021), esp. 105–133.

[25] I am indebted to Pierre Bourdieu's demystified reformulation of Max Weber; Pierre Bourdieu, "Genesis and the Structure of the Religious Field," *Comparative Social Research* 13 (1991), 1–44; idem, "Legitimation and Structured Interests in Weber's Sociology of Religion" in *Max Weber: Rationality and Modernity*, ed. Scott Lash and Sam Whimster (London: Allen and Unwin, 1987), 119–136; idem, *The Rules of Art: Genesis and Structure of the Literary Field* (Cambridge: Polity Press, 1996); idem, *The Field of Cultural Production* (New York: Columbia University Press, 1993).

pole. The traditionally legitimized specialists, in their view, had been corrupted by depending upon the money, power and prestige that belonged to the dominant pole. Truth and morals could only come from those who had not sold out, those who showed disinterest in money, wealth and power. Experts on this dominated side had no position by inheritance or bestowal and could only gain legitimacy by outdoing other experts in displaying disinterest and novelty. Unsurprisingly, these entrepreneurs criticized reciprocity as a mode of relating to the gods.[26] The gods could not be bribed, bargained with or honored through petty offerings. The gods wanted true beliefs and the right inner formation of individuals.

In the case of classical Athens, the poets were the literate experts who stood closest to the everyday religion and civic religion. Epic, tragedy and comedy were in many ways conservative, but literate experts by definition followed norms inherited from other experts in the field that operated by literary, interpretive, and textual principles that were semi-autonomous in relation to the RESE and civic religion. Thus, Zeus in epic and comedy was often lusty, adulterous and in a troubled marriage with Hera. This Zeus fit ancient storytelling conventions of the relevant genres and their entertainment values. In the religion of everyday social exchange, by contrast, and in the religion of the polis, Zeus and Hera were the most sober models of marital propriety.[27] How remote is Zeus in Homer or Aeschylus from the Zeus of the Possessions who had little or no myth and did not need personality? Yet poetry was performed publicly, and poets lived by public patronage. The underlying conservatism of the poets allowed their textual innovations on religion to exist in a semi-autonomy alongside the RESE in civic religion. If the Homeric epics or Athenian drama had disappeared, the religion of everyday social exchange would have been little affected in the way that it worked, although the specifics would have differed in the way that everyday religiosity interacted with civic religion.

The other pole of the field of literate specialists in Athens was occupied by philosophers of various sorts, certain so-called sophists, independent religious entrepreneurs and traditions such as Orphism.[28] This pole was important for the future because it was necessary to the formation of Christianity. Many of these literate specialists centrally criticized both poetry and the RESE. The opposition of philosophy and poetry is well known to us. For all of the differences that separated the legitimized poets from the religious entrepreneurs and philosophers, it is important to recognize that they were – excuse the metaphor – playing

---

[26] Ullucci, *Christian Rejection*.
[27] Parker, *Polytheism and Society*, 393, 441.
[28] On Orphism, see Wendt, *Temple Gates*, 129–135. Parker has discussed some appropriate evidence under the category of "Unlicensed Religion and Magic" (*Polytheism and Society*, 116–152). Important is Fritz Graf and Sarah Iles Johnston, *Ritual Texts for the Afterlife: Orpheus and the Bacchic Gold Tablets* (London: Routledge, 2007).

versions of the same game on a common field. This shared game can be seen among other ways in their sense of opposition to one another, one pole of the field to the other. One side guarded traditional religious sensibilities and the other attacked these as false religion. Their reading, writing and interpretive practices and generalizing, even universalizing, points-of-view allowed both sides to take intellectualist positions on religious matters. The Greek farmer in the religion of everyday social exchange did not take competing positions on the true nature of Demeter or Zeus of the Possessions or the origins and meaning of some civic cult as an essential part of his religiosity.

Drama in virtue of its proximity to the less independent side of the field, only took positions in indirect ways, often by voicing difficult theological questions and providing kinds of explanations, including the invention of memorable foundation stories for established civic cults.[29] The questioning and explaining took place safely inside the different world and time of heroic myth. In this mythic time and world, gods could be imagined as demanding human sacrifice by a writer who inhabited this literary world. But such imagining was utterly remote from everyday sacrificial practices and not the perception of some essence or origins to sacrifice. The literate products of drama also created other novelties for both civic religion and the religion of everyday social exchange. In the world of myth, the gods were often irrationally angry, vengeful, seemingly unjust and undependable. Athenians in their civic religion never spoke of the gods in this way, however.[30] In the public religion of the city, the gods were always good, gracious and trustworthy. Furthermore, the gods loved Athens in a way that the gods did not love individuals in the religion of everyday social exchange.

Robert Parker makes another point about drama's difference from everyday religion. In contrast to the rich divine and heroic personalities of drama,

> In daily life the experience of the gods was muted and anonymous. One might suspect a divine element in many aspects of life, but one never or hardly ever saw an identifiable god at work. In ordinary speech accordingly one normally spoke of 'the divine' or 'the gods' or an unspecified 'god/the god/some god,' not of named Olympians.[31]

These speech practices that Parker describes, with their implied modest epistemology, comes from what I have argued is the religion of everyday social exchange, a default basic religiosity that was built upon and modified in the religion of literate experts and in civic religion. Fitting with drama's location toward the dominant pole of the field of literate specialty, which is most closely

---

[29] Mikalson, *Honor Thy Gods*; Sourvinou-Inwood, *Tragedy and Athenian Religion*.
[30] Parker, *Polytheism and Society*, 146.
[31] Ibid., 140.

connected to civic and everyday religion, its position-takings about religion took place in the bracketed arena of fictionality and of a fabulous yonder-world of myth. Here knowledge about the gods presented itself as a story told by someone from some place. This approach connected with the often-richer divine personalities and language of secure knowledge favored in a civic cult, but in terms of the semi-autonomous literate practices of this kind of expert.

By contrast, Zeno of Citium *knew* that Zeus was the one deity who had created this cycle of the cosmos and who pervaded the world as the structuring *pneuma*, and explicitly argued that other positions were quite wrong.[32] Moreover, he knew that Homer had craftily presented his gods as symbols for this underlying reality. The popular and civic understanding of the poets was theologically wrong and immoral. Proper interpretation was required. The priest who wrote the Derveni papyrus laments the ignorant literalist views that most people have.[33] Just as one might expect, Aristophanes in turn ridicules such literate specialists who come from the independent and non-legitimized side of the field. On this kind of analysis, his famous criticisms of Socrates are predictable. In *Peace* (38–49), a slave who has to tend the disgusting dung beetle wonders if some angry god has given him the job as a punishment. Then his fellow servant says,

> But perhaps now some spectator, some beardless youth who thinks himself a sage, will say, What is this? What does the beetle *mean*? And then an Ionian, sitting next to him, will add, I think he refers this *enigmatically* to Cleon, who so shamelessly feeds on filth all by himself.[34]

Of interest here are the aspirant student sage, the Ionian next to him and the practice of seeking the meaning of enigmas. The second is surely a reference to the many Ionian philosophers and similar intellectuals who came to Athens in the fifth century or perhaps especially to one of them. Many of these operated by the allegorical or symbolic interpretation of texts, finding deep meanings not found in civic religion and the religion of everyday social exchange. To use Gregory Nagy's language, such practices often participated in an "ideology of exclusiveness."[35]

---

[32] Keimpe Algra, "Stoic Theology," in *The Cambridge Companion to the Stoics*, ed. Brad Inwood (Cambridge: Cambridge University Press, 2003), 153–178.

[33] See note 46 below and the associated text.

[34] For the example and translation see, Peter T. Struck, *Birth of the Symbol: Ancient Readers at the Limits of Their Texts* (Princeton: Princeton University Press, 2004), 39–41.

[35] Gregory Nagy, *The Best of the Achaeans: Concepts of the Hero in Archaic Greek Poetry*, rev. ed. (Baltimore: Johns Hopkins University Press, 1999), 239; Struck, *Birth of the Symbol*, 41. On such allegorical and symbolic interpretation, in addition to Struck, see Donald A. Russell and David Konstan, eds., *Heraclitus: Homeric Problems* (Atlanta: SBL Press, 2005), xi–xxx; G. R. Boys-Stones, *Metaphor Allegory and the Classical Tradition* (Oxford: Oxford University Press, 2003); Wolfgang Bernard, *Spaetantike Diktungstheorien: Untersuchungen zu Proklos, Herakleitos und Plutarch* (Stuttgart: Teubner, 1990).

The tension between traditional religion and the claimed authority of the expert with his books and interpretive practices is wonderfully captured in the *Birds* of Aristophanes (959–990). Pisthetaerus is about to sacrifice a goat for the founding of the new city in the sky when an oracle-speaker (*chresmologos*) appears:

> Oracle-Speaker: Let not the goat be sacrificed.
> Pisthetaerus: Who are you?
> Oracle-Speaker: Who am I? An Oracle-Speaker.
> Pisthetaerus: Get out!
> Oracle-Speaker: Wretched man, insult not sacred things. For there is an oracle of Bacis which exactly applies to Cloudcuckooland. . . .
> Oracle-Speaker: *But when the wolves and the white crows shall dwell together between Corinth and Sicyon* . . . –
> Pisthetaerus: What do the Corinthians have to do with me?
> Oracle-Speaker: Bacis enigmatizes this to the air (*aer*).
> *They must first sacrifice a white-fleeced goat to Pandora, and give the prophet who first reveals my words a good cloak and new sandals.*
> Pisthetaerus: Does it say sandals there?
> Oracle-Speaker: Look at the book.[36]

Beyond the standard joke about the greedy motives of seers in this exchange, Aristophanes gives some interesting details about this particular oracle-speaker. The latter interprets a book of oracles by the famous oracle-speaker of the fifth century from Boeotia who was credited with important prophecies about the Persian War and prophecies under his name were important during the Peloponnesian War. Books of his oracles circulated widely and were used at least as late as the second century CE. The figure in the *Birds* is an expert interpreter of a book that is an accumulation of literate knowledge-practices. It is not clear whether these are supposed to be ecstatic prophecies Bacis committed to writing or prophecies he collected from elsewhere. But the specialist in the *Birds* applies to the situation of Cloudcuckooland an interpretation that Bacis gave to an oracle in another context, a move highly familiar from ancient Jewish and early Christian writings. Peter Struck has pointed out that Aristophanes uses the same technical language for interpretation here as he does of the Ionian philosopher in *Peace*: "Bacis enigmatizes this to *aer*."[37] The specialized language comes from the symbolic interpretation of texts. We should not universalize and naturalize symbolic interpretation as has been done in much literary and anthropological theory. The symbolic interpretation of writings has a beginning and a history.

---

[36] The translation is adapted from Eugene O'Neill, *The Complete Greek Dramas* (New York: Random House, 1938) and Struck, *Birth of the Symbol*, 175–176.

[37] Struck, *Birth of the Symbol*, 176.

Its modern practitioners have bedeviled the study of sacrifice. In the *Birds*, *aer* is, of course, the lower atmosphere where Cloudcuckooland was to be. But what symbolic interpreters of Homer and other writings had found at least as far back as the sixth century was that the ancient writers had left enigmas in the text with symbolic meanings. The real meanings of these enigmas were often physical and cosmological truths such as the idea popular from Empedocles to the Stoics that Hera represented *aer*, both the element and the heavenly realm.[38] In the examples from his *Peace* and the *Birds*, Aristophanes makes light of a kind of claim to literate interpretive knowledge that is particularly annoying to him; that of the annoyingly independent and unsanctioned fellow expert in texts, literature and opinions about what is right and true.

Such experts often criticized the religion of everyday social exchange by claiming that their textually based knowledge disclosed the true and deeper meaning of everyday practices. Rather than the mundane local perspectives and interests of the first mode of religiosity, the literate expert, especially that of a more entrepreneurial kind, sought to discover the deep meanings and hidden wisdom about the gods, the cosmos, the structure of the world and human nature. Paul's words in Romans 12:1–2 provide an example, "present your bodies as a living sacrifice (*thusia*), holy and well-pleasing to God which is your rational worship. And do not be structured by this age, but be transformed by the renewal of your mind so that you might test for what is the will of God. . . ." The "rational worship" of the exhortation implies a contrast with the non-Judean ritual practices that Paul excoriates in chapter one (1:21–25). Specifically, he claims that practices – surely including animal sacrifice – that employ carved and variously formed representations of gods in anthropomorphic, theriomorphic and other iconic forms are foolish, dishonor God, represent a corruption of rationality and lead to gross immorality. From the perspective of this self-proclaimed expert interpreter of Judean writings, these common practices featuring gods of many locales miss the truth of one transcendent universal god who should be worshipped with the right conceptions, a mind in the proper disposition and with the right moral character. Religion here is not about the everyday interests of family, clan, friends and neighbors, good crops, the health of a child, the powers of revenge for a perceived injustice, and so on. Rather it concerns products of mind, the right belief about the divine, the true nature of the self and discernment of one's place in the drama of world history. These intellectualist origins of Christian religion are why it took centuries for Christians to develop distinctive life-course rituals such as for weddings, funerals and local agricultural festivals. In the religion of literate experts, sacrifice is often not festively eating an animal in the presence of the gods. It is rather a cipher for supposedly deeper meanings.

---

[38] Peter Kingsley, *Ancient Philosophy, Mystery, and Magic: Empedocles and the Pythagorean Tradition* (Oxford: Clarendon Press, 1995), 24–35.

Of course, all of these deeper truths required the interpretive skills of the expert – who alone could decipher the meaning of things by means of abilities with books. One could include here Zeno, who thought that there was no need for temples at all, and Chrysippus who read traditional Greek representations of the gods as symbols that pointed to the one theistic-pantheistic god. Cynic philosophers populated the markets and public places with critics attempting to bend the ears of the masses. Plutarch used similar methods to find a different sort of god in a vastly more hierarchical universe. Or it could be Lucian of Samosata who ridiculed animal sacrifice and ordinary religious practices. The list is very large. The important thing to bear in mind is that Paul, Zeno, Plutarch and Lucian, in spite of the competitive opposition that they would have had toward each other by virtue of being experts whose raison d'etre was staking positions about what is true, right and good, shared more with each other than they did with the Greek farmer or Egyptian Jewish weaver.[39] Above all, the practices about the gods that they valued most highly and upon which their power depended were their competitive literate skills.[40]

Plato takes the literate specialist's point-of-view on the religion of everyday social exchange when in the *Laws* (909e–910b) he proposes to do away with practices that he sees as too private, local and reflective of misunderstandings about the nature of the gods:

> It is not easy to establish temples and gods, and to do this properly requires great intelligence (*dianoia*), but it is customary for all women especially, and for people who are sick everywhere, and people in danger or trouble – no matter what kind of trouble – and conversely, when people have some good fortune, to consecrate whatever happens to be at hand right then, and to vow sacrifices and promise the building of sacred places or objects for gods, daemons and children of the gods: and because of fears caused by apparitions while awake or dreams . . . they chance to found altars and sacred sites, filling every house and every village with them, and open spaces too, and every spot that was the place of such experiences (*Leg.* 909e–910b).[41]

True religion must show a disinterest in the private and local and show an interest in the city as a whole, the universal and the true nature of the gods.

The expert thinks that what is essential to a practice is its meaning. Meaning here is some determinate proposition or set of propositions about the practice that usually derives from the expert's textual activities.[42] Such propositions often come with criticisms about sacrificial practices being too local, too interested

---

[39] For the competition see Wendt, *At the Temple Gates*.
[40] By contrast, the practices of animal sacrifice, as I have argued, were related to agriculture, animal husbandry, and the land.
[41] My translation.
[42] Ullucci, *Christian Rejection*.

and too literal. "Literal" here means supposedly ranking the traditional activity, understood as mundane interaction with the gods, over meaning. The most important practices of the literate expert were acts of translation. Even their writings depended upon interpretive reading activities involving books deemed to have authority of various types. The earliest known Greek example involving such translation is Pherekydes of Syron, who wrote about 544 BCE. Fragments of Pherekydes show him interpreting passages from Homer as truly about the fundamental nature of the cosmos. Between Pherekydes and Aristotle one finds Metrodorus of Lampascus, Theagones of Rhegium, Anaxagoras, and Stesimbrotus of Thasos treating Homer in similar ways.[43] The act of translation works like this. The shallow person, probably the average participant in the religion of social exchange or civic religion, understands Homer, and presumably rituals, at the surface. But these literate specialists know that "difficult" passages in Homer are "enigmas" and "symbols" that reveal truths about the nature of the soul, the cosmos, and other wisdom. So Aristobulus, Philo of Alexandria and numerous other Jewish literate experts treated the Books of Moses. Christians would translate from Judean scripture into truths about the true nature of the world order, its future, true worship and a particular figure from recent history. In each case, what ordinary people practiced as local, particular and unsystematic, the specialist translates into another idiom that tends toward universalizing, the non-local and harmonized knowledge.

The writers of the rabbinic literature produced another translation that can be used to illustrate the range of creative possibility available to the experts. They imaginatively "replaced" a temple-centered religion of plant and animal offerings with a non-locative, highly portable religion. But ironically, in the name of civic religion they undermined key aspects of both civic religion and mundane religion. They accomplished this under the guise of being the expert interpreters of civic religion. They would codify and interpret the laws of the Judean people including of a temple and a capital city that no longer existed. They silently assimilated the religion of everyday social exchange to an ethnicizing but paradoxically non-locative religion of upholding the commandments of the sacred books. Performance of acts with textualized significance became central. In an example of one way of doing this, Jonathan Z. Smith writes,

> attributed to Rabbi Gamaliel: 'Whoever does not say these three things on Passover has not fulfilled his obligations,' with the first of these being the sacrifice of the Paschal lamb (*M. Pesachim* 10.5). This is a sentence about ritual speech that, by virtue of its inclusion in the later *Passover Haggadah*, has itself become ritual speech.[44]

---

[43] Struck, *Birth of the Symbol*, 26–29.
[44] Jonathan Z. Smith, *Relating Religion: Essays on the Study of Religion* (Chicago: University of Chicago Press, 204), 223.

Moreover, this latter move makes the ritual speech into a substitute for animal sacrifice.

In ways that remind me of the Attic tragedians, central practices connecting with everyday practices of the household – like prayer and meals – were set in an epic mythic framework that intertwined the mythic world with contemporary interpretation and practice. So, with sacrifice, the myth of a portable temple in a wilderness and its ritual laws from the Hebrew Bible was projected onto the imagination of two temples built and destroyed before any of the "Rabbis" lived. The Mishna and Talmuds encourage the study and discussion of laws imagined for a conflation of these mythic temples as if they were laws for the present. The bloody contingency, mind-numbing repetition, and fatigue of priests slaughtering, dismembering and reducing hundreds and even many thousands of animals a day in a historical "second" Judean temple must not be confused with learned imaginative study and lawmaking. The religion of sacrifice finally gets fully transformed into something else when rabbis insist that one might sacrifice, but it would only be a righteous act before God because it was the keeping of a commandment.[45]

Another early Greek example of such specialists comes from the Derveni Papyrus.[46] The fourth-century author of this commentary on an Orphic cosmological poem was a divinatory priest, who mentions his oracle reading activity (col. v, xi) and alludes to other divinatory practices. In the manner of the literate specialist, he has textualized ritual. He expresses unhappiness with the people who come to him for rituals. The truly pious have a full understanding of the rituals through the proper interpretation of the texts, while others perform the rituals without the right thoughts (col. xx). The author harshly criticizes the normal person's participation in ritual as ignorant and impious. What they must have for the proper rituals that include animal sacrifice (cols. ii, iv – to the Erinyes; vi – preliminary sacrifice to the Eumenides; bird to the "gods") is a proper allegorical understanding of meaning. The author-priest interprets the writings of Orpheus as oracular, full of enigmas, riddles to be translated into cosmogonic and cosmological truths. Work by David Konstan has convincingly argued that ancient reading practices in general, and not just the work of allegorists and the like, featured the search for riddles, problems to be solved and underlying meanings in the text.[47] High literacy in general then fostered the kind of outlook on the world featured in the religion of literate experts.

---

[45] See the extremely important dissertation of Aaron Glaim, "Reciprocity, Sacrifice, And Salvation in Judean Religion at The Turn of The Era" (PhD diss., Brown University, 2014), doi.org/10.7301/Z0GF0RWN.

[46] The critical text is still unpublished. I am following the textual numbering of André Laks and Glenn Most, *Studies in the Derveni Papyrus* (New York: Oxford University Press, 1997).

[47] David Konstan, "The Active Reader in Classical Antiquity," *Argos* 30 (2006): 5–16.

A more general tendency for the religion of experts entails not only claiming that rituals are about meanings revealed by translation, but also textualizing rituals. Practices of claiming a fixed text as the truth of a ritual introduce a far different dynamic than the mythic fragments to which the practices of the RESE might allude or the endless strategic variation of oral mythic storytellers. To say that a text – from Hesiod, Paul's institution text for the Lord's supper or a liturgy – has a privileged meaning not only aims to limit interpretation, but also tends to move the emphasis from everyday local goals to truths and ritual actions that concern supposedly deeper universal human and cosmic issues.

I believe that modern scholarship on animal sacrifice has been too close to the habits of the ancient literate experts. That the meaning of sacrifice is about guilt and atonement, that life is sacred, sacred violence, the scapegoat mentality, and the idea of the sacred and the profane are among the very large number of such translations.[48] But are meanings the essence or important thing about social practices that are not themselves literate textual practices? What is the meaning of lunch? Lunch has as many meanings as it does diners and those meanings are secondary to the everyday goals of acquiring nutrition, pleasure in eating and in sharing these ends with others. Of course, someone can always say that lunch on a certain day will be eaten so as to commemorate a certain story. The problem would come from claiming that the essential or basic or important thing about the everyday practice of eating lunch was that story or its meaning. The Greek gods were participants in the everyday social world of the Greeks. The activities of living with the gods, including cooking and eating animals, did not need the texts and the meanings of the specialists in order to carry on that imagined divine-human sociality. This is not to say that sacrificial practices did not do social work by indexing types of participants, for example, men/women, young/mature, Greek citizens/non-citizens by assigning them a hierarchy of roles and social places.[49] That was certainly powerful and often experienced as natural. Nor does my approach deny that individuals might sometimes have had various symbolic or propositional associations and intuitions. But these will be too indeterminate, varied, and changing to be *the* meaning of the sacrificial practice or what is important about it for its participants. Like lunch, sacrifice did not encode its own interpretation apart from the implicit shared practical understandings that constituted it as an act of cooking, eating, giving and honoring. For Greeks, Romans and others it was interpretive because it involved divinatory practices: reading the inner organs

---

[48] See for instance, most of the approaches in Carter, *Understanding Religious Sacrifice*.
[49] For that sort of social work, see Stowers, "Greeks Who Sacrifice."

of the animal, watching the burning and movements of the fire, the tail and the bladder, and the behavior of the animal as it processed to the altar. All of these and more might indicate messages from the gods, but in the form of signs and traces, not the certain propositions or legal opinions of privileged texts and interpreters.

Finally, I will make some brief comments about sacrifice and the four sub-kinds of the analytical typology. As outlined in the Introduction, civic religion, the religion of the literate experts and the religion of literate experts with political power depend upon the religion of the RESE that gets its persistence and relative stability from intuitive cognitive tools, on the one hand, and the agricultural environment, on the other. The environment elicits the cognitive patterns that make likely imagined exchange with gods and such beings. Civic religion builds on and reshapes the religion of everyday social exchange in specific ways. The key factor is an aristocracy of some sort that claims to control and operate on religion for the whole population of the city. Civic religion thus builds upon the RESE with its central practices of offerings and various gifts, divinatory practices and prayer practices, but shaped by the wealth and power of aristocracies with their particular "civic interests." The scale and resources allowed for the grand and extensive elaboration of social formations, practices, and rites built upon the foundations from mundane religion. Even though the physical/social context was now urban, the offerings were still agricultural, and still featured grains and animals. Once one treats the reinterpretations of the literate experts critically by endowing them with their own characteristic interests and perspectives, the problem of sacrifice for civic religion disappears just as with the religion of everyday social exchange.

But scholarship has not usually seen things this way. Writers have rightly devoted vast amounts of attention to civic religion with its temples, calendars, festivals and so on, but until recently too often through the lenses of ancient and later literate experts with their interest in the meaning of sacrifice. So, for instance, their writings have hidden the nature of the hugely important practices and institutions related to the Lares in Roman religion and even led certain scholars to treat the Lares as a minor cult for the dead.[50] Standard accounts of Roman prayer based on the ancient writers have depicted it as consisting of fixed unalterable formulas that had to be said perfectly with no room for personal and situational creativity by individuals, when such creativity was actually the norm.[51] The vast amounts of ink spilled on Judean religion

---

[50] Harriet I. Flower, *The Dancing Lares and the Serpent in the Garden: Religion at the Roman Street Corner* (Princeton: Princeton University Press, 2017).

[51] Maik Patzelt, *Über das Beten der Römer: Gebete im spätrepublikanischen und frühkaiserzeitlichen Rom als Ausdruck gelebter Religion* (Berlin: de Gruyter, 2018).

from the Persian period until 70 CE has often portrayed it as a religion where individuals related to their one God by study, and personal obedience to the laws of books.[52] The truly important religious experts were supposedly literate interpreters leading the masses, not temple priests. The temples in Jerusalem, Elephantine, Leontopolis and perhaps other places were of little interest except as reflections of the book religion. Sacrifice symbolized or enacted purification or atonement from personal sin, but prayer for forgiveness would also work and was more spiritual. The real meaning of sacrifice was about the heart. "Judaism" seemed nothing like civic religion, and the seeming centrality of sacrificial exchange in the temples did not make it similar to other civic religion in the Mediterranean and West Asia. But I would argue that there was no "problem of sacrifice" in the civic religion that most Judeans considered to be central to their religiosity.

Civic religion often used literate experts working for the interests of the city, kings, empires, and aristocratic households, but it did not require literate experts in some essential way. Offerings, divinatory practices and prayer do not require them, although they could certainly have important bureaucratic and administrative roles and create literature to further the ideology of the city. But cities have existed without them. Like much else of the social, religion comes in formations of more and less. The third sub-kind only appears at the point where literate experts develop their own social formations – e.g., networks and social fields – of intellectualist interaction that is semi-autonomous from civic religion and civic experts. We must not miss the enormously important change here. Unlike the religion of mundane social exchange and civic religion, the religion of writings, interpreters and so on does not situate itself in the agricultural environment centering on exchange with gods who give goods from the land. Such experts often denounced plant and animal offerings as carnal, bloody, crude, primitive and material. Their semi-autonomy as freelance figures forged in the creative fires of literary imagination allowed them critical distance from the normal.

But the religion of the literate religious experts still centered on exchange with gods and similar beings who for them tended to be on the more abstract side. The gifts that the god wants are mental, behavioral, matters of character, having the right and true teachings, and so on. God delights in obedience, devotion from the heart, moral goodness, inner transformation, loyalty, following the way things truly are, keeping the commandments, aligning with the principles of the universe and so forth. For these gifts of the self the return involves things like eternal life, happiness, flourishing, a world to come, a

---

[52] Chapter Three in this volume.

better rebirth, a tranquil mind, union with the divine, the spiritual life, and so on. The literate experts kept the central pattern of exchange but now everyday goods such as food and sociality got decentered by goods and practices more mysterious in two ways. First, the goods that the divine delights in are personal and inner, of the heart, mind and soul. Second, the truths that the obedient or devoted self deals in are truths that can only come from the expert interpretation of special writings. Instead of sacrifice consisting of cooking cakes or meat on an altar for the god's delight and honor, we get ideas such as that sacrifice is self-giving altruism, or a mystery to be embraced, or truly only devout prayer, or a rite that binds together the essence of the people, a symbol only for the enlightened to understand and so forth. Now we have the problem of sacrifice.

The fourth mode based itself upon the religion of literate experts, but with political and institutional developments. I call this the religion of literate experts and political power. The Christian churches, beginning roughly in the third century, are the most obvious ancient Mediterranean examples, a religion distant from the agricultural life and economy and requiring experts with books.[53] When Jews became governed by learned religious authorities rather than aristocratic families – a contentious issue – Judaism would have also been of this fourth mode. In the Christian example, the religion of freelance entrepreneurial specialists like Paul, Valentinus, Tatian, Justin and numerous others received institutionalized forms and political organization that also changed the mode of the religiosity. These semi-autonomous experts either lost their autonomy or the new political power classified them as heretics, charlatans, and sorcerers.

This mode of politically and institutionally organized literate specialists did not completely leave behind the RESE, but attempted to intellectualize it and tried to subordinate it to the control of the political-institutional literate experts like priests and bishops. Thus, it reintroduced a dominated version of everyday religion. By the fifth century, those in power were developing or at least allowing a religion that would mediate between the religion of the literate specialist with political power and a religion of everyday social exchange with the places of saints, martyrs, miracles and other holy sites spreading across the urban and rural landscape, but with ultimate authority resting with the interpreters of books. It was important, if difficult, to enforce the right meanings of rituals, of doctrines and to control the entrepreneurial activities of

---

[53] Stanley Stowers, "Why Expert Versus Non-Expert is Not Elite Versus Popular Religion: The Case of the Third Century," in *Religious Competition in Late Antiquity*, ed. Nathaniel DesRosiers and Lilly C. Vuong (Atlanta: SBL Press, 2016), 139–53.

the literate experts. At the same time, the mode organized institutions for education in the right meanings produced by the church's literate experts, employing the constant repetition of approved teachings, partly thorough rituals that featured approved meanings connected to authoritative written texts. Doctrines and rites attempted to fix the mystery of sacrifice and save it from endless interpretation. Now the butchering, cooking and eating of animals came to seem like a primitive and crude gesture that had failed to grasp some deeper proposition or symbols revealed in texts that had been the true essence of the practice all along.

CHAPTER TWO

Locating the Religion of Associations

Historians agree upon the great importance of so-called "voluntary associations" such as *synodoi, koina, eranistai, hetaireiai, collegia, sodalicia* and *corpora* in the Hellenistic age and Roman Empire.[1] The ubiquity of religious practices in such groups forms another area of agreement, although an older scholarship often characterized such activities as mere pretexts for drinking, eating and good cheer. How to construe the category of associations with its many varieties of social formation has proven more difficult. The work of John Kloppenborg, alongside his colleagues and students, has marked an advance on this problem of the category and other issues.[2] Here the criterion of social networks has been a methodological aid to finding a broadly convincing fivefold typology based on relations of the household, of ethnicity or geography, of neighborhoods, of occupations and of "cults."[3] As this and earlier scholarship has shown, there

---

[1] For the ubiquity of associations in the Empire and importance for understanding the non-elite see Andreas Bendlin, "Gemeinschaft, Öffentlichkeit und Identität: Forschungsgeschichliche Anmerkungen zu den Mustern sozialer Ordnung in Rom," in *Vereine in der römischen Antike: Untersuchungen zu Organisation, Ritual und Raumordnung*, ed. Ulrike Egelhaaf-Gaiser and Alfred Schäfer (Tübingen: Mohr Siebeck, 2002), 9–40.

[2] E.g., John S. Kloppenborg, "Collegia and Thiasoi: Issues in Function, Taxonomy and Membership," in *Voluntary Associations in the Graeco-Roman World*, ed. John S. Kloppenborg and Stephen G. Wilson (Oxford: Routledge, 1996) and the other articles in the volume and Philip A. Harland, *Associations, Synagogues and Congregations: Claiming a Place in Ancient Mediterranean Society* (Minneapolis, MN: Fortress, 2003). Very helpful is Richard S. Ascough, Philip A. Harland and John S. Kloppenborg, eds., *Associations in the Greco-Roman World: A Sourcebook* (Waco, TX: Baylor University Press, 2012) with bibliography and the important website http://philipharland.com/greco-roman-associations. Abbreviations for inscriptions and papyri follow G. H. R. Horsley and John A. L. Lee, "A Preliminary Checklist of Abbreviations of Greek Epigraphic Volumes," *Epigraphica* 56 (1994): 129–69; J. F. Oates et al., eds., *Checklist of Editions of Greek Papyri and Ostraca*, 5th ed., BASPSup 9 (Oakville, CT: American Society of Papyrologists, 2001).

[3] Kloppenborg and Wilson ed. *Voluntary Associations*, 16–30; Harland, *Associations, Synagogues and Congregations*, 28–53. John Kloppenborg's definitive *Christ's Associations: Connecting and Belonging*

can be little doubt that many synagogues and Christian groups were seen as and understood themselves as associations.

Although the wide agreement on the importance of religion in associations prevails, one finds remarkably little discussion of their religious activities, associated goals or beliefs, especially within some account of how ancient Mediterranean religion worked. An enormous amount of research meanwhile exists regarding their organization, sense of fellow belonging, legal status, relation to the polis/civic and imperial order, occupational forms, patronage by the well-to-do, and practices of honoring members and benefactors.[4] If one rejects the ideas that all religion in antiquity was adherence to the official public norms of cities, ethnicities or "the Church" or that one cannot detect differing modes or types of religiosity, then the alternative compels the historian to imagine a complex and dynamic map of interactive practices, institutions and sites of religiosity. This theory stands in opposition to the once dominant "polis religion" theory, and the similar "common Judaism" theory.[5] In this chapter, I aim to address the question of where the religiosities of associations lie on such a map. The tools for this endeavor come primarily from my theory of religion as a social kind with eventually four dominant sub-types in the ancient Mediterranean religion.[6]

Reviewing the Theory of Mediterranean Religion

I will assume the accounts of the four sub-types of religion outlined in the first two chapters of this book. The cognitively and socially most basic of the modes upon which the second and third depend is the religion of everyday social exchange (the RESE). The second is civic religion, the religion of cities, kingdoms, priestly aristocracies, and similar formations controlled by elites who shape religion according to their interests as the self-proclaimed guardians of the religion of the whole population in question. The third mode arises from competitive highly interactive fields of semi-independent literate and usually literary religious experts such as Paul who write, interpret, and teach complex texts,

---

in the Ancient City (New Haven: Yale University Press, 2019) appeared after this article had been written and was in process for publication. I have not been able to update this piece in light of that book's treasures, but some of my comments at the close of this chapter have the book in view. I found it distressing that the book rejects the category of religion.

[4] The bibliography is huge. A good source for these topics is the Harland web site and the annotated bibliography, both in n. 2 above.

[5] Among the critiques of the polis religion theory, see Jörg Rüpke, *Religion of the Romans*, trans. and ed. Richard Gordon (Cambridge: Polity, 2007), 5–38; Julia Kindt, *Rethinking Greek Religion* (Cambridge: Cambridge University Press, 2012), 12–35. See Chapter Three in this volume.

[6] See the Introduction and Chapter One in this volume.

often narratives and law. In the fourth mode, literate experts rule over institutions featuring their interpretive power with non-expert members. Each of the modes represents different interests, clusters of practices, and social networks.

Four criteria that aid in distinguishing these modes require brief mention: (1) interests (2) modes of production (3) physical environment and (4) social environment. The interests of most people in everyday life are often not the same as the interests of cities, ethnicities, and the elites and aristocrats who controlled these two. These two sets of interests can coincide, but often do not. For the present purposes, I will simply note the last two criteria but comment on modes of production. This criterion proves central to understanding ancient Mediterranean and West Asian religion. That religion was thoroughly enmeshed in what we now call "the economy." Economic production and consumption were seen as entailing social exchange (not mere monetary), usually reciprocity, not only between humans but also between humans and gods/NEBS (non-evident beings, in the same intuitive category as gods).[7] The gods gave the good and necessary things of life and culture. The economy was inseparable from the religion of everyday social exchange because most economic production took place within households, involving family members, dependents such as slaves and apprentices, neighbors, and social allies, and on land or in shops that belonged to households. The practices of divination, prayer and offerings to the gods/NEBS were exchange relations usually modeled on ways of maintaining social relations in the culture between more and less powerful humans.

The central sites of religious production in civic religion were temples and sacred spaces with associated practices related to calendars of festivals, processions, spectacles, and entertainments for the gods and so on. This religion entailed the sacralization of time that punctuated lives with regular and special religious days. The massive collection, distribution, redistribution, storage and consumption of wealth took place at temples. Aristocrats claimed to represent the whole citizenry or ethnic population in their control and conduct of civic religion. Temples collected, redistributed and consumed mostly agricultural goods produced on land centered on households.[8] Civic religion thus tied

---

[7] A large bibliography exists on non-commercial non-monetary (i.e., by price equivalence) exchange, especially in anthropology beginning with Mauss. See Jan van Baal, "Offering, Sacrifice and Gift," *Numen* 23 (1976): 161–78; Daniel Ullucci, "Contesting the Meaning of Animal Sacrifice," in *Ancient Mediterranean Sacrifice*, ed. Jennifer Wright Knust and Zsuzsanna Várhelyi (New York, Oxford University Press), 62–67; idem, *The Christian Rejection of Animal Sacrifice* (New York: Oxford University Press, 2012), 24–30; Richard Seaford, *Reciprocity and Ritual: Homer and Tragedy in the Developing City State* (New York: Oxford University Press, 1994); Jennifer Larson, *Understanding Greek Religion* (London: Routledge, 2016), 40–47.

[8] The massive slave estates that arose mostly in Italy and Africa represent a partial exception to this model.

itself structurally to the non-elites, the agricultural economy and the religion of everyday social exchange.

The production of the independent or semi-independent literate religious experts consisted of intellectual practices related to literate forms of cultural production.[9] The expert's products were writings, textual techniques, learned interpretations, position-takings about what is true, just. and good, narratives, forms of teaching, and transmitting knowledge and so on taking form from existing literary and literate traditions. Such production, in contrast to that of civic religion and the RESE, was distinctly separate from the agricultural economy and its products. The writer's study could be anywhere, and writings could circulate anywhere. Experts accrued social capital rewarded in various ways. While the RESE sprang from intuitive cognition, as did much of civic religion, the literary experts depended heavily upon reflective and rationalizing thought that was not intuitive.

The Place of Associations among the Kinds of Religion

In light of this admittedly brief sketch of the sub-types of the kind "religion," where does the religion of associations fit? The religion of a large proportion, if certainly not all associations, appears to be an extension of the interests, sites, production, distribution, consumption and exchange of the religion of everyday social exchange, while being frequently networked with and making alliances with aspects of civic religion and civic power. Before discussing evidence for this thesis, a word needs to be said about how most scholarship has treated the religion of associations, often according to modernist assumptions.

Scholarship on the religious elements of associations has suffered from the modern division between the individual's and the social's relation to the world into semi-autonomous life spheres such as the economic, the political, the artistic and the religious. Underlying this division was another, the division between the instrumental areas of life and society and the symbolic areas. Art, including literature, were on the symbolic, non-instrumental side with religion often seen as epitomizing the symbolic. Part of this separation had to do with the principles of modern science becoming dominant for which divine causality was not admissible such as thunder and lightning caused by Zeus or Yahweh. Religion had to be relegated to the symbolic and non-instrumental. It produced meaning for individuals and social groups or perhaps identity and social solidarity instead.

---

[9] There was much use of literacy in civic religion that did not participate in some literary field or serve freelance religious entrepreneurs. See, for example, Mary Beard, "Writing and Religion: Ancient Literacy and the Function of the Written Word in Roman Religion," in *Literacy in the Roman World*, ed. Mary Beard (Ann Arbor, MI: Journal of Archaeology, 1991), 35–58.

Pervasively, scholars write that associations like the ancients in general naturally practiced "worship" as if worship were a self-explaining concept. "Worship" in our western tradition involves a kind of total honor and devotion and fits the god imagined for western monotheism or the ancient idea of god as an ultimate cosmic emperor. The ancient vocabulary for worship comes from words that mean prostration before the powerful, say a high god or an Assyrian king. But how does the concept help when attempting to understand beings, albeit usually much superior to humans, but conceived as locally present and active social partners? However much honor one gives, the work that the imagined divine human relationships do in the world stems from the practices of intense social exchange with them, especially long-term reciprocal relations. The ship owner risks the voyage because he is confident of the relation built on gift exchange that he cultivated with Poseiden and the Dioscuri. To simply talk about the worship of Heracles or Demeter or the Judean god in an association does not explain anything and attributing only total adoration and honor misreads such activities. Adoration and honor certainly occurred, but they did so in a context of the ongoing imagined interaction of persons.

With the theoretical tools outlined above, I think it easy to see why the religion of a large proportion of associations belongs largely to the RESE. Indeed, two great categories of associations entail this conclusion; those based on household connections and on occupational groups. To these, one can add associations based on neighborhoods. With the theory, the former case is almost definitional and can be illustrated by two atypical examples. Although unusual, the religion of the two examples operates according to principles of the RESE and will illustrate creative possibilities for family and household associations.

Epikteta of Thera founded an association (*koinon*) probably sometime in the early second century BCE (*IG* XII, 3.330; *LSCG* 135; Laum 1914 II, no. 43).[10] Her family was wealthy and likely among the local elite. Following the death of her two sons and her husband, she took control of the household. A sign of the family's status lies in their construction of a private Mouseion, a shrine to the Muses, a group of goddesses who gave powers and abilities to poets, philosophers and practitioners of other arts.[11] Ideas had also developed linking the Muses to the afterlife of the illustrious.[12] Cults of heroines and heroes

---

[10] Andreas Wittenburg, *Il Testamento di Epikteta* (Trieste: Bernardi, 1990). For a recent discussion, see Larson, *Greek Religion*, 289–91.

[11] For the convoluted debate about whether Athenian philosophical schools were *thiasoi* dedicated to the Muses, see Matthias Haake, "Philosophical Schools in Athenian Society from the Fourth Century to the First Century BC: An Overview," in *Private Associations and the Public Sphere: Proceedings of a Symposium Held at the Royal Danish Academy of Sciences and Letters, 9–11 September 2010,* ed. Vincent Gabrielsen and Christian A. Thomsen (Copenhagen: Det Kongelige Danske Videnskabernes Selskab, 2015), 57–91.

[12] Larson, *Greek Religion*, 290–91 and the whole chapter.

were common in Greek civic religion, but this family distinguished itself by the heroization of its own members and establishment of a cult to them. Yet we can recognize this as a fancy and perhaps status-seeking Greek version of family funerary/mortuary practices seen elsewhere across the Mediterranean. Epikteta's husband and two sons died before her and were treated as heroes, kinds of NEBS.

The wording of the inscription in the form of a will that founds the association shows great care in attributing authority for the completion of the Mouseion to her husband and son, fulfilling their intentions, and mentions her legal guardian (*IG* XII 3.330, 7–15). She describes the group as the "men's association of relatives" that seems to be a clever way of instituting a family-based association duly described as ruled by men, but actually involving women and even women friends and children of the extended family.[13] In spite of all of this official deference, clearly Epikteta founds and authors the association. She also owns and runs the household: "I shall administer what belongs to me."[14] The association is to meet in the Mouseion that apparently housed the tombs of the heroes. Only the family members are allowed to use the shrine except for relatives of Epikteta's daughter, Epiteleia, in the case of a wedding. Weddings, of course, were religious rites and important to the religion of everyday social exchange.[15] This stipulation illustrates the connections, alliances and forms of exchange between families that was important for the RESE, in this case by marriage. Another example appears in the detailed list of family members in the association, including mention of those by adoption, that ends with four unrelated women, apparently friends of Epikteta. These women are to be admitted along with their husbands and children. Clearly this is a family association, and yet friendships, alliances and social networks that reach out are important to what families were and important for the RESE, which was much more than the religion of families and households in any narrow sense.

The major religious practices of the *koinon*, whose assembling is called a synagogue (*synagoge*), were to take place during the three days of annual meeting that featured offerings given to the Muses and the three heroes, with Epikteta to join their ranks at her death (177–94). Thus, in a Greek conception one sees an exchange with a group of gods whose activities were closely related to a cluster of specific human activities and their products and to a category of NEB that Greeks

---

[13] Anneliese Mannzmann, *Griechische Stiftungsurkunden* (Münster: Aschendorff, 1962), 142.
[14] Translation from Ascough, Harland and Kloppenborg, *Associations*, 145.
[15] The specifics of weddings varied among Greeks and others, but see John Oakley and Rebecca Sinos, *The Wedding in Ancient Athens* (Madison: University of Wisconsin Press, 1993); Karen K. Hersch, *The Roman Wedding: Ritual and Meaning in Antiquity* (Cambridge: Cambridge University Press 2010).

usually did not think of as gods, but more as being like gods in some respects.[16] Heroines and heroes – dead humans – were normally unseen but living beings who could watch humans and often had many great powers. Most importantly, one could carry on reciprocal relations with them like with gods. Other ancient Mediterranean cultures had similar NEBS without a specific category for them that appears in literary sources or inscriptions, but with similar practices. Judean cults at the tombs of the Patriarchs form one such example.[17] They were of great importance in the everyday religion of Romans.[18]

The focus of the three days were two sets of offerings corresponding to the two categories of NEB. The decree of the association, its laws, specified offerings of an animal in "the usual way," plus cakes and cheese to the Muses on the first day. On the second day the hero and heroine Phoenix and Epikteta, and on the third, the two sons were to be given the same with the addition of a loaf of bread, a different sort of cake and three fish. The latter items were customary funerary offerings, not appropriate for immortal goddesses, but marking the status of the family members as heroes. Both categories were to get crowns, probably placed on statues of the Muses and perhaps at a sculptural relief of the family dining together in the afterlife. Although not spelled out in detail in the rules, each day's offerings would have been shared by the members of the *koinon* in a celebratory feast in honor of the NEBS. The decree of the *koinon* also mentions a meeting in which the first drink of the meal will be poured as a libation to the Muses and the heroes and heroine. Epikteta endowed these practices of the association of family and friends to go on indefinitely, long term reciprocal relations practically imagined with these non-evident beings.

Prayers certainly occurred to accompany the offerings. All of the NEBs would have been praised and probably asked for some sort of help or oversight. Much evidence exists for intensive reciprocity with heroes and heroines in civic religion.[19] But these were often founders of cities, civic institutions and of aristocratic families. How recently dead rather ordinary individuals would have been approached is not entirely clear. Yet, even more ordinary families typical of the RESE without the wealth and high-status infrastructure gave gifts to their dead and expected help, of course, with variation according to

---

[16] Larson, *Greek Religion*, 263–91.
[17] Pieter W. van der Horst, *Japheth in the Tents of Shem: Studies on Jewish Hellenism in Antiquity* (Leuven: Peeters, 2002), 119–37.
[18] For a recent account that typically downplays the abundant evidence for interaction with the dead, see Rüpke, *Pantheon*, 247–50.
[19] For a good discussion of heroes and heroines with excellent bibliography, see Larson, *Greek Religion*, 263–309.

time, place and ethnicity. The dead were asked to "send up good things."[20] The Jewish writer of Tobit (4:17) throws out "Pour your bread and your wine on the tomb of the righteous, and do not give to sinners," as if the maxim was well known common sense. Information provided by the dead through dreams may have been the most widespread gift.

Unfortunately, we do not know anything about purity practices of the association. The topic, however, raises some important and interesting issues. The religion of funerary practices and tombs belonged to the RESE, specifically to the family and not civic religion. Everywhere across the Mediterranean until Christians eventually changed things, cemeteries and burial of the dead occurred outside of the city walls so as to protect the purity of the city's temples, the foci of civic religion. For Greeks, Romans, Judeans and others, to even enter a house where someone had died and where there was a corpse resulted in pollution of the person that could only be remedied variously by time and bathing.[21] Households were also regularly subject to the strong pollution of childbirth and more minor sources of defilement that were considered a part of everyday life. We lack clear evidence about purity notions attached to houses in various cultural areas. But one likely wanted places of household offerings and associated meals to be pure on the model of civic temples.

Strikingly, with Epikteta's association, the tombs of the recent deceased enter into a sacred space devoted to deities. Even in Greek civic religion, the possible pollution from heroic tombs was an issue, at least in certain periods and places. At certain times and places tombs of some and not of other heroines and heroes were considered polluting. Some priests were forbidden to approach heroic shrines, usually considered tombs, because it would compromise the high level of purity that their offices required.[22] All of this ambiguity resulted from both the paradoxical nature of the dead as NEBs and the ways that civic religion marked the RESE as sometimes problematic. But hero cults were very popular, often with a local quality that fit the RESE. They were fixed by family place, a tomb and these imagined counterintuitive agents were former living human beings. As such one could readily imagine them as understanding personal, local and familial problems. Yet the dead paradoxically shared basic characteristics with the highest of

---

[20] Larson, *Greek Religion*, 292 n. 16. Larson may be correct that the emphasis in classical Greek cities was on gifts to the dead and not from them, but reticence in talking publicly about the agency of the dead may be the real factor. Much evidence for reciprocity exists for the Roman Empire, including for Christianity. See Ramsey MacMullen, *The Second Church: Popular Christianity A.D. 200–400* (Atlanta: SBL Press, 2009).

[21] Robert Parker, *Miasma: Pollution and Purification in Early Greek Religion* (Oxford: Clarendon, 1983), 48–55.

[22] Parker, *Miasma*, 39. For a summary discussion of the ambiguities of god and hero "cults" in earlier Greek religion, see Robert Parker, *On Greek Religion* (Ithaca, NY: Cornell University Press, 2011), 290–92.

NEBs, gods, despite lacking immortality marked through entry into their new state by death.²³ In many cultures, including the ancient Mediterranean's, gods were repelled by death.

Many associations of various types included the support of funerary and memorial practices as a part of their constitutions. Some even state these duties in a way that entails stressing the pollution of death. The charter of an association from Tebtunis in 43 CE, probably of tenant farmers, specifies that, "If one of the leaders should die, or his father or mother or wife or child or brother or sister and any of the undersigned men does not defile himself, he shall be fined four drachmas payable to the association." A guild of sheep or cattle herders also from first century Tebtunis required members to "defile themselves" and place wreaths at the tomb (*P. Mich V 243*). "To defile oneself," means to come into proximity with the dead through funerary and mourning rites. With this and other sorts of practices, associations intertwined themselves with quintessential rites of family religion, of the RESE. What everyone knew, but what would have rarely come into public discourse, was that most people intuitively with varied kinds and levels of cultural reinforcement believed that their beloved dead became a kind of NEB who was present near the tomb and who might send signs or messages, desired gifts of drink, food and entertainment, could look into the lives of the living unseen and might give certain sorts of help to the living.²⁴

Like Epikteta's example a rather famous inscription (*SIG 985*; *LSAM 20*) from Philadelphia in Lydia also illustrates how family and household associations reached out to those who were not family or household members.²⁵ This reaching out and extension should be seen as intrinsic to the religion of everyday social exchange, and therefore also intrinsic to associations closely related to families, households and other similar locative social formations. Quite apart from civic religion, personal and family friendships, alliances, and networks should be seen as natural to the social organization of the RESE. As in the RESE where one reached out to establish and maintain long term relationships of generalized reciprocity with gods/NEBs so also individuals, families, and households sought similar relationships with other individuals, families, and households.

---

[23] Stanley Stowers, "What is the Relation of God to the Ghost that Saul Did not See?" in *With the Loyal You Show Yourself Loyal: Essays on Relationships in the Hebrew Bible in Honor of Saul M. Olyan,* ed. T. M Lemos, Jordan D. Rosenblum, Debra Scoggins Ballentine, Karen B. Stern (Atlanta: SBL Press, 2021), 385–400.

[24] For an important study of the phenomenon in ancient Israel, see Kerry M. Sonia, *Caring for the Dead in Ancient Israel* (Atlanta: SBL Press, 2020).

[25] It is dated from late second century to early first century BCE. An important article with translation, that in my view overplays similarities to Christianity is S. C. Barton and G. H. R. Horsley, "A Hellenistic Cult Group and the New Testament Churches," *JAC* 24 (1981): 7–41.

The association from Philadelphia has been widely interpreted as a precursor to purported characteristics of Christianity with a large cult site and meeting place.[26] The group was supposedly egalitarian, open to all – "men, women and slaves" – with a membership recruited from the wider society. But as I have argued elsewhere, the evidence better fits the elaboration and extension of a large household cult that has become an association.[27] Its rules do not proclaim an "advanced morality" and social equality but reinforce the hierarchical order and security of the household. Scholars have confused openness to participation by various categories of people with equality. Participation and equality are not the same thing. Differentiated participation according to gender and rank is precisely how the hierarchical social order reproduced and maintained itself. Free males participated as free males, free women as free women, slaves as slaves and so on.

Unlike most inscriptions with the rules of associations, this one was not the result of a meeting and a vote cited in the inscription. Rather the inscription purports to be instructions given by Zeus the Kindly in a dream to a certain Dionysius for an association to be set up in his house with some members also from the outside.[28] Among its religious practices, the great emphasis given to ritual purity is also odd, but makes sense in light of the anxiety that Dionysius expresses about the conduct of those who enter his house.[29] "Zeus has given commands to this one [Dionysius] for the purifications and the cleansings and the [mysteries?]" as the regulations introduce. Again, oddly for an association, the monthly and yearly sacrifices are mentioned almost inadvertently at the end. There is also nothing about the dues and finances that often dominate other inscriptions about associations. The rules of Zeus/Dionysius express great

---

[26] For this interpretation and bibliography see Barton and Horsley, "Hellenistic Cult Group,"; also, Stanley Stowers, "A Cult from Philadelphia: *Oikos* Religion or Cultic Association?," in *The Early Church in Its Context: Essays in Honor of Everett Ferguson*, ed. Abraham J. Malherbe, Frederick Norris and James W. Thompson (Leiden: Brill, 1998), 287–301.

[27] Stowers, "A Cult from Philadelphia." The title of my article draws the contrast between household religion and associations too sharply, although the contrast is more muted in the article. My error is usefully noted by Korinna Zamfir, "The Community of the Pastoral Epistles: A Religious Association?," in Gabrielsen and Thomsen, *Private Associations*, 214–15.

[28] For a translation, see Ascough, Harland and Kloppenborg, *Associations*, 82–84 (#121).

[29] Also somewhat unusual, the moralizing of purity should not be overplayed, especially in light of the required oath that calls on gods to watch behavior more generally. The later Hellenistic and Roman periods saw the influence of philosophy and the spread of purity as a moral metaphor. See, Angelos Chaniotis, "Reinheit der Körper – Reinheit der Seele in den griechischen Kultgesetzen," in *Schuld, Gewissen, und Person: Studien zur Geschichte des inneren Menschen*, ed. Jan Assmann and Theo Sundermeier (Gütersloh: Gütersloher, 1997); John S. Kloppenborg, "The Moralizing Discourse in Greco-Roman Associations," in *"The One Who Sows Bountifully": Essays in Honor of Stanley K. Stowers*, ed. Caroline Johnson Hodge, Saul M. Olyan, Daniel Ullucci, and Emma Wasserman (Providence, RI: Brown Judaic Studies, 2013), 215–28.

anxiety about possible corruptions of the household such as adultery and an odd emphasis on the gods punishing those who break the rules, even requiring that members take an oath. All of this oddness can be explained if the association grew out of a purely household cult with Dionysius's anxieties about expanding it to outsiders. The oddness points to an important characteristic of the RESE: Individuals, families, and privately formed groups had room for religious creativity that civic religion did not have. Their choices and patterns of activity were often highly strategic, idiosyncratic and therefore particular, within the constraints of family tradition, degrees of privacy, and broader social convention.

The religion of Dionysius's association displays normal reciprocity with the gods, but more stress on sanctions by the gods than is typical as part of these exchange relations. In addition to the founder's anxieties about his household and the purity that the presence of gods in cultic exchange required, the stress on bathings and other purifications may be related to mysteries that were part of the association's religious practices. The text is difficult on this point and some possible restorations would denote other practices, but "mysteries" seems the most likely.[30] These religious practices became widely popular in the Hellenistic age, including in private groups. If following normal patterns, Dionysius's mysteries would have involved some sort of initiation in which a high level of ritual purity would have been required and the revelation of some piece of sacred knowledge with the whole process promising an advantage in one's future guaranteed by some god or gods.[31]

In my, admittedly speculative, imagining of the cult site, Zeus and Hestia (goddess of the hearth), a quintessentially Greek household pair, had altars (mentioned in the text) at the center of the cultic layout.[32] Alongside, and redundantly, was Agdistis who in parallel with Zeus was "guardian . . . of the household (*oikos*)" and apparently had the inscription at her altar or shrine. After other examples from the period, the nine "savior gods" (including Eudaimonia, Ploutos, Hygeia, Agathe and Tyche) may have had their names inscribed on one altar. All of this is typically Greek from the period with similar examples from household sites except Agdisitis, a form of the Great Mother popular in Phrygia and Anatolia where Lydia is. This site, probably in a courtyard of some type, would have been the place of Dionysius's household religious practices with his family, dependents and slaves and the place for the religious activities of the association.

---

[30] I still see difficulties with reading "mysteries," but now favor it instead of others as in Stowers, "Cult from Philadelphia," 291 n. 31.
[31] On mysteries and associations, see Harland, *Associations*, 45–49, 70–74, 128–32. On "private" mysteries, see Larson, *Greek Religion*, 254–63.
[32] Stowers, "Cult from Philadelphia," 288–93.

The gods/NEBS side of reciprocal relations entailed that they watched and remembered what humans did and therefore would often give bits of information useful to humans who appealed to them. Zeus gave instructions for founding the association to Dionysius in a dream, something seen in the founding of other associations.[33] It seems likely that divinatory signs and messages would largely play a different role in the life of associations than for individuals. Apart from foundings by individuals, issues of authority would seem to have arisen for individuals appealing to bird flights or other typical signs to argue for some point in the decision-making of an association, but none of this is clear. The corporate activity of offering meat did feature reading the entrails, noting the way the fire burned and the behavior of the animal, all regular means of obtaining clues to the god's will.[34] One inscription (*MDAI* A 1941, 228) honors a certain Serapeion for performing "good omened sacrifices" for the association, including "the wives and children."

Divine oversight also came to Dionysius's association in the case of the oaths to obey the rules that members had to take. Oaths appealed to the ability of Gods/NEBS to see people's behavior. Oath-takers asked the god to punish them if they broke their promise, here all seemingly for the security and prosperity of the founder's and member's households with special anxiety about the behavior of women. Almost as an afterthought, the inscription mentions the regular animal and other offerings to the association's gods that typically included libations, food offerings, incense burning, singing, praise in prayers and other gifts. This household-based group shows all of the practices and patterns of everyday social exchange, but with quite particular emphases. As shown by the examples discussed below, the Philadelphia association's stress on good behavior *even outside its meetings* is not unique in spite of scholarly claims.[35] Attempts to create networks of trust desired by households best explains the phenomenon, but of course, with the help of gods familiar to the people and site.

The religion of occupational associations also frequently belongs to the RESE, and is made especially clear by the illuminating evidence of inscriptions and papyrus documents from Egypt. Most occupational work, workshops and retail shops were located in or otherwise connected to homes and based on the labor of the household.[36] To this one must add farming and pastoralism based

---

[33] See James C. Hanges, *Paul, Founder of Churches: A Study in Light of the Evidence for the Role of "Founder-Figures" in the Hellenistic-Roman Period* (Tübingen: Mohr Siebeck, 2012).

[34] Sarah Iles Johnston, *Ancient Greek Divination* (Oxford: Wiley-Blackwell, 2008), 125–28.

[35] An advance on this issue is Kloppenborg, "Moralizing Discourse."

[36] Miko Flohr, *The World of the Fullo: Work, Economy, and Society in Roman Italy* (Oxford: Oxford University Press, 2013); Clare Holleran, *Shopping in Ancient Rome: The Retail Trade in the Late Republic and the Principate* (Oxford: Oxford University Press, 2012); Andrew Wilson and Miko Flohr, eds., *Urban Craftsmen and Traders in the Roman World* (Oxford: Oxford University Press, 2016).

on land belonging to or leased by the family. These ancients believed that their production was only possible with the aid of the gods. The relevant archeological sites with work areas in good states of preservation often have altars and cult sites for thanking and honoring the gods. These religious household/work sites have been clearly revealed especially at Ostia and Pompeii.[37] But the walls of houses and workshops or the minds and interests of individuals do not circumscribe the religion of everyday social exchange. Occupational associations illustrate this principle.[38]

Scholarship has dispelled the idea, occasionally seen, that guilds were kinds of trade unions, but even more distorting has been the once dominant idea that associations were attempts to compensate for the supposed loss of meaning, breakdown of family life, and individualism of the Hellenistic age due to the supposed degeneration of the polis.[39] Writers once waxed eloquent about how the socially rootless masses of the poor would band together in burial clubs so they could at least have a place of final rest. The idea of even the category of burial societies has since been disproven.[40] Many specialists now find instead that associations gave members bigger and more luxurious funerals than on average.[41] More importantly, like compensatory and deprivation theories of religion, compensatory theories about the motivations for associations have been strongly criticized.[42] Because the RESE centrally involves positive socio-economic exchange with the gods embedded in human socio-economic interaction, one seriously misunderstands such religiosity by construing it as something only designed to mollify social and psychological deprivation. But deprivation theories grow easily out of the Western and Christian polemics that separated the social from the economic, the long term generalized relationship with the god from gift-giving, the economic portrayed as a commercial relation.

---

[37] Jan Theo Bakker, *Living and Working with the Gods: Studies of the Evidence for Private Religion and its Material Environment in the City of Ostia (100–500 AD)* (Amsterdam: Gieben, 1994); W. Van Andringa, *Quotidien de dieux et des hommes. La vie religieuse dans la cités de Vésuve à l'époque romaine* (Rome: École française de Rome, 2009).

[38] On guilds see, Jean-Pierre Waltzing, *Étude historique sur les corporations professionnelles chez les Romains depuis les origènes jusqu' à la chute de l'empire d'Occcident*, 4 vols. (Louvain: l'Academie Royal de Sciences, des Lettres et les Beaux-Arts Belgique, 1895–1900); Onno M. van Nijf, *The Civic World of Professional Associations in the Roman East* (Amsterdam: Gieben, 1997); Harland, *Associations*, especially 38–44.

[39] See Philip Harland, "The Declining Polis? Religious Rivalries in Ancient Civic Context," in *Religious Rivalries in the Early Roman Empire and the Rise of Christianity*, ed. Leif Vaage (Waterloo, ON: Wilfred Laurier University Press, 2006), 21–50.

[40] Kloppenborg, "*Collegia* and *Thiasoi*," 20–23.

[41] Philip F. Venticinque, "Family Affairs: Guild Regulations and Family Relationships in Roman Egypt," *GRBS* 50 (2010): 293.

[42] Venticinque, "Family Affairs," 273–94.

A related misreading comes from the habit of reading the rules of associations as attempts to forestall the interventions of state authorities supposedly always suspicious of associations.[43] A more promising approach comes from the sociologist Charles Tilly's theory of "trust networks" that have strong social and economic effects.[44] The theory would help to explain a fact puzzling in light of traditional scholarship on associations: dues and other costs for membership were often very high so that the poor and less well to do would have been unlikely to afford membership.[45]

A few associations were large, with thirty or more members, but these frequently cited examples of large memberships belie the fact that most associations were small, with 10–25 members, usually all male. Much evidence illustrates the ways that associations, including occupational guilds, stabilized households and supported their interests, but not because the institution of the family was in trouble. I have already noted the way that associations enlarged the social circles involved in funerary and mortuary rites. The following charter (*P.Mich.* V 243) from the early first century CE institutes monthly common meals at which we can assume offerings and prayers took place, but many of the regulations consist of rules that have families and households directly in view.[46]

> If anyone marries, let him pay two drachmas [if he does not celebrate the rites], for the birth of a male child two drachmas, for the birth of a female child one drachma, for the purchase of property four drachmas, for a flock of sheep four drachmas, for cattle one drachma. If anyone neglects another in trouble and does not give aid to release him from his trouble, let him pay eight drachmas . . . If anyone prosecutes another or defames him, let him be fined eight drachmas. If anyone intrigues against another or corrupts his home, let him be fined sixty drachmas. If anyone is given into custody for a private debt, let him go to bail for him up to 100 silver drachmas for thirty days., with which he will release the men. May health prevail! If one of the members dies, let all be shaved and let them hold a feast for one day, each bringing at once

---

[43] Venticinque, "Family Affairs," 287–88; Jonathan S. Perry, "'L'État intervint peu à peu': State Intervention in the Ephesian 'Baker's Strike,'" in Gabrielsen and Thomsen, *Private Associations and the Public Sphere*, 183–205.

[44] Charles Tilly, *Trust and Rule* (Cambridge: Cambridge University Press, 2005). The following have used Tilly's theory: Andrew Monson, "The Ethics and Economics of Ptolemaic Religious Associations," *AncSoc* 36 (2006): 221–238; Venticinque, "Family Affairs"; Kloppenborg, "Moralizing Discourse," 217, 226–27.

[45] Venticinque, "Family Affairs," 274–75, with bibliography in notes 4–6.

[46] I owe this example and the stress on families to Venticinque, "Family Affairs," 279–83. The translation is from A. E. R. Boak, editor of *P. Mich*. For similar rules see P. Mich.V 244 that adds the funerals of parents.

one drachma and two loaves, and in the case of other bereavements, let them hold a feast for one day. Let him who is not shaven in case of death be fined four drachmas. Whoever has no part in the funeral and has not placed a wreath on the tomb shall be fined four drachmas. And let the other matters be as the society decides.

It would be a misunderstanding to think that the fines indicate laxness or difficulty in maintaining good relations and in the fulfillment of duties among members. The opposite is in fact the case. That, by voluntarily binding themselves with concrete rules and sanctions they show their commitment to other members and their families. Undertaking this self-binding eliminated the unreliable and uncommitted and left those who could be trusted. Such associations thus extended the trust that belongs to the household into a larger network important both for positive social relations and for business and commerce. But how did mundane religiosity fit into this?[47]

The rules above imply that numerous events and practices of the RESE were all enlarged and enriched by the participation of the association. Generalized reciprocity with the gods mirrored reciprocity with others in the association, albeit a reciprocity among equals instead of gods, and relationships of long-term generalized reciprocity are epitomized by trust. Weddings among the Mediterranean ethnicities were events with prayers, offerings to gods and numerous other activities related to gods/NEBS.[48] Births usually involved pollution, purification, celebration, thanksgiving, apotropaic practices, prayers and offerings.[49] Purchasing property, sheep, or cattle were major events that called for thanksgiving and celebration with the gods in view and the assumption of reciprocal exchange.

A scene from Plautus, who is known for his realism about the family and religion, illustrates everyday assumptions about what to do when good things happen. In *Rudens* (1205–07), a celebration breaks out when parents are reunited with their long-lost daughter and the father says, "We ought to stop this kissing at some point, my wife, and put me in finery so that I can make an offering when I go in and approach the household Lares, because they have added to our household. We have unblemished lambs and pigs at the house." Plautus assumes that an offering of celebration and thanksgiving to the divine guardians of the household is the natural reflex. In some of these events, including when a member died, a meal of bereavement and memory

---

[47] I am generally following Venticinque and Monson (notes 41 and 44 above) in this paragraph.
[48] We know nothing about Jewish weddings in the second temple period, but see Hersch, *Roman Wedding*; Oakley and Sinos, *Wedding in Ancient Athens*.
[49] Parker, *Miasma*, 63–64; Larson, 138–41, 158, 162–63; Maurio Bittini, *Women and Weasels: Mythologies of Birth in Ancient Greece and Rome*, trans. Emlyn Eisenbach (Chicago: University of Chicago Press, 2013).

or of celebration and thanksgiving of the whole association would have been held that included the normal gifts to the appropriate god or gods such as food offerings, libations, incense, singing/music, flowers, prayers and so on. It would be remiss not to mention that birthday rituals also fit into such celebrations of the RESE.[50]

Looking at only the associations clearly marked by close ties to families and households leaves aside a great deal of evidence, even when we limit ourselves to those only organized by occupations. Especially those organized by ethnicity or geography and by focus on a particular deity might be seen as based on principles closer to civic religion. The goals of the ethnic association would in this case be the maintenance of culturally particular practice of the city and civic or ethnic ideology. But such a conclusion would be hasty. One rarely finds in associations a monopolistic principle of ethnic ideology or recognition of only one deity to the exclusion of a world full of gods/NEBS related to the mundane interests of the RESE.

The associations of Romans and Italians of late Hellenistic Delos, for example, combine elements in ways that show everyday and local interests together with the ethnic and geographic.[51] The choice of gods and festivals entailed central everyday and local interests. Three of four associations were named after deities: the *Apolloniastai*, the *Hermaistai* and the *Poseidoniastai*. Apollo was the ancient god of Delos. Choosing Apollo meant reciprocity with the historic and present god of place, even if it was not one's place of origin. Hermes or Mercury was the god of trade, commerce and banking, together the chief activities on the island and those that brought the Italians there. Poseidon, of course, was ruler of the sea, and exchange relations involving protection for ships and shipping would have marked that group. Cults directed toward Hermes would have been important in many ways, including the practice of contracts between parties taking place with an oath and a sacrifice to the god calling him to be guarantor.[52] There were certainly religious practices of these groups that appealed to and reinforced Roman or Italian identity, but the more directly practical and strategic aims are also clear.

---

[50] For example, Karl Aretsinger, "Birthday Rituals: Friends and Patrons in Roman Poetry and Cult," *ClAnt* 11 (1992): 175–93.

[51] The definitive guides are Philippe Bruneau and Jean Ducat, *Guide de Délos*, 4th ed. (Paris: Boccard, 2005); *Recherches sur les cultes de Délos à l'époque hellénistique et à l'époque impériale* (Paris: Boccard, 1970). For the Lares, the compitalia and the associations, see Claire Hesenohr, "Les Compitalia à Delos," *BCH* 127 (2003): 167–249, and especially Harriet I. Flower, *The Dancing Lares and the Serpent in the Garden: Religion at the Roman Street Corner* (Princeton: Princeton University Press, 2017), 175–91.

[52] Nicholas Rauh, *The Sacred Bonds of Commerce: Religion, Economy, and Trade Society at Hellenistic Roman Delos, 166–87 B.C.* (Amsterdam: Gieben, 1993).

The fourth association, the *Competaliastai* (those who celebrate the Compitalia), is interesting. The names on inscriptions show that most of the members were slaves, with a few freedmen. In Rome and other places in Italy, the Compitalia was a moveable-date mid-winter festival for the Lares. The Lares were gods of place and Compital shrines (*compita*) were at the crossroads that defined the meeting of neighborhoods and neighbors.[53] On farms the shrines were at the corners of the property where neighbors would come together. The Lares were central to households where they protected and helped everyone who belonged to the household and not just those with blood family relations as tended to be the case with the Penates. This means that slaves and resident freed persons related to them strongly. Household shrines were typically in the kitchen or cooking area where slaves labored and the food for the household was prepared. In Pompeii, most houses had a painting in the cooking area of two dancing Lares, with a genius making an offering and frequently a small altar.[54] In Rome and other cities, the Compitalia was meanwhile an inclusive festival of the city beloved by slaves and freed persons. The compital shrines of neighborhood crossroads beautifully illustrate how civic religion and the RESE could work together. Even though the neighborhood magistrates (*vicomagistri*) of Rome were in charge of the shrines and the festival, the *compita* were places that defined neighborhoods and anyone, Roman or Greek, Jew or Phrygian, female or male, could make daily and personal situational offerings at their altars.

After the Romans defeated Perseus, the Macedonian monarch, in the battle of Pynda (168 BCE) they gave control of Delos to Athens and made the island a free port.[55] This means that the island had no Roman organization or administrative structure with Compitalia shrines throughout and the civic festival. Nevertheless, the *Competaliastai* whose members were mostly Greek slaves born in the East were dedicated to the Lares and to organizing a purely private festival. The religious and other interests of these slaves were not primarily civic interests, but surely related to their sense of place, the sites of their day to day lives on Delos.

As the Lares illustrate, neighborhoods and places form another principle for organizing associations related to the religion of mundane social exchange. Local and locally strategic interests often guided those who organized for social exchange with the gods/NEBS based on shared place. Sometimes occupation and place coincided for associations due to the habit of the same sorts of

---

[53] Flower (*Dancing Lares*, 40–75 and throughout) is superb on the local nature of the Lares.
[54] For powerful arguments that the domestic Lares are above all gods of the hearth and kitchen see, Federica Giacobello, *Larari Pompeiani: Iconografia e culto dei Lari in ambito domestico* (Milan: University of Milan, 2008). See also, Flower, *Dancing Lares*, 46–70.
[55] Bruneau and Ducat, *Guide de Délos*, 41–43.

commercial enterprises clustering on particular streets and neighborhoods as with the "Purple-Dyers of Eighteenth Street" in Thessalonike (*IG* X 2.1 291). One *collegium* in Rome went by the name *montani*, the people or men of the mountain, meaning the association of those who live atop the Oppian Hill (*CIL* 1.2 1003). They left an inscription noting their work on an open-air shrine (*sacellum*) that would have been significant for the people of the neighborhood. The fragmentary inscription mentions priests of the association, but no god in what remains. Clearly reciprocity with some god/NEBs was important to the group and it likely would have been a local deity or one with a locative interpretation. Andrew Wallace-Hadrill and others have shown that neighborhoods in Greek and Roman cities were perhaps even more than houses in some ways sites of intensively interactive everyday life and identity, each a village of its own.[56] The divinatory, offering/honoring, praying, apotropaic, and other practices of residents belonging to neighborhood associations are native to the RESE, even if they sometimes also entailed civic religious interests and practices, but with the every day and local interests clearly primary.

Early Christianity and Associations

Associations of the later Hellenistic and early Roman imperial periods display great cultural and social variety. I have argued that the types of religion prove analytically helpful in showing that a significant portion of these groups primarily exhibit the religion of everyday social exchange. I also suspect that the argument could be extended to other kinds of associations and to a larger proportion of them. These conclusions cohere with the scholarly habit of describing them as private, although sorting out the quite different nature of the private in antiquity remains a challenge. But counting gods and cults is not enough, the kind of religion with its characteristic goals and practices needs to be explained, and in relation to other religious arenas of the societies. The long history of Christian propaganda that misrepresented ordinary Mediterranean religion as based on a crass and selfish commercial relationship with implausible gods has supported both the neglect and the misrepresentation of that religion in modern scholarship.

I have no quarrel with the idea that associations usually related positively to their civic environments and reflected these in their own expression, but the idea has of recent, I think, been overemphasized to the detriment of

---

[56] E.g., Andrew Wallace-Hadrill, *Rome's Cultural Revolution* (Cambridge: Cambridge University Press, 2008); idem, *Houses and Society in Pompeii and Herculaneum* (Princeton, NJ: Princeton University Press, 1994). Richard Last is conducting pathbreaking research on neighborhoods and early Christianity in Last, "The Neighborhood (*vicus*) of the Corinthian *Ekklesia*: Beyond Family-Based Descriptions of the First Urban Christ-Believers," *JSNT* 38 (2016): 399–425.

everyday religiosity.⁵⁷ That associations sought the financial backing and support of well-to-do patrons and honored the civic achievements of such people should surprise no one. Their social world worked as a studied hierarchy with needed benefactors always above you. The gods were such benefactors, but also the elite in the cities who normally considered regular membership in an association as below their dignity. Even emperors, almost as distant as heavenly gods, who were perceived as bestowing goods such as peace, prosperity and just government might find god-like honors returned by an association. But none of this negated the basic social exchange and everyday interests of the associations.

This analysis, with a theorized approach to religion, casts some light on Judean and Christian groups organized as associations. Religious tradition and modern scholarship have overwhelmingly characterized Judaism and early Christianity in terms that fit my third and fourth modes, the religion of literate experts and experts with political power. Almost all of Jewish and Christian religious practices supposedly followed laws and scripts from the Hebrew Bible, the New Testament and other early writings. It was all about the meaning endowed on cultic practices by texts and expert interpreters. The cult of the temple followed Leviticus and other scripture. The Lord's Supper and Eucharist followed Pauline and Gospel texts. Ritual was about the communication of *meaning* usually conveyed as a narrative about Israel or Christ that the experts taught. The masses of highly educated Jews went to synagogues to study Torah and follow a liturgy. Jewish life in the so-called second temple period was dominated by expert interpreters of religious law. All of this would have required the dominance of a highly literate body of expert interpreters and a huge educational system for which we have no evidence. I believe that this story only contains a nugget of truth at best, but I want to make a different point here. Neither the religious practices nor the central religiosity of reciprocal gift-giving seen above in associations requires or features written literary texts and expert interpreters. The associations did not focus on literary texts, their teachings and interpretation with dominating roles for experts in particular literate traditions. We do not find associations organized under figures like Paul, Justin, Valentinus, or Irenaeus with their intellectualistic practices, interests and intense competition about which teachings were true or false.

Rather than once again declaring the Jews and Christian groups unique, we would do better to read the early Christian and Jewish writings more critically and especially with the understanding that in the context of ancient Mediterranean religion they represent a particular social and cultural perspective. Groups

---

⁵⁷ For instance, in the views of the editors discussed throughout Gabrielsen and Thomsen, *Private Associations*.

of Christ followers may in general not have described themselves in quite the way that their highly literate and entrepreneurial would-be leaders did. And because our only access to that movement, if that is what it was, comes by way of a tiny collection of writings from the literate experts, we have little direct evidence for the everyday religiosity of the majority. The writings themselves, however, constantly criticize practices that seem to arise from the RESE while also projecting visions of an ideal people of God that the non-experts should be or become. As some scholars have done, it is easy to imagine, say Paul, struggling to mold into shape a preexisting association that welcomed him, but not with passive acceptance on the part of those people who had their own interests, habitual practices, and religious intuitions. That hypothesis has a good deal of explanatory power.

Scholars have frequently compared the assemblies of Christ people to associations. So-called elective cults such as Mithraism and the so-called "oriental cults" have also been seen as comparable to early Christian groups. In making these judgments, scholars view the social formations as stand-alone entities notable because individuals supposedly chose to join them, like joining a modern church or social club. Being in the same category supposedly made these religious formations competitors for members. I judge this line of thinking at best misleading and at worst inscribing Western modernist assumptions onto antiquity.

A further related line of thinking wants to compare Christian groups and Christianity to the "religious system of paganism." So, for instance, some argue that priests of pagan cults come up short in comparison with Christian priests and officials.[58] When plagues and other catastrophes occurred, Christian bishops organized relief, but priests of "pagan" temples did not do that sort of thing. Also, pagan priests and cults made no ethical demands on their devotees. Christianity required exclusive commitment and was therefore strong, but "pagans" could shop around and, for instance, find a suitable association to join. E. R. Dodds wrote, "A Christian congregation was from the first a community in a much fuller sense than any corresponding group of Isiac or Mithraist devotees. Its members were bound together not only by common rites but also by a common way of life . . ."[59]

The writings of the ancient Christian experts almost unanimously, and with some variety, attempt to create a social formation that is disembedded from the larger society to various degrees. Mediterranean religion was the worship of idols and demons. For this and other reasons, the society was deeply morally corrupt. Jesus was said to have taught: "If anyone comes to me and does not hate his father, mother, and wife and children, brothers and sisters, and even

---

[58] Rodney Stark, *The Rise of Christianity* (Princeton, NJ: Princeton University Press, 1996), 88.
[59] E. R. Dodds, *Pagan and Christian in an Age of Anxiety* (New York: Norton, 1970), 136.

his own soul, he cannot be my disciple (Luke 14:26)." Civic religion and the religion of everyday social exchange were everywhere in the organization of the societies: households, families, places of work, entertainment, the political forms, and so on.

While Christians still lived in households with families – although optionally – the family and household was not necessary to churches in the way that it was to the RESE. Christian religion was not essentially embedded in households and so on. The life and organization of the cities and towns was also not necessary. You could not have the RESE without the social forms of households, families, farms, neighborhoods, associations, and individual members with norms and obligations connected to those social forms. Nor could you have civic religion without cities run by aristocrats and elites and the norms and obligations related to being an individual citizen in a city. But you could have Christian groups disconnected or relatively disconnected from these social forms intrinsic to ancient Mediterranean religion.

The fundamental social form of Christian groups was organized around literate experts (such as freelance teachers, presbyters, bishops) in authoritative books, teachings and behavior, with non-expert learners collected around them and forming an exclusive, and in theory, totalizing group. But the social form of civic temples, household cults and associations simply was the social organization of the city, family, household and occupations. Reciprocity with the gods cut across those units and interconnected. Instead of disembedding one from the wider norms and obligations around patterns of exchange with the gods as Christian groups did, membership in associations connected one with those wider patterns of household, city and so forth. It misleads to pull a temple or cult or association out of these social forms and compare it to a Christian group. Religion, if you will, was distributed throughout rather than concentrated in rather small populations surrounding experts in books, teachings, and rites who made such claims as being the true Israel and as being destined to rule the cosmos. To say that the priests of Apollo somewhere did not teach ethics or organize famine relief, and therefore unlike Christians, failed – misleads. The civic priest's job was to carry on reciprocity with a particular god on behalf of the city. The city of Rome and other cities imported grain for their citizens, and members of associations pledged to help needy members. Grammar teachers, parents, and philosophers taught morals in ways not unrelated to thinking about norms and obligations to the gods. What was concentrated in the rites, teachings, and guidance of Christian literate experts in Christ assemblies was distributed across the social forms of the city, town, and farm.

My account here may to some ears sound functionalist, structuralist, or like the polis religion model, but my theoretical apparatus undermines such social holism. The cognitive and social dynamics of the RESE make it most basic and necessary for civic religion, and in a complex often messy relation to the latter, as also to the religion of literate experts and intellectuals. The researcher best charts the social mass by analyzing the ever-changing networks and tangles of social practices, including the multitude of practices for interacting with an imagined world of gods and similar non-evident beings who lived with humans. The stresses and the factures are as important for the historian as the connections.

    I have tried to show that looking by way of this theory at the religion of associations reveals their embeddedness in the RESE, just as much scholarship has shown that they were also embedded in the civic social forms. We are held by an illusion in thinking that people in the RESE and citizens did not make religious choices and that genuine religious choice has to be about the one big commitment. They constantly made choices. At what temple shall I make my votive offering? What god can I invoke to cast a spell? Should the family sacrifice a sheep on the master's birthday? Shall I become a member of an association for my trade? Should I follow my passion for devotion to Demeter by becoming an initiate? Associations were not somehow disembedded from their social fabric because individuals made choices about them. But the teachings of the Christian teachers in the first two centuries required members to disembed themselves from the social organization of ancient Mediterranean religion across families, households, cities and so on, and to various degrees according to the particular Christian writer and authority. What counted as idolatry, superstition, immorality and so on?

    Did people often resist or attempt to adapt the teachings of the Christian experts to their own interests and purposes? Of course they did, and recent scholarship by Caroline Johnson Hodge, Éric Rebillard, Ramsay MacMullen and others has graphically displayed such resistance and selectivity through the analysis of non-literary sources and by reading such experts as Tertullian in a critical way.[60] It was messy. Ordinary Christians mostly did not live in a separate Christian world in spite of totalizing claims often made by the experts. The literate experts around which Christian groups formed faced a structural issue; their followers, mostly without the deep habituation into the non-intuitive knowledge and practices of the intellectual, remained deeply affected by the intuitive religiosity of the RESE. The non-experts, for example, tended to find the emerging practices of interaction (e.g., messages in dreams, healings) and exchange (food and drink offerings) with saints, martyrs and the beloved

---

[60] Caroline Johnson Hodge, *My God and the God of This House": Christian Household Cult Before Constantine* (University Park, PA: Pennsylvania State University Press, forthcoming); Éric Rebillard, *Christians and Their Many Identities in Late Antiquity: North Africa, 200–450 CE* (Ithaca, NY: Cornell University Press, 2012); Ramsay MacMullen, *The Second Church*. See Chapter Four in this volume.

dead more relevant and attractive than devotion to a distant more abstract God marked by difficult doctrines of the Trinity. Presbyters and bishops would eventually try to solve the problem by embracing saints and martyrs and bringing them inside the church. Associations did not have this kind of structural issue because they were not organized around authoritative teachers of books and doctrines; their teachings marked by a competitive dynamic among various teachers. Rather their patterns of reciprocity with the god or gods of the particular association followed the intuitive religiosity characteristic of the RESE and much civic religion.

But what about the good evidence of Christian groups organizing as associations and Christians being members of associations?[61] Some Christians adapted to the demands of the experts by deciding that membership in an association was compatible with their understanding of devotion to Christ. We know this because writings from the experts sometimes complain about such believers participating in associations or even threaten damnation on Christian participants.[62] I know of no ancient Christian writing that would allow that, say, offerings made to Heracles in rites of an association, was acceptable. But some Christians seem to have disagreed. An assembly of Christ could also think of itself as a kind of association with a constitution, a patronized God or gods, leaders, regular rituals, banquets, a common fund and so on. There is some evidence for this. But the kind of exchange with gods and non-evident beings of the Christian association was different than the offering of food, drink, and other gifts traditionally from the land deemed given by the gods in palpable local patterns of imagined interaction. The Christian experts, freelance or developing clerical, put forth various schemes of salvation in narratives of human need and divine rescue that always involved those who believed in the story doing certain things and living a certain kind of life as a whole in order to qualify for such rescue. So both the Christian and non-Christian association had religion, cognitive patterns and practices involving exchange with gods and non-evident beings (such as the human dead, martyrs, angels), but intellectualized and literary Christian forms broke from the ancient Mediterranean reciprocity of goods from the land and womb returned in gratitude to the gods of such places.

---

[61] Now see, Kloppenborg, *Christ's Associations* with exhaustive evidence and arguments about Christians and associations.
[62] Kloppenborg, *Christ's Associations*, 275–76.

CHAPTER THREE

Why "Common Judaism" Does Not Look Like Mediterranean Religion

In a volume celebrating the scholarship of Ed Sanders, Shaye Cohen considered the evidence of Greek and Roman writings for Sanders's notion of "common Judaism."[1] There he makes a point important for my effort here: These writers mention things distinctive to Jews, but have almost nothing to say about what was common across the Mediterranean. Thus, for instance, they say nothing about Jewish hymns and prayers. But what exactly is the price to pay for characterizing Jewish religion by difference only?

Ed Sanders's idea of common Judaism has been a hit, albeit with a number of dissenters.[2] The idea beautifully expresses intuitions underlying conceptions of Jewish and Christian origins that have been and still are normative for many. In my estimation, there is clearly something right about common Judaism. There were, for instance, social mechanisms that allowed for ethnic-religious self-identification and identification by others. But the idea contradicts much of the scholarship about social groups that has become dominant in the social sciences, parts of the humanities and the mind sciences in the last several decades. The academy is in the midst of a major revolution in thinking about social groups.[3] I will briefly discuss why the common belief/practice model that "common Judaism" assumes cannot adequately deal with the dynamics of ancient Mediterranean religion.

Psychology and other fields have shown dramatically that we know far less than we think we know.[4] With unrealistic confidence individuals hold

---

[1] "Common Judaism in Greek and Latin Authors," in *Redefining First-Century Jewish and Christian Identities: Essays in Honor of Ed Parish Sanders*, ed. Fabian Udoh, Susannah Heschel, Mark Chancey and Gregory Tatum (Notre Dame, IN: University of Notre Dame Press, 2008), 69–87.
[2] *Judaism: Practice and Belief 63 BCE–66 CE* (Philadelphia: Trinity Press International, 1992), 45–314.
[3] Rogers Brubaker, *Ethnicity Without Groups* (Cambridge, MA: Harvard University Press, 2004).
[4] A pioneer and Nobel Prize laureate has been Daniel Kahneman, e. g., *Thinking Fast and Slow* (New York: Farrar, Straus and Giroux, 2011).

fragmentary outlines of knowledge and what is known varies greatly across individuals in a population. This overconfidence has in many ways served our species well. The unfounded confidence has made us bold about acting and going forward even when we really do not know. The mentally efficient fragments and outlines often pay off because they allow us just enough information to discover where to go for types of expertise or to technologies of knowledge for answers. Brains/minds with intrinsic limits can not survive unless they are efficient and adapted to the resources of their social environment. The key resource of social environments comes in that many people in any culture are experts in some small corner of knowledge. They know a lot about a little. Humans have been successful not because all share deep funds of common knowledge, that is, cultures, but due to the networks that connect individuals to experts, and now especially to knowledge technologies such as books, libraries, television, the internet, computers, smartphones. Even though the technologies of writing and literacy had already had a transformative effect on Mediterranean cultures in the relevant period of antiquity here under examination, few individuals were highly literate. So revolutionary has this new understanding been about cognitive constraints that it has affected the way that securities and bonds are managed and traded as well as numerous other technical areas of business, government, and the military. These consistent and well-established findings about – to cite a recent book title – *The Knowledge Illusion*, are important both for the practices of historians and for the way that historians understand cultures and the knowledge/knowledge practices that characterize them.[5] Conscientious historians can no longer rely only on their instincts in light of – to cite another title – *Why Our Intuitive Theories About the World Are So Often Wrong*.[6]

In a 2008 book, the anthropologist Scott Atran and the psychologist Douglas Medin write, "... it is just a non-starter to treat or define cultures and groups in terms of shared properties."[7] What could be more counterintuitive to us traditional historians! The ways that humans, including us twenty-first century academics, think intuitively about social groups has also been the object of some intensive cross-cultural study. We intuitively attribute something like essential natures to both natural kinds and social groups and create stories like "common Judaism" to make plausible such massive social coherence and commonality.[8] Critically self-reflective biologists, for instance, frequently write about how difficult it is for them to think about species in Neo-Darwinian

---

[5] Steven Sloman and Philip Fernback, *The Knowledge Illusion: Why We Never Think Alone* (New York: Riverhead Books, 2017).
[6] Andrew Sthulman, *Scienceblind: Why Our Intuitive Theories About the World Are So Often Wrong* (New York: Basic Books, 2017).
[7] *The Native Mind and the Cultural Construction of Nature* (Cambridge, MA: MIT Press, 2008), 265.
[8] Ibid., 20–23.

rather than essentializing ways.[9] Scholars in many areas of the academy have long understood aspects of this problem of essentializing and tried to introduce variation into descriptions of social groups. So one begins with the idea of an integrated entity such as a culture or a religion and then talks about variation within the unity, but with no escape from the mode of thought. Social theory in the last two centuries was dominated by three ideas that surely had something to do with those centuries being the great age of the nation-state: societies or cultures as super-organisms, as machines with functional parts and as integrated systems. These models have been largely abandoned in light of vast quantities of detailed data about some cultures and the increasingly powerful methods of analysis.

The historically typical idea of an unchanging core to some entity is not the "essentialism" decried by post-modernism and post-structuralism that often consists of an opposition to any kind of generalization. "To generalize is to essentialize." But as Jonathan Z. Smith has said, there is no thinking or membership in the academy without generalizations.[10] The other notion of essentialism seen in the post-isms holds that to claim that a cultural or social formation has any sort of stability across cultures or time is essentializing. Thus, to claim that sixteenth century India or the Roman Empire had religion is to attribute an essence to the parochial modern western notion of "religion" and then to violently impose this upon the other.[11] But to claim enough stability in a social formation to recognize some significant continuity is not to claim that there has not been change and variation over its history. We could learn here from Darwinian thinking. Cats were once quite different animals than they are now, and there has only been variation on certain themes over the period of cat history. Cats are always changing with sub populations moving in different directions, but it would be absurd to deny that it makes sense to call that animal both in China and the UK "cats" or to deny that these existed in ancient Egypt. Even with all of the change and variation, there is enough relative stability of this population over a certain period of time to understand cats as a natural kind. Recognizing relative degrees of stability in social formations does not amount to claiming invariant essences.

But traditional social analysis in the humanities and social sciences has proceeded by the principle of synthesis. As Bronislaw Malinowski wrote,

> We are not interested in what A or B may feel *qua* individuals . . . we are interested only in what they feel and think *qua* members of a given community [where] their mental states receive a certain stamp, become stereotyped by the institutions in which they live.[12]

---

[9] Michael Ghiselin, "Categories, Life and Thinking," *Behavioral and Brain Sciences* 4 (1981): 269–313.
[10] *Relating Religion: Essays in the Study of Religion* (Chicago: University of Chicago Press, 2004), 174.
[11] See the Introduction to this volume.
[12] *Argonauts of the Western Pacific* (New York: Dutton, 1922), 23. See Atran and Medin, *Native Mind*, 220.

This largely ahistorical consensual view of cultures, or of religions, based on intuitive ideas, treats individuals as passive recipients of the culture by causally opaque and rather uniform kinds of absorption such as imitation, instruction and rule following. This intuitive model simply assumes that habits, procedures, beliefs and norms are transmitted intact. But empirical investigation of cultural learning has found just the opposite.[13] Cultural transmission instead involves constant and large amounts of error, variation and change.

Historians of antiquity have no way of performing large and representative studies of cultural matters, but we can learn from our colleagues who do have such data and use less intuitive and more realistic models of culture. Philo and Josephus, to take examples that have been central to dominant constructions of "Judaism," can speak with great confidence about what Judeans think and do. They often generalize about Jews with little hesitation. But even before the recent revolution regarding knowledge in cultures, we knew on some level that they could not have known these things about the millions of Jews living across the Mediterranean and West Asia. They could not have had a representative basis for most of their claims. Their confident statements and descriptions combine characteristic overconfidence with the impulse of literate elites to institute the normative, that is, to say what they think Jews ought to think and do. I believe that the blending of the normative and the descriptive characterizes much scholarship on ancient Jews and Christians. It would be one way to explain statements such as the following, from a recent volume on Sanders's notion of common Judaism:

> Jews from Italy, Egypt, Mesopotamia, and Jerusalem believed that God had given the Torah to Israel, rescued Israel from Egyptian bondage, and would in some fashion free Israel in the future again. Included within common Judaism was a commitment to the sacrificial system, the temple, observance of Sabbath and festivals, circumcision, purity, dietary laws, and charity. True, profound differences existed. While Torah, synagogue and purity were important for all Jews, their language, function and significance differed.[14]

Okay, and Roman Catholics revere the authority of the Vatican, obey the Church's teachings, do not practice artificial birth control and share a common religiosity around the world.

In sociology, history and other areas the new approach to similarity and difference, to stability and change across groups and cultures, has usually been some

---

[13] Jean Lave and Etienne Wenger, *Situated Learning* (New York: Cambridge University Press, 1991). Dan Sperber, *Explaining Culture* (Oxford: Blackwell, 1996); Scott Atran, "The Trouble with Memes: Inference Versus Imitation in Cultural Creation," *Human Nature* 12 (2001): 351–81.

[14] *Common Judaism: Explorations in Second-Temple Judaism* ed. Wayne O. McCready and Adele Reinhartz (Minneapolis, MN: Fortress, 2008), 219–20.

form of network theory and network analysis.[15] Meanwhile in anthropology and areas of cognitive studies, epidemiological methods that chart the acquisition, transmission and distribution of knowledge (beliefs/cognitions/discursive artifacts) and practices have become important, and are often used together with the network theory.[16] These areas, when using the two different but related approaches, typically find vastly varied distributions of knowledge across putative cultures with a central role for networks of experts and connections or lack of connections by degree to these networks by non-expert populations.

Atran and Medin with their research teams, for instance, spent two decades studying the Itza' Maya, the Spanish speaking Ladinos, and the immigrant Q'eqchi' Maya of the great Petén forest region, populations vastly less socially and culturally complex than the Jews of the ancient Mediterranean.[17] Their focus was on folk biological knowledge of these populations who have depended on agroforestry for livelihoods and culture. They consciously began with conceptions not too different from "common Judaism" in identifying the peoples above as cultures. But the researchers crafted various experiments with the goal of understanding the distribution of knowledge, practices, the relations of such distributions to social formations, and the causal processes involved.

The resulting "maps" rendered visually as three-dimensional topologies showed the pathways along which knowledge has been stored, lost, distributed and assimilated. Sometimes subgroups appeared clearly as in the genders among the Ladinos. Itza were the least interconnected socially, but had the most prestigious experts that the Ladinos and their expert networks depended upon for the flow of knowledge. Knowledge clearly clustered in densities among the Itza and the Ladinos with certain individuals (experts) being hyperconnected in some network. One surprise came from finding that the Itza and Ladinos, but not the Q'eqchi' networks, even cultures, were blending, especially due to the Ladino dependence on Itza experts. As the authors write, "Analyses within the Itza' sample revealed little residual agreement and this agreement was inconsistent across different tasks. In no case could we discern relationships between residual agreement and social or expert network proximity."[18] The Ladinos showed the most convergence of social and expert networks. The Q'eqchi' are highly corporate and focused on local social relations with few native experts. The Itza example shows that experts can form rather autonomous networks of experts who only indirectly affect the broader culture. In this case, there were two distinct networks of forest/farming/hunting/fishing experts.

---

[15] Charles Kadushin, *Understanding Social Networks: Theories, Concepts and Findings* (New York: Oxford University Press, 2012).
[16] Ibid., 136–61; Atran and Medin, *Native Mind*, 209–23.
[17] Atran and Medin, *Native Mind*, 161–223 and bibliography.
[18] Atran and Medin, *Native Mind*, 213.

The point here is only to illustrate how their and other network and epidemiological research shows that our intuitive ideas about the commonality and boundedness of cultures and groups ranges from misleading to radically distorted. Vital takeaways appear from this sort of analysis, lessons for how historians should envision the cultures of the ancient Judeans and their religion. For one, there can be broad agreement across a population of individuals who identify most strongly with X group and the widely shared belief that the X group shares beliefs and practices, when in reality there are actually huge differences and a lack of commonality in many areas. Identifications also shift and overlap much more readily than in our intuitive ideas about social groups. Individuals will claim shared identity with different groups in different contexts and times. Asking a Josephus or a Philo, self-identifying experts on Judeans, needs the caution that they often likely project themselves onto Jews in general.

In addition to the histories of the populations, the environments, the cultural materials and social organization, such network approaches consider the constraints of broadly human mental organization to be a key factor. An enormous amount of progress has been made in cognitive studies that can only be ignored at the risk of making the humanities into esoteric clubs.[19] Structuralists and post-structuralists believed that the only significant mental organization was that binary oppositions structured language/thought. In a 1974, interview, Lévi-Strauss, who largely invented this view, said when asked about these binary operators, "When I started there was still no science of mind. Saussure, Marx, Mauss, and music were my guides. Since then things have changed. Psychology now has something to say."[20] That this binary view of language still has great influence in parts of the humanities, but none in linguistics, witnesses to the former's sometimes extreme isolation from the rest of the academy. All ideas and theories about how cultural items are produced, transmitted and acquired presuppose some view of mind, even if it is the modernist idea of mind as the blank slate and culture sponge.

Atran and Medin follow the consensus in cognitive studies. Their focus was the distribution and variation of folk biological knowledge. Anthropologists have studied folk biology in numerous cultures and found a common cognitive structure. Independently, psychologists have found the basic categories upon which folk biology depends in young children. For example, "From an early age, it appears, humans cannot help but conceive of any object they see in the world as either being or not being an animal, and there is evidence for an early distinction between plants and nonliving things."[21] With such categories go

---

[19] Edward Slingerland, *What Science Offers the Humanities: Integrating Body and Culture* (Cambridge: Cambridge University Press, 2008).
[20] Atran and Medin, *Native Mind*, 283, n.4.
[21] Ibid., 29.

certain inferential structures. They are not dogmatic about this evidence for an evolutionarily developed mind, but follow consensus in thinking it strong enough to use it as a hypothesis, a part of possible explanations. It certainly has vastly more evidence than the blank slate model. The nested taxonomy found in all cultures so far studied is kingdoms, life forms and generic species. Where great culturally specific variation occurs is within species. There can also be intermediate taxa between life form and generic species. For the Maya and Ladinos, these categories are hugely important and shape their central practices, the way they relate to their environment and their everyday reasoning. Three elements come together to shape their reasoning and knowledge: mind, culture and the causal relation to the natural environment. The latter, such as actually perceiving and relating to trees, is required to activate mental structures and cultural knowledge. Atran and Medin write, "We suggest that much of the cultural transmission and stabalization of ideas . . . involves the communication of poor, fragmentary, and elliptical bits of information that manage to trigger rich and prior inferential structure."[22] Here the two are agreeing with a conclusion based on a great deal of empirical research in psychology. Minds do not passively absorb information but individually shape it so much that commonality that does exist within and across cultures is best explained as the result of certain relatively common features of the brain's architecture organizing input. Commonality would yield such things as easy belief in a category of gods and similar beings and not something like monotheism or rest on the Sabbath or broadly common intuitions about polluting and disgusting things and not specific rules about them. My attempt to theorize aspects of Mediterranean religion also attempts to relate tendencies of mind, culture and environment.

I will briefly review my arguments that religion across the ancient Mediterranean shared common patterns so that it can with profit be analyzed into three and then four types.[23] These sub-kinds of religion partly follow from an understanding of the ancient cultures as distributed, even if we possess the evidence to see only fragments of social and cultural networks. My approach draws on theories of social practices and attempts to chart ways that religious practices clustered and interconnected or did not connect in the larger social landscape, partly based on propensities demonstrated by cognitive scientists. On this view, all the cultures of the ancient Mediterranean were in many ways distinctive, but none were unique, or incomparable. But this is not the scholarly consensus. The notion of common Judaism illustrates a wider approach in which Judaism is so different that it only marginally counts as a Mediterranean religion, if at all.

---

[22] Ibid., 158.
[23] See the Introduction and Chapter One in this volume.

Religion in Judea during the three centuries before the Roman destruction of the temple in Jerusalem was a combination of broader Mediterranean and West Asian religion with certain peculiarities. My three modes are analytically useful precisely because they fit broadly across the cultures. This allows one to then study the interaction of the three modes that characterizes the religion of the various cultures. This approach, I believe, encourages thinking about the religion of ancient Jews without constructing "Judaism" according to an always-essential exceptionalism.

For cognitive and social reasons that I cannot discuss here, but that I have outlined in earlier chapters, the mode I call the religion of everyday social exchange (RESE) is most basic.[24] It can and frequently does exist even apart from the other two modes, but those modes base themselves partly on the RESE. The religion of everyday social exchange features approachable deities and similar non-evident beings (NEBS) such as local gods, the beloved dead, the familiar heavenly bodies, angels, demons, ghosts, divinized humans, and "spirits." Participants imagine that these beings affect their lives in personally relevant and tangible ways such as giving humans the offspring of animals and plants, children, good and bad weather, health and illness, help and hindrance with the contingencies of life and so on. Humans in turn want to build and maintain positive long-term relations with the beings most relevant to their lives. Some ancients thought of these beings as serving under a high ruling god, but that did not eliminate the everyday and local qualities.

People intuitively deemed it right and fair to give gifts and thanks for the benefits that the gods and NEBS gave to them. Practices of gift-giving (e.g., food and drink, votives, incense, praising by prayer, recognitions at meals, blessings, lamp lightings) and reciprocity are central, but also healings, exorcism, divinatory practices, apotropaic objects and so on. Some beings were imagined to have characters making them not so positively approachable, which had to be placated or avoided. This mundane religion characterized farms, neighborhoods, households and their members, including slaves. This mode was important to women and slaves. The optimal social and physical environment for the religion was agricultural although extension of the practices to contexts of non-agricultural production was normal. At least ninety percent of Jews lived in agricultural contexts.[25] We should not confuse the ways that God was represented in some places in the writings of Judean intellectuals as high and rather remote with the intuitive sense in the RESE, even seen many places in writings that became scriptural.

---

[24] See the Introduction and the first Three Chapters in this volume.

[25] A figure widely agreed upon for the whole Empire. See, Catherine Hezer, *Jewish Literacy in Roman Palestine* (Tübingen: Mohr Siebeck, 2001), 34–5, 476.

The most important practices of the RESE were gift-giving to gods/NEBS, divinatory practices in which gods/NEBS provided information in the form of signs and traces, and prayer. In this mode people were typically modest about their knowledge of gods/NEBS, their intentions and moods. This contrasts sharply with the claims to certain knowledge of the second mode of literate religious experts who often appealed to texts. Individuals, however, can participate in more than one mode, especially in different situations and contexts, without noticing contradictions. Psychologists find such compartmentalizing to be a central characteristic of the mind.[26]

What I call "civic religion," a kind closely related in many ways to the RESE, features practices from the RESE such as prayer, offerings, signs and messages, but reshapes them and organizes them together with other practices according to civic interests and principles of civic power. I use "civic" as a catchall for the religion of cities, kingdoms and similar social formations based upon the prestige and power of hereditary classes. As a central underlying principle of this mode, some portion of the aristocracy claimed the authority to represent the whole ethnic/citizen population before the gods. Thus, for instance, a small portion of the Roman elite ran the so-called "religion of Rome"; so also for the Judean temple in Jerusalem. Most of the population never directly participated in many of these official cultic activities. These elites conducted the rites on behalf of Rome, Judea and their entire populations. The masses mostly carried on the practices of everyday social exchange, but the RESE especially came together with civic religion in offerings made by individuals and families in temples and in festivals set in calendars. In rituals, festivals and many other practices celebrating cities, kingdoms and ethnicities, civic religion was the major producer of ideologies that justified and naturalized the rule of aristocracies and that aimed to crystallize the solidarity of the relevant populations. The Judeans like the Egyptians and many West Asian cultures had a priestly aristocracy.

Civic religion tended to make these practices splendid and big. Offerings were made in temples, not houses, and set apart by being purified from birth, death and other pollutions of the house and family. Civic religion thus created a structural hierarchy over the religion of families and households. The impurity of the latter was a threat to the presence of the gods on behalf of the city. Altars, libation cups and divine representations often became magnificent works of art. Prayers and hymns became literary pieces to glorify the city, the ethnicity, their histories, their futures and the city's gods. Festivals, although often agricultural, also celebrated the same, drawing in the participation of the non-elite on a large scale. Civic religion shared long-term generalized

[26] Shtulman, *Our Intuitive Theories*.

reciprocity with the RESE. The gods of the city gave benefits to the city and its inhabitants. The city in turn gave back gifts to thank and honor them. Events and circumstances might be read as signs of stresses and fractures in the city's relationship with a god. Thus, rites to re-establish the relationship and thus reinstitute normal exchange might be carried out. Both everyday religion and civic religion related to the gods/NEBS within an environment that was largely agricultural with fruit, grain and animal offerings from the land. By contrast, the religion of literate experts focused on intellectual practices in an urban context.

The religion of literate experts, specialists in texts, their interpretation and production constituted a distinct religiosity. The religions that we moderns know and often simply equate with religion and religions such as Judaism, Christianity, Islam, Buddhism are institutionalized social formations dominated by literate experts in texts. The number of truly literate people – sufficiently to write or competently interpret complex texts – was very small in antiquity. Yet nearly all of our conceptions of Judean, Christian and other religion in antiquity come from this tiny, but powerful caste to whom we owe the literary sources. But for game changing finds like the Dead Sea and Nag Hammadi manuscripts, all of the literature that was transmitted – 1 to 3% of what existed – has been highly selected, shaped and edited by the traditions that built upon the ancient literate and literary intellectuals.

But the person who offered a sacrificial animal did not need to be literate, and the practice did not depend upon writings or their interpretation. Any illiterate farmer could offer cakes, light a lamp, beg a NEB for help, receive a divine message in a dream, ask a deity to bless or curse someone, pray for the success of crops and so forth. While the religion of the expert might include the practices of the RESE, or even be parasitic upon them, the religion of the literate specialist could not exist without writings, high literacy and networks of literate production and exchange.

Two things must be kept in mind in order to understand the effects of literate experts on religion. First, any textual practice, including writing, reading and interpretive practices, introduces changes into, or over against, the RESE and civic religion.[27] To write about the rules for sacrificing in a temple is not the same thing as sacrificing in the temple. Scholars have constantly confused creating norms via writing or stipulating a meaning with the practices themselves. Second, the kinds of novelty and degree of difference from the RESE and civic religion varied greatly among kinds of experts in the field. The field had many sub-fields according to ethnicity, social rank

---

[27] Jack Goody, *The Logic of Writing and the Organization of Society* (Cambridge: Cambridge University Press, 1986).

or educational opportunity. It also had two poles: dynamic and creative tension. On one side, experts were not very entrepreneurial and depended upon kings, aristocratic priesthoods, patrons and the scribal needs of aristocrats. Experts on this pole tended to intellectualize and textualize religious practice, but they took a much less radical position than those on the other pole. By the second century CE, for instance, the dominant Greek and Latin rhetorical culture, the orators and writers of the "Second Sophistic," and certain kinds of philosophers represented the dominant pole. Judeans like Ben Sira, Philo and Josephus were of this type. An opposing pole of certain sorts of philosophers, Christian teachers and many sorts of independent operators defined themselves in opposition to the dominant pole. The traditionally legitimized experts in their view had been corrupted by the money, power and prestige that belonged to the dominant pole. Truth, morals and the legitimate interpretation of texts could only come from those who had not sold out, those who showed disinterest in money, wealth and power and who possessed a greater devotion, more faithful to the texts and their truth. The Gospels use John the Baptist as this sort of ideal semi-autonomous pole figure to legitimate the claims of Jesus and Josephus writes that he spent three years with a similar figure named Banus (*Vita* 2). Experts on this side had no position by inheritance or bestowal and could only gain legitimacy by outdoing other specialists in displaying disinterest and novelty. Unsurprisingly, these entrepreneurs often criticized reciprocity as a mode of relating to the gods. The gods could not be bribed, bargained with or honored with petty offerings. The gods rather wanted obedience, true beliefs and the right inner formation of individuals. Both poles said that proper religious activities needed the rulings, interpretations and judgments of the keepers of texts.

This breezy reminder of the kinds – distinctive concentrations of linked practices partly shaped by cognitive constraints – of ancient Mediterranean religiosity, has aimed to bring standard conceptions of Judaism, including common Judaism, into comparison. In addition to an exaggerated commonness across this "Judaism," other broad features stand out. These include the supposed highly literate and intellectualistic nature of the common religion and its relative lack of reciprocal exchange with God and the other Judean deities, especially apart from the temples. The RESE is nearly invisible within such accounts of Judaism. More broadly, while localism – local variation and the importance of place/local context (not just the idea of Jerusalem) – was central for all other peoples, for Jews, on this view, common trans-local belief and practice massively eclipsed localism. If this picture is true, ancient Judaism was radically different from the religion of everyone else in the Mediterranean and West Asia. It would have looked more like the religion that has emerged in western modernity. Of course, this exceptionalism is precisely what scholars often want and frequently explain as due to the unique "Bible-based" monotheism of Judaism. Jews unlike everyone else did not live in a world filled with all sorts of unseen beings in a grand hierarchy reaching up to the highest god. Unlike all other peoples, Jews lived in a disenchanted modern-like world.

Looking more closely at the three interacting modes of religion from the vantage of its theorization, the most important civic religion seems to have organized itself around the temples, especially the Jerusalem temple, of course, but also the temple at Leontopolis. The most important aristocracy for civic religion was the priesthood that formed a hierarchy from the highly aristocratic down to common priests who were only marginally so based on certain inherited prerogatives. The non-priestly aristocracies of Judea and surrounding areas were similar to others in West Asia and the Eastern Mediterranean. A key difference from most areas of the Mediterranean, excepting Egypt, appears in how the hereditary priesthood monopolized the claim to religiously represent the whole ethnic population. The hereditary priesthood and temple in Jerusalem with its legally mandated economic support from Judean agriculture largely but not totally pre-empted the typical kind of economic basis for civic religion in the benefactions of the aristocracies. The non-priestly aristocracy could not claim to represent the whole population before God.

Reciprocity with the Judean supreme god was also the central principle in Judean civic religion and its RESE. This claim runs counter to the way that scholarship has represented the temple anachronistically as either an occasion for "the life of Torah" or as a system for dealing with human sinfulness.[28] The goal of generalized reciprocal exchange in both the RESE and civic religion is the maintenance of long-term relationships with the divine. The god who gives the bounty of the land, human and animal offspring and offers aid and support to those in the relationship including the ethnicity or city in turn gets goods, thanks and honors from humans. Of course, in a typical way, a calendar of festivals was also central to the Jerusalem temple's civic religion.

This reciprocity has been demonstrated for the representations of the Jerusalem temple and offerings in the Hebrew Bible and Jewish writings in the extremely important scholarship of Aaron Glaim.[29] He shows how the Hebrew Bible on offerings in the Jerusalem temple overflows with the language of gift-giving and reciprocity. Glaim gives an analysis of the so-called critique of sacrifice in the prophets showing that the real concern is the issue of God not accepting gifts when the relationship has been violated, a classic topic in ancient reciprocity. Chapters demonstrate that Philo, the Dead Sea Scrolls, Paul and the early Rabbinic texts also have the temple/offerings focused on reciprocity, even though each of these adds certain twists characteristic of literate experts.

---

[28] Sanders, *Practice and Belief*, 92-118 and variously through 119-278.
[29] "Reciprocity, Sacrifice, and Salvation in Judean Religion at the Turn of the Era." PhD diss. Brown University, 2014 (https://doi.org/10.7301/Z0GF0RWN).

The religion of literate experts with its intensively interactive field of exchange was clearly important during the so-called Second Temple Period. The tiny but sometimes influential schools of Sadducees, Pharisees, Essenes and probably others formed associations or networks of literate experts. For good reasons, Josephus found these people to resemble Greek philosophers. At times, schools and individuals were part of the heteronomous pole of the field as they advised rulers, the high priesthood and aristocracy. At other times, individuals and groups were rather freelance actors working to create their own legitimacy among interested fellows and followers. The Dead Sea Scrolls people worked, it seems, in semi-autonomy over against the pole legitimated by established institutions. Josephus and other sources mention many teachers and freelance figures working out of Judean literate exchange. Heidi Wendt has shown that freelance Jewish religious experts in such things as divinatory practices, healing, purifications and so on were so common across the eastern Roman Empire that "a Judean" like "a Persian (a Magus)," "a Chaldean" and sometimes "an Egyptian" became a word for a type of ethnically coded religious expert (I sought out a Judean/Chaldean/Magus to discover what the god wanted me to do.).[30] Many of these were literate experts. Roman authorities were anxious about such freelance operators. Wendt shows that the supposed expulsions of the Jewish population from Rome were actually expulsions of such Jewish experts.

The role of the priesthood in literate exchange presents enormous questions with quite limited evidence, but at least the more well-to-do portions of the priesthood were moderately to highly literate and the temple itself probably a center of textual learning. The presence of the temple and the importance of the sacred writings created conditions for freelance teachers and schools to thrive and compete in Jerusalem and elsewhere. This temple culture participated in broader West Asian and Mediterranean patterns. Of course, we also have much evidence for an extensive and vigorous Judean sub-field of literate production and exchange in Greek that largely follows Hellenistic literary traditions and practices with expertise often focused on Greek translations of the scriptures.

The extant sources for Judaism in this period focus overwhelmingly on the civic religion of temple and the religion of literate experts. Almost everything we know about Judean religion comes from highly educated writers. Likewise, the interests of the later Mishnah and Talmuds is in the civic religion of the temple and their own tradition of literate exchange focused on law. Even when they write about what happens in households, their interest is in legal interpretation and in extending the practices of civic religion with its focus on celebrating the people and on corporate ethnicizing social thought into the domestic sphere

---

[30] *At the Temple Gates: The Religion of Freelance Experts in the Roman Empire* (New York: Oxford University Press, 2016).

(e.g., marriage, purity, festivals, prayer). Interestingly, the RESE does show up here and there in all of these sources but usually when, as for example, Josephus narrates events from everyday life in "historical" story telling. For a well-known instance, he touts his own divinatory skills and their role in the war with Rome (*BJ* 4.629). It would be foolish to believe that he never practiced divinatory skills in order to make decisions about his own life. Literate experts with their central interest in determining what should be normative, also frequently mention everyday Jewish practice when they criticize practices from the RESE.[31] They otherwise have little or no interest in it. Josephus and Philo occupy most of their pages with anachronistic writing about representations of the temple, laws and narratives from scripture as if they represented the way things were for Judeans in their contemporary world. Rabbis write as if the system of the temple and its law were still in effect just as contemporary Greek and Latin writers looked back to the writings, culture and language of classical Athens as if these were contemporary. Jewish writers lived out fantasies about the presence of the Judean past in a rarified world of literary and legal imagination. The religion of everyday social exchange was too basic and too commonplace to even be noticed by our sources except incidentally or when writers wanted to extend their particular book religiosity over those outside their caste.

But incidental mention in writings and non-literary sources provides much evidence. I will briefly mention some of these practices. But to grasp the RESE, these practices must be understood as part of a local and everyday world full of gods and non-evident beings with whom people imagined living day to day and often treated with patterns of long-term exchange. That exchange most centrally concerns coping with life, family and farm.

It has been standard in the past to describe Jews in this period as "strict monotheists." Scholars should now know better, and I will not re-argue matters.[32] I have no doubt that Jews generally revered their "one god" as the legitimate object of honor and as the high god. Psychologists who have studied cognition about gods have shown quite convincingly that even though literate authorities tend to advocate non-intuitive ideas about God, as for example, transcendent, omniscient, omnipresent, three in one and as an incomparable cosmic emperor, people not highly educated into such conceptions use intuitive thinking that treats even God as local, limited by time and space and possessing human-like desires and moods.[33] Thus God can be treated as fitting the conditions of the

---

[31] A theme of Wendt, *Temple Gates*.
[32] See the excellent treatment of Paula Fredriksen, "Philo, Herod, Paul and the Many Gods of Ancient 'Jewish Monotheism,'" *HTR* 115 (2022): 23–45.
[33] Justin L. Barrett and Frank C. Keil, "Conceptualizing a Non-Natural Entity: Anthropomorphism in God Concepts," *CognPsych* 31 (1996): 219–47; Justin L. Barrett, "Theological Correctness: Cognitive Constraints and the Study of Religion," *MTSR* 11 (1999): 325–39.

RESE. Further, scholars have, I believe, argued convincingly that most Jews in this period believed in the existence of the gods of the cities and the other peoples.[34] They also often thought that these gods should be respected, but perhaps not honored in any way comparable to the Judean high god. Certainly, there were exclusive conditions and rules for God's temple in Jerusalem. In reality there were probably a range of ways to react to and relate to these gods frequently considered to have been appointed by God. A few of the numerous practices of relating to God and gods for which evidence exist follows below.[35]

The instance of a certain Moschos who identified himself as a Jew in an inscription (*Inscriptiones Judaicae Orientis* 1, Ach45) is probably not atypical. In a dream, two local gods had commanded him to place the inscription in the temple. Moschos announces his obedience to the divine commands of Amphiarios and Hygieia but, there is no reason to conclude that Moschos saw his acts as diminishing his dedication to the Judean god.[36]

Karen Stern has shown how scholars have resorted to the most specious arguments in attempts to render those who wrote graffiti at a temple of Pan either subtle monotheists or bad Jews.[37] But both of the inscriptions and perhaps a third witness to the intuitive localism and sense of gratitude that belongs to the RESE. She shows that without a sense that they would be considered heretics they proudly proclaimed themselves Judeans and following the conventions of other such common graffiti, thanked and blessed this god of the desert for safe travel. What was their theology? We know little about this except that they presumably honored the Judean god and did not see thanking Pan for help in his territory as a conflict. In all likelihood the epistemological modesty of the RESE is at play here. Unlike the literate experts, they had little or no investment in beliefs that were not practical and palpable.

Even Second Isaiah, supposedly the pinnacle of an evolution to monotheism, has God with hosts in heaven and a sea god enemy.[38] Yahweh was not without other gods, even if literate authorities sometimes told people that God was in a class of his own, and the other "gods" should not be called gods. In addition to many texts in the Hebrew Bible, Philo speaks of gods and certain of the Dead Sea scrolls describe the gods in God's heavenly court or temple.[39] In Josephus' story (*War*, 6.300) about the withdrawal of divine presence from the temple, a voice "as of an assembled army, says 'we are leaving here.'"

---

[34] Paula Fredriksen, *Paul: The Pagan's Apostle* (New Haven, CT: Yale University Press, 2017), 32–60.
[35] For examples see Fredriksen, ibid., n. 13 and throughout.
[36] Ibid., 46.
[37] "Vandals or Pilgrims? Jews, Travel Culture, and Devotional Practice in the Pan Temple of Egyptian El-Kanais," in *"The One Who Sows Bountifully": Essays in Honor of Stanley K. Stowers*, ed. Caroline Johnson Hodge et al., (Providence, RI: Brown Judaic Studies, 2013), 177–88.
[38] Saul M. Olyan, "Is Isaiah 40-55 Really Monotheistic?," *JANER* 12 (2012): 190–201.
[39] E.g., *The Songs of Sabbath Sacrifice*; Philo, e. g., *Spec.* 1.13–15.

Josephus has no problem with the idea of an army of NEBS stationed in the temple of the one God. He does not worry that the story might suggest a god unable to fight alone. Through Christianity we have inherited a strictly dualistic picture of God with his administering angels opposed to Satan with his demons. But the very numerous types of NEBS that work for God and those who were seen as ambiguous, unreliable or even in rebellion were not divided into two neat camps during the "Second Temple Period."[40] Even in the writings of the literate elite, this wide range of beings play important roles, including when writers depict life on the ground, so to speak.

The literate experts whose imaginations thrive from texts with long interpretive traditions and the elite of civic religion who are entirely focused on the divine histories of specific sites tell stories and execute rites with definite claims about identified deities involved such as God, Michael, Mastema, Artemis. But in everyday life it is not like that. In Greek religion one has the same contrast between the writers, official civic contexts and everyday life. In the latter one rarely called on or identified a particular god or NEB. Rather, one spoke of "whichever divine one" or "the one who hears" or "the divine one."[41] One might get a message in a dream or see a sign in the sky or role the dice for a yes or no from a NEB, and yet not know – at least for certain – which god or NEB sent the message, and yet be nevertheless confident that it was a divine message. A person might call on "all who watch over us" or "God and all his holy ones" or to "the spirit who has helped us in the past." These ambiguous identifications are not the kinds of things that a Philo, a Josephus or a rabbi would write in books, but they were probably typical of the RESE. The farmer who acted so modestly at home would likely feel not the slightest contradiction in reciting lines about the God of Abraham, Isaac and Jacob in a civic context, but might hesitate at the presumption that the one God who ruled the universe had spoken directly to him. Yet an angel, or dead hero or beloved familial dead one might make perfect sense in the farmer's environment.

One does indeed need to mention the famous dead, the beloved dead and the annoying dead. Across the Mediterranean massive evidence exists, especially archeological, for exchange with the beloved dead in varied forms and with varieties of local practices that range from leaving clear evidence to activities that would barely leave traces.[42] This topic for Judaism usually gets confounded and bypassed in that scholars slide quickly into discussions of supposed Jewish beliefs about the afterlife. Evidence shows that even when people officially held some view such as that the dead became stars or slept until the resurrection that they

---

[40] Emma J. Wasserman, *Apocalypse as Holy War: Religious Polemic and Violence in the World of Paul* (New Haven, CT: Yale University Press, 2018).
[41] Robert Parker, *Polytheism and Society at Athens* (Oxford: Oxford University Press, 2005), 140.
[42] For bibliography, see Hans-Josef Klauck, *The Religious Context of Early Christianity* (Minneapolis, MN: Fortress Press, 2003), 68–69, 70.

also thought the dead to have an existence near their tombs. In such cases, the cognitively intuitive overpowers the cognitively difficult on a practical level. The husband felt the presence of his wife at the tomb and saw her in a dream.

If a Judean woman whose husband had recently died appeared to her in a dream and warned her about an impending business transaction and complained of his thirst, I suspect that many, especially among the ninety plus percent who lived in rural areas with little influence from literate experts, would have gone to the tomb and poured a libation. She probably would have considered the exchange a private matter between her and her husband. There would be no trace in the archeological record. How often did individuals in situations like the woman's go to tombs and talk to their beloved dead? Frequently, I think. The reaction to the text where Tobit exhorts (4:17), "Pour your bread and your wine on the tomb of the righteous, and do not give to sinners," should not be reflection on some rabbinic prohibition with the conclusion that the text depicts a practice that good Jews did not countenance. Rather such gift-giving and exchange with the dead was probably so basic and common that the author of Tobit mentioned it without a thought. To interaction with the beloved dead one can add the famous dead such as the patriarchs whose supposed tombs had a vigorous history. Scholars have detailed the evidence and arguments for such tomb practices and, as Pieter W. van der Horst emphasizes, it is likely that Jews went to these tombs for intercessions and miracles.[43] Finally, similar arguments could be made about the unhappy dead, ghosts, and practices to keep them away.

Very quickly I will mention some practices important to the RESE for which we have evidence. One of the most important, with much evidence in this period, are votive offerings.[44] Here one requests some help or benefit from a god or NEB and promises to give a gift in return when the boon has been granted. We hear in the literary sources and inscriptions especially about votive gifts given to the temple in Jerusalem, sometimes to synagogues and in public settings, but surely more important to everyday religion were small and more private exchanges. A mother promises to light lamps in honor of the deity for a month if her son recovers from an illness. A farmer whose crop was bountiful pours wine at the base of a tree where he had heard words of encouragement in the wind. Afterwards he might repeat yearly.

---

[43] *Japheth in the Tents of Shem: Studies in Jewish Hellenism in Antiquity* (Leuven: Peeters, 2002), 123, 135–36; Jack N. Lightstone, *The Commerce of the Sacred: Mediation of the Divine among Jews of the Greco-Roman World* (New York: Columbia University Press, 2006), 41–62.

[44] Michael Satlow, "Giving for a Return: Jewish Votive Offerings in Late Antiquity," in *Religion and the Self in Antiquity* ed. David Brakke and Steven Weitzman (Bloomington, IN: Indiana University Press, 2005), 91–108; Anne Katrine de Hemmer Gudme, *Before the God in this Place for Good Remembrance: A Comparative Analysis of the Aramaic Votive Inscriptions from Mount Gerizim* (Berlin: Walter de Gruyter, 2013).

Other practices include healing *via* a god or NEB, local funerary rites, hundreds of forms of divination, oaths calling on the divine as witness, exorcisms, apotropaic practices (such as against evil eye, spirits of illness, ghosts), numerous methods of honoring or other gift-giving to NEBS in homes and fields, prayers focused on local needs, some household purifications, incantations, spells, and various local (rather than civic) life passage and life crisis rites.[45] Against common assumption, some evidence also exists for domestic sacrifice of animals.[46] For Jews, keeping the Sabbath was a practice of the RESE that also linked to civic religion and the book religion of literate experts. The book, Tobit, attempts to depict episodes from everyday life, albeit in a theologically correct way. Tobit exhibits numerous links to literature and literate traditions of religious experts. The angel Raphael receives one of Tobit's prayers – named angels not likely in the RESE – and heals Tobit and Sarah. Disguised as a human, the angel also provides practical strategic information to Tobit about Sarah. The narrative has a focus upon issues regarding family and marriage. In one episode, a carefully prepared fried fish liver becomes an apotropaic device that drives demons away. In spite of the highly intellectualized theological framework, one can see in Tobit practices of the RESE.

A more thorough discussion of the sub-kinds of ancient Mediterranean religiosity would emphasize their often dynamic and interactive character, including the ways that the RESE interacted with the festivals and offering practices of the temples. So-called voluntary associations would also play a major role in the picture of Jewish religion. Many pre-70 CE synagogues or houses of prayer would fall into this category. Such associations typically involved extensions of the RESE and were sometimes even based in homes, neighborhoods or organized by trades with local religious practices relevant to the sites (see Chapter Two in this volume). But such extensions, especially away from Judea, through patronage by local elites and as community centers, connected the mode of everyday religion with civic religion. Literate experts also sometimes had roles as teachers, leaders and advisors in connection with associations and thus involved interaction with the field of literate experts.

Common Judaism generalizes to Jews in general the religion of literate experts whose writings have survived. It seems that nothing is more central to the imagination of this supposed religiosity than the image of millions of Jews across the Mediterranean pouring into synagogues to study the Torah

---

[45] Jennifer Eyl, *Signs, Wonders and Gifts* (New York: Oxford University Press, 2019); Gideon Bohak, *Ancient Jewish Magic: A History* (Tel-Aviv: Tel-Aviv University Press, 2011); John H. Elliott, *Beware the Evil Eye: The Evil Eye in the Bible and the Ancient World* (Eugene, OR: Cascade, 2016).

[46] Jordon Rosenblum, "Home Is Where the Hearth Is? A Consideration of Jewish Household Sacrifice in Antiquity," in *"The One Who Sows Bountifully,"* 153–63; Aryay Bennett Finkelstein, "Julian Among Jews, Christians and 'Hellenes' in Antioch: Jewish Practice as a Guide to 'Hellenes' and a Goad to Christians," PhD diss. Harvard University, 2011, 38–83.

and pray each Sabbath, Philo and Josephus' image of a nation of philosophers. I obviously cannot critique this model here, but at least, I can point to its role in creating the idea of a religion in which the central practices of its individual members focused upon deep knowledge of extensive writings and the idea that these writings minutely governed the lives of individuals. It seems to me that such a religion would require an enormous infrastructure for which we lack evidence. It would require nearly universal literacy, individual possession of the writings and an educational system in which the probable millions of Jews spent large amounts of time on a regular basis hearing instruction from experts. Literate experts would have to have been in charge of the religion of Judeans as they apparently became centuries later. Instead of the handful of remains of Jewish meeting places, we would be finding many thousands of buildings able to accommodate numbers very much larger than in most finds. Again, this sounds suspiciously like conditions that only emerged in western modernity with the printing press, universal education and so on. Of all the ethnicities in the Mediterranean, only the Jews would not possess a basic religiosity that focused upon interaction and exchange with gods and NEBS who inhabited the local environments of their lives.

Studies of modern religious populations where universal literacy prevails, where religious institutions have large comprehensive educational systems (e.g., catechism through university) and which have built infrastructures that can accommodate a large proportion of their population at any one time, do not lend credibility to the idea that even such conditions would succeed. A large-scale survey in 2010 by the Pew Research Center showed that Protestants and Roman Catholics had appallingly poor knowledge of basic information about the Bible and their own traditions.[47] Other studies have consistently yielded similar results. It is not that these people have not heard the correct teachings. Rather, just as the cognitive scientists predict, some religious representations rely on intuitive mental tools and others use non-intuitive mechanism supporting teachings only acquired and held with great difficulty and needing constant reinforcement.[48] Perhaps the religiosity of the Jews of the centuries before 70 CE was unique and shared little with everyone else in their world, but the modes of religiosity based upon clusters of practices and cognitive propensities should at least raise questions about models like common Judaism.

---

[47] Daniel Ullucci, "Competition between Experts and Non-Experts," Nathaniel DesRosiers and Lily C. Vuong, *Religious Competition in the Greco-Roman World*, (Atlanta, GA: SBL Press, 2016), 133–36 for references and discussion.

[48] Jason Slone, *Theological Incorrectness: Why Religious People Believe What They Shouldn't* (New York: Oxford University Press, 2004).

PART II

Paul As Freelance Expert

CHAPTER FOUR

Kinds of Myth, Meals and Power: Paul and the Corinthians

Jonathan Z. Smith's comparison of the Corinthians, as known from Paul's letters and the Atbalmin of Papua New Guinea, provides a remarkable opportunity for scholars of early Christianity.[1] The study of the New Testament has understandably been dominated by the internal perspectives of Christian theology. This means that approaches to Paul's letters continually reinscribe a notion of incomparable uniqueness and irresistible relevance. Privileged meta-narratives ensure that the ways scholars imagine Paul and the Corinthians elide many of the human social and cognitive processes that students of a contemporary culture or a scholar in a department of history would assume as requirements for construing the people in question as human. Smith's bold comparison breaks through these constraints and creates an opening for imagining Paul and the Corinthians in ways that are quite normal in the humanities and the social sciences.

I want to take advantage of the opening created by Smith's article to raise some questions about certain social and cognitive processes that traditional approaches usually hide. In a more comprehensive study, I would theoretically develop the concepts of *doxai*, interests, recognition, and attraction that I believe need to be added to Smith's concepts of incorporation and resistance.[2] I understand all of these as attendant to the processes of ongoing mythic formations that Smith's paper allows us to imagine for the Atbalmin, and for Paul and the Corinthians. For the purposes of this chapter, I will stipulate the following. A "doxa" is a body of taken-for-granted beliefs, practical skills, assumptions and understandings that the researcher through historical investigation imagines that the people in question brought to a social situation.[3] Interests are the most basic and important projects and ends that motivated

---

[1] Smith, "Re: Corinthians," in *Relating Religion: Essays in the Study of Religion* (Chicago: University of Chicago, 2004), 340–61.
[2] Smith, "Re: Corinthians," 347.
[3] I borrow the concept from Pierre Bourdieu as used by him throughout his career.

the people in question. "Most basic" should be a matter of debate and corrigible for scholars. "Recognition" meanwhile is the process of someone taking someone else or another group to be someone of a certain type or identity that to various degrees makes sense to them, and that often entails to some degree of legitimacy or social capital. "Attraction" is the process of recognizing some sort of mutuality of interests that can be the basis for individuals or groups engaging in common practices or entertaining the possibility. One rightly assumes that individual participation is differential and that individuals do not bring exactly the same skills, understandings and so on to practices in common with others, even while they share certain common practical understandings with all those who participate in a particular practice.[4] I will presuppose these notions as I first engage some facets of Smith's paper and then use Paul's discussion of the Lord's Supper as a case to explore how one might imagine the mythmaking and ritualization of Paul and the Corinthians as dynamic social activities. At the end, I will return to Smith's construal of the incommensurability that he sees between the religion of Paul and the Corinthians and suggest another interpretation.

I characterize the dominant approach to Paul and the Corinthian letters as one of academic Christian theological modernism.[5] This approach has made enormous contributions to the study of the New Testament and contributes substantially to this chapter, but its limitations are, I think, clear. The tradition is thoroughly grounded in the situation developing from the aftermath of the Protestant Reformation, but took form as a part of the crystallization of European modernity in the nineteenth century and the institutionalization of confessional faculties in the universities. The approach trades centrally on the dualisms of material/spiritual and orthodox/heretical. With regard to science and cosmology, the ancients and the early Christians are other in a rather absolute sense, but with regard to religion, morals, sociality and subjectivity, the early Christians are the same as us. They are same people in different clothes, with a different "science." The early Christians are not only generally the same as modern Europeans, but also the same as the professors and Christian scholars who study them in their focus on specialized intellectual interests such as doctrines, theology, ideas.

The basic moves are familiar. One first reads the letter for Paul's explicit criticisms of the audience encoded in the rhetoric of the letter. Secondly, and much more importantly, one reads passages with irony and sarcasm, and where Paul seems to oppose something or seems defensive as reflections of an opposing point-of-view, often with supposed behavioral manifestations. Two moves,

---

[4] For practical understanding, see Theodore Schatzki, *Social Practices* and *The Site of the Social*.
[5] E.g., as in Werner Georg Kümmel in *The New Testament: The History of the Investigation of its Problems* (Nashville: Abingdon Press, 1972).

mirror reading and asserting that Paul uses the language of his opponents – of course he doesn't really mean what he says in such cases – prove central to this enterprise. With these methods, one constructs opponents and reaches the goal of outlining the theological or ideological positions of these opponents or deficient Corinthians. Typically, the scholar will identify this false teaching with some intellectual position in Greco-Roman or Jewish culture often represented in the most extreme caricature. Then, in a second major move, the academic theological modernist reads Paul's rhetoric, and the theology supposedly behind the rhetoric, over against and as a response to the ideology of his opponents. Inevitably, the opponents turn out to be suspiciously similar to contemporary religious opponents of the scholar such as pietist enthusiasts, evangelical or fundamentalist spiritualists, ascetic world renouncers, sacramentalists, worldly philosophers, libertine intellectuals and so forth.

The central pattern here is the model of orthodoxy and heresy. Religion is a matter of right belief and wrong belief. Doctrines are formalized or semi-formalized teachings. People consciously adopt beliefs and are conscious of their beliefs/positions as beliefs/positions. Thus, a historian could, on this view, without anachronism ask, "what was Paul's or his opponent's position on, say, justification by faith or ecclesiology and so on." But there is an unanalyzed social phenomenon involved in taking positions. To provide perspective on this assumption, I would argue that it would be highly misleading to ask this question of, for instance, a typical Roman, Greek, or Jew. Greeks ordinarily did not have "positions" on the doctrine of Zeus or the gods and Judeans on Yahweh or the nature of belief. There are social conditions for this kind of religion supposed as natural and universal in much scholarship. Rather, I will admit below that Paul does have some interest in religion with a certain focus on right and wrong positions, but one can only explain his interest within the social conditions of a field of intellectualist competition.

A key assumption in most theological modernist interpretation is that the people whom Paul addresses and whom he represents as the church at Corinth form a community. The idea of a community is the idea of a highly integrated social group based on a common ethos, practices and beliefs. Paul preached the gospel, people converted, and Paul welded them into a community. With this assumption, Paul's words in 1:10 become the basis for asking the question: how did the Corinthian community become divided? What false doctrine from inside the community, or infiltrating from the outside, corrupted the community or seduced a portion of it? Usually, the corrupting ideas have an external ideological or theological source, often false beliefs "left over" from "the pre-Christian environment." The concept of community has been enormously constraining for scholarship on ancient Christianity (Chapter Ten in this volume). "Community" is a highly ideal and ideological concept. There are very many kinds of social formations that are not communities.

The approach that I characterize assumes not only Christian community and Christian subjects, but also that the pre-Christian religious interests and formations would have to a substantial degree coincided with Paul's own interests and formation. The Corinthians were looking for the truth about salvation, say, and Paul provided the true beliefs. But are all people just naturally looking for salvation? This approach overlooks the fact, long established from ethnography and the history of religions, that the vast majority of religious people have "practical" religious interests focused on the household and family rather than specialized intellectual interests, such as explaining the nature of the cosmos and human destiny, the true doctrine of God, right worship, the true interpretation of authoritative texts and the nature of the ideal human community. In fact, it takes a massive cultural-institutional structure, say with something like bishops, textually oriented religious education, the massive production and religious use of texts, and so on in order to reproduce religions that focus on intellectual practices and doctrines of need and salvation. Greek and Roman religion and the religion of the Judean temple were not such religions. It is unlikely that Paul's formation and interests substantially overlapped with those of most of the Corinthians.

On the modernist reading, Paul's first contact with the Corinthians must have been somewhat as follows. Paul knocks on a door in Corinth. Gaius comes to the door. Paul says, "Jesus Christ has died for your sins, and you have been justified by God." Gaius joyously proclaims, "Thank God I am saved!" Now this may be an exaggeration of what is naively unexamined, but only a small one. The theological modernist approach fails to address the sociological questions of recognition – what are the conditions for someone recognizing someone else as a particular someone representing something; and similarly the questions of the coincidence of interests, of attraction, practical participation, negotiations of individual self-understanding, and social formation. All of these remain unasked as the scholar posits Christian subjects and community.

In my view, two things are clear from the evidence of the Corinthian letters: First, Paul very much wanted the people to whom he wrote to be a community and held a theory proclaiming that God had miraculously made them into a community "in Christ"; Second, the Corinthians never actually sociologically formed a community, and only partly and differentially shared Paul's interests and formation. In my estimation, it is very unlikely that the Corinthians ever had any more social organization than households that may have had previous ties with other households, and after Paul, a roughly shared knowledge that Paul wanted them to be an *ekklesia* in Christ and that he kept telling them that God had transformed them into one.[6] But Paul's relation with a fraction of the

---

[6] I do not find likely that the Corinthians formed an association either before or after Paul for a host of reasons. Paul's language (e.g., 1 Cor 11:18, 19–33, 14:26–38 and places throughout the letters) suggests meetings of households and fractions thereof.

Corinthians that we know included some elites in the sense of being heads of households and potential heads was different and more cohesive.

That the primary social formations Paul encountered were households does not mean that there were not many other social formations that either cut across households or that involved individuals and sub-populations within households. The possibilities are numerous such as circles of friends, trading networks, cultic associations, neighborhoods, ethnic identifications. One of which we have firm evidence is a field of literate competition and cultural production that I will discuss below. In spite of our romantic notions, even households might not be communities, and the individuals associated with Paul might not have ever belonged to any community. I follow contemporary social thought in holding that "community" or even groupness more broadly is something to be demonstrated rather than to be assumed.[7] Community and groupness – that the category X (such as Jews, Christ followers, Corinthians, local aristocrats, a particular clan) actually constituted a group – should not be axioms of analysis. Holding to this approach typically yields two results: firstly, a separation of social ideology from social practice, and secondly the discovery that individuals participate in numerous social formations.

In addition, I want to insist that individuals under specific social conditions produce and interpret myths, not communities. One cannot simply identify the interests of the mythmakers and myth interpreters with the collective minds and wills of communities and peoples. One often best thinks of a mythmaker as a kind of entrepreneur attempting to produce and shape groupness. Eytan Bercovitch in his analysis of Atbalmin religion, I think, attempts to encompass some of these distinctions with his concept of "social multiplicity," the idea that "people possess several, often contradictory, sets of beliefs and practices."[8] He is explicitly trying to avoid an old fashioned, and now discredited, identification of a posited group with its purported culture seen as a whole and notably including its myths. Of course, we can know a great deal about Paul's views, but must be very modest about those of the Corinthians.

Smith's comparison gives permission to the scholarly imagination to construe the social situations reflected in the Corinthian letters in new ways. I want to engage three central aspects of the two situations in which he finds similarity and a basis for further comparison: localism, simultaneous experimentation, and changes in a small homogenous community. The relevant statements from the article are:

> Two major elements stand out in which the New Guinea materials make more plausible the imagination of some early Christian social formations.

---

[7] Rogers Brubaker, *Ethnicity Without Groups* (Cambridge: Harvard University Press, 2004).
[8] Eytan Bercovitch, "The Altar of Sin: Social Multiplicity and Christian Conversion among a New Guinea People," *Religion and Cultural Studies*, ed. Susan L. Mizruchi (Princeton: Princeton University Press) 211–35.

The first is the ability of a small relatively homogenous community to absorb a stunning series of situational changes within a brief span of time through strategies of incorporation and resistance . . . The second element is the capacity of a small relatively homogenous community to experiment, simultaneously, with multiple modes of religion. (Bercovitch described four.) The Atbalmin have exhibited, within their social and religious history, the dialectical relations of processes of reproduction and transformation that constitute, with particular clarity, what Sahlins has termed "structures of conjuncture."

As a generalization, all of this makes more plausible the presumption of the coexistence of multiple experiments by early 'Christian' communities as well as their localism. It alerts us to the presence of sorts of changes not necessarily captured by the historical record.[9]

By "localism," I take Smith to mean, in the case of the Corinthians, their practice of the religion of place manifest in their concern for the dead, for spirits, for kinship and ancestry and for their common meals.[10] The letters clearly give evidence of the Corinthian practice of religion of the household and family and religion of the temple.[11] Thus interpreters should take these, and especially the first, as expressing the religious interests of the people to whom Paul wrote and think of Paul's religion of "anywhere" as at least novel for most of the Corinthians and perhaps with Smith as a problematic intrusion.[12] This then makes explaining mutual interests, recognition of Paul, and attraction – processes that precede Smith's issues of incorporation and resistance – a central task for the scholar. Even a problematic someone is a someone to the other, but always under conditions. In the minds of at least some of the people whom Paul addresses, what authorized Paul as a purveyor of certain cultural products and practices? In order to follow this approach, New Testament scholars will have to denaturalize their understandings of religion and not assume a contextless universal meaningfulness and attraction to Paul's gospel. It is simply a fact of ethnography and the history of religions that the religious interests of most people focus on the locative religion of household and family.[13] I will argue that Paul's teachings and mythmaking were centrally about kinship and ancestry, even if not in a typically locative way, and integrally connected to

---

[9] Smith, "Re: Corinthians," 347.
[10] Stanley Stowers, "Theorizing the Religion of Ancient Households and Families," in *Household and Family Religion in Antiquity*," John Bodel and Saul Olyan (Oxford: Blackwell, 2008), 5–19; Smith, "Here, There and Anywhere," *Relating Religion*, 323–39.
[11] 1 Cor 8:10 and the discussions of meat sacrificed to non-Jewish deities.
[12] Smith, "Re: Corinthians," 351–52.
[13] See n. 10 above.

his discourse about the spirit (a poor translation) or *pneuma*. An implication of this argument is that modes of religion that are distinctive enough to classify as types may not be pure. Tension, inconsistency and modes of hybridity ought to be taken as the norm. The kind of religion imagined and advocated in Paul's letters embodies tensions. It denies many of the principles and practices of the locative religion of land, temple and home precisely by thinking, including mythmaking, about family, kinship, and descent. Is Paul simply incomprehensible to many or all of the Corinthians as Smith and Burton Mack suggest? Or does the very evidence of creative differential reaction and resistance to Paul on the part of the Corinthians argue for varied degrees of comprehension and creative response in light of that comprehension? We can conclude with confidence that even if the Corinthians had fully understood what Paul wanted them to do, they would have been selective about what they wanted to do, and could not have given up their religion wholesale, even if they had wanted to do so. This means that there is a very large gap between the idealized descriptions of the Corinthians as "in Christ" and the real situation. The deep failures that Paul sees among the Corinthians are likely the result of their selective and mixed appropriation and outright resistance to Paul.

Smith describes the social formation subject to these changes as "a small relatively homogeneous community." While this certainly fits the Atbalmin and to some extent fits Paul's Corinthians, I think it helpful to make some further specifications and modifications of the description. Although complicated by the intrusion of Western modernity and the Indonesians in New Guinea, I would argue that the society of Roman Corinth was in important ways more differentiated and certainly more diverse than traditional Atbalmin society, even with the intrusions.[14] Slavery, for example, and a multi-ethnic urban context make a difference, but I want to draw attention to one feature of the culture/social organization of the Roman Empire in particular. Trans-local fields of knowledge with experts who served as producers and distributors and a niche of people socialized as consumers of this culture had long been a feature of the Mediterranean. By "field," I mean a space of norms and practices, a game if you will, that had gained a semi-autonomy from kings, patrons and the economy in general.[15] The dominant and broadly legitimized form of this knowledge and practices is well known to us as Greek and Roman *paideia* or according to the myth, a single paideia whose commonality to Greeks and Romans was based on an ancient shared ancestry.[16] The Augustan classicism

---

[14] See Smith's qualifications and differences, "Re: Corinthians," 347–48.

[15] I discuss the notion of fields, especially in relation to Pierre Bourdieu and his critics in "Pauline Scholarship and the Third Way in Social Theory" (an unpublished paper read at various venues).

[16] Simon Swain, *Hellenism and Empire: Language, Classicism, and Power in the Greek World, AD 50–250* (Oxford: Clarendon, 1996).

and the classicism of the so-called Second Sophistic, for instance, both celebrated ancestral cultural heritage. The two major traditions of this paideia were found in rhetoric or sophistry and philosophy.[17] But there were clearly other bodies of knowledge with producers, distributors and interpreters. Most obviously, these appear as ethnic knowledges, the wisdom of the Egyptians, Syrian and Jews, for example. Forms of these knowledges with their authoritative texts and interpretive practices ceased to be merely local and both competed with and overlapped with the dominant paideia at points. Translation of key texts into Greek and writing in Greek were conditions that facilitated the participation of ethnic fields or sub-fields in the dominant field. The myth of the barbarian origins of Greek wisdom grew during the Hellenistic period and became very influential under the early Empire.[18]

The abundant evidence shows that only a relatively small number of people aspired to become producers, distributors and even dedicated consumers of paideia. The key point is this: two kinds of religion existed only by way of specific social conditions and in relative autonomy. "Autonomy" here refers to the larger fields or arenas of the modes setting and contesting their own rules and practices. Autonomy does not mean that the modes for individuals were mutually exclusive. The beliefs and practices of normal Mediterranean religion such as Greek, Lydian and Judean were doxic: it was given; for the most part, taken for granted.[19] This sort of religion was embedded in the everyday life of farm, family, household and the order of the city, and thus focused on place. The religion promoted among those in the fields in question was different in that contestation for defining what was true about the gods and the cosmos, and what was the true written tradition, created a dynamic struggle to produce intellectual and cultural products to promote the legitimacy of established or challenging experts and their consumers. In this social space and game, religion is something contested rather than given. There must always be defenders of the current form of the dominant intellectual tradition and challengers. Greek philosophies once challenged traditional paideia and then became part of the dominant legitimized tradition. Dominant Greek paideia was challenged, especially in many local arenas, by claims that Greek wisdom derived from more ancient cultures. "Why not go to the original sources," the challenging specialists said. Greek and Roman traditions kept reinventing

---

[17] The classic discussion has been Hans von Arnim, *Leben und Werke des Dio von Prusa, mit einer Einleitung: Sophistik, Rhetorik, Philosophie in ihrem Kampf um die Jugendbildung* (Berlin: Weidmann, 1898).

[18] G. R. Boys-Stones, *Post-Hellenistic Philosophy: A Study of its Development from the Stoics to Origen* (Oxford: Oxford University Press, 2001).

[19] I owe the sociological conceptions of doxa, orthodoxy and heresy to many works by Pierre Bourdieu such as *The Field of Cultural Production*.

themselves and facing new challengers. But none of this meant that those outside of these games felt that the givenness of their gods, temples, and practices was normally a matter of debate.

At the same time, it would be a mistake to imagine a hard impermeable boundary between the specialized writing and interpretation of the field and normal local culture outside of the field. Indeed, a typical process of domestication often prevailed. The odd specialized productions of the field often become domesticated to culture outside the field. So, for instance, a generation of French people who found the paintings of the Impressionists shocking and incomprehensible was followed by another that viewed them as challenging and appealing.[20] In typical fashion the field moved on far ahead of the general population. The Impressionists became orthodox, and a succession of rebelling movements arose such as Cubists, Dadists and Surrealists. Of course, most farmers and workers, for instance, may never have found the products of some of these field movements comprehensible, but some did, and it was always possible for individuals to be educated into the taste for such products by entrepreneurs of art in the field.

A field is a social space that floats free of certain kinds of place, the reference to fixed objects and locations in the world made meaningful by human imagination. A family shrine has a context conditioned by its fixed site, but a text circulates without the context of its creation, although it must have a context of certain practices embodied as skills such as reading in order to be and remain a text. One does not have to be in any particular place to read or write a book or debate an idea. Once written, a text might go anywhere and does not need to have an author attached to it. Literates different from and far away from the time and place of a text's writing can modify it. As with markets, cultural products circulate and have effects within fields that are mostly unseen by their producers and modifiers. Because producers in fields compete over the true, the good, and the beautiful and because the field cuts across particular places, the products tend toward universalizing knowledge and rhetoric.[21]

Where does Paul fit into this? His work was to find Greeks, Romans and other non-Jews whom he could convince that their religious and moral practices were utterly false and evil. The only true and living god was the God of the ancient Judean writings that recounted the world's nature and beginnings, and the history and fates of all the world's peoples. Christ was a being possessed of God's own *pneuma* and chosen humans could possess a share of this divine

---

[20] Pierre Bourdieu, *The Rules of Art: Genesis and Structure of the Literary Field* (Cambridge: Polity Press, 1996).

[21] See Andrew Wallace-Hadrill, "*Mutatio morum*: The Idea of a Cultural Revolution," in *The Roman Cultural Revolution*, ed. Thomas Habinek and Alessandro Schiesaro (Cambridge: Cambridge University Press, 1997), 1–22.

stuff that God had given to Christ. Paul was certainly not a sophist legitimated in the dominant fraction of the field, but belonged to one of the aspiring, competing illegitimate fractions that were every bit as necessary to the existence of the field as a field of cultural-production-as-contestation.[22]

By way of illustrating one kind of specialist, an instance of whom we know a good deal is Lucian of Samosata, a Syrian whose first language was probably Syriac rather than Greek. He came from a family of stone carvers and yet he describes how paideia lifted him into the elite dominant field known via Philostratus as the Second Sophistic. Even though this was an archaizing movement of Greek linguistic and literary purity, Lucian suggests the potential power of dominated fields by writing about the Syrian goddess of his homeland and in several writings by constructing his authorial persona as that of the marginal disinterested educated barbarian who as outsider can critique other specialist producers of cultural products.[23] In his writings, one encounters every sort of cultural specialist such as sophists, philosophers, astrologers, prophets, experts in foreign books, whom Lucian skewers as would-be competitors in the field of paideia. One vivid portrait of the expert consumer's desire for the status brought by paideia appears in the aspiring target of the *Ignorant Book Collector*, another in the form of well-to-do householders who take in experts of various sorts to bring the status of learning to their homes (*On Salaried Posts*). It seems to me that even the arrival of Christian missionaries in New Guinea did not create a comparable cultural field.

I also see another relevant difference between the situation of Christianity among the Atbalmin and Paul's coming to the Corinthians. Christian missionaries and teachers in New Guinea, even when they were natives bringing domesticated forms of the religion, carried the background authority of an enormously powerful imperial culture from the west that exerted both attraction and repulsion. Paul, the diasporate Judean, carried no such background authority. The Corinthian reception of Paul needs explanation.

To explain Paul's recognition by, and attraction of, some Corinthians, one needs three elements. The first condition is a field, or perhaps, a set of

---

[22] I find fantastic Bruce Winter's attempt to make Paul into a Sophist in *Philo and Paul among the Sophists*, 2nd ed. (Grand Rapids: Eerdmans, 2002). For suggestions about locating Paul's rhetoric and education see, my "Apostrophe, ΠΡΟΣΩΠΟΠΟΙΙΑ and Paul's Rhetorical Education," in *Early Christianity and Classical Culture: Comparative Studies in Honor of Abraham J. Malherbe*, ed. John T. Fitzgerald, Thomas H. Olbricht, and L. Michael White, (Leiden: Brill, 2003) 359–61. On how Paul's thought and practice places him in the "unorthodox" sociological fraction originally staked out by philosophy, see my, "Does Pauline Christianity Resemble a Hellenistic Philosophy?," in *Paul Beyond the Hellenism-Judaism Dualism*, ed. Troels Engberg-Pedersen (Louisville: Westminster John Knox, 2001), 81–102, and "Social Status, Public Speaking, and Private Teaching: The Circumstances of Paul's Preaching Activity," *NovT* 26 (1984): 59–82.

[23] On authorship, C. P. Jones, *Culture and Society in Lucian* (Cambridge: Harvard University Press, 1986), 41. For barbarian identity, see *The Double Indictment, The Dream and The Dead Come to Life*.

overlapping fields of knowledges and intellectual practices in which experts employed their skills to compete in the production and interpretation of oral and written texts and discourses that contest the truth and legitimacy of both traditions and novel doctrines. These practices aimed at a niche of consumers who found social distinction and other benefits in acquiring such paideia. Second, one needs to suppose a number of people among the Corinthians who desired an alternative paideia. This desire for an alternative esoteric and exotic paideia may have had a basis in their minority or mixed ethnic statuses or other status inconsistencies that both alienated them from the dominant legitimate paideia and attracted them to an alternative.[24] Beyond this, we know that certain people now and then have been attracted to the esoteric and the exotic because attachment to the different can involve social distinction in the eyes of the adherent and others. Such adherence can also express a person's broader social and cultural sympathies, a kind of cosmopolitan outlook beyond one's local and inherited culture. Lucian's ambition to leave stone carving in order to gain fame and see the larger world illustrates this motivation. Third, one must view Paul as a producer and distributor of an alternative esoteric paideia different from the dominant sophistic or philosophical kinds, yet still recognizable as a form of the same broader game of specialized literate learning. With these assumptions, it makes sense that some Corinthians would have shared interests with Paul, recognized him as a person with a certain kind of legitimacy, and found an attraction to some of his performances. It remains to show how Paul's mythmaking and other practices might have made sense to such people.

If a minority among Paul's Corinthians shared various degrees of this attraction to the "intruder," there is every reason to believe that this attraction was not easily shared by the majority. Those who did not aspire to such paideia and did not see it as a feature of their roles, statuses and aspirations, would have had interests focused on the religion of household and family. They would likely have understood Paul on their own terms and exhibited both repulsion and attraction at points related to their strategic concerns. For instance, if those who were attracted found interesting Paul's cosmic *pneuma* doctrines and teachings about the nature of the gods and the one true god and the myth of a heroic martyr who created a mode of access to the most powerful and sublime kind of *pneuma* and to a renowned ancestry, the majority may have reacted differently. As Smith suggests, they may have seen in Paul's talk of ancestors and baptism, a pneumatic link to ancestors, an opportunity to experiment with a technique for accessing their own significant dead.[25] Baptism for the dead

---

[24] On many of Paul's people being freedpersons, *A Rereading of Romans: Justice, Jews and Gentiles* (New Haven: Yale University Press, 1994), 74–82 and Wayne A. Meeks, *The First Urban Christians: The Social World of the Apostle Paul* (New Haven: Yale University Press, 1983), 55–63.

[25] Smith, "Re: Corinthians," 349–51.

may have been seen as a way to improve the status of the recent or untimely dead, a well-documented concern of families.[26] Further, Smith is right that experimentation with ritual must have involved the Corinthians in their own mythmaking, both among those who did not aspire to be specialized consumers of Paul's cultural production and the attracted.

Who were these people attracted to Paul's myths, pneumatic doctrines and performances, and moral-psychological teachings? It has been a temptation of recent scholarship to make Paul into a champion of the underclasses and a critic of the elite. This preaches well, but goes against all of the evidence that Paul was a person of his age and cultures. Likewise, it might be tempting to make Paul simply a mentor and client of the elite. The letters name some of these people and provide valuable information about their activities with the "intruder." Paul admits that the Corinthians understood their baptisms in different ways, leading to a lack of unity, and he is glad that he only baptized Gaius, Crispus and the household of Stephanas (1 Cor 1:10–16). But the choice of these people for baptism by Paul does not appear to be arbitrary (in spite of 1 Cor 1:17) because these are precisely those who are noted as sharers in Paul's specialist's activities. At the end of the letter one reads:

> Brothers, you know that the household of Stephanas is the first fruit of Achaia and they have organized themselves for the service of those who are holy. I beg you to subject yourselves to such people and to all those who work and labor with them. I rejoice at the coming of Stephanas and Fortunatus and Achaicus because they have made up for what you haven't done (or your failings); for they have refreshed both my *pneuma* and yours. Give recognition to such kind of people. (1 Cor 16:15–18)

First, Stephanas and his peers and companions whom Paul describes as "such kind of people" (*toioutoi*) are participants in Paul's teaching and organizing activities. Second, this gives them a kind of capital and legitimacy in Paul's view so that the Corinthians who are not distinguished in this way ought to be under their authority. Third, Paul compares the valorized activities of these people to the lack of valorized participation on the part of the rest of the Corinthians. When Paul later wrote Romans from Corinth, he sent greeting from one of the other named three he baptized, Gaius (16:23). Gaius is Paul's host and host to the whole assembly. Paul also mentions an *oikonomos* of the city who from contemporary evidence is probably something like a city treasurer. Gaius is

---

[26] The public festivals of the Greek Anthesteria and the Roman Parentalia and Lemuria concerned relations between the living and the dead; Sarah Iles Johnston, *The Restless Dead: Encounters Between the Living and the Dead in Ancient Greece* (Berkeley: University of California Press, 1999).

certainly an elite with a house large enough to host all of Paul's Corinthians and to provide extended hospitality to Paul. Some of these men are heads of households and in that sense elites. Only they could open the door to Paul. There would have been no "Paul and the Corinthians" without these people and their recognition of him and attraction to his productions.

The basis of this attraction should be clear in the extensive evidence to which I have alluded that elites at various levels often, but certainly not always, strove for the distinction of learning and culture. Dare I cite Petronius' proverbial Trimalchio, the wealthy freedman who invites experts into his house in order to pose as interested in the distinction of paideia. As outrageous as it might first seem to compare Paul's situation to the world of Petronius, there are some important analogies relevant to the issue at hand in this work that was probably written about the time that Paul wrote Romans. Paul employs his ethnicity in a way different from the characters in the Satyricon and the content of his learning is of a different tradition, that is of a dominated wisdom of a people and not the dominant legitimized paideia. Paul also wants to organize people socially in a way that is rather distinctive.[27] But regarding fields of specialized cultural producers and consumers and attraction of the latter to the former, the analogy is helpful.

In the influential interpretation of Gian Biagio Conte, the *Satyricon* is a parodic comic novel about *scholastici*, a word for which there is no English equivalent or near equivalent.[28] The word is a term for the primarily amateur devotees of Greek and Latin literature, learning and oratory.[29] The hero or rather anti-hero Encolpius seems to be some sort of itinerant lecturer. The fragmentary nature of the novel means that we have lost some information about him. His companion, Agamemnon, heads a rhetorical school for older boys and has an assistant Menelaus. Eumolpus is a poet and poses as a moralist so as to be invited into a prosperous house in Pergamum as a kind of teacher advisor that the text compares to an old-fashioned philosopher (*Satyr.* 85). Encolpius meets Agamemnon outside of a hall where *scholastici* have been delivering speeches and launches into a learned tirade against the way declamation is taught and practiced and about the general decline of speaking (1–2). *Scholastici* were people who took themselves and their enterprise very seriously. This is why Petronius is able to so effectively satirize and parody them. At their

---

[27] Paul's letters are not religious while the Satyricon is supposedly secular. Not only are the gods and religious practices prominent in the latter, but the anti-hero's relation to the god Priapus is central to the plot. A genuine difference would stress that humor and satire involving the divine are inconceivable in Paul's tradition.

[28] Gian Biagio Conte, *The Hidden Author: An Interpretation of Petronius' Satyricon* (Berkeley: University of California Press, 1996).

[29] George Kennedy, "Encolpius and Agamemnon in Petronius," *AJP* 99 (1978): 171–78.

meeting, Agamemnon improvises lofty words in Lucilian style – not the style of the Septuagint – about the calling of *scholastici*: "Ambition to fulfill the austere demands of Art, the mind moving to mighty themes, demands discipline, simplicity – distain the haughty seats of the mighty, humiliating invitations to drunken dinners, the addictions, the low pleasures . . ." (*Satyr.* 5).[30] Here he expresses the field ideals of autonomy. The true intellectual does not produce for a patron, or for money or to please the powerful, but for the sake of truth or beauty or God. It is precisely these moral and intellectual ideals that the novel subverts as it makes the "heroes" exact opposites of the ideal.

Edward Courtney persuasively argues that the *Satyricon* is overall about educated freedmen and slaves.[31] He shows that Encolpius, Giton, Ascyltos, Agamemnon, Menelaus and Eumolpus are highly educated former slaves. The *Satyricon* trades on a social phenomenon that is important for understanding Paul and his reception by certain kinds of people. Only a small percentage of people in the empire were truly literate, but slaves were disproportionately represented among the educated.[32] A literate slave was very valuable to a master and owners often educated them just to increase their value. Because Roman education developed under the influence of Greek education and by the first century CE most aristocratic and prosperous families wanted their sons to be educated bilingually, Greek-speaking urban slaves were considered ideal tutors and teachers. Slaves and freedmen, then, in some sense, dominated most areas of learning, but faced a glass ceiling that kept them from the ranks of the aristocratic dominant culture of people like Virgil, Pliny and Aelius Aristides. Courtney shows that Petronius enforces this glass ceiling. Even though his freedmen characters have a higher education, instead of possessing the virtue and noble character that such education was supposed to bring, they are utterly debased and out of control. They can create poetry, interpret their experience by myths and epics, and produce learned speeches, but Petronius makes these skills opportunities to show that theirs is a pathetic parody of true culture. Courtney also shows that Encolpius and Ascyltos, who are said to make their livings by their educations, are not *scholastici*, but are only mistaken for such by being in the company of Agamemnon. Unfortunately, just what cultural specialty characterized their itinerant lives is lost to the fragmentary

---

[30] The translation is by J. P. Sullivan, *Petronius, The Satyricon: Seneca, The Apocolocyntosis* (New York: Penguin Books, 1986).
[31] Edward Courtney, *A Companion to Petronius* (Oxford: Oxford University Press, 2001).
[32] Stanley Bonner, *Education in Ancient Rome* (Berkeley: University of California Press, 1977), 65–75; Courtney, *Companion to Petronius*, 41. Johannes Christes studied forty-one slaves and freedmen who became famous enough to be remembered in the sources and who bore the titles of either *grammaticus* or *philologus*. See his, *Sklaven und Freigelassene als Grammatiker und Philologen im Antiken Rom* (Wiesbaden: Franz Steiner, 1979).

nature of the text. Looking past Petronius' aristocratic slur of these characters, they represent the most successful of freedmen who aspired to paideia. We must imagine many more who never had their own school or were able to make livings through paideia, yet possessed it in various forms and degrees.

Good reasons exist, then, for thinking that among freedmen there would be people alienated from the dominant culture who would be attracted to an alternative wisdom and the autonomous pole of the cultural field. One option that illustrates the attraction of the autonomous cultural pole and seems to have been followed by growing numbers during the early empire was the life of Cynic philosophy. From his perspective of the elite dominant paideia, Lucian spends many pages depicting such people as charlatans who were inevitably runaway slaves, base freedmen and, like Paul, of the despised artisan class. If such people got no respect, there is much evidence to think that they often tried for respectability. Trimalchio, of course, is the cliché. He owns a huge twin Latin and Greek library, but cannot read (*Satyr.* 48.4). He invites *scholastici* to his house who turn out to also be of slavish character. Both Trimalchio and Ascyltos pose as members of the equestrian class by wearing gold rings. When one of Trimalchio's freedmen friends takes offence at Ascyltos' pretensions, he says, "You're a Roman knight, are you? Well, my father was a king" (*Satyr.* 57.4). Courtney thinks that the reason why so many slaves in this era were mockingly named Malchio, "little king," is that slaves and freedmen (and freedwomen?) had become proverbial for their obsession with ancestry.[33] So either posing as of a higher rank or claiming to have been enslaved though from some noble line was common enough that Petronius could make casual jokes about it. Such freedmen/women and slaves would surely have heard Paul's gospel of ancient wisdom, the *pneuma* of God, and Abraham's lineage "in Christ" in a different way than we moderns might understand it.

It would be a mistake, however, to think that only elites – in the special sense that I have been using the term – might want to be consumers of Paul's learning and performances. A definitional feature of cultural fields is their semi-autonomy from the economy and outside order of sociality and power. They constitute a game that has its own distinctive order of power, of social and symbolic capital, through the skills, productions and prestige of its practices. Thus, being a head of household might allow one to give hospitality and patronage to an expert, but that status alone did not confer an aptitude for skillful learning and literate practices. The elite certainly had advantages such as leisure for cultural activity, but anyone who could master the skills and learning could gain the capital that gave one power and place in the game. Admittedly, non-elites who made it into the cultural field usually had the

---

[33] Courtney, *Companion to Petronius*, 52.

advantage of a relatively prosperous household. In addition to the examples suggested above, one famous example is Epictetus, the slave who became the head of his own philosophical school.

It may be significant that Paul singles out not just Stephanas, the lord of a household, in order to praise him for his participation in activities that Paul promotes, but also praises his household for such activities. They have done what the rest of the Corinthians have not (1 Cor 16:17). Stephanas's household has organized itself (*etaxan heautous*) for serving those who are holy (1 Cor 16:15). They are fellow workers and laborers (1 Cor 16:16), terms that Paul uses for assistants in his expert's activities. Stephanas's companions, Fortunatus and Achaichus, may have been relatives, freedmen of Stephanas, or trusted slaves. It is easy to imagine a slave whose literacy had been encouraged in order to facilitate management of the household and family business having the ambition to become learned in Paul's wisdom and pneumatic practices. Except for Stephanas' people and some household heads that Paul singles out, then, he can generalize about the other Corinthians so as to imply by contrast his disappointment in the way that they have received and participated in his practices. I see no reason to posit some uniform ideology or reason for their resistance beyond attachment to their own interests and practices, and certainly not the corrupting outside heresy such as a fantastic "Gnosticism" or "pneumatic enthusiasm" or "realized eschatology" imagined in academic theological modernism.

I want to insist that instead of a simple model of myth and community, one should imagine the groups as socially and culturally differentiated. All of the Corinthians may have shared a similar doxa to a point, but the elites and the non-elites had some different interests, and some of the elites and others strove to be participant consumers in the field, or overlapping fields, of specialized knowledge that might make them cultured. Unlike in New Guinea, specialized book-learning and literary/rhetorical production was an important means for distinguishing a whole class of elites from the masses, and fostering competition for honor among elites of various sorts. Paul almost certainly in his letters intellectualized issues for the sake of attracting such people. So, for example, what might have been quite mundane interests in the extended family of ancestors and the dead for the non-elites was addressed by Paul with the culturally ambitious in view as an opportunity to expound on human nature and the science of the cosmos through the Christ-*pneuma* myth in 1 Cor 15. Paul treats issues among the Corinthians about the pros and cons of competing teachers (1 Cor 1:10–16) with a long discussion about the nature of divine and human wisdom. Many of the passages that the Christian church has cherished as theological are less anachronistically described as Paul appealing to the interests of aspirants to paideia by showing his stuff in intellectualizing issues that were "practical" and strategic for most of the Corinthians. The letter treats issues about prostitutes, marriage and sacrificial meat that might have been quite local and mundane for most Corinthians as issues about moral freedom and correct worship of the truly conceived deity.

Some recent scholarship argues that Paul's teachings about *pneuma* and about Christ as the link to the lineage of Abraham have not been fully understood in scholarship and their centrality to his gospel not recognized.[34] These are also the themes, as we have seen, that in different ways most likely attracted the interest of the people Paul tried to make his audience. I will provide some comments about my understanding of these narratives in a list of components of Paul's mythmaking. The central vehicle for much of his mythmaking is Paul's interpretation of Judean scripture. His access to books, ability to read and write proficiently and exegetical practices gave him intellectual skills that few if any of the Corinthians were likely to have had. What follows is based on my work and on an important book by Caroline Johnson Hodge.[35] The components of the myth that Paul formed from scripture and other sources is fairly clear, but the order and relationship of the components is more difficult, and the following could be arranged in a number of ways with emphases in different places.

- Ancient prophecy said that a descendant of Abraham, ancestor of the lineage chosen by the true God of the cosmos, a righteous forbearer out of a world of sinful nations, would bring a great blessing to the other peoples.
- In God's plan, Paul would be appointed to teach the non-Jewish peoples about this promise and its fulfillment.
- This blessing makes non-Judeans into descendants of Abraham by means of their penetration by the divine *pneuma* that God used to refashion Jesus Christ when he raised him from the dead. Divine *pneuma* interacts with ordinary human *pneuma*, but is a vital substance of a vastly superior quality, the highest of all substances in the cosmos.
- Christ is thus the *pneuma*-bearer whose heroic martyrdom became an occasion for God to reconcile the world's peoples to himself and to perfect the human species.
- Since Christ was "in Abraham" as seed, and chosen Gentile believers through baptism gain a material connection to Christ, participating in his *pneuma*, they have a material contiguity with Abraham back through the lineage of Christ just like any descendant.

---

[34] See Chapters Six and Seven in this volume and Pamela Eisenbaum, "Paul as the New Abraham," in *Paul and Politics: Ekklesia, Israel, Imperium, Interpretation*, ed. Richard Horsley (Philadelphia: Trinity Press International, 2000), 130–45; "A Remedy for Having Been Born of Woman: Jesus, Gentiles, and Genealogy in Romans," *JBL* 123 (2004): 671–702.

[35] Caroline Johnson Hodge, *If Sons, Then Heirs: A Study of Kinship and Ethnicity in Paul's Letters* (New York, Oxford University Press, 2007).

- At the end of the current phase ordained for the cosmos, divine *pneuma* will entirely replace flesh (*sarx*) and blood in the constitution of at least chosen individuals, perhaps all. Until then, divine *pneuma* only mixes or communicates with human *pneuma*, but gives special powers to such people who are to understand that their true selves are pneumatic and not of flesh.

Someone might reasonably object that there is nothing about Abraham and gentiles becoming a lineage of Abraham in the Corinthian letters. One must go to other letters for these. This is true, but evidence does exist to show that Paul presupposes the myth and speaks as if the Corinthians know it. First, it is necessary to establish that Paul thinks of the Corinthians to whom he writes as gentiles. 1 Cor 12:2 is clear: "Now concerning pneumatic things, brothers, I do not want you to be ignorant. You know that when you were Gentiles (*ethnē*), you were taken and led away by speechless idols." If Paul were writing according to scholarly consensus that follows Acts and dogmatic definitions of the nature of "the church" or "Christianity," he would have written, "now brothers and sisters, to the portion of the congregation that converted from a gentile background, I want to say." The language of 5:1 carries the same assumption that the Corinthians are people who used to be Gentiles – of a non-Jewish ethnicity as seen from the perspective of Jews.

But what are they now? The evidence of the letters, I have argued, overwhelmingly militates against Paul having the idea of Christianity as a distinct religion.[36] Rather, Paul thinks of Gentiles who are "in Christ" as a new but separate line grafted into the lineage of Abraham, Isaac, and Jacob. Thus, one reads in 1 Cor 10:1, as Paul interprets the Exodus legends, "I do not want you to be ignorant, brothers, that our fathers were all under the cloud, and all went through the sea, and all were baptized into Moses in the cloud and in the sea and all ate the same pneumatic food and all drank the same pneumatic drink." Many interpretive challenges arise here, including the assumption that the Israelites were already in some way given the divine *pneuma*. The relevant point for the present argument is that Paul speaks of the Corinthians as former Gentiles who are now descendants of the Israelite patriarchs, but not Jews.

Caroline Johnson Hodge has shown that Paul employs a way of thinking well known to the Greco-Roman world; ethnic mythmaking that employs an aggregative strategy.[37] No one thought that contemporary Romans and Greeks constituted the same social, political or religious entities, but a myth made them related by an ancient ancestor.[38] They were distinct, but related in ways thought to give them important privileges and commonalities, including supposedly

---

[36] Stowers, *Rereading of Romans*, 23–25, 133.
[37] Johnson Hodge, *If Sons, Then Heirs*.
[38] Johnson Hodge, *If Sons, Then Heirs*; Stowers, *Rereading of Romans*.

the same gods and sacrificial practices. Paul is engaged in a complex and highly negotiable practice of making distinctions by ethnic-religious mythmaking. In his rhetoric, the Corinthians are not Gentiles, but were Gentiles who are importantly different from Gentiles and who are now related to Jews, but are importantly different from them. As Smith writes in another essay, especially reflecting upon the kinship system of the Hua people,

> Meaning is made possible by difference. Yet thought seeks to bring together what thought necessarily takes apart by means of a dynamic process of disassemblage and reassemblage, which results in an object no longer natural but rather social, no longer factual but rather intellectual. Relations are discovered and reconstituted through projects of differentiation.[39]

The appropriation of Paul's discourse under the category of "theology" makes Paul's writing sui generis and therefore unique. But the category of "mythmaking" renders it an ordinary human activity familiar to discourses that refer to gods, ancestors and other non-obvious beings from cultures all over the world and across history. Moreover, it is a form of speaking-writing-thinking that implicates itself in familiar human ways of making social distinctions involved in social formation and power.

One other point: In both 1 Cor 10:1 and 12:1, Paul employs the expression "brothers, I do not want you to be ignorant." In the latter, this is followed by, "*You know* that when you were Gentiles." "I do not want you to be ignorant," is the voice of the specialist in esoteric knowledge giving an authoritative interpretation of a discourse or story that the readers or in reality some of the readers – the class of those distinguished by consuming such knowledge – know, but need interpreted. At least in Paul's rhetoric, the Corinthians know that they are now descendants of Abraham through *pneuma*, by participating in Christ. As I will show, participation in Christ is presupposed by Paul's discussion of the Lord's Supper and talk of the social body and the body of Christ.

A further clue to Corinthian interests might be found in their practice of baptism for the dead (1 Cor 15:29). Paul brought baptism to them, but they made their own uses of it, as Smith argues.[40] Paul taught them that they could share in the *pneuma* of the *pneuma*-bringer, Christ, and that the divine *pneuma* would connect them to the renowned ancient ancestor, Abraham. They saw another ritual means for improving the lot of their more immediate ancestors. Baptism for the dead would incorporate those dead into the distinguished lineage and ancestry. Without baptism for the dead, their own baptisms might cut them off from their extended families of the significant dead. This scenario

---

[39] Jonathan Z. Smith, "Differential Equations: On Constructing the Other," in *Relating Religion*, 246.
[40] Smith, "Re: Corinthians," 348–51.

makes sense, if the Corinthians or some of them were people concerned about their own ambiguous and ignoble ancestry, a point to which Paul alludes politely in 1 Cor 1:26 ("not many of you are of good ancestry"). Smith points out that the resettlement of Corinth in 44 BCE involved importing large numbers of freed slaves from Greece, Syria, Judea, and Egypt.[41] Such people would not only have had the stain of slave origins, but also have been cut off from ancestral burial grounds.

Imagining Paul and the Corinthians with the aid of Smith's comparison and also the insistence on the differentiation of interests, recognition and attraction leads to imagining plausible religiously contextualized interactions. It allows reading the letters from non-Pauline perspectives. Yet that sort of reading provides a richer and more historically plausible sense of what Paul was about and up against because it casts both Paul and the Corinthians in terms of interests, practices and discourses from their time instead of in terms of the later and contemporary church's interests. The Corinthians reacted in different ways to Paul's mythmaking and ritual practice, partly with their own mythmaking and ritual experimentation. Much more could be said about such things as speaking in tongues, but by way of an example I will focus on the fact that Paul spends much of 1 Corinthians 8–11 worrying about Corinthian eating practices, his own meal practices and sacrificial meals. Can we also tease out likely Corinthian responses to Paul's discourse and practices regarding meals and especially what he calls "the Lord's Dinner"? In what follows, I will attempt an approach toward that end by first analyzing the senses of the practice and then by telling a just so story about the strategically differentiated reactions (such as interested recognitions, appropriations, resistances, accommodations) of the Corinthians.

Much scholarly interpretation of the Corinthian letters naturalizes the specialized intellectual interests and intellectual practices concerned with contesting truths, traditions, and practices of the Corinthians rather than demonstrating them and makes theological ideas the significant essence of the activity imagined of Paul's addressees. At the same time, interpreters misrecognize and vastly under-appreciate the power of Paul as an expert in intellectual practices. An antidote to these approaches begins with imagining the religious interests of the Corinthians as intelligible in a vast web of practices that made up a whole way of life and to do the same for Paul. The second aspect of the approach is to imagine the logic of the practices that were important to these people and to think of their beliefs, ideas, and texts as embedded within these ongoing activities.

Most of human life unfolds in kinds of activities based on practical skills that the individual did not invent. As such, practices are the primary unit that

---

[41] Smith, "Re: Corinthians," 248.

a culture or society reproduces over time. On this view, a society or culture is not greater than the sum of its parts, but a large number of practical skills are assembled and linked in characteristic ways that actors pass down from generation to generation. Thus, I want to focus upon practices rather than beliefs, texts, structures, symbols or particular actions and events. I say focus because beliefs, texts, actions and events will not disappear from the account. They are components of practices.

Eating a meal is a practice. Mythmaking and numerous other kinds of activities in which agents produce discourses are practices. In taking this perspective on a culture, it becomes clear that the wills of individuals do not control practices, nor are the supposed instruments of minds such as symbols, beliefs, intentions, texts, myths and theories the meaning or basis of practices. What is the meaning of dinner or of lunch? You would not persuade me if you said that *the* meaning of dinner for participants, the essence to which it reduces, was a determinate set of beliefs, or a foundational myth or meeting needs for nutrition or fellowship, although all of these might be involved. Practices are so complex that participants are never aware of all the implications, consequences, possible meanings, or effects of their activity in a practice. To take the perspective of practice is to become aware of the high degree of indeterminacy in both the participant's own interpretations of their activities, and in the interpretations of participants' activities and interpretations by scholars. But such actors have great intuitive knowledge. They know how to participate, to play the game. Such practical skill can be the object of analysis and historical imagination.

I will begin the task of locating the Lord's Supper as represented by Paul within the range and relation of practices in the cultures in question. To what other discourses were meals and mythmaking practices near, distant, comparable to, and differentiated from at that time? How was mythmaking deployed in relation to and as a part of other practices? This move helps the historian to avoid one of the illusions created by focusing upon the beliefs, symbols, and texts of particular groups or upon narratives of events. The illusion natural to focusing upon these is the essential or non-reciprocal uniqueness of the community in question. If the meaning of the Lord's Supper is the words of institution that Paul and the gospels provide, then it might easily seem incomparable. Those words should be situated first of all in writing practices rather than eating practices. But if I choose to imagine Paul's writing as representing an eating practice, then I immediately notice that it shares central and numerous similarities with practices common to cultures throughout the Mediterranean. Any person from that world would immediately recognize it as a type of eating practice and one that already possess many of the skills necessary to participate, even if they found a particular expert's interpretation of it implausible, uninteresting or confusing.

Paul's discussion of the Lord's Dinner can then be seen as one interpretation of a broader practice. But the practice belonged to the culture and was not under his control, as various people participated in that activity employing practical skills that may have involved a huge variety of social abilities, bodily skills, beliefs, symbols and strategic interests. The key to the question of why the Corinthians gave some recognition to who Paul was, and to what he did, and had some interests in him, is not that his message of a crucified Christ and the power of Christ's *pneuma* met a universal intrinsic need or was inherently intelligible or attractive. Rather, the Corinthians possessed fine-grained practical understandings, skill intelligibility, if you will, of most of the practices that Paul advocated, albeit differentiated in various ways such as by age, gender, free/slave, elite/non-elite and individual proclivity. They therefore already had practical dispositions toward the genres of Paul's doings and sayings, but not necessarily toward his particular interpretation of these practices.

The Lord's Dinner is a meal, one form of people eating together in the Greek East of the early Roman Empire. A meal has much of its potential for meaning to participants and observers simply because it is recognizable within the logical possibilities of eating socially in that culture. However, Paul might have used, interpreted and modified the meal practices, which were not his or the assembly's invention; nor did his or the assembly's will control such cultural formations with their enormous amount of inertia. The question, then, is what sort of eating practices would ancient participants and observers have been likely to compare and contrast with the Lord's Dinner in order to make sense of it, if they were to reflect upon their implicit and instinctive knowledge of it as a practice? Three types of meals seem absolutely basic for locating the possible senses of the Lord's Dinner: the common meal at home; meals involving animal sacrifice; memorial meals for the dead. In Paul's time, one can find Greek, Jewish and Roman versions of all three, although the Greek types were clearly dominant in the world of the Pauline groups.[42] A common idiom of meal practices and symbols transcended the particularity of ethnic practices and provided the possibility for articulating those distinctions.[43] Commonality in practice, in other words, was the condition for the endless elaboration of difference in practical meaning through ritualization or ad hoc strategic activity by individuals and groups.

---

[42] Stanley K. Stowers, "Elusive Coherence: Ritual and Rhetoric in 1 Corinthians 10–11," in *Reimagining Christian Origins: A Colloquium Honoring Burton L. Mack,* ed. Elizabeth Castelli and Hal Taussig (Valley Forge, PA: Trinity Press International, 1996), 68–83. Most Jewish animal sacrifice took place in the temple, but the Passover, when celebrated outside the temple, was a domestic sacrifice. On Jewish meals for the dead, see Hans-Joseph Klauck, *Herrenmahl und Hellenistischer Kult: Eine religionsgeschichtliche Untersuchung zum ersten Korintherbrief,* 2nd ed. (Münster: Aschendorff, 1986), 86–88 and 66–67 or everyday Jewish meals..

[43] Kathleen E. Corley, *Private Women, Public Meals* (Peabody, MA: Hendrickson, 1993) 68–69.

The ordinary everyday meal and the meal involving the sacrifice of an animal formed the two most important poles for the meaning of meals in virtually all cultures of the ancient Mediterranean. This is not a distinction between secular and religious meals. At center stood the differentiation of gender: women and slaves managed by women cooked bread or grain porridge at home for everyday meals; men sacrificed animals at home and at other sites for special meals, feasts.[44] Eating meat constituted the highest form of eating in relation to the gods and involved some form of sharing of the meat with the gods. Food offerings stood in a hierarchy with meat at the top and grain and vegetable products normally below. According to the evidence from 1 Corinthians, the Lord's Dinner was constituted so as to distinguish itself from both an ordinary meal and a sacrificial meal, but was markedly closer to the ordinary meal than to the sacrificial meal in featuring bread instead of meat.

If the Lord's Dinner seems to have some ambiguous status between sacrificial meals and everyday meals, then perhaps one can clarify the way it worked as a practice by comparing it to a practice for which we have much evidence: Greek alimentary animal sacrifice. I will use examples from classical Attika because they are so rich and so well documented. My main points here will be analogical and not genetic. Some of the most interesting sources come from the court speeches of the Attik orators.[45] That fact is interesting in itself. Although the Athenians kept deme and other records, they surprisingly do not appeal to these when arguing cases concerning identity. These cases about identity – for example, citizen status, lineage, status as heir – make up the bulk of the cases in the orators. Instead of appealing to a birth or marriage record, the orators call upon witnesses who were present at various events such as festivals, funerals, weddings, rituals of entry into *oikoi, gene, thiasoi, orgeones*, phratries, and demes. All of these events involved *thusia*, animal sacrifice as a meal.

An example from Isaeus 8 (*Kiron*) is interesting because it explicitly draws attention to the physical contact with the meat that was crucial to the way that sacrificial rites indexed groups of people.

> We also have other proofs that we are sons from the daughter of Kiron. For as is natural since we were male children of his own daughter, he never performed any sacrifice (*thusia*) without us, but whether the sacrifices were great or small, we were always present and sacrificed with him ... went to all the festivals with him. But when he sacrificed to

---

[44] Stanley K. Stowers, "Greeks Who Sacrifice and Those Who Do Not: Toward and Anthropology of Greek Religion," *The Social World of the First Christians: Essays in Honor of Wayne A. Meeks*, ed. L. Michael White and O. Larry Yarbrough (Minneapolis, MN: Fortress, 1995), 299–320.

[45] See my "Truth, Identity and Sacrifice in Classical Athens," (paper presented at the Ancient History Documentary Research Centre, Macquarie University, June 1996).

> Zeus Ktesios he was especially serious about the sacrificial rite (*thusia*), and he did not admit any slaves or free men who were not relatives but he performed all of the sacrificial rites himself. We shared in this sacrifice and we together with him handled the sacred meat and we put offerings on the altar with him and performed the other parts of the sacrifice with him. (8.16)

Here, participation in the sacrifice constitutes membership in a certain social formation, the household (*oikos*) or family-lineage (*genos*) of Kiron. Zeus Ktesios is god of the household property. The speaker claims that his grandfather was very pious about this sacrifice to one of the gods of his *oikos* and therefore allowed only his close blood relations to participate.[46] He emphasizes the close participation in the rite such as touching meat with his hands; placing the meat on the altar.

The truth in such examples from the orators relates to the continuity of blood and of flesh from parent to child. This truth is determined through a particular medium, the body of a domestic animal. Like family members and citizens, such animals were members of the community and thus duly decked out in garlands as they "willingly" gave their bodies as food for gods and men. These were animals bred by the Greeks to produce the best individuals from the best lineages. Greeks in theory only sacrificed the most perfect products of their breeding practices and put these animals through rigorous testings and scrutinies.[47] The ritualized use of the flesh and blood of animals with whom humans had a kind of kinship, precisely because they both were of flesh and blood, offered excellent ways of thinking about social relations deemed to be in some essential way based upon flesh and blood kinship.

Sacrificial meals involved very complex types of truth practices. The animal had to behave well and give the proper signs of assent before the altar or hearth. Next, the animal was killed, not because the meaning of its sacrifice had anything to do with death or ritual violence, but because it is very difficult to eat a live animal. Then came the precise division of the animal into portions that would create relations of differentiation and hierarchy among those eating dinner. The higher-ranking citizen males of whatever group the dinner represented would gather around the altar and roast the sacred *splanchna* – heart, liver, lungs, kidney. Before they ate, they placed the god's portion on the altar

---

[46] The speaker claims to be the son of Kiron's daughter and to be fighting for the estate over against a son of Kiron's brother. The speaker is ignorant of Athenian law, which gave priority to the male line and tries to give the impression of closer kinship.

[47] Inscriptions use the same terms (e.g., *krinein, diakrinein, dokimazein*) for testing these animals to determine if they were perfect enough for sacrifice that the Athenians used for the testings that determined one's purity of lineage and descent from a pure Athenian mother and father."

and their feasting on the sacred *splanchna* coincided with the god's portion ascending in smoke. Any person being tested must be present at the altar, taste, and touch the holy meat. If the individual was not who he claimed to be, the god would give signs and the men's barbecue would be aborted. To proceed would not truly be to have the god's dinner.

The men inspected the *splanchna* for signs. The liver received special attention. Both the animals that Greeks deemed proper to sacrifice and humans shared the same *splanchna*, with each organ given the same name. It makes sense that the *splanchna* was the locus of messages and effects from the gods when one observes that fifth and fourth century Athenians spoke of human *splanchna* as organs of consciousness and receptivity to the gods.[48] Feeling, mood, desire, emotion and thought were located not in a non-physical mind but in the organs that made up the *splanchna*. This was a discourse of intelligent flesh and blood, not body and mind.

One first poured blood on the altar, then removed and divided the *splanchna*. The word for "divide" can also mean "distribute" as in sacrificial portions, distinguish, decide, define and interpret. All of these activities can take place in conjunction with the division, interpretation, and distribution of the *splanchna*. Animals and their *splanchna* are indeed good to think with. Plato compares the logical division of dialectic to division in *thusia*: "let us divide by parts as we divide a sacrificial animal" (*Pol.* 287C). Everyone watched closely as the god's portion of tail, fat and bones burned on the altar. The movements of the tail and the color and motions of the flame were full of signs of the god's disposition toward the particular social group and the testing.[49] Those celebrating could also establish the truth by touching the *splanchna* while taking an oath. The orators frequently mention such oaths and in various contexts every Athenian took them as a part of feasts of *dokimasia*, of testing. In Paul's time, such sacrificial testing was still important. The future citizens or elites of the Greek cities, for example, sacrificed with testings (*dokimasiai*) as they feasted and took oaths upon graduation from the ephebic training that made them adult citizens.

The feast entered a second stage as the wider group of men and sometimes women and children who had watched the episode around the altar or hearth were given portions of boiled meat from the thighs. All then merrily feasted on meat and accompanying dishes. Numerous versions – simpler or more complex – of this procedure for meals with meat took place in settings such as temples, clubs, at private parties, and banquets.

---

[48] Ruth Padel, *In and Out of Mind: Greek Images of the Tragic Self* (Princeton: Princeton University Press, 1992), 12–48.

[49] F.T.Van Straten, *Hiera Kala: Images of Animal Sacrifice in Archaic and Classical Greece* (Leiden: Brill, 1995), 122–24.

Now what does all of this have to do with understanding the Lord's Dinner? We can be certain that for most of the Gentiles who constituted Paul's communities that any special meal such as a birthday, a friend's dinner party, a holiday at home, a wedding, a public feast, consisted of a version of the practices that I have described. Paul discusses Corinthian participation in sacrificial meals in chapters 8–10. Paul presents himself as attempting to train these Hellenized Corinthians in something called the Lord's Dinner that he relates to his Christ myth and that is also a special meal. Neither the Corinthians nor Paul could have made sense of it without at least implicit comparison with sacrificial meals. Indeed chapters 8–11 are replete with comparisons to *thusia*. Furthermore, even though I cannot tell you what beliefs and interpretations of the Christ myth that these people held when they feasted at the Lord's Dinner, I can describe many of the skills they possessed that allowed them to participate. They already possessed many of these skills merely by inhabiting a culture that centered on *thusia*. I will focus on four sets of these skills: testing and truth making skills; group formation and social differentiation skills; skills in interpreting signs and symbols; and skills at relating fragments of mythic narratives to the preceding activities.

Paul's interpretation of the Lord's Dinner shares a basic assumption with sacrificial practice: In both meals, participants make themselves liable to divine judgment and signs reveal truths about one's identity. In 1 Corinthians 11:19, there must be factions so that those who are tested might be revealed (*oi dokimoi phaneroi genontai*). An inscription from a cult to Zeus and other gods from late second or early first century BCE. Philadelphia, in the house of a certain Dionysius, makes an interesting case for comparison.[50] The inscription encourages participants of this extended household cult "who have confidence in themselves" at the monthly and yearly sacrifices to touch the stele near the altar upon which the cult regulations have been written so that "those who obey the ordinances and those who do not may be revealed" (*phaneroi ginetai*). As in Paul's account, it will be dangerous for those who have not passed the test of self-examination to participate.

Paul seems to say (11:27) that the one who eats the bread or drinks the wine in the wrong way has taken sides with those who betrayed Jesus and is thus guilty of destroying his body and blood. He is attempting to shape eating practices and testing practices by an interpretation of a kind of martyr myth that ties a specific manner of ritual practice to social loyalty and unity. The individual participant must test him or herself (*dokimazein*) and then eat only if the person's disposition toward the body and blood of Christ are correct (11:29). The person who does not distinguish the body, that is perform an action with a certain social and ideological disposition, will bring down the

---

[50] See Chapter Two in this volume.

judgment of the god who is present in that ritualized eating environment. Paul explains that many have been weak and sick, and some have even died because they ate the bread and drank the cup without this disposition (11:30). If the individual makes herself/himself an object of self-examination and is able to discover the truth about her/his loyalty and disposition for ritual action, then the person can decide that it is safe to participate or decline and save herself/himself from God's testing that might result in illness and a revelation to the community of the person's false disposition (11:28–29, 30–32).

In *Against Neaera*, Demosthenes says that when Phrastor attempted to admit his son by a woman not of Athenian citizen blood, his phratry, and his *genos* refused and voted against admission. Phrastor then challenged the rejection, but when he was required to swear an oath at the altar on a perfect sacrificial animal, he backed down and refused. Phrastor also had to decide about the truth of his disposition toward a body that was to become the body that constituted the social body in the act of eating: for Phrastor it was the body of a sheep to be rendered as food; for Paul's implied actor, bread that symbolizes the body involved in a martyrdom on their behalf. Unlike Paul's, Phrastor's truth cannot be located in his own inner disposition by an act of self-examination.[51] Phrastor's truth was not about his loyalties and the correctness of his beliefs.

Strange as it may sound to the modern ear, unlike the flesh and blood body of the sheep and of Phrastor and his purported offspring, the body that is in question in the Pauline text is not a flesh and blood body. Nor is it a merely metaphorical body. According to Paul's mythmaking, the body in which the Corinthians share and with which they have the most literal contact is the pneumatic body of Christ that he gained when the *pneuma* from God replaced his soulish (*psychikos*) flesh body at his resurrection. As Paul explains by good physics of his day (1 Cor 15:44–7; Chapter 6 in this volume), in the cosmic hierarchy of being, various earthly creatures have bodies of different qualities of flesh, and higher in the cosmos bodies are made of qualitatively better materials. Christ, the first fruit, died with a soulish flesh body made of dust and was raised with a pneumatic body (1 Cor 15:44–47). Chapter 6 develops the argument that for one who has been baptized into Christ, to be physically joined with a prostitute means joining the prostitute to Christ: "do you no know that your bodies are members of Christ. . . . the one who joins with a prostitute is one body with her . . . 'the two shall become one flesh.'" (Gen 2:24; 1 Cor 6:15–19). Those who are in Christ feel what he suffered and can thus "participate in the body and blood of Christ" (1 Cor 10:16) because they have a part of

---

[51] Paul places the self-examination practices in the context of another myth, God's final judgment of the world. Chastening is an educational punishment to save the person from the final and absolute punishment.

him, his divine *pneuma*, in them. Thus, in the cosmic physics/myth by which Paul desires to gain legitimacy from Corinthians, those "in Christ" are physically connected both to Christ and to all other baptized people. There is one body and for one individual to divide from it in any way is an attack on Christ and the entire body. This is a pneumatic body composed of a stuff belonging to a higher order of existence.

The Greek and Christ myths that ancient interpreters used to manipulate and rationalize the skills of actors in ritual practice are different stories, but the Corinthian actors and the citizens of Athens exercised some of the same skills, skills that connected eating to truth practices and community formation. Note that Paul uses exactly the same terms for testing and self-examination that Greeks used for the testings involved in sacrificial practices: to become manifest (*phaneroi genontai*), tested (*dokimoi*), to test (*dokimazein*), to distinguish (*diakrinein*) and to judge (*krinein*).[52] Athenian failure to use deme records did not stem from poor record-keeping, but from considering identity to be ritually constituted and confirmed. In the Lord's Dinner and in Greek sacrifice, who is in and outside of the community is not simply predetermined in some juridical or definitional way, but is negotiated in the very exercise of the skills of mythmaking, testing and eating. Phrastor's son did not become a member of his phratry because Phrastor feared that the god would know the truth. Therefore, he would not swear on the animal and allow it to be cooked and distributed so as to form a feasting community. Other court cases show that if the community had eaten with him, then that fact would be compelling evidence of his son's identity and his truthfulness. Those who claimed to be Kiron's kin said (in my words) "we sacrificed with him to his household god, touched and ate the meat. No one else in the household did that. We are therefore the ones who are truly of his flesh and blood."

Paul assumes that the Corinthians possess similar skills, but does not like the way that they have used them. What more precisely is Paul's complaint? Some of the Corinthians used their skills to form eating groups that excluded others (1 Cor 11:18–22). Was the criterion social rank, family connection, ethnic origins? I do not know, but most of the possibilities suggest that the rules of the game followed by the Corinthians might have been for meat meals instead of bread meals, the ordinary meals cooked by women that were much less intently focused on social differentiation. Meat meals organized groups on the basis of characteristics deemed by the ancients to have been based on blood, on ancestry. To add to the confusion, Paul taught a cult myth for baptism in which having fellowship with this new god connected one to a great ancient ancestor and lineage. Paul's account of what the Corinthians were doing

---

[52] Stowers, "Truth, Identity and Sacrifice," 8–9.

attempts to make the ritual focus of the meal the bread and wine, but also supposes a more elaborate meal. Perhaps some of the Corinthians, in Paul's view, had allowed the other cuisine, possibly even some meat to become the focus. Paul contrasts eating with the goal of satiating appetite in everyday meals to the correct manner of the Lord's Dinner (1 Cor 11:21–22, 33–34). He associates eating meat with passion, desire, idolatry, and sexual immorality in his warnings from the story of Israel in the wilderness (10:1–22).[53]

It seems to me dead wrong to take his account of the Dinner's institution as a script or liturgy for the ritual. If we did not know that the later church had incorporated these words into its liturgy, we would have no clue to even suggest that the words were repeated in worship. Furthermore, we also have no reason to think that Paul recounted the story in the same way with exactly the same words, even if the story was traditional and certain elements had become essential. The account is also an etiological myth, but that observation may lead us to miss the important point which is the way it functions in Paul's rhetoric. I suggest that the account is the specification of a genre of eating.[54] Paul is saying that they have confused a genre of eating that focuses on the desire for food and drink and that produces a certain pattern of social differentiation with the genre of the Lord's Dinner.

But as I have tried to show, the signals and expectations suggested by the Lord's Dinner might be read as confusing and contradictory in the context of the codes of eating in Greco-Roman culture. Paul's account of the institution unquestionably shares in the genre of mortuary foundations right down to the words: "do this as a memorial."[55] This is so even if it is odd for the dead to also be alive and to promise a return as judge of the world. Paul's account yields a very peculiar yet familiar memorial feast for the dead. On the level of practices, whereas one expects a memorial feast for the dead to be a sacrificial feast, the Lord's Dinner features bread. Where one expects filet minion, there is white bread. In this light, one can understand Paul's need to insist that the Dinner is not an ordinary meal like one eats at home.[56]

I suggest that Paul's martyr myth, by which he attempts genre specifications about ritualized eating practices, plays on a disjunction between the flesh and blood body and the self. The Greeks and Paul were concerned about

---

[53] Stowers, "Elusive Coherence," 76–78.
[54] He presents the problem of the misapplication of eating skills in 1 Cor 11:17–22 and says he will not praise such behavior. Then he introduces the account as if it were a demonstration of the reason (*gar* in 11:23) why such eating is not the Lord's Dinner. He draws the conclusion (*hoste*) from it that unworthy eating places those dining among the betrayers of Christ.
[55] Stowers, "Elusive Coherence," 82 n. 49.
[56] One hundred years later, Justin Martyr (1 *Apol.* 65-67) has to insist on the same point as he tries to describe the meal to outsiders.

group social formation and the identity of those who ate together. That truth was about the identity of one's flesh and blood.[57] The god provided signs about this truth during the skillful cooking, sharing and eating of meat in honor of the god. The medium for communicating this truth about flesh and blood was the flesh and blood of an animal from the best lineages that Greek animal husbandry could provide. For the kind of Greeks that we meet in the Attik orators, it would be nonsensical or inconceivable to say, "you can kill my body, but you cannot touch me." Body and identity are one.

Paul's Christ myth and ritual, on the other hand, work around a disjunction between the truest self and the body. Instead of the community being constituted and tested by eating meat, it exists by eating bread that is a symbol of an absent body that points both to the significance of giving up that body and to the loyalty of the social body toward that symbol. In the martyr myth, the martyr's obedience, will and benevolent intention triumphs over the body. The body symbolizes both what is expendable and the obedient resolve that triumphed. Because of this triumph of will and obedience to God, Christ lives on a new level of existence transcending the old existence of the body, a pneumatic existence.

The social group does not test for the truth about the identities of its members by observing the signs made by flesh and blood, but by making the true self an object of self-examination. "Flesh and blood cannot inherit the kingdom of God" (1 Cor 15:50). In testing oneself to see that one can discern the body, the true self consists in being beyond oneself just as the martyr surpassed himself in giving up his body.[58] Discerning the body means both entertaining Paul's *pneuma*-Christ myth and also acting so as to acknowledge the priority of the social body over the desires of one's body. "Because there is one bread, we the many are one body. Consider Israel according to the flesh; are not those who eat of the sacrifices partners in the altar?" (1 Cor 10:17–18).

The self-surpassed is the kind of self seen in traditional Greek sacrificial practice that maintains no disjunction with the self as body in the act of constituting the social body. No wonder that Paul contrasts the Lord's Dinner to meals with meat.[59] Notice for example the implicit contrast with merely bodily *thusia* in Romans 12:1–3: "present your bodies as a living and holy sacrifice (*thusia*) acceptable to God which is your rational cultic practice. Do not be conformed to this age but have your form changed by the renewal of

---

[57] Did the claimants to Kiron's household share his flesh and blood? Were the ephebic candidates truly of aristocratic or citizen blood?

[58] The ritual actors inspect their own dispositions toward the eating to make certain that their actions will manifest the meaning of the martyr's death which is the triumph of the will over the body for the benefit of others.

[59] Stowers, "Elusive Coherence," 76–79.

your mind so that you might test (*dokimazein*) what is the will of God." Here true *thusia* is the surpassing and mastery of the body by "rational" practice and a mind that has gained the skills to test for the truth. Verses 3–8 employ the metaphor of the body and its parts to explain that this means consciously defining oneself as a part of a differentiated social body.

What is the yield of this analysis? Above all, I think this analysis can suggest a holistic interpretation of two historical moments. The goal of this type of study is the sense of an interpretation thick enough and with enough of our modern analytic contexts such as religious, social, political, economic and semantic that we can warrant some degree of success in bridging the gap between a distant culture and our own requirements for understanding. Comparison provides the leverage to dislodge the text from the categories and questions internal to the tradition that appropriated it and to display it in a new way.

The way of life in the ancient Greek polis worked through practices, including ritual and discursive practices, concerning place and the products born from that place. Sacrificial practice was saturated with physical contiguity: altars on the land; meat of animal lineages from the soil; smoke rising from the altar sending the bodies of animals from the land to the god who owns and occupies the land; the differentiated social body united around and touching the altar while ingesting flesh; meat passed from hand to hand; the god testifying to the truths about the continuity of flesh from parent to child.

If, in this ideological construction, meat is the natural product of men according to the patrilineal principle of the seed of the founding ancestor passed on as flesh, then bread is the fabrication of food by art, like spinning wool, the artifice of women and slaves. In Greek sacrifice, the body is present to be touched and eaten. But where is the body in the Lord's Dinner? It is present in its absence. The bread of human art, is the reminder of a body that occupies no place. Christ, who by the art of his obedience and will triumphed through God's power, lives on a new plane of pneumatic existence where a body that one can touch seems superfluous. Where is the dead and torn merely human body of the martyr? There seems to be a certain fit between a ritual of a body surpassed by the will and the kind of people associated with Pauline Christianity. Many, like Paul himself, were artisans without ties to the land, who lived lives characterized by physical mobility. They also represent a new class of people in a polyethnic world with a predilection for transcending their ascribed local and ethnic places.

Paul is above all an expert in a new knowledge and the practices that go with this knowledge. Paul's power is that of an intellectual. He is a purveyor of knowledges and truths in a way that the typical Greek citizen, even the priest of a particular cult, was not. The truths of Pauline Christianity are not common everyday truths about one's social groups and the signs seen in the cooking and eating of an animal, but instead truths about a person's interior, soul and mind, and the relation of these to the destiny of the cosmos. So instead of the social group watching the body of an animal, each individual looks inside and strives to obtain a newly socialized mind by reflecting upon a symbol for an absent body.

But how does this interpretation play out in terms of the historical particularities of the differentiated interactions between Paul and the Corinthians? I am half-facetiously calling what follows a "just-so story" to indicate its status as an explanatory proposal. Daniel Dennett has stolen the phrase from jaundiced critics of the stories that adaptationist Neo-Darwinian biologists tell as hypotheses about evolutionary episodes.[60] By the expression, I do not mean that the account, or such accounts, are just made up, are "merely" interpretations, or that they cannot in principle be justified by evidence and theory, or imply post-modern confusions such as there is no truth or falsehood, we are trapped in a prison house of language or that meaning is too slippery to pin down. Rather, instead of claiming a justified explanation of the historical situation among Paul and the Corinthians, it is an account to be tested by the refinement and debate over theorization and assessments of the evidence that ought to go on and on. This ought to be a process in which the activity of theorization transparently makes data into evidence.

Paul's message in 1 Corinthians (but not in 2 Corinthians, where he battles with other specialist producers) is unequivocal: the Corinthians have become one body by baptism into Christ and common participation in the *pneuma* of Christ; they remain one body and total unity is required.[61] His caveat in the Dinner text, however, suggests that there may be unidentified individuals or groups who are not truly of the one body: "When you come together as the assembly I hear that there are divisions among you, and I partly believe it because there must be sects (*hairesies*) among you so that those who have been tested and approved can be revealed" (1 Cor 11:17–18). I find four hypotheses or parts to the story.

First, Paul drew elites to participation in the field, and that involvement in the field practices had the effect of causing or exacerbating a social distance from the unity of the locative religion and household organization of the Corinthians, in spite of the baptism of whole households at the behest of their heads and other elites. As discussed above, some of these people get named such as Gaius, Crispus and the household of Stephanas, Fortunatus, and Achaicus.

---

[60] Daniel Dennett, *Darwin's Dangerous Idea: Evolution and the Meaning of Life* (New York: Simon & Schuster, 1995), 242, 245–46, 308–9, 454–56, 461–66, 485.

[61] Margaret M. Mitchell, *Paul and the Rhetoric of Reconciliation* (Louisville: Westminster John Knox, 1991).

My second hypothesis is that Paul places the responsibility for unifying the rest of the Corinthians and enforcing their proper participation in the practices that he advocates on the elite named fellows. Paul addresses the Lord's Dinner text most directly to the elites: "Do you not have houses in which to eat and drink; or do you despise those who have nothing" (1 Cor 11:22). This cannot be addressed to everyone because in the previous verse he has distinguished people who have meals and don't get enough to eat and drink from those who feast. The latter have to include or be the elites. Moreover, only the elites truly have houses in the sense that they can control who eats and how people eat. I suggest that the rest of the text is primarily for them with the "institution" passage a model for their organization, leadership and ideological focus. In Chapter 12, where Paul outlines a hierarchy of skills and specializations, the elite experts are the leading and more important body parts in the metaphor, like the head, and they are urged not to think that the less important, less honorable, parts are dispensable. The list that follows places at the top experts who are cultural producers involving intellectual practices with recognized identities that he ranks – missionaries, prophets, teachers – and follows these with less well-defined and perhaps single skills.

Third, the less or non-elite Corinthians resisted full participation in Paul's practices and reacted by experimenting with their own mythmaking and ritual activities based on their strategic locative interests. Thus 11:21 contrasts genres of meals that the Corinthians are having to the one true united Lord's Dinner. Scholarship agrees that all of chapters 11–14 are about ritual activities of the Corinthians. The body metaphor in 12:14–27 suggest that in Paul's view, some of the Corinthians are saying or indicating with their actions, "I don't belong to the body." I could develop the thesis that the trouble Paul sees with women participating in various ritual activities and the tongue speakers who need expert interpreters to make their noises or words rational and intelligible are such non-elite resisters and experimenters. As I have argued, Paul's meal is gendered toward women's practices by lacking meat and featuring grain. The Dinner seems very domestic, like a grain meal at home and memorial meal for the dead, recalling the important participation of women in funerals and memorial practices. This might have been read as a signal by women that elicited their own creativity and participation. Paul clearly thought that it went too far. More broadly, since Paul's meal sent mixed messages, pointing to various common locative practices, it likely encouraged creative interpretations of just such practices.

Fourth, in addition to placing weight on the elites to weld the non-elites into one body, Paul addresses what he sees as the problem, by adding the testing practices that are typically part of sacrificial practices to his meatless meal of the Dinner. But as I have noted this not only sent mixed messages, but also meant a translation into a new mode of religion that brought the texts and interpretations of literate experts to bear on an inner-judging. This religion shaped by the field would become a religion in which a certain kind of self and self-policing would play a central role.

I will summarize some central points of my argument and underline the tensions in my proposals that need to be addressed. Paul's esoteric mythmaking and ritualization depend upon his claims to be a chosen spokesperson for the deity. But we can only imagine social legitimacy attaching to these claims by virtue of a field widely attested in ancient sources in which Paul played a position both recognizable and attractive to some Corinthians. Apart from the broad terms of debate within the field, such as the nature of the cosmos and its elements, critique of traditional religion and the nature of the gods, ancient epic and ancestry, the therapy of the passions and the means to self-mastery, the specifics of Paul's discourse were probably unfamiliar and therefore both exotic and esoteric. The core of Paul's legitimacy and thus his power among some of the Corinthians, derived rather from his skillful display of abilities native to the field, such as his education in ancient books, his interpretive skills, his reading, writing and speaking abilities, and his pneumatic demonstrations, whatever those were. I have specifically argued that Paul's message and appeal focused on Christ as the bearer and dispenser of the most perfect stuff in the cosmos, the *pneuma* of God. These ideas were tied to a prophetic genealogical myth regarding Abraham's lineage and the non-Jewish peoples. The Pauline ritual of baptism gave initiates a share of the *pneuma* that God had given to Christ, by connecting with his *pneuma*. Being "in Christ" or having Christ in you gave the baptized a physical connection back to Abraham. I also discussed the significance of the Lord's Dinner as a ritual practice in the context of everyday meals at home, sacrificial meals and memorial meals for the dead. I concluded that Paul's version of the practice would have sent mixed messages connected with issues of food and gender. His use of the Christ myth in advocating an interpretation of the meal for the Corinthians points to a self marked by a disjunction between its true self, its body and its place.

Jonathan Smith's comparison shows how the local interests of the religion of place were likely to have provided the Corinthians with a basis for a limited and differentiated hearing of Paul. His practices became the occasion for creative mythmaking and ritual experimentation among his hearers shaped both by the encounter itself and the interests and doxa of the Corinthians themselves. But for there to have been a sustained encounter between Paul and the Corinthians at all requires the existence of a group among the Corinthians who were already habituated, not so as to want to be saved or become Christians, but so as to want to become consumers of Paul's foreign paideia, a known commodity supported by a dynamic social arena.

According to the key contributions of Smith and Burton Mack, Paul just misunderstood the Corinthians and their locative religious interests due to his utopian understanding. Smith, in scholarship over many years, has developed the idea of locative religion over against utopian religion. He uses the latter with reference to its sense of the a-topic; the without place. Such categories appear especially as part of discussions about historical persistence and change and have proven an enormous advance over the idea that all religion is about salvation or about nature. Smith describes the two as "worldviews."[62] The locative

> is concerned primarily with the cosmic and social issues of keeping one's place and reinforcing boundaries. The vision of stability and confidence with respect to an essentially fragile cosmos, one that has been reorganized, with effort, out of previous modes of order and one whose appropriate order must be maintained through acts of conscious labor. We may term such locative traditions, religions of sanctification.[63]

Purification and healing are two central modes of labor for keeping this order. Corpse pollution is the model for all sorts of impurity. The living belong to the world of the living and the dead to the place of the dead. On this view, Paul's central idea of a resurrection of the dead is utopian and utterly antithetical to the basic premises of the locative worldview. Although in what Smith calls "locative ideology," everyone is responsible for the labor of maintaining and rectifying the boundaries, the thought suggests rigid social stratification.

By contrast, a worldview that finds the patterns and structures of the cosmos to be "fundamentally perverse" and that good and reality are to be found above and beyond this cosmos is utopian.[64] The utopian mode of salvation involves reversal and rebellion. On Smith and Mack's interpretation, Paul fits the utopian mold. Unsurprisingly, they base this interpretation largely on the Paul of modernist theological New Testament scholarship, which since Albert Schweitzer has been constructed as centered on two aeons, the domination and conquest of demonic powers, cosmic sin, personal transcendence, and related familiar themes. The demolition of this Paul, or at least major parts, is already well under way.[65] Smith writes regarding Paul: "Any pretense of remediation, of rectification, of healing and sanctification is absent."[66] I find it

---

[62] Jonathan Z. Smith, *Drudgery Divine: On the Comparison of Early Christianities and the Religions of Late Antiquity* (Chicago: University of Chicago, 1990), 121.
[63] Ibid., 121.
[64] Jonathan Z. Smith, "Birth Upside Down or Right Side Up," History of Religions 9 (1969–70), 302; idem, "When the Chips are Down," *Relating Religion*, 15.
[65] Caroline Johnson Hodge and Denise Kimber Buell, "The Politics of Interpretation: The Rhetoric of Race and Ethnicity in Paul," *JBL* 123 (2003): 235–51; Johnson Hodge, "*If Sons Then Heirs*."
[66] Smith, *Drudgery Divine,*" 142.

interesting that these are precisely what the divine *pneuma* does in the Christ-*pneuma* myth, and the rectifications are psychological, social and cosmic. I will not, however, try to argue for a new Paul beyond what I have already done and I do not simply want to deny that Paul is in some sense utopian. The latter may depend on how much of x and y it takes to push one into the "utopian" category. Instead, I want to raise some questions about the locative/utopian concepts that I hope will contribute toward what Smith calls "the rectification of categories." I have both criticisms and an explanatory proposal.

The categories, I believe, are under-theorized. I also have some worries that with minds less brilliant than Smith's, such categories might prove dangerous. "Locative" partly originated in Smith's correction to Mircea Eliade's interpretation of cosmogonic myth and his "patterns of archaic religion." He sought to bring Eliade's timeless "archaic" into history and to show evidence of a change in both directions between the locative and utopian types of religion.[67] My first worry is that without more satisfactory explanations of the two that locative might against all of Smith's efforts seem to be primordial and utopian essentially psychological. After all, locative is the religion that most people and families just have, while utopian seems to be an unnatural rebellion against it. But how does locative religion come about? It can easily seem like it is based upon the natural attitude toward the world. By insisting that these are rather like existential attitudes without further social explanation, the two categories could also seem at base to be psychological in origin and essence. According to Smith, then, Paul works out his thought "from a perspective of alienation and *ressentiment*, to a thoroughly utopian understanding."[68] Smith is also admirably aware of the limitations of his suggested explanations. In an earlier note he writes that, "I am aware that, in this formulation, I am offering a tentative and, undoubtedly, partial causal explanation for the co-occurrence of the shift to utopian interpretations, in the case of the Cybele-Attis cult, and of Paul, in terms of alienation and *ressentiment*."[69]

My proposal is that much of what is or seems utopian in Paul and other ancient writers is a field effect. Indeed, utopian thought may be the result of the semi-autonomy and disinterestedness produced by the conditions of cultural fields. In Bourdieu's account of cultural fields, he attributes much of their creative dynamism to their characteristic of possessing opposing dominant heteronomous and dominated autonomous poles. Some philosophy, for example, defines itself as autonomous in opposition to the dominant philosophy and rhetoric and thus occupied the other pole of the field. Both sides of the field claimed to value

---

[67] Smith, *"When the Chips Are Down,"* 13–16.
[68] Smith, *Drudgery Divine*, 141.
[69] Ibid., 134 n. 35 adding: "However, as indicated above, it is my belief that the determination of such matters 'will be the work of a generation'."

autonomy as Agamemnon's speech above on the ideals of the *scholastici* asserts. But one side defined itself as truly autonomous over against the other side that had sold out. Literate experts on the autonomous pole derive their legitimacy and prestige – their ability to attract others – from demonstrating that they and their cultural products are pure and not compromised by the backing of power, money or conventional legitimacy. Classic figures who modeled the autonomous form of philosophy would include Socrates, Diogenes the Cynic and Zeno the Stoic, all known for their radical rejection of the wealth, honor, prestige and institutional power sought by other sorts of intellectuals. Their own prestige and power derived from their practices of disinterestedness regarding wealth, power, and honor. Above all, they developed sharp critiques of traditional Greek religious beliefs and practices as attempts to buy the good will of gods, gods falsely represented as having human-like interests and motivations. Diogenes and Zeno banished temples, priests and offerings altogether from their *Republics*. The right relationship with the divine was not to be one of traditional reciprocity.

Bourdieu's famous example of the field of art well illustrates the autonomous pole. The museums, academic artists, artists supported by patrons, the state and by the market formed the heteronomous pole. With the development of the idea of pure and true art – art for art's sake – a succession of artistic movements and individuals defined themselves and their work in contrast to the heteronomous who they claimed produced for money, conventional approval and power. The ideal of the poor starving artist arose. The bohemian lifestyle expressed disinterest in conventional values, approval and material possessions. In the view of the autonomous pole specialist, true art – as opposed to mere craft – was of unlimited value, beyond economic price. Since the social and symbolic capital of the autonomous pole producer is only derived from comparison to those who are cast as more heteronomous than they are, autonomous producers must continually and competitively define themselves as even more disinterested than others who claim disinterest. Sociologically perhaps the most striking thing about Paul's letters is the astounding number of competitors – false apostles, evil workers, proponents of false gospels, super apostles, law binders of gentiles, "dogs" and so on – that the letters mention. And here is the interesting point: there is almost no discussion of the content of the "false teachings." Rather, the letters refer to their false motives regarding money and gain, and desire for human prestige and approval. I see a fit between such disinterestedness and a religion focused on the myth of a teacher without teachings, whose totalizing act was to die faithfully, only for the interests of God with no interests of his own.

My proposal therefore entails that the attitudes and practices that Smith describes as utopian derive from the conditions of experts whose religion is that of bookish interpretation and norms produced by the interactions with other such specialists in various degrees of distance and autonomy from everyday religion outside of the field. The most utopian would be those competing to outdo other producers of disinterested religion on the autonomous pole. In Smith's *Drudgery Divine*, the central example for comparison to Paul is the Cybele-Attis cult. He shows its locative forms and their later utopian interpretation. The locative evidence is relatively extensive and largely archeological, but the utopian interpretations come from highly literate intellectuals with known locations in the cultural field.[70] The interpretations of the cult that take a utopian direction use intellectualizing conventions that are specialized skills such as allegory, allusion to philosophical doctrines and intertextual interpretation.

None of this means that people who were not players in the cultural fields could not give intellectually sophisticated, creative and thoughtful practice and interpretation to their religion. It does mean that such people would not be constrained and habituated by the norms and social dynamics of experts whose intense interaction produced and even required distinction from the normal, everyday, locative perspective on religion. I think it likely that Corinthians, including especially people who did not aspire to paideia, gave locative interpretation to Paul's Christ-*pneuma* myth. When 1 Corinthians 15:12 refers to some who say there is no resurrection of the dead and the long discussion that follows vigorously argues on a number of points about the reality of a resurrection of those in Christ, and not of Christ only, locative logic over against utopian thinking seems the best explanation for Paul's efforts.[71] After all, a hero who had broken the bounds of place and become a heavenly god was a familiar idea in Paul's world. The two best-known examples are, of course, Heracles and Asclepius.

Heracles can help us to think about the resources that the Corinthians might have had for doing their own thinking and mythmaking about Christ.[72] Heracles was enormously popular in extremely complex varieties of myth, cult and literature. Most often his cult was heroic in form, but he had the unheroic characteristic of possessing no tomb. Heroes were normally intensely local, given cult where they were buried. Sometimes he was worshipped as an Olympian god, who had received apotheosis and ascended to heaven. The apotheosis was widely seen as a reward for his suffering and virtue. Myth and literature dealt with this category-breaking figure in several different ways.

---

[70] Smith, *Drudgery Divine*, 133. The figures that Smith mentions are Sallustius, Julian, Firmicus Maternus, Damascius.

[71] Paul's argument assumes that the same people who deny the more general resurrection had no problem with Christ's resurrection.

[72] David E. Aune, "Heracles and Christ: Heracles Imagery in the Christology of Early Christianity," in *Greeks, Romans and Christians: Essays in Honor of Abraham J. Malherbe*, ed. David L. Balch, Everett Ferguson, and Wayne A. Meeks (Minneapolis: Fortress, 1990), 3–19.

Pindar coined the oxymoron, hero god (*Nem.* 3.22). Rationalizing writers sometimes claimed that there were two different Heracleses. One died and became a hero; the other was a god. Homer has his shade (*eidolon*) in Hades while he dwells on Olympus with the gods, another unresolved contradiction. About the time that Paul was in Corinth, Seneca wrote of Heracles, "He has crossed the torrents of Tartarus, subdued the gods of the underworld, and returned" (*Heracles Furens*, 889). Here a writer can even have Heracles conquer death, but there is no reason to think that this would have disrupted the normal locative religion. He was treated as a singular figure and he did not change the normal course of human life and death, as Paul's Christ did. Paul taught that Christ had been rewarded for his faithfulness with a body of divine *pneuma* vastly superior to mortal flesh. By ritual means others could have some of his *pneuma* and become physically connected to Christ and a distinguished ancient lineage blessed by God. Only the claim that all the dead with this *pneuma* would soon come back from death and that the living would never die would have perhaps been non-sensical and have certainly contradicted the principles of locative religion.

Most of the Corinthians may have treated Paul's Christ-*pneuma* myth as an interesting and challenging opportunity for thinking about their religion of household, ethnicity and city. Christ, like Heracles, embodied opposites and contradictions that might be treated as exceptions and singularities, but also opportunities for thought. Most of the ways that writers, cultural experts at least, treated Heracles did not eliminate the tensions, but led to novel and creative formulations. In a cult, apart from the practices of writing and literate fields, a person might be faced with giving heroic cult to Heracles one day and celebrating him as a god the next. Sometimes the cults were as mixed and as ambiguous as the Lord's Dinner. I would argue that both Heracles myth and cult could provide opportunities for thinking about boundaries, their transgression, and maintenance. So also for the Christ myth and cult.

What I have been suggesting only makes sense if one sees this thinking with myth and cult as socially useful thinking. In view of my analysis of the Lord's Dinner, Smith writes, "Some Corinthians may have understood Paul as providing them, in the figure of Christ, with a more proximate and mobile ancestor for their new nonethnic 'Christian' *ethnos*."[73] "Non-ethnic ethnos" can be taken in various ways. Some of these would obscure rather than clarify the kind of social creativity for which I want to argue. One could follow the

---

[73] Smith, *Relating Religion*, 351. The quotation draws on Burton Mack's response to my paper, "On Construing Myths, Meals and Power in the World of Paul," (now partly incorporated into this article) read at the Consultation on Ancient Myths and Modern Theories of Christian Origins at the annual national meeting of the Society of Biblical Literature, in New Orleans, 1996. The expression drawn from Mack is: "Christ the first father of a non-ethnic genealogy."

popular interpretation of Galatians 3:27–28 and say that Paul discovered the principle of non-ethnic liberal individual identity. But among other things, this ignores the argument beginning in 3:6. The gospel is the promise that all the gentiles will be blessed in Abraham's seed, Christ. The content of the Abrahamic promise, the blessing, is the divine *pneuma*. This argument culminates with words of 3:29, "If you are of Christ, you are Abraham's seed, heirs according to the promise." "All are one in Christ" is not a liberal erasure of gender, ethnicity and social status, but the claim that all of those in Christ share the same superior ontological status, possession of Christ's *pneuma*, in spite of other differences. Thus "non-ethnic" should not be given this popular interpretation through 3:27–28.

Another interpretation of "non-ethnic" might make ethnicity fixed, given, primordial and essential over against Paul's mere ethnic language – that is just made up. Here Paul represents the modern voluntaristic conception of religion over against the persistent conception of ethnicity as fixed and primordial.[74] Such an interpretation would mystify both religion and ethnicity and hide the fact that both are the result of human activity and social processes. Much recent scholarship in the social sciences has worked at explaining these activities and processes and critiquing the essential and primordial conceptions of ethnicity. Two points from one of these scholars will be helpful for interpreting "nonethnic ethnic." Rogers Brubaker writes, "The genealogical construction of relationality offers possibilities for extension that are obscured by the contemporary scholar's tendency to look for a neat boundary between inside and outside."[75] Further he says, "In almost all societies, kinship concepts serve as symbolic and ideological resources, yet while they shape norms, self-understandings and perceptions of affinity, they do not necessarily produce kinship 'groups.'"[76] These are useful maxims for an area of scholarship that begins with premises about the existence and inherent qualities of groups such as "the Corinthian community," "the Jews" and "the Romans." Brubaker's sentences occur in a discussion of "the Nuer" and "the Dinka" of East Africa, peoples that earlier scholarship had constructed as neatly bounded ethnic groups. Recent scholarship, especially from Sharon Hutchinson, has shown that no such ethnic group as "the Nuer" ever existed.[77] Rather practices of creative genealogy, endogamy, and fictive kinship allowed varied populations over a huge region to relate in complex and flexible ways. In light of this, and that of many other such examples,

---

[74] Denise Kimber Buell, *Why This New Race: Ethnic Reasoning in Early Christianity* (New York: Columbia University Press, 2005), 5–6 and throughout.
[75] Brubaker, *Ethnicity Without Groups*, 50.
[76] Ibid., 51.
[77] Sharon Hutchinson, *Nuer Dilemmas: Coping with Money, War and the State* (Berkeley: University of California, 1995).

Paul's entrepreneurial activities employing genealogical myth and concepts and practices appealing to kinship may not appear as pseudo over against the real ethnicity and religion of the Corinthians, but as rather forms of ordinary social activity. So also, the varied resistances, appropriations and negotiations of the Corinthians in the face of Paul's efforts seem unexceptional. Group-making and group-resisting are activities with varied kinds of actors who employ, categories, schemes of classification, organizations, activities of mobilization, cognitive schemas, taken-for-granted practices, expectations regarding patterns of proximity and distance and so forth.[78] The way I read the work of Smith and Mack, "non-ethnic ethnic" would best be interpreted as pointing to Paul's activity as an attempt at group-making in view of the constructedness of social formations, including locative and ethnic. So, I would claim that the tension between a Paul focused on genealogical and kinship mythmaking and his interpretation of the Lord's Dinner/Christ myth with its implications of breaking socio-religious boundaries is not so odd or rebellious and just the kind of tension required by the social workings of the ethnic and the non-ethnic. I say not so odd only with the caveat that we see Paul's activity within another quite ordinary form of human sociality, the rather more autonomous pole of a field of cultural expertise.

[78] Brubaker, *Ethnicity Without Groups*.

CHAPTER FIVE

The Social Formations of Paul and His Romans: Synagogues, Churches and Occam's Razor

In this chapter, I discuss traditional conceptions of the social formations that scholars imagine as having been in Rome and that present themselves as explanatory for understanding Paul's letter. I then outline an alternative scenario. I undertake this project as an experiment in what I take to be the best critical practices of the historian who works in the study of religion. Of course, "best practices of the historian" and "the study of religion" are rightly debated activities.

Among several possible critical issues one could raise about scholarship that tries to argue for social formations in Rome that would partly explain Paul's letter, I want to focus here upon the issue of parsimony. Many people are familiar with the Rube Goldberg cartoons depicting extremely complex sets of gadgets, levers, pulleys on a contraption designed to perform some simple task. These drawings are amusing because a good mousetrap does not need eighty working parts. Given the varied constraints of different fields of knowledge – and the application of the principle of simplicity does vary by field – among relatively plausible contenders, the more economical explanation is generally to be preferred. This is one of the bedrock principles of knowledge both in the academy and more generally.[1] The historian wants to explain particular relatively-known outcomes in terms of antecedent processes (types of causes including human activities). The parsimony here is not reduction to some totalizing theory such as psychoanalytic, crude forms of Marxist ideology, or a Foucauldian idea that "all language, culture and practice is politically loaded," but preferring that which most fully explains the antecedent processes with the greatest economy, the fewest assumptions. This is in no way to deny the great complexity and multiple causes in history. Romantic historiography such as R. J. Collingwood's revels in the irreducible complexity of the historical and

---

[1] Alan Baker, "Simplicity," *Stanford Encyclopedia of Philosophy* (Berkeley: University of California, 2010), 1095.

the intuitive understanding of the historical interpreter, but even these historians rather inconsistently use the principle of parsimony in their actual historical work.[2] In the case before us, the relatively known to be explained is Paul's letter to the Romans. I will argue that numerous scholarly accounts, taken as explanations, resemble Rube Goldberg contraptions. This I think is partly due to confusing the necessary and important task of richly imagining historical hypotheses (often called "historical contexts") with the justification of such hypotheses as explanations.

The traditional approach places Paul writing his letter on one side and the church in Rome with the Jewish community, understood in terms of synagogues, on the other side. The latter two are in some way supposed to be explanatory of the former. But these large and complex social formations in Rome are tips of yet more massive icebergs, the religion Judaism, the synagogue, worship, conversion, Christianity or the Christian religion, the church and the sub-concepts house churches, Jewish Christians, the Jewish and Christian communities in Rome, and the apostolic mission. These conceptions dominate commentaries on Romans and writing about "the church in Rome" and Paul's letter. It is important to understand what I take to be the broader historical issues. I am convinced that the myth of Christian origins begun by Paul and then Acts, Irenaeus and others in the second century and fully developed by Eusebius and others in the fourth century, dominates scholarship on early Christianity. The critical counter principle is simple. New social formations come into being by normal social processes out of already existing social formations and cognitive processes. Accounts with *sui generis* social formations that have no fit with the wider social world are mythic and not critical history. The powerful impulse to find justifying antecedents for later Christian and Jewish institutions, practices and denominations in the enchanted time of origins has built a large and unwieldy edifice. In addition to this stress on the process of contextually understandable social formation, my scenario depends upon reinterpreting three key pieces of evidence central to dominant interpretations of the letter's historical setting: namely the supposed expulsions of Jews under Claudius, the greetings in Romans 16, and the explosive growth of the Christian movement.

The following is a synthetic summary of the standard account that has many variations. The Judeans in first century CE Rome adhered to the religion of Judaism that centered on meetings at synagogues where the chief activity

---

[2] Robert Jervis, "International History and International Politics: Why Are They Studied Differently?" in *Bridges and Boundaries: Historians: Political Scientists, and the Study of International Relations*, ed. Colin Elman and Miriam Fendius Elman (Cambridge: MIT Press, 2001), 385–402; Paul W. Schroeder, "International History: Why Historians Do It Differently than Political Scientists," in Elman and Elman, *Bridges and Boundaries*, 403–16, at 405.

was monotheistic worship.[3] This Judaism and monotheistic worship attracted large numbers of non-Jews, some of whom converted to the Jewish religion. Such attraction and conversion of Gentiles was the likely source of much Roman anti-Jewish feeling and the chief reason for the periodic expulsions of the Jews from Rome. Christianity began as a natural correction and perfection of Judaism so that the first Christians were ethnically Judeans but whose religion was Christianity or in another formulation, their Judaism was fused with, but subordinate to their Christianity. The new religion of Christianity began in Rome when Jewish Christians came there and converted other Jews and Gentiles to Christianity. The church may have begun in the synagogues, but became mostly Gentile in house churches after Claudius expelled the Jews from Rome in 49 CE. The churches offered a highly attractive alternative to Jewish worship in synagogues and the Jewish religious system because they lacked the ethnic limitations of Judaism but still offered monotheism. When Paul wrote Romans, he envisioned this fluid situation of emergence from the synagogue and competition over the attraction and conversion of Gentiles and lack of clarity about the rules of membership in the two religions. Above all, the letter was shaped by the stresses between Jews and Gentiles in the several house churches and synagogues of which Christianity in Rome consisted.

Almost everything about this account is wrong and a great deal of excellent recent scholarship has persuasively criticized one aspect or another of the picture without challenging the overall picture and providing an alternative. Judeans were an ethnic people like Greeks, Phrygians and Egyptians and not a religion in the sense that Christianity became a religion, or that Buddhism and Islam are religions. Much has been written about the history and limitations of the concept of "religion" and "a religion," but it is only now beginning to have an impact on the study of ancient Christianity and Judaism. Judean religion was not separable from Judean ethnicity and certainly not a semi-autonomous sphere as in modernist conceptions of religion and as often imagined in scholarly ideas about synagogues. The recent book by Matthew Thiessen, *Contesting Conversion*, is another blow to the idea that Judaism was a religion that one could normally

---

[3] A few scholars hold to a less anachronistic view of synagogues as primarily school-like rather than liturgical, a case argued by Peter Wick, *Die urchristilichen Gottesdienste: Entstehung und Entwicklung im Rahmen der früjüdischen Tempel, Synagogen und Hausfrömmigkeit*, (Stuttgart: Kohlhammer, 2002). The actual evidence for Rome is for Judean *collegia*, associations in their well-known forms. See, Peter Richardson, "Augustan Era Synagogues in Rome," in *Judaism and Christianity in First-Century Rome*, ed. Karl P. Donfried and Peter Richardson (Grand Rapids: Eerdmans, 1998), 17–29; "Early Synagogues as Collegia in the Diaspora and in Palestine," in *Voluntary Associations in the Graeco-Roman World*, ed. John S. Kloppenborg and Stephen G. Wilson (London: Routledge, 1996), 90–109; L. Michael White, *The Social Origins of Chirstian Architecture: Building God's House in the Roman World: Architectural Adaptation among Pagans, Jews, and Christians* (Valley Forge, PA: Trinity Press, 1996).

convert to, much less one that had a mission to the Gentiles.[4] The idea that first century Judaism was a religion goes hand in hand with the idea that this religion centered on Sabbath day worship in synagogues suspiciously like going to church on Sunday. Obviously, this enormous topic is controversial, and I can here only suggest a case. Joseph Fitzmyer evokes the standard picture when he writes that the Jewish population in Rome has been estimated as about fifty thousand "grouped into several synagogues."[5] But there is no evidence that the Jewish population of Rome was organized according to synagogues. A survey of scholarship on synagogues shows two things clearly.[6] First, traditional scholarship, especially using evidence from the periods after Paul, wants to depict a rather uniform institution across the Roman empire for which Sabbath worship is a version of "going to church on Sunday" and like what is known from medieval evidence of synagogue services. But this begs the question about several things including the origins of the "great synagogue" that emerges in the fifth and sixth centuries. Second, there is no evidence for this scenario in the Rome of Paul's time and scholarship on synagogues is far from agreeing on even what a synagogue was, much less that there was a common church-like institution rather than great regional variety in Jewish meetings and meeting places.[7] The other rather startling factor is that Paul's letters never mention synagogues or anything like them, as one would surely expect from the premises of traditional scholarship and the book of Acts. We instead hear of households and non-Jewish temples and feasts, but nothing that can be identified as a reference to a synagogue apart from the wildest conjecture. The appeal to synagogues is an argument from the unknown to the unknown, claiming that synagogues in Rome explain the processes and events that led to Paul's letter.

The most common explanatory argument goes like this. Christianity was first established in the synagogues of Rome and included some Gentile Godfearers. When Claudius expelled the Jews in 49 CE, Gentiles had to meet in houses and the church became predominantly Gentile even after the Jews started to return to the city. Scholars present this scenario as an explanation for why Romans supposes "a predominantly Gentile audience," yet why the letter is very Jewish.[8] In this account, Paul cryptically alludes to this situation when he mentions the

---

[4] Matthew Thiessen, *Contesting Conversion: Genealogy, Circumcision, and Identity in Ancient Judaism and Christianity* (New York: Oxford University Press, 2011).

[5] Joseph A. Fitzmyer, *Romans: A New Translation with Introduction Commentary* (New York: Doubleday, 1993), 27.

[6] For a helpful survey, see Anders Runesson, Donald D. Binder, and Birger Olsson, *The Ancient Synagogue from its Origins to 200 C.E.: A Source Book* (Leiden: Brill, 2008), 1–15.

[7] Runesson, Binder, and Olsson, *Synagogue*, 230–37. It is not clear that any of the catacomb inscriptions that mention Jewish groups are earlier than the second century.

[8] Romans actually describes its audience as only Gentile, although this fact is widely ignored by scholars.

weak (Jews) and the strong (Gentiles) in 14:1–15:6. This explanation contains a very large number of unsupported or poorly supported assumptions, one linked to another. There is no evidence for Christianity first being in synagogues in Rome, not even in Acts, much less good evidence for what being a Christian in a synagogue would even mean. The character of Roman synagogues in Paul's time is far from clear.

We need to explain both the ancient evidence and the scholars who interpret it. The problem that emerges as most palpable for me is not sheer numbers such as the numerous house churches and imagined tallies of Christian members. Even more, Roman Christianity gets imagined as a non-Pauline foundation of a movement and an institution that was well on its way to becoming the Church that would come to dominate the West. The imagination of the Roman church in Paul's time gets bolstered by connecting it with 1 Clement supposedly in the 90s evidencing a bishop of Roman with hierarchy and apostolic succession.[9] This, in radical opposition to Paul's vision, is an institution designed for enduring the long haul in the world. The culprit, I submit, is the very foundation myth of Christianity that gave it the identity, boldness and audacity to assert itself in the Roman Empire and later, what some have called the big bang theory of Christian origins.[10]

This myth had its beginnings with the earliest Christian writings and still influences the scholarly imagination about the scale of early Christian population. And Rome has been such an important center for Christianity that it had to be a significant church from the beginning. Writing almost a century after the events, the author of Acts has the movement begin when two sermons result in more than eight thousand individuals joining together with such commitment that they sell their possessions and form a community of radical dedication (Acts 2:25–47; 4:5, 32–35). The story goes from "the assembly" having no existence to nearly ten thousand radically dedicated in

---

[9] For instance, Jan N. Bremmer, *The Rise of Christianity Through the Eyes of Gibbon, Harnack and Rodney Stark* (Groningen: Barkhuis, 2010), 50 writes that 1 Clement, for which he gives the traditional Eusebian dating, also gives the same impression of a substantial church. A number of scholars have shown that 1 Clement cannot be plausibly dated that early and probably comes from the 120s: Otto Zwierlein, "Petrus in Rom? Die literarischen Zeugnisse," *Petrus und Paulus in Rom: Eine Interdisziplinäre Debatte,* ed. S. Heid et al. (Freiburg-Basel, 2009), 468–91. According to Eusebius's impossible scheme, Clement was the third bishop of Rome from the twelfth year of Domitian (93 CE) until about 100. Clement's talk of persecutions in Rome and the supposed one under Nero have been mutually reinforcing for scholars, each text the reason for dating the other early.

[10] Robyn Faith Walsh, *The Origins of Early Christian Literature: Contextualizing the New Testament Within Greco-Roman Literary Culture* (Cambridge: Cambridge University Press, 2021), 22–23 n. 7 for use of the expression; "Q and the 'Big Bang' Theory of Christian Origins," in *Redescribing the Gospel of Mark* ed. Barry S. Crawford and Merrill P. Miller (Atlanta, GA: Society of Biblical Literature, 2017), 483–533.

a matter of days. This is indeed a big bang. And, of course, the assumption among readers has been that the large and constantly growing number of believers led by apostles continued as the norm. Already in 6:1–7 the community has expanded so much that various administrative issues arise, and large numbers of priests join under the direction of the apostles. The larger story has Paul trek fearlessly and triumphantly from Jerusalem to Rome overcoming constant obstacles and fierce opposition. Large numbers of hearers form churches along the way. After two years of teaching in Ephesus "*all the residents of Asia, both Jews and Greeks, heard the Lord's word*" (19:10). Researchers guestimate the population of the province of Asia to have been 8-15 million.[11]

Paul's death, likely in Rome, surely known to the author, gets skillfully elided from the triumphant story. The author, like Paul, attributes such growth and community instead to God. But what Paul and Acts present as a miracle of God, scholars have often taken as sociological data, though perhaps with a bit of exaggeration. The kernel of the story still stands – whatever that means. Acts, I would argue, received its audacity from the letters of Paul. The historian, of course, should resist the literature's enthusiasm and make a more sober assessment, weighing the historical realities against the audacious mythology. But admitting exaggerations and then proceeding as if the story is mostly sound history will not do. Otherwise translators and commentators simply ignore or cover up the over-the-top claims as when the *New Revised Standard Version* translates the Greek's "how many ten thousands there are among the Judeans all believing and all zealously keeping the law" of Acts 21:20 with "how many thousands of believers there are among the Jews."

Paul himself initiated the myth of explosive beginnings because of his confidence that Christ would return any day to transform the cosmic order, and that God was currently bringing about the earthly preparations for which the apostle was playing a major role.[12] Paul tells us that he is *the* apostle to the non-Jews, the Gentiles (e.g., Gal 2:7–8 cf. 1:15–16; Rom 1:5). Gentiles made up all but a tiny bit of the earth's population. But 1 Thessalonians was likely written a mere twenty years after the death of Jesus. A few years later, although the number of Pauline Christ-people must have been pitifully small, with seeming equanimity he envisions that his mission might be successfully finished any day (Rom 15:19) and that it had already been successfully completed from Jerusalem to present day Croatia. In Matthew, Jesus commissions the disciples to

---

[11] Bruce W. Frier, "Demography," in *The Cambridge Ancient History XI: The High Empire, A.D. 70–192*, ed. Alan K. Bowman, Peter Garnsey, and Dominic Rathbone (Cambridge: Cambridge University Press, 2000), 827–54.

[12] E. g, 1 Thess 4:13–5:11.

go to every nation in the world and convert the populations (Mt 28: 16–20). Christ promises to be with the effort so that success seems assured. But the actual Christian population when the author of Matthew wrote perhaps three decades after the first Judean war with Rome must have been small.

Eusebius takes this myth and makes it into history. He creates a detailed story with sources used as evidence of the Church's big bang and inexorable growth. Already in 211 CE, Tertullian made the outrageous claim that 50% of the Empire's population was Christian (*Ad Scap.* 2:10). Eusebius picks this up and continues the mythmaking of Acts. During his life Jesus was famous in "all of Palestine" (*E.H.*, 2.2.11). He further repeats a story as history from Tertullian (*E.H.*, 2.2.7–24; Tert. *Apol.* 21). The emperor Tiberius wanted to declare Jesus a Roman god and put it before the Senate where the Senators rejected the proposal on semi-procedural grounds. Tiberius reigned 14–37 CE, while Jesus died around 30 CE. Seven years later, the doctrine of his godship was public and known across the empire. Apostles and missionaries went across the whole earth. "In every city and village churches were established completely filled with thousands of men" (*E.H.*, 2.3.6–7). Shortly after Jesus' crucifixion the whole known world had heard the gospel and teeming churches could be found in every city and village. The Christian takeover of the Empire had made decisive headway just years after the messiah's death with what has to be a substantial portion of the Empire's population. It is time to downsize the historical imagination, and although the idea of eight to fifteen house churches and other Christians in synagogues has chastened older more naïve scenarios, even more modest proposals deserve a hearing.

Scholars have based the knock down argument for a large, developed and noticeable Roman church on Tacitus (*Ann.* 15.44) who writes of an immense multitude (*multitudo ingens*) of martyred Christians under Nero in connection with the great fire of 64 CE. Tacitus's story of Christians used as torches, crafted by later Christian historians as the beginning of the "Age of Persecution," has long been treated as the linchpin of the saga about the explosive growth of Christianity. Sure, Acts exaggerates, however Nero certainly found and executed an "immense multitude" of Christians a few years after Paul's death. If the church had gained such prominence that Nero could recognize the existence of the Christian organization, yielding after police action an enormous multitude of those arrested and executed for crimes supposedly well known as characteristic of that population, then ten thousand and growing in the movement's first days in Acts seems plausible.

But Tacitus's story remains wildly implausible. To go over all of the reasons would take us too far afield. But recognition of an entity "the Christians" seven or so years after Paul wrote his letter to some in Rome makes no sense. There is no evidence that the term "Christian" was even used until much later and the social form in the letter consists of a few Judean teachers meeting with small numbers of non-Judeans in homes. How would Roman authorities even know to distinguish these groups from Judean groups long accepted in Rome? It is also implausible that the minute number of Christ people in Rome already had a reputation for such criminal activity and were known by the masses. The list of problems could go on and on.

Scholars have come up with two plausible ways to treat Tacitus's report. For a long time, a growing list of scholars have proposed a Christian interpolation into Tacitus's text. He wrote the Annals 50 to 60 years (115–120 CE) after the supposed events and it is suspiciously the only source for it, even though others describe the great fire of 64 CE.[13] We know of Christian interpolations in Josephus and elsewhere. After all, Christians preserved and transmitted these "classical texts." One scholar proposes that the line translated as, "The author of this name, Christ, was executed by the procurator Pontius Pilate in the reign of Tiberius," was added.[14]

In the second plausible approach, Candida Moss, for instance, argues that Tacitus projects backward things that he knows or thinks that he knows from his own time onto Nero's Rome.[15] Precisely at the beginning decades of the second century we can see much evidence of the proliferation of Christian teachers, writings and groups organized around such leaders. In 2015, Brent Shaw wrote a major article arguing that Tacitus sincerely retrojected knowledge of Christians recently gained in his social circles and tied these to Nero. Overall, the argument is impressive. Christian presence in Rome in the 60s would not have been large enough or of the character to have drawn the attention of Roman officials to the existence of a group distinct from the large Judean population. A response criticizing Shaw displays the weakness of the traditional uncritical treatment of Tacitus.[16]

Shaw's case for the emergence of the term "Christian" and recognition of Christians as a group in the period 110–120 CE is of special interest. Tacitus and the younger Pliny were good friends and Suetonius was also in their circle.

---

[13] Later Christian writers who link the fire to Nero persecuting the Christians depend upon Tacitus.

[14] R. Carrier, "*The Prospect of a Christian Interpolation in Tacitus, Annals 15:44*, Vigiliae Christianae 68 (2014): 264–83.

[15] *The Myth of Persecution: How Early Christians Invented a Story of Martyrdom* (New York: HarperOne, 2013), 138–39.

[16] Christopher P. Jones, "The Historicity of the Neronian Persecution: A Response to Brent Shaw," *New Testament Studies* 63 (2017): 146–52. Both Shaw and Jones make uncritical use of Acts. Jones seems to think that Rom 1:8 seals the case. Here Paul gives thanks that his addressee's "faithfulness is announced in the entire world." The kindest characterization would be to call this hyperbolic praise. The entire world of many millions did not hear about the faithfulness of this small loose collection of people. The line is typical of Pauline audacity.

In his exhaustive book on dating Acts, Richard Pervo concludes on c. 115 CE by an anonymous writer.[17] Acts and the three historians are the first to use the term, Christians. Pliny had served as a praetor and consul in Rome and long practiced as a lawyer, and yet he tells Trajan that he had never witnessed a trial of Christians and did not even know if just membership in the group was punishable or only specific crimes. Such ignorance hardly supports the notion of a well-developed and long standing official Roman policy toward Christians. If Eusebius can be trusted, Aristides and Quadratus addressed their apologies to Hadrian, who ruled from 117–138 CE, indicating the more public appearance of Christians. Roughly in this period 1 Peter writes "if any of you suffer as a Christian" (4:16) as if it were a known outsider's term for a group. *Christianus* (in Tacitus *chrestianus*) is a Greek word with a Latin ending that often meant a follower of so and so, and frequently of political leaders, but not devotees of a god.[18] The designation has a perfect fit with a category created by Roman elites or officials once they had had enough encounters to need a category for members of the group. Ignatius's letters, dateable from the mid-120s to the 140s, show the clearest early evidence of Christians embracing the term. Acts, of course, and 1 Peter, both sometime in the early second century, use the term, but it still seems primarily an outsider's designation in both.

Something new seems to have been happening. On my theory, Christian teachers, writers and their followers came to public recognition as experts in the field of literate production. The period begins at the turn of the century with the wide circulation of Paul's letters and the writing of the gospels, both read as containing models of intellectualist competition in the field, Paul with his contending fellow-workers and Jesus and his students.

My alternative scenario requires understanding the greetings in Romans 16 in a way that differs greatly from standard scholarly treatments. Scholars widely understand the individuals greeted there as direct evidence for the composition of Paul's addressees and of Christianity in Rome with clusters of names and reference to households often taken as evidence of house churches. Many scholars find four house churches in the chapter, but others find seven to ten, and one contemplates possibly 15.[19]

In their enthusiasm, commentators on Romans have misunderstood the nature of greetings in both the letters, and in Romans. I find it bizarre that

---

[17] Richard I. Pervo, *Dating Acts: Between the Evangelists and the Apologists* (Santa Rosa, CA: Polebridge, 2006).

[18] Pervo, *Acts*, 295.

[19] An extensive treatment with five house churches in chapter 16 that represent Paul's addressees is Robert Jewett, *Romans: A Commentary*, Hermeneia (Minneapolis: Fortress, 2007), 951–94, 55–74. For 15 house churches, see Thomas H. Tobin, S. J., *Paul's Rhetoric in Its Contexts: The Argument of Romans* (Peabody, MA: Hendrickson, 2004), 37–39.

scholars have consistently ignored what those specializing in epistolography have said, including Terence Mullins, whose work is well known in the field. He writes of the second-person greeting, "In this way, the writer of the letter becomes the principal and the addressee becomes his agent in establishing a communication with a third party who is not intended to be among the immediate readership of the letter."[20] Paul's words in Romans 16:1–16 make it clear that those named to be greeted are not among the audience toward which the letter was aimed. Those greeted, at least in theory, could be contacted by the audience. The people greeted are distinctly not that particular group of people whom Paul addresses in an uncharacteristically indefinite way as "all of those in Rome loved by God who are called to be holy" and as fruit he wants to obtain from among the Gentiles. As every commentator notices, he does not describe these people as a Christ assembly, a church, or churches, even though there is one in the residence of Prisca and Aquila that he mentions in asking that his audience relay greetings to the couple. It would be very strange for Paul to mention only one church if the groups of people in chapter 16 were also churches. And the letter does not address itself to this acknowledged assembly that he knows. The letter envisages others, who are the targets of his most complex surviving letter. I am convinced that any contemporary ancient reader would have understood the people addressed by Paul as a group quite distinct from those mentioned in chapter 16, clearly including the only church mentioned in the letter, the assembly in the house of Prisca and Aquila.

Uniquely among the letters, the epistolary opening of Romans foregrounds "God's good news" as foretold in the holy writings by God's prophets and relates this to his audience of certain gentiles in Rome who are loved by God and called by Christ to be holy ones. The audience of the letter consists of non-Jews who have an interest in prophecy, the ancient holy writings and whom Paul treats as chosen by God.[21]

Discussion of the supposed expulsion of the Jews from Rome under Claudius leads directly to the first alternative social formation. Critique of the highly dubious case for an expulsion of the Jewish population or a large part of it in the year 49 CE has been laboriously detailed several times.[22] But that thesis tied to texts about the weak and the strong, supposedly Jews and Gentiles, has proven irresistible. Now a historically plausible interpretation of the texts about the expulsions has appeared in the work of Heidi Wendt. In a book on the phenomenon of freelance religious experts at Rome and a journal article

---

[20] Terence Y. Mullins, "Greeting as a New Testament Form," *JBL* 87(1968): 418–26, at 420.
[21] Runar M. Thorsteinsson, *Paul's Interlocutor in Romans 2. Function and Identity in the Context of Ancient Epistolography* (Stockholm: Almqvist & Wiksell, 2003), 34–37.
[22] Most extensively in H. Dixon Slingerland, *Claudian Policymaking and the Early Imperial Repression of Judaism at Rome* (Atlanta: Scholars Press, 1997).

on the Jewish expulsion texts, Wendt shows that *Ioudaioi* or *Iudaei* is used in those texts like *Chaldeans*, *Magoi* and sometimes *Egyptians* as a term for an ethnic subset of freelance religious experts.[23] She studies the anxieties on the part of the Roman state about this class of specialists in certain kinds of religious knowledge and practices and the developing legal and administrative policies toward them. These were individuals who acted on the basis of their own skills instead of a temple, city or some official capacity. They had expertise in such things as healing and especially all sorts of divinatory activities, including prophesies and signs from sacred books. There was a great demand for this sort of thing in Rome and elsewhere. Rome was the city of the Sibylline Oracles. Augustus, Tiberius and later emperors from time to time banned and collected all kinds of books used for prophecy and divination. Livy has a magistrate say that one of his jobs included searching for and burning prophetic books.[24] Wendt points out that Juvenal tells the story of the woman who interpreted the Jewish laws in a list of other experts such as a eunuch of Bellona, one who dressed as an Egyptian god, Armenian and Commagenian *haruspices* (entrail diviners), and Chaldean astrologers. The satirist says that Judeans will interpret a dream for a fee. Wendt shows that such specialists appear each time that writers mention Jewish expulsions. So in 139 BCE *Chaldaei* and *Iudaei* are expelled together and in 19 CE people performing particular Judean and Egyptian religious practices along with *mathematici*, that is, astrologers.[25]

When Suetonius writes that *Ioudaioi* constantly made disturbances at the instigation of Chrestus, he is not talking about fights between Jews and Christians over Christ, but freelance Judean religious specialists and a particularly prominent one named Chrestus. Both Wendt, and Pauline Ripat, who writes about *magoi*, astrologers and various diviners, show clearly that the Roman authorities did not oppose the astrology or divination or ethnic versions of these practices as such, much less the ethnicities themselves, but a certain class of freelance practitioners.[26] Paul clearly belongs to this class of freelance religious expert. Claudius did not expel the estimated 15–60 thousand Jews from Rome, but instead such independent and often itinerant practitioners.

Understanding Paul within this social formation of freelance experts places him in a broader and well-known historical phenomenon that cuts across ethnic formations like Judaism and that can be known confidently as a social

---

[23] Heidi Wendt, *At the Temple Gates: The Religion of Freelance Experts in the Roman Empire* (New York: Oxford University Press, 2016); eadem, "*Iudaica Romana*: A Re-Reading of the Evidence for Judean Expulsions from Rome," *JSJ* 6 (2015), 97–126.

[24] Livy, *Ab urbe cond.* 39.16.8–9.

[25] Suetonius, *Tib.* 36; Tacitus, *Ann.* 2.85.11–17.

[26] Pauline Ripat, "Expelling Misconceptions: Astrologers at Rome," *Classical Philology* 106 (2011): 115–54.

fact.[27] Understanding this social phenomenon requires something like a field of social competition and self-definition. A field is a particular sort of social arena where, instead of control by patrons or official institutions, players contend over what the rules are and set these norms themselves. To play, one has to be educated or socialized into the particular skills that give one more or less prestige and thus power in the game or the ability to consume an expert's products. Such writers wrote, and speakers spoke, in relation to other writers and competed with positions on topics that claimed to be truer or more just than the positions in the writings of others. Paul's competition with his opponents is well-known. He certainly had specialist skills that were not primarily literate practices such as prophecy, tongues, healing practices and performing wonders, but his literate skills with the Judean holy writings placed him in such a social field and made him attractive to people who desired the products of these niches of literate knowledge.

The addressees targeted in Paul's extremely learned and complex letter were such people from this tiny number of those educated and interested in this niche. Romans can in no way be explained as a writing for supposed general Christian and Jewish populations, something that could be read publicly to the "every person" with any hope of comprehension. The letter can only be explained by a scenario in which Paul imagines and targets a much more educated and specialized audience. Whether that audience understood and desired Paul's message of salvation or not, they would have recognized him as a social type of one who had knowledge about prophecy from ancient writings, who taught their relevance to the present, and who commanded the special wisdom of an ancient people. This self-selected and small population of people interested in types like Paul and with skills to interact with him might be conceived as a part of the field of literate specialists, namely the consumers of their services. Being one of these consumers required certain social and educational conditions that historians can investigate. This is an argument from the known to unknown. The argument, unlike traditional suppositions, does not assume the universal intelligibility or appeal of Paul's message.

One can approach the other necessary social formations for explaining Romans through the concept of social networks. We can assume, and Paul's letters provide much evidence to suggest, that households and families constituted another key social formation in addition to a field of specialists, of literate experts. Paul belonged to networks that connected him with at least some in the audience and also connected him to the people whom he asks the audience

---

[27] Wendt, *Temple Gates*; Jennifer Eyl, *Signs, Wonders, and Gifts: Divination in the Letters of Paul* (New York: Oxford University Press, 2019); Stanley Stowers, "Does Pauline Christianity Resemble a Hellenistic Philosophy" in *Redescribing Paul and the Corinthians*, ed. Ron Cameron and Merrill P. Miller (Atlanta: SBL Press, 2011), 219–43.

to greet in chapter 16. Households and various kinds of economic activity overlapped significantly since most business activity was located in households. Aquila and Prisca might have formed a household and also have been artisans working from their home as well as literate experts. The key connection, however, is between members of households, especially *kurioi*, heads, and the field of literate experts in ancient books. Households would then be connected with other households at the level of power by way of the friendships between heads of different households. Women might sometimes, at least, have been de facto heads of households, as Phoebe perhaps was. Other members of households and families might also connect to a field in virtue of the *kurioi*'s approval or tolerance and certain qualifications of education and socialization to the skills and knowledge of the field. In spite of our often-naïve ideas about the universal power and attraction of Paul's message, the appeal of messages and messengers required certain socio-cultural conditions.

With this bare-bones sketch in view, one could make up a number of possible scenarios that would not invoke the often-blatant historical anachronisms of the traditional religions, the synagogue, the church, and so on. So here is one scenario that the historically known social formations might allow. One *kurios* of a moderately well-to-do household had a decent Greek education and a long-standing interest in ancient books, ancient wisdom and the interpretation of prophetic writings. He may have studied some of the numerous collections of oracles that circulated in Rome, consulted experts in the *disciplina Etrusca* (Ertuscan divinatory arts), or Chaldean and Egyptian books in the past. But he had come to have a major interest in ancient Judean writings, perhaps by way of a Judean expert. In the recent past, he had also studied with an itinerant Judean expert who taught the idea that the Judean writings focused on the figure of a Judean martyr, Jesus Christ. And this freelance interpreter was networked somehow with Paul or with one of Paul's associates and was able to convey some of the teachings for which Paul was known. At any rate, someone had communicated to Paul that the circle around this *kurios* had found Paul's version of the Christ myth persuasive and the apostle took this as a providential opportunity to develop supporters for his work in Spain.

This *kurios*, let us call him Demetrius, had a grown son, and two slaves whom he had educated, and all three were part of a longstanding study circle. Other members of the rather large household may have listened in the shadows from time to time, and understood a little of what was said. Further, Demetrius had a close friend, head of a similar household who was a sometimes-dedicated participant of the study circle who brought with him auditors and discussants, especially when various Judean experts might be passing through Rome and willing to expound on topics of interest. Through his network, perhaps by way of Prisca and Aquila, who had a Pauline *ekklesia* in their house in Rome,

Paul may have heard about Demetrius and his circle and his acceptance of or openness to his Christ interpretation of the Judean writings. Some associated with the circle probably had been baptized by one of itinerant teachers of the new movement. Altogether the "interested" formed a loose but substantial circle of people centered on two substantial households.

Paul then wrote Romans, a dense letter intensely interpreting the scriptures in complex ways that would have impressed and challenged just this sort of circle, making Paul stand out from other freelance teachers. Paul knew that they were not fully indoctrinated followers of his version of the Christ message, but sought by way of the letter to mold them into followers, to describe and address them as fellow travelers so as to evoke a Pauline self-understanding. As chapter 15 suggests, Paul's strategy included enticing these people to become strategic supporters of his mission to Spain. The letter's rather open-ended address to interested Gentiles in Rome aimed to make them into committed Pauline Gentiles in Rome as he prepared to visit. The message about the future of Jews and Gentiles in God's prophetic plans for world history aimed at the interests of people like Demetrius; so also, the teachings about self-mastery and self-transformation by way of Christ and his *pneuma*. Over against other Judean experts, the letter urges the gentile hearers not to aspire to become Jews, but to join in God's special plan for chosen gentiles.[28] Paul, at the end of the letter, also tried to encourage Demetrius and his circle to connect with Paul's own network in Rome by asking people in the circle to carry his greetings to these Pauline associates of various sort.

Why is this a more plausible historical scenario and explanation than the traditional church or churches in Rome or Christians in synagogues? First, I invoke Occam's razor, the principle of parsimony in explanation. The approach involves many fewer assumptions and still explains the letter. Second, this economy relates to the approach's principle of social formation from what is known to exist socially to what is in the process of being formed. The specifics of my scenario are just speculation, but the social and cultural formations and processes are well known and plausible. In traditional accounts, Christianity and the church are always already there. Third, the approach employs categories such as social networks, freelance religious experts, literate intellectual practices, divinatory practices, households and so on that cut across the concepts of Christianity and Judaism and thus do not continually reinscribe historically implausible uniqueness and *sui generis* social formation. Instead, the unknowns – Christianity and Judaism – get redescribed in terms that make them understandable in the ancient historical context. Fourth, the

---

[28] *The So-Called Jew in Paul's Letter to the Romans* ed. Rafael Rodriguez and Matthew Thiessen (Minneapolis: Fortress, 2016).

scenario avoids the myth of the apostolic gospel seen in Acts and Eusebius, but also in Paul's letters. In this myth, the message automatically produced communities of fully agreeing and committed believers rather than the humanly plausible degrees of acceptance and rejection and appropriation of the message to one's own understandings and interests.

PART III

Paul's Message and Objectives

CHAPTER SIX

The Dilemma of Paul's Physics: Features Stoic-Platonist or Platonist-Stoic?

Paul of the New Testament letters was not a philosopher, but more than a century of scholarship has shown that he nevertheless knew and used philosophical terms and concepts.[1] The letters possess a philosophical element, but how to construe both the philosophical affinities of those features and the degree of coherence among them remains a matter of debate. Troels Engberg-Pedersen has made a brilliant case for a substantial and coherent Stoic element.[2] Others, including myself, have argued for significant Platonic features also and an appropriation that is more piecemeal and adapted to Paul's particular interests.[3] The bulk of scholarship on Paul and philosophy has focused on moral psychology, ethics and educational-psychagogic elements in the letters. Very recent work has meanwhile taken up features that we can rightly think of as involving physics and ontology.[4]

---

[1] A large bibliography exists on Paul and philosophy, e.g., the bibliographies of Troels Engberg-Pedersen, *Cosmology and Self in the Apostle Paul: The Material Spirit* (Oxford: Oxford University Press, 2010); Abraham J. Malherbe, *Paul and the Popular Philosophers* (Minneapolis: Fortress, 1989).
[2] Troels Engberg-Pedersen, *Paul and the Stoics* (Edinburgh: T&T Clark, 2000); idem, *Cosmology and Self*.
[3] Stowers, *Rereading of Romans*; Chapter Eight in this volume ("Paul's Four Discourses About Sin"); idem, "The Apostle Paul" in *The History of the Western Philosophy of Religion*, ed. Graham Oppy and N. N. Trakakis, vol. 1 (Oxford: Routledge, 2009), 145–57; and especially idem, "Paul and Self-Mastery," in *Paul in the Greco-Roman World*, ed. J. Paul Sampley, vol. 2 (London: T&T Clark, 2016); Emma Wasserman, *The Death of the Soul in Romans 7*, WUNT 2/256 (Tübingen: Mohr Siebeck, 2008); idem, "Paul beyond the Judaism/Hellenism divide? The Case of Pauline Anthropology in Romans 7 and 2 Corinthians 4–5," in *Christian Origins and Hellenistic Judaism: Social and Literary Contexts for the New Testament*, ed. Stanley E. Porter and Andrew Pitts, TENTS 10 (Leiden: Brill, 2012); George H. van Kooten, *Paul's Anthropology in Context*, WUNT 232 (Tübingen: Mohr Siebeck, 2008); M. David Litwa, *We Are Being Transformed*, BZNW 187 (Berlin: de Gruyter, 2012); Laura Dingeldein, "Gaining Virtue, Gaining Christ: Moral Development in the Letters of Paul" (PhD diss., Brown University, 2014).
[4] See Chapter Seven in this volume ("What is Pauline Participation in Christ?"); van Kooten, *Paul's Anthropology*; Engberg-Pedersen, *Cosmology and Self*; Litwa, *We are Being Transformed*.

Paul ranks by broad scholarly agreement as a thinker centrally informed by Judean apocalyptic beliefs and he interprets Jesus Christ according to these beliefs. My own thesis about the genesis and sense of the major physical ideas in Paul's thought is as follows. Sometime in the 30s CE Paul came into contact with people who organized themselves around the belief that the executed Judean teacher, Jesus, had returned to life and had become a god serving the Judean high god. His resurrection was the beginning of a crisis in history that would eventuate in a resurrection of the righteous dead. Paul came to accept these beliefs and claimed that he had a vision in which Christ commanded him to teach about this scenario to non-Jews. After so many centuries of Christian culture in the West, this may not seem a striking idea, but the very notion of a "salvation" movement of Judeans for non-Judeans based on ideas about a Jew who became a god should be odd for the critical historian and in need of explanation. I would argue that central to this puzzle is Paul's conviction that when God brought Jesus Christ back to life he had been remade of a particular substance, a very special kind or quality of πνεῦμα (hereafter *pneuma*). This idea of Christ as what one might call the *pneuma*-bearer made Paul's teachings distinctive and adaptable to audiences of Greeks and Romans. Thus, at the very genesis of a movement that would involve making a local Judean figure into a god who was forcefully marketed throughout the Roman Empire lies a particular physical doctrine.

There have been numerous apologetic attempts to construe Paul's idea of divine *pneuma* as purely Jewish, but these attempts fail badly and the apologetic strategy of using the idea of a pure Judaism to protect Christianity from "pagan" influence is now well known and critically deflated.[5] Paul certainly draws on ideas of God's breath and divine breaths from the LXX and Judean literature, but interprets these with Stoic features as Engberg-Pedersen has shown.[6] I cannot argue a case about the relation of the Judean traditions to the Stoic here, but some brief points are in order. The Judean ideas are far from uniquely Jewish, but versions of folk beliefs about the role of wind/air/breath in the way that the world works, especially regarding human life, the nature of gods, and their "breaths." These beliefs were common to all cultures of the ancient Mediterranean and West Asia.[7] These folk beliefs were the starting point for what Greek philosophers, beginning with the Presocratics, said about *pneuma* and would theorize about pneuma. The folk uses in the Hebrew Bible and LXX, mostly in narrative literature, are hardly philosophical theorization and they are open to numerous interpretations.

---

[5] Smith, *Drudgery Divine*. Litwa (*We are Being Transformed*, 131–33) does a good job of answering one of the "Jewish only" naively modernist apologetics.

[6] Engberg-Pedersen, *Cosmology and Self*.

[7] On the West Asian, Egyptian and Akkadian background to Psalm 104 and Yahweh as creator by his breath, see Mark S. Smith, *The Origins of Biblical Monotheism: Israel's Polytheistic Background and the Ugaritic Texts* (Oxford: Oxford University Press, 2008), 69–75, with bibliography.

Stoic-like and Platonic-like Features

What follows is an attempt to sort out some of the Stoic-like and Platonic-like features with the goal of understanding Paul's ontological ideas.[8] This assessment, however, will require seeking clues from the letters in several areas of thought such as moral psychology and eschatology, that are inseparable from Paul's notions about physics. Engberg-Pedersen admits Paul's use of Platonic language in places, but finds a consistent Stoicism underlying such texts. I want to take a different approach and allow the Platonic-like features to stand unless I find clear reasons to give them another reading. Engberg-Pedersen's approach may well be the best one, but I want to avoid the possibility of forcing an underlying consistency and allow for other sorts of explanations, one of which I will propose below. The hope is that this treatment will make comparison with Engberg-Pedersen's reading possible and illuminate the issues of interpretation.

Strategically, I will begin with an area of thought that scholars usually pass over with a couple of comments, which is Paul's thought about the Judean God – the god of the universe. Typically, scholars assert that Paul's God has no ontology or is beyond ontology.[9] Suspiciously, the same view about God has become the standard modern Christian theological position and seems blatantly anachronistic. Paul does not shy away from predicating properties and conditions of God that involve physical ideas. The old strategy of declaring such language merely metaphorical or symbolic cannot be applied cogently or consistently and would not be used by scholars for non-Christian writings. I have two major points for this large topic.

First, Paul's basic conception of God is that of an incomparable cosmic emperor who rules within the universe that he made from preexisting matter.[10] One sees this conception in writings from the Hebrew Bible that scholars have shown to follow West Asian traditions, especially Neo-Assyrian and Neo-Babylonian.[11] But one can find similar ideas about Zeus in Greek materials.[12] God exercises

---

[8] These categories only fit from our modern and ancient philosophical perspectives.
[9] Engberg-Pedersen, *Cosmology and the Self*, 59, 61, 83.
[10] Emma Wasserman, *Apocalypse as Holy War: Divine Politics and Polemics in the Letters of Paul*, (New Haven: Yale University Press, 2018). Smith (*Origins*) is excellent on Israelite beliefs about their high god (and Judean in *God in Translation: Deities in Cross-Cultural Discourse in the Biblical World*, [Tübingen: Mohr Siebeck, 2008]) in spite of his conceptually tortured attempt to redeem a concept of monotheism. Stowers ("Gods, Monotheism and Ancient Mediterranean Religion" [paper presented at the Brown Seminar for Culture and Religion of the Ancient Mediterranean, 2012, and the Columbia University New Testament Seminar]) shows that the idea of monotheism was invented in the mid-seventeenth century and is impossible to square with ancient Jewish and Christian beliefs.
[11] Smith, *Origins*, 149–85.
[12] Jonathan L. Ready, "Zeus, Ancient Near Eastern Notions of Divine Incomparability, and Similes in the Homeric Epics," *ClAnt* 31 (2012): 56–91.

control over the cosmos by means of the cosmic order that he established, including the norms, properties and materials of the cosmos, and by means of innumerable legions of divine underlings. This openly anthropomorphic understanding of God and other gods is impossible to square with Stoic non-anthropomorphic doctrines. God also expresses emotions and acts unpredictably in ways that the Stoic or Platonic god could not. God's fit with the created cosmos rules out a later Platonic high god. It is difficult to imagine a distinct noetic realm with Paul's conceptions, but this renders the letters' Platonic-like ideas difficult to explain. Paul predicates a very large number of activities in the cosmos and the human scene to his god. God is busy like the Stoic god, a characteristic much criticized by Platonists, but in an anthropomorphic way rather than only by immanent rational ordering of the details of the cosmos and its processes.[13]

When Paul writes of God's throne, Christ at his right hand and battles with heavenly armies, the language is not a code for some less anthropomorphic, philosophical view. Nothing in the letters indicates such symbolic discursive practices and readers could not have known from what Paul writes about God in the letters that a non-anthropomorphic conception was Paul's. After all, the anthropomorphic understanding of the gods was the default belief for most people in Paul's time and not the theology of philosophers.[14]

One feature of Paul's language about God, Christ and Christ-people usually overlooked or treated as symbolic comes in the extensive use of δόξα, following traditions from the Hebrew Bible, meaning visual splendor or glowing or brightness, sometimes described as a kind of fire.[15] I am convinced that Plato and Platonists invented the idea of bodiless gods, and the opposite was the standard Mediterranean and West Asian assumption. Gods had very special bodies that were normally invisible to humans. In the J materials for the Hebrew Bible, in Ezekiel, and the Priestly Source, God unambiguously has a body often characterized as shining or glowing.[16] There is no evolution to "a more spiritual understanding." Scholarship has conventionally considered the P source as one of the latest, usually exilic or post-exilic, and as responsible for putting together

---

[13] Thomas Bénatouïl, "How Industrious can Zeus be? The Extent and Objects of Divine Activity in Stoicism" in *God and Cosmos in Stoicism*, ed. Ricardo Salles (Oxford: Oxford University Press, 2009), 23–45.

[14] See Chapter One in this volume.

[15] Helpful, in spite of its modernist theological hermeneutic, is Carey Newman, *Paul's Glory-Christology: Tradition and Rhetoric* (Leiden: Brill, 1991); Litwa's (*We are Being Transformed*, 119–36) discussion of divine bodies and glory is astute and brings in both Greek and biblical comparative material. He, however, misses Paul's differences from celestial immortality and makes the idea too important for Stoics.

[16] Benjamin D. Sommer, *The Bodies of God and the World of Ancient Israel* (Cambridge: Cambridge University Press, 2009), 1–57; Newman, *Paul's Glory-Christology*. Unfortunately, Sommer confuses aniconism with bodiless gods and believes that the Israelites became monotheists.

most of the Pentateuch. Greek, wider Mediterranean and West Asian materials also attest to the idea that gods had very special kinds of bodies characterized by bright splendor.[17] Paul proclaims (Phil 3:20–21) that the citizenship of his Philippian followers is in heaven. They await Christ who will transform their bodies of humiliation so as to conform to Christ's body of splendor, "an eternal degree of splendor far beyond measure" (2 Cor 4:17). In 1 Cor 15:43, the corruptible body is sown in dishonor, but it will be raised in splendor. This splendor will be like that of the sun, moon and stars (15:41). The good news announces the light of Christ's splendor, Christ who is the image of God (2 Cor 4:4). *Pneuma* and visible splendor seems to be a common denominator between God, Christ and Christ-people with their new bodies. Platonists might have to explain the visibility of incorporeal and therefore invisible heavenly bodies above the moon, but it was not a problem for Stoics, for whom glowing might be a natural property of aether or pure *pneuma*.[18]

Paul does not flinch from using language about God that implies ontological assumptions. As Engberg-Pederson has emphasized, Paul's language about the materials of the universe features *pneuma*.[19] Jesus Christ was refashioned in the resurrection from *pneuma* and Christ followers will receive a body of *pneuma* when Christ returns.[20] The pneumatic body that Paul suggests will have qualities similar to or superior to the stars and planets will replace a body made from earthy material.[21] This "*pneuma* of God" or "holy *pneuma*" is clearly higher and distinct from the *pneuma* related to ordinary consciousness and cognition that all human beings possess.[22] So Paul assumes something like differing qualities of *pneuma* – at least two – divine and human. He also writes of the "*pneuma* of the cosmos" as opposed to divine *pneuma*.[23] The sentence makes it difficult to construe the phrase, but the idea of a Stoic-like *pneuma* organizing the world is one possibility.

In light of later Christian theology, 1 Cor 2:10–13 would seem to make similarity and contiguity between humans and God too strong if read literally, yet there are no good historical or philological reasons for a symbolic reading:

> God has revealed [the mysteries of his plans for the world] through his *pneuma*. For the *pneuma* searches everything, even the depths of God.

---

[17] Jean-Pierre Vernant, *Mortals and Immortals: Collected Essays*, ed. Froma I. Zeitlin (Princeton: Princeton University Press, 1991), 27–49; Smith, *Origins*, 86–97.
[18] Zeno described a heavenly body as "rational and wise, burning with designing fire" (*SVF* 1.120).
[19] Engberg-Pedersen, *Cosmology and Self*.
[20] For Rom 1:4; 1 Cor 15:42–49, and texts that imply both points, see Engberg-Pedersen, *Cosmology and Self*, 41–58.
[21] 1 Cor 15:38–41. The substances of the cosmos have degrees of splendor and lack thereof. The most splendid are the highest stars and the resurrection body is from heaven (1 Cor 15:47–49).
[22] Rom 8:16; 1 Cor 2:11; 1 Thess 5:23; cf. Rom 1:9.
[23] 1 Cor 2:12.

> For what human knows the things of a human except a human *pneuma*? So also no one knows the things of God except the *pneuma* of God. But we have not received the *pneuma* of the cosmos, but the *pneuma* out of God so that we might understand the things given to us by God.[24]

Paul goes on to write that the person with God's *pneuma* is able to understand these mysteries by means of that *pneuma*, but the soulish person who presumably only possesses normal human *pneuma* cannot understand them. Elsewhere he speaks of a "soulish body" (1 Cor 15:44). Both "soulish person" and "soulish body," I think, mean something like the Platonic irrational soul in its attachment to the body. Paul writes (1 Cor 2:15–16): "The pneumatic person critically judges all things, but is critically judged by no one. 'For who has known the νοῦς (mind) of the Lord so as to instruct him? But we have the νοῦς of Christ.'"

We learn a number of things here. The passage highlights the impossibility of treating "the *pneuma* of God" as only an objective genitive, the *pneuma* that God gives to people. God has or is a type of *pneuma*. God's *pneuma* has cognitive and communicative powers. Those who have been baptized into Christ also have this *pneuma* in them and thus share its cognitive and communicative powers. This situation contrasts with the cognitive and communicative limitations of people who have only an ordinary human soul, that Paul later in the letter describes as mortal, decaying and made of earthy material (1 Cor 15:45–49). The analogy between the God of the universe and Christ followers is quite striking: "The *pneuma* searches everything even the depths of God" and humans share in this *pneuma* so that they share some of God's privileged knowledge. Paul's language here indicates contiguity and extension. One might imagine a Platonic explanation for the contiguity, if *pneuma* were taken to be νοῦς in which humans share, but not the extension, of course.

At this point the reader probably wants to object that I am taking loose metaphorical language too literally. My response is that one simply cannot but do violence to the letters by invoking metaphor in this way. One example comes in 6:12–20 of this letter. There Paul tells the Corinthians that if they have sex with prostitutes, they will be joining Christ to the body of the prostitute because believers share one *pneuma* with Christ. Using metaphor, he says their bodies are body parts of Christ and are temples of the divine *pneuma*. The connection with Christ by way of the *pneuma* is like that of an individual's hand to its arm. "Body" and "temple" are metaphors here, but the contiguity with Christ cannot be. Paul's teaching on the divine *pneuma* has a strong emphasis on contiguity – one *pneuma* shared – and extension. *Pneuma* occupies

---

[24] On this text and its context, see Dingeldein, "Gaining Virtue, Gaining Christ."

time and space and has causal effects on physical entities. Paul does not speak of the holy *pneuma* as if it were some sort of spirit or ghost, an anthropomorphic agent that flies back and forth between God, Christ and believers. Rather, as Engberg-Pedersen has argued, his conception suggests Stoic ideas about *pneuma*. One could also add the evidence of Paul's extensive realistic language about the baptized being "in Christ" and Christ being in them. As noted above, he also makes *pneuma* the stuff of the resurrection body of Christ and of Christ followers, that is, on the opposite end of the scale of substances in the cosmos from earth as the lowest.

But what then is the mind? In the text above (1 Cor 2:10–14), after claims about the abilities of the divine *pneuma* to provide knowledge regarding God's plans and critical discernment, we hear that believers have the mind, the νοῦς, of Christ (2:16). They will have the same kind of pneumatic body as Christ in the future, but in the present they have the νοῦς of Christ. I think it unlikely that the mind of Christ is anything other than the portion of holy *pneuma* that occupies the current flesh bodies of Christ followers as 2:10–16 and other texts imply.[25]

If the transformed mind is divine *pneuma* from Christ, then it is striking to find Platonic-like features in connection with νοῦς in the letters. These appear especially in texts about moral psychology and about the transformation of those who are in Christ. It seems very difficult to construe Paul's many texts about the mind/body relation and the relation of the mind to the appetitive desires and emotions in any other way than Platonic. Romans 6–8 has been popularly construed by way of twentieth century categories of existence as a primordial dimension of human being and tied to a symbolist reading of "Sin" and "Death," but I am quite sure that Paul never read Martin Heidegger or his Marburg colleague Rudolf Bultmann.[26] The key to Romans 7 has been decisively described in the scholarship of Emma Wasserman: the individual in the chapter represents a case of total moral failure in Platonic terms.[27]

In sharp contrast to the Stoic moral psychology, which stresses psychophysical holism, Paul has a parts-based psychology.[28] In Romans 7, the "I" constructed with the rhetorical technique of προσωποποιία disassociates itself from its own flesh, that is, body, earlier called "body of sin" (6:6).[29] The true self in a rebellious body of flesh does not do what it wants to do (7:14–20). In fact, it does what it hates. No good lies in the true self's flesh (7:18). In other

---

[25] Litwa, *We are Being Transformed*, 206 n. 27.
[26] Among critiques, see Paul S. Macdonald, *History of the Concept of Mind: Speculations about Soul, Mind and Spirit from Homer to* Hume (Aldershot: Ashgate, 2003).
[27] Wasserman, *The Death of the Soul*.
[28] Christopher Gill, *The Structured Self in Hellenistic and Roman Thought* (Oxford: Oxford University Press, 2006).
[29] On the rhetoric, see Stowers, *Rereading of Romans*, 264–72.

words, the true self has been so overpowered by appetitive desire (ἐπιθυμία) and passions (πάθη) that it no longer controls what the body does. The condition is worse than simple ἀκρασία. The true self has been taken captive, enslaved and lives in a "body of death" (7:24). As is typical with a parts psychology, Paul constantly attributes features of mind to the irrational soul or body. Wasserman has shown that from Plato to Philo, Plutarch and Galen, Platonists employed metaphors and images of captivity, attack, enslavement and so on to depict the emotions and appetites, the irrational soul, when unchecked by the mind. By contrast, Stoicism does not have distinct rational and irrational parts. The whole psychophysical human being is ordered by rationality. In spite of passages in Epictetus and other Roman Stoics that negatively contrast the body to moral purpose, Stoicism does not ordinarily treat the body and emotions as inherently irrational. Roman Stoics, most importantly Epictetus and Seneca, do sometimes use the language of parts as if there were an inherently irrational element.[30] But there is an important difference in comparison with Paul. These Stoics elsewhere make it clear that they reject a parts-based moral psychology, and the language in question appears only to be incautious rhetoric. But Paul's letters show no reticence about such dualism.

What is the true self in Romans 7? Paul's language is unambiguous. It is the mind, the νοῦς (7:23, 25). Moreover, Paul also calls it the "inner person" (7:22). This image comes from Plato's story of the beast, the lion and the little person inside (the mind) in the *Republic* (9.588c–591b). Regarding Paul's physics, I find it important that although the mind here has totally lost control of the passions and appetites of its own body, it still intrinsically desires the good and the law of God. This strongly suggests an ontological difference from the body and an ontological connection to the good and with God. Admittedly, Paul does not spell out this connection explicitly, but it seems to be implied. The mind "wants" the good (7:14–20). The inner person "delights in its connection with" (συνήδομαι) the law of God (7:22) and "agrees" that God's law is good by its innate desire to do what is right (7:16). The νοῦς still serves God's law, the good, even as its flesh and body-parts serve the law of sin (7:25). In the argument of the letter, chapter 7 tries to show that the Judean law is of no help to the non-Jew without the *pneuma* of God to empower their mind. But the moral psychology used in this rhetoric is Platonic with a mind of a different order than its body/irrational soul.

Numerous texts suggest a Platonic-like mind or true self in that it is distinct from the body and at home in a higher realm. Paul writes (2 Cor 12:2–3) that he once traveled to the third heaven, likely where the court of God is.

---

[30] See Inwood in n. 60 below. I find both a parts based moral psychology and a dualism of mind/ *pneuma* versus flesh body/irrational soul of earthy material in Paul.

Whether this trip occurred while he was in his body or outside of his body, he does not know (v. 2). "In the body" suggests a miracle of God such as in other Jewish writings in which a person is taken up bodily into the heavens.[31] But it also seems easy for Paul to talk of his self as capable of leaving his body. He would rather be away from the body and with Christ. Christ lives a pneumatic existence in the heavens, so being in the body means being away from him (2 Cor 5:6–9). At present, Christ people live in an earthly tent, but they will soon live in an eternal heavenly tent not made by hands (2 Cor 5:1–2).[32] The current state of mortality weighs them down (2 Cor 5:4), but the *pneuma* given now is a guarantee of the full pneumatic existence (v. 5). At present, they see only enigmatically in a mirror, but finally they will see face to face (1 Cor 13:12). What can be seen is temporary, but the unseen is eternal (2 Cor 4:18).

The pneumatic body awaits the near future. That which is empowered, lifted up and transformed now is the mind and not the body. In Romans 8, the νοῦς (mind) overpowered by appetites and emotion gets power from God's *pneuma* that allows its own thinking to control the thinking of the flesh. As noted above, 1 Cor 2:11–16 makes clear that the divine *pneuma*, rendering one pneumatic instead of soulish, is the same condition as having the mind of Christ. Romans 12:1–3 calls on the readers to serve God rationally (τὴν λογικὴν λατρείαν) and to be transformed by a renewal of the νοῦς that entails discernment of the good and God's will with a range of virtues (vv. 2–21). Scholars have often noted the Platonic tone of 2 Cor 4:16–18, but treated the ideas dismissively as mere linguistic borrowing:

> though the outward person is rotting away, our inner person is being renewed from one day to the next. For this minor momentary suffering is equipping us for an eternal degree of bright splendor far beyond measure, not gazing at what can be seen but what is invisible, for the visible is transitory, but the invisible is eternal.

Here again one meets Plato's image for the mind, the inner person, together with the idea of its gradual renewal and language that could be understood as

---

[31] Engberg-Pedersen's (*Cosmology and Self*, 89) interpretation of the passage with the idea of types of pneumatic bodily states seems unconvincing to me. "Out of the body" can only refer to Paul's true self, his mind, to be sure, made of *pneuma*. "In the body," must mean his current flesh body.

[32] I agree with Engberg-Pedersen (*Cosmology and Self*, 48–50) that the heavenly dwelling is the pneumatic body, but the true self in the terrible earthly dwelling must be a Platonic-like mind in a Platonic-like body of a different ontological order. The contrast here is not a Stoic one between one's character and choices that are under one's control and externals such as the body that are not. The underlying problem for Paul is the decaying nature of the substance(s) that make up the body.

contemplation of the intelligible realm by the mind, although I have already pointed out the difficulties with the sensible/noetic split in Paul. The transformation and the contemplation must be physical, or quasi-physical, if such an idea might be permitted. The mind that is daily being transformed does not want to be naked at death, but to be clothed with a heavenly dwelling (5:1–5). This dwelling could be understood as a pneumatic vehicle for a rational soul/ mind as in later Platonism, but texts indicate that the person will be entirely of *pneuma* as the mind itself seems to be.[33]

Paul's language for God's *pneuma* and the empowerment of the mind is part of an equally important idea for Paul of assimilation to Christ.[34] But the material in the letters for this Platonic motif only exacerbates the problem of Stoic-like material *pneuma* in a Platonic-like framework, or as Engberg-Pedersen has argued, Platonic-like language in a Stoic framework. A key text is 2 Cor 3:18. The chapter has typically been read in anachronistic ways as describing the supersession of Judaism by the new religion, Christianity. More plausibly, and with abundant textual evidence, Paul has been attacked in Corinth by other Judean Christ teachers for his character and his teachings.[35]

Chapter 3 seeks to undermine their claims to be interpreters of Christ by way of the Judean scriptures. Paul contrasts their approach through textual interpretation to his direct access to Christ who is God's *pneuma* (already in 3:1–3). The chapter presents Moses both as the recipient of the law and the prototype of one who is transformed by seeing God. The message of Paul's competitors is only the reiteration of the dead letter that has missed the direct vision of the divine. The Israelites were not able to bear the shining splendor of Moses's face after he had seen God because their thoughts (νοήματα) were petrified. By contrast, Paul's faithful Corinthians (3:18) "all with unveiled faces seeing the Lord's glory as if reflected in a mirror are being transformed into the same image from shining splendor to shining splendor as from the Lord, the *pneuma*."

Paul seems to be claiming that his labor is distinctively powerful in that it brings about transformation by the contemplation of a god. His acolytes are in

---

[33] For the person as totally pneumatic, Engberg-Pedersen (*Cosmology and Self*) and Litwa (*We are Being Transformed*). For Litwa, deification is assimilation to Christ's pneumatic body.

[34] Assimilation to Christ also encompasses what is widely called "participation in Christ." See Chapter Seven in this volume. Best on assimilation in Paul is Litwa *We are Being Transformed*, but also van Kooten *Paul's Anthropology*. Litwa and van Kooten do not sufficiently situate assimilation in Platonic thought and tend to blur it with the very different Stoic idea of imitation of God. They also rather strangely focus on what they call "moral assimilation" as if there were some distinction between the ontological and the moral in Platonic ideas about assimilation.

[35] On the letter's integrity and argument, see Ivar Vegge, *2 Corinthians – a Letter about Reconciliation*, WUNT 2/239 (Tübingen: Mohr Siebeck, 2008). For Paul's opponents, see 2:17–3:3, and 11:4–5, 13 ("super apostles," "false apostles, "deceitful workers"). On their identity as Jewish teachers about Christ, see 11:22–23.

the process of divinization by seeing Christ with the eyes of the mind. Christ is divine *pneuma*, and those who gaze on him gradually become pneumatic beings beginning with the divinization of their minds and developing the character of Christ. Four verses later he writes (4:4–6):

> the god of this age has blinded the thoughts (νοήματα) of the unbelievers so that they might not see the illumination of the good news of the shining splendor of Christ who is the image (εἰκών) of God ... [Christ] who is the illumination of the knowledge of the shining splendor of God in the face of Jesus Christ.

These passages raise a great may issues, but clearly Paul is still playing on the idea of Moses's face being transformed into glowing splendor by seeing God. In Christ's case, those dedicated to him can see the glory by seeing it in his face. By seeing Christ's splendor, they see God's splendor. The texts seem to contain a remarkable combination of Stoic materialism and Platonic mentalism, with the latter seemingly rendered material. The text suggests something like Philo's Logos or second god through whom one can have a mediated knowledge of God. But Paul does not isolate God, and the possibility of Christ's pre-existence is one of the most difficult and controversial issues in Pauline scholarship.[36] Christ has God's shining splendor as he also has God's *pneuma*. Shining splendor would seem to be a feature of holy *pneuma*. Believers will participate directly in Christ's *pneuma* that Paul repeatedly calls God's *pneuma* in reference to human recipients. That God, Christ and certain humans will all participate in God's *pneuma* is the cause of all three having splendor. Humans obtain this pneumatic condition gradually to some degree before death or before Christ returns by means of focusing on Christ with the mind's eye.

The result is participation in Christ likened to the conformity of a copy to its original, again Platonic notions. Likewise in Rom 8:29, "Those whom he knew beforehand, he also planned beforehand to be conformed to (συμμόρφους) the image (εἰκόνος) of his son so that he might be the first born among many brothers." Christ is the archetype of a new pneumatic species (v. 29). The text concludes a long discussion of how the divine *pneuma* transforms the minds of Gentile adherents. When Christ returns from God's heavenly court, those who are in Christ will be "conformed to the body of his shining splendor" (Phil 3:21).[37]

I will come back to the idea of Christ as the archetype of a new species, but first a few reflections on making sense of Paul's Stoic-like and Platonic-like

---

[36] James D. G. Dunn, *Christology in the Making: A New Testament Inquiry into the Origins of the Doctrine of the Incarnation*, 2nd ed. (Grand Rapids: Eerdmans, 1996).

[37] Likewise in 1 Cor 15, the image of dust from the prototype of Adam will be replaced by the image of Christ's heavenly pneumatic body. See Litwa, *We are Being* Transformed, 149.

ideas. If we think of Platonism as characterized by a clear distinction between the intelligible and the sensible and related distinctions such as corporeal/incorporeal, Paul's ontological and cosmological thought seems a confused jumble of philosophical terms and commonplaces. But there is evidence that among philosophers from the first century BCE through the second century CE who sought to "rediscover" the ancient teachings of Pythagoras and Plato that the lines noted above were more fluid and less clear than often thought. Paul's Judean contemporary, Philo of Alexandria, is exhibit one.

Philo and Paul

As already noted, Paul does not have a god who, like Philo's, is beyond all attributes but one who deals rather directly and constantly with the lower world. But if one brackets the distinct intelligible realm, then a comparison of the two figures is useful. I suspect that the immanent physicality and constant activity of Yahweh, El and Elohim in the Hebrew Bible, not hidden by the Greek translations, may have encouraged Philo to develop an ontology that had an unnamed ontological area between the sensible and the noetic, sharing some of each as a background for divine activity. In other words, it may have made intuitive sense to Philo that there be a higher yet more immanent ontological correlate to the roles of the Logos, angels, rational souls (minds) and the heavenly bodies. Where later Platonists gave analogous noetic beings bodies of pure fire, sometimes thought of as pure *pneuma*, Philo made these dwellers of the sub-intelligible realm souls/minds consisting of pure fire or pure *pneuma*.[38] Philo also complicates things further by attributing such an ontology to heavenly bodies above the moon in a way that seems more Stoic than Platonic.[39]

Philo's writings afford many striking illustrations. Unfortunately, we cannot be sure of the Greek from the extant Armenian of *Questions and Answers on Genesis*, but with what seems an ontological contradiction, Philo writes, "the substance of angels is spiritual . . . sometimes he calls the angels 'sons of God' because they are made incorporeal through no mortal man, but are spirits" (QG 1.92). The relevant Greek words here are likely to have been πνευματική, ἀσώματοι and πνεύματα. What does it mean for *pneuma* to be immaterial and the substance of sons of Gods? Even stranger from the perspective of a more standard later Platonism, Philo has the mind, the Logos in its immanent role, the stars and planets made of *pneuma* or pure fire.[40] At *Fug.*

---

[38] John Dillon, "ASŌMATOS: Nuances of Incorporeality in Philo," in *Philon d'Alexandrie et le langage de la philosophie*, ed. Carlos Lévy (Turnhout: Brepols, 1998), 99–110, at 110 and n. 3. For pure fire and *pneuma*, see the Dillon article and below. Sometimes Philo writes that the soul consists of aether (*Leg.* 3.161).

[39] Dillon, "ASŌMATOS," 104–6.

[40] Also Dillon, "ASŌMATOS."

133, the mind (νοῦς) is said to be "hot and burning *pneuma*" and the substance of the rational soul is "divine *pneuma*" (*Spec.* 4.123). Scholars have often treated such passages as inconsistencies or as forced upon Philo by Gen 2:7.[41]

I find two possible ways of understanding Philo's challenging language to be less plausible than what I will present below. The first would find him to be simply confused, a philosophical bungler who could not keep his concepts straight. But this goes against the consensus of specialists on Philo, who find that he fully understands Plato's ideas about the noetic and the sensible and texts where Plato has the mind leave behind the sensible world to join the noetic.[42] The second approach treats Philo's language as perhaps sloppy and incomplete, but as having a coherent Platonic thought hidden behind it. When Philo writes that an angel or the mind is made of fire or *pneuma*, he forgets to mention that these are incorporeal noetic beings. The fire or *pneuma* here would be like higher kinds of bodies for the noetic essence. But this reads too much into Philo. His language in these texts equates fire/*pneuma* and incorporeal existence.

Another solution, following arguments made by John Dillon, is to conclude that ἀσώματος (immaterial) meant something somewhat different for Philo than has usually been assumed.[43] In the way it is commonly used, a body or something material has three-dimensional extension, offers resistance, and can act on or be acted on causally. As Dillon argues, Philo's fire and *pneuma* is almost certainly a version of Stoic designing fire (πῦρ τεχνικόν).[44] That fire is unchanging and indestructible. I would add that it is also invisible. Changelessness, indestructibility and invisibility to sensible vision are characteristics of Platonic noetic substance. Philo's *pneuma* or pure fire of minds, angels and heavenly bodies is not the ordinary *pneuma* that for the Stoics was a combination of the divine fire and the element air.[45] It is the divine fire alone. For Philo, then, ἀσώματος may have been a category encompassing substances that have extension and can act on other substances, but that are indestructible, unchanging, and invisible.

Philo's example then implies that Paul would not have to have had a thoroughgoing Stoic physics to have held that heavenly bodies, some divine beings, and human minds consisted of *pneuma*, albeit a form inferior to God's *pneuma*, but nevertheless inherently orienting human minds to God.[46] With

---

[41] So, Thomas Tobin, *The Creation of Man: Philo and the History of Interpretation*, CBQMS 14 (Washington, DC: Catholic Biblical Association of America, 1983). On Gen 2:7, see David T. Runia, *Philo of Alexandria, On the Creation of the Cosmos according to Moses: Introduction, Translation and Commentary* (Leiden: Brill, 2001), 321–29.

[42] David T. Runia, *Philo of Alexandria and the "Timaeus" of Plato* (Leiden: Brill, 1986), 332–33.

[43] Dillon, "ASŌMATOS."

[44] Dillon, "ASŌMATOS," 106–10.

[45] Plato, of course, wrote that the heavens were made mostly of fire and specifically the fixed stars (*Tim.* 40a).

[46] For the heavenly bodies, see Engberg-Pedersen, *Cosmology and Self*, 27–28.

Paul's contrast between restored mind/divine *pneuma* and lower elements such as earth and flesh, his ontological and cosmological inspirations might have come from those contemporaries in the first century who were seeking to discover the ancient teachings of Pythagoras, Plato and even Moses, but mixed with a good deal of Stoicism. Of course, in this scenario, Paul went his own way by replacing the duality of the sensible and the noetic with a duality of lower changeable, mixed, and decaying elements versus the divine *pneuma* as pure, unchanging and indestructible. It was also invisible to normal human vision, although having a radiant splendor to those with eyes of the mind or to special humans to whom God, Christ or an angel might choose to reveal themselves. This fiery divine substance would make sense to Philo and Paul whose sacred scripture often had God appear as a kind of fire as, for instance, in the highly influential vision of Ezekiel (1:4, 13–14, 27).

Both Philo and Paul, I believe, have lower and divine forms of *pneuma*. Both writers say that divine *pneuma* is a substance that belongs in the heavenly realms (1 Cor 15:40–49). Philo emphasizes that it is light, ethereal and naturally "wants" to rise to its home in the heavens (*Aet.* 28, 33). Both also at least imply that its nature is to be unmixed. The future body in Paul is made only and fully of *pneuma*, as is the mind already in the present. Paul's idea seems to be that the divine pneuma gradually replaces the natural human *pneuma* of the mind. Paul has no highly transcendent god. Like other West Asian high gods, he created the cosmos out of pre-existing stuff, and he rules it through legions of intermediaries, cosmic substances and laws. There is no intelligible realm, but there is a cosmic hierarchy of substances that explains, among other things, the human tendency to disobey God and have decaying bodies even though the mind is inherently drawn to God. Philo's hierarchy of substances below the moon has similarities to Paul's and does some of the same explanatory work. But as I will argue, I do not think that Paul's cosmology and physics is simply hierarchical.

Similarities also appear between Christ's pneumatic role in relation to Christ followers and Philo's notions about *pneuma*. One could conduct substantial discussions about similarity and difference, but one example (*Det.* 83) will suffice to suggest an outline:

> To the power that we have in common with the irrational beings blood has been assigned as its substance (οὐσία), but to the power that flows from the spring of reason *pneuma* has been assigned, not moving air, but like an impression and stamp of the divine power, to which Moses gives the appropriate name "image" (εἰκών), making it clear that God is the archetype of rational nature and the human being is the copy and likeness, not the animal of double nature, but the best form of soul that is called mind and reason.

Here *pneuma* is the substance of mind and mind is the image (εἰκών) of God, the archetype. The formulation reflects Philo's account of human creation in Genesis.[47] In spite of constant attempts by scholars to make "the image of God" and a fall-restoration schema central to Paul, neither of these fit.[48] The only time that Paul refers (1 Cor 11:7) to creation in the image of God, it is something that only men have, not women, and means something like the authority to rule. Christ brings a new creation not a reworking or restoration of the old one. Adam's problem was that he was created out of earth of flesh and animal soul that are prone to passion, and thus sin and decay, as almost every commentator up to Augustine emphasized.[49] "Flesh and blood cannot inherit the kingdom of God (1 Cor 15:50)." Paul's Christ is like Philo's unmixed human being who is mind of *pneuma* in the image of God. But with logic similar to later Platonists who gave their minds/souls free from flesh-bodies vehicles, sometimes of *pneuma*, Paul gives pneumatic bodies to pneumatic minds at the resurrection.[50] The transformed humans will be just as bodily as God and the heavenly retinue are in the Hebrew Bible and much Jewish literature. God recreated Jesus Christ out of his own *pneuma* in the resurrection to be the archetype of a new species.[51] This is why when Paul speaks of conforming to Christ and assimilating to Christ, he talks of transformation of the mind by Christ's *pneuma* and of Christ's *pneuma* possessing or controlling the body. The key to understanding both the origin and sense of Paul's ontology, however, lies in his apocalyptically shaped program.

Paul's Apocalypticism and Physics

What about the mission of Christ? This question introduces Paul's apocalyptic thought and distance from Philo. A great deal of recent scholarship on ancient Christianity has rejected the traditional idea that Paul sought to found a new religion of salvation to replace the inadequate religion of salvation, Judaism.[52] Paul understood himself as the Judean messenger sent by God to the non-Jews to prepare the way for Christ's return as warrior, judge and ruler, the agent for God's disciplining of the recalcitrant human and divine beings in the cosmos. He had no inkling of a new religion or of being anything else as a human

---

[47] Runia, *On the Creation*; Tobin, *The Creation of Man*.
[48] E.g., van Kooten, *Paul's Anthropology*.
[49] Stowers, "Paul's Four Discourses."
[50] This is the implication of 1 Cor 15 and the texts discussed above about the mind. The true self is what will be embodied.
[51] Thus, Paul's stinging criticisms: you are acting like a human being (1 Cor 3:3).
[52] Helpfully, Magnus Zetterholm, *Approaches to Paul: A Student's Guide to Recent Scholarship* (Minneapolis: Fortress, 2009), esp. 127–63.

than a Judean "in Christ" or that the Judean temple in Jerusalem would be destroyed. He claims that the ultimate goal of his work with the Gentiles was the salvation of his people, the Judeans (Rom 11:13–16, 25–26).

Recent scholarship has shown that later Christian dualisms pitting the kingdom of God against the kingdom of Satan misread Paul's and Jewish apocalyptic thought.[53] Indeed the constant message of the apocalyptic writings is that although it may seem from some limited local point of view that God has lost control of a part of his empire, he is still in control. Some of the subordinate lower divine beings – who do not even deserve to be called gods – have indeed run the domains allotted to them by God as break-away kingdoms, but mostly such administrators have just done a poor job overseeing the earth's peoples and have not shown the proper subordination and humble obedience to God. This is where the central theme of Christ's obedience and humility comes in. Christ is the archetype of a new species of divine beings.[54] Jesus Christ, even allowing himself to be humiliated and crucified to fulfill God's plans, was totally obedient toward God and appropriately humble before the ruler of the cosmos. Thus, God transformed him into a creature made of divine *pneuma* and brought him to his court to administer his empire (e.g., Phil 2:5–11; 1 Cor 15:23–28).

No issue more divides current scholarship than the nature of Paul's universalism.[55] I side with scholars who argue that Paul's apocalyptic scenarios have surviving humanity still divided into peoples led by the Judeans with their central temple to the supreme God around which all the nations will unite.[56] This, of course, is a case that I cannot argue here, but it has important implications for how one interprets the teachings in the letters addressed to Paul's Gentile followers.

The standard assumption that Paul teaches a new universal religion of salvation in which those converted go to heaven will not hold up in that form. The

---

[53] Emma Wasserman, "Beyond Apocalyptic Dualism: Ranks of Divinities in *1 Enoch* and Daniel," in *The One Who Sows Bountifully: Essays in Honors of Stanley K. Stowers*, ed. Caroline Johnson Hodge, Saul M. Olyan, Daniel Ullucci, and Emma Wasserman (Atlanta: Society of Biblical Literature, 2013), 189–199; *Apocalypse as Holy War*.

[54] Here I disagree with Litwa's argument (*We are Being Transformed*, 213–16) that the meaning of "moral assimilation" to Christ is his model as one humble toward other people. Paul can use Christ as model to exhort for the social solidarity of the saints, but Christ's humility is in contrast to those who have not been properly subject to God, the point of the so-called Philippian hymn (2:9–11). Christ's humility results in every creature in the cosmos prostrating themselves before him.

[55] Zetterholm, *Approaches to Paul*; Johnson Hodge, *If Sons, Then Heirs*.

[56] James M. Scott, *Paul and the Nations*, WUNT 84 (Tübingen: Mohr Siebeck, 1995); Terence L. Donaldson, *Judaism and the Gentiles: Jewish Patterns of Universalism (to 135 CE)* (Waco, TX: Baylor University Press, 2007), 499–513; Paula Fredriksen, "Judaism, the Circumcision of Gentiles, and Apocalyptic Hope: Another Look at Galatians 1 and 2," *JTS* 42 (1991): 532–64, at 544–48.

first problem comes from Paul's announcement at the end of Romans that he has completely finished his mission in the Eastern Mediterranean and will soon go to Rome and Spain to complete his work in the West (15:16–24). With his conviction that Christ's return is imminent – most of Paul's followers will be alive (1 Cor 15:51; 1 Thess 4:15) – and only a few hundred adherents in an Empire of millions, such a small number of saints does not fit the idea of world evangelism. Rather, Paul's Gentile Christ people, "conformed to his image," are being made into brothers of Christ who is the "firstborn" (Rom 8:29) and thus they have been prepared to play a special role in the apocalyptic scenario that Paul assumes. They are sons of God and co-heirs with Christ (Rom 8:17) in a secret plan (Rom 8:29–30; 1 Cor 2:7–10, 15:51–52) that will have Christ and his fellow sons of God subjugating every power in the cosmos as brothers who cannot be separated from Christ (Rom 8:35–39; cf. 1 Cor 15:23–28) and who will always be with him (1 Thess 4:17). At present, Christ sits beside God's throne in a position of power that includes testifying to God on behalf of his fellows in the process of transformation on earth (Rom 8:34). Paul thought he was facilitating the creation of a heavenly contingent of Christ-like beings, unlike many angels and gods, truly obedient and submissive to God. They would also likely be the Gentile representatives from the nations who would show the world's submission to God by bearing gifts to the temple in fulfillment of prophecy when Christ had subdued the rebellious humans, gods, and angels so as to restore Israel.[57] Other apostles were presumably responsible for assembling a contingent of Christ-like beings from the Judeans to also cosmically serve God under Christ's lordship. Whatever universal events might address the general human condition would occur after these things had happened. The first contingents of cosmic Christ people from Jews and the other nations might be the model for a general transformation of the righteous, but Paul's few hints in that direction are unclear and conflicting.[58]

If this scenario is plausible, then it explains both why Paul's followers will be remade of divine *pneuma* with direct knowledge of God's plans (1 Cor 2:10–16) and why assimilation to and participation in Christ are so overwhelmingly central to Paul's thought. Jesus Christ, in contrast to the angels and gods, is a perfectly obedient and humble (before God) character remade with a perfect material to whom Paul's Gentile's "in Christ" assimilate in character and in substance. The incorruptible *pneuma* would seem to guarantee the permanence of the character. Rom 8:23 equates full sonship with "the redemption of our bodies" and as we have seen, that means becoming fully beings made of God's *pneuma*. Paul writes that those who are in Christ will rule together

---

[57] E.g., the scriptural allusions and quotations of Rom 11:25–32; 15:7–13 and the centrality of Jerusalem (e.g., the collection from the Gentiles) to Paul's plans.
[58] E.g., Rom 5:19; 1 Cor 1:18; 15:22, 25, 51; 2 Cor 2:16–17.

with Christ, judge the cosmos (1 Cor 6:2), including even judging angels (1 Cor 6:3). Those remade in Christ's pneumatic image will be administrators under Christ's rule.[59]

When Christ descends from the heavenly court, Christ people will pass through the clouds and meet Christ and his angelic army in the ἀήρ, the region between the moon and the lower atmosphere (1 Thess 4:16–17). Joining up with this heavenly contingent headed to set things right on earth must imply that Paul's Christ people will participate. Now beings fully made of God's *pneuma* like Christ, they will be well equipped to travel about the entire cosmos and act like more perfect kinds of angels and other gods. Paul's Gentile assemblies represent non-Judeans who are more than faithful to the one supreme god, reversing the degeneration of the non-Judean peoples into iconic worship and worship of the subordinate gods.

With this scenario, one is in a position to understand why Paul used his philosophical resources about ontology in the way that he did. That ontology, I think, looks more like a dualism than like the Stoic qualified monism for the following reason.[60] In Paul's cosmos, shaped by Judean apocalyptic thought, both human and divine beings have proven unable to be fully obedient to God. Even the divine beings, who serve God's court and his administration of the world, have done poorly, not all such beings, but all have the potential to disobey as the behavior of the gods/angels that God himself appointed to rule the nations (e.g., Deut 32:8; Ps 82) shows. God has done two things to create a new species of perfect obedience. First, though merely a human, Jesus in God's secret plan was perfectly obedient. Second, God remade Christ from his own holy *pneuma* eliminating the passions, desire and general weakness of the flesh that allow disobedience. The chosen humans, who have assimilated to Christ's character/mind and have obtained a pneumatic body like his, will have formed a new species of God's servants. All other beings in the cosmos are made of some inferior grade of substance, even if it is a lower form of *pneuma*. Thus, there are two essentially different grades of material in the cosmos, corruptible and incorruptible, God's *pneuma* and everything else.

---

[59] One of the groundbreaking features of Litwa's *We are Being Transformed* is to bring the deification of Christ followers theme in relation to their future cosmic role under Christ (see, 182–88).

[60] I find Jean-Baptiste Gourinat's ("The Stoics on Matter and Prime Matter: Corporealism and the Imprint of Plato's Timaeus," in Salles, *God and Cosmos*, 46–70, at 48, 68–69) formulations to be most apt for Stoic ontology. Matter and god are both bodies and yet form an irreducible pair. The Stoic view is neither materialist monism nor dualism. One could certainly develop this as a dualism between human beings and nature as Seneca did, but that is not a substance dualism. On the latter see, Brad Inwood, *Seneca: Selected Philosophical Letters* (Oxford: Clarendon, 2007), 150–57.

Paul and the New Terrain of Philosophy

The philosophical ideas in the letters serve Paul's apocalyptic interpretation of Christ. The ideas are also fitted to his Mediterranean-West-Asian-Judean cosmology of a world filled with varied divine beings in an expanding three-story universe ruled by a supreme emperor. But *pneuma* and assimilation to a god are not just forms of window dressing. They are central to that interpretation of Jesus Christ. Before David Sedley's arguments that Antiochus's physical and cosmological ideas derive from the early Academy instead of Stoicism, one might have pointed without controversy to Antiochus as ushering in a Platonic-Stoic synthesis that could be a background for understanding Paul's appropriations.[61] Sedley has complicated things. But this debate aside for the moment, Paul lived in the period of an emerging philosophical terrain in which working with Plato's complexly literary, often contradictory, and unsystematic dialogues instead of the piles of systematic treatises by Zeno, Chrysippus and Epicurus helped to create a new intellectual ethos.[62]

Three characteristics of this first century intellectual movement that might have been attractive to Judean intellectuals bear emphasis: the relative openness and flexibility of the thought in first century CE; the importance of religion; and the idea that the best philosophy might be found in ancient wisdom often transmitted by way of books. If one did not want to commit to the whole of the highly articulated Stoic or Epicurean systems and ways of life, one could join in a more flexible search for the wisdom that Plato had transmitted from Pythagoras, and perhaps even look for older sources that Pythagoras had depended upon. Many of those from the late first century BCE through the first century CE who sought to find the earliest and therefore purest and truest teachings by way of the writings of Plato and the teachings of Pythagoras did come to depend upon tradition and the symbolic exegesis of books in a central way.[63] Moreover, as much recent scholarship has emphasized, such thinkers could claim that the books and traditions of the Egyptians, Judeans, Chaldeans or other peoples contained primitive truth or even the oldest and truest philosophy.[64]

---

[61] David Sedley, "The Origins of Stoic God," in *Traditions of Theology*, ed. Dorothea Frede and André Laks, PhA 89 (Leiden: Brill, 2002), 41–83. See the cautions of Brad Inwood, "Antiochus on Physics" in *The Philosophy of Antiochus*, ed. David Sedley (Cambridge: Cambridge University Press, 2012), 188–219.

[62] Dingeldein, "Gaining Virtue, Gaining Christ."

[63] Peter Struck, *Birth of the Symbol: Ancient Readers at the Limits of Their Texts* (Princeton: Princeton University Press, 2004); George Boys-Stones, *Post-Hellenistic Philosophy: A Study of its Development from the Stoics to Origen* (Oxford: Oxford University Press, 2001).

[64] Boys-Stones, *Post-Hellenistic Philosophy*, 60–98.

With the challenge of understanding historical changes in the intellectual life of the early Roman Empire, especially regarding Stoicism and Platonism, where do Philo and Paul fit in? Much recent scholarship agrees that there was no standard or orthodox Platonism in the first century CE. Further, it is frequently difficult to pin down the philosophical allegiances of figures in this period. At least partially excepting avowed Stoics and Epicureans, they often identify with those whom they hold to be originators of truth, especially Pythagoras, Socrates and Plato rather than with schools. In Philo's case, it is Moses from whom Pythagoras and Plato got their truth. I have suggested that precisely the lack of a standard Platonism or Platonic-Pythagoreanism encouraged creative uses of the philosophical traditions. I think it important to distinguish between professional philosophers, who fit the model of such people going back to classical Athens, and individuals who appropriated philosophy for other intellectual and practical projects. Philo and especially Paul were of this sort. Such uses are probably misdescribed as eclecticism and syncretism because the thinkers well understood the doctrines that they adapted and endeavored to integrate these into their larger intellectual and practical projects.

Some instances from Rome where both Philo and Paul were well connected illustrate the practical and creative intellectual uses of the complex post-Hellenistic movements. Moderatus of Gades claimed that Plato had plagiarized his metaphysics and other teachings from Pythagoras (Porphyry, *Vit. Pyth.* 53). One of his followers, a certain Lucius, called himself an Etruscan and claimed Etruscan wisdom and religious practices as Pythagorean.[65] The Etruscans were the true heirs of Pythagoras and practiced his ancient *symbola*. This ethnic and practical interpretation bears a very general similarity to Paul. Moderatus was preceded in Rome by Nigidius Figulus and his circle. At the same time as Moderatus we have Apollonius of Tyana, and I wish that we had some secure knowledge of him.[66] But certainly he had a practical freelance religious side to his Pythagoreanism.[67] I would add Thrasyllus the Platonic court philosopher, diviner and astrologer of Tiberius who was also a significant textual scholar.[68] In the time of Augustus, Quintus Sextius the senior is described as a Stoic and a Pythagorean, apparently implying some sort of synthesis. Seneca intriguingly says that Sextius was a Stoic but that he would deny it (*Ep.* 64.2). I am not

---

[65] Plutarch, *Quaest. conv.* 727b–728d and Books 7–8 for context.
[66] I am skeptical about finding any information in Philostratus's *Life of Apollonius* that we know we can trust.
[67] Graham Anderson, *Sage, Saint and Sophist: Holy Men and Their Associates in the Early Roman Empire* (London: Routledge, 1994).
[68] Harold Tarrant, *Thrasyllan Platonism* (Ithaca: Cornell University Press, 1993). The importance that Tarrant gives to Thrasyllus as a Platonist is controversial, but his detailed discussions of the sources and the figure are excellent.

suggesting that Paul was such a Platonist or Pythagorean, but he likely knew people influenced by these currents and found an environment of rich resources for his project in the broader post-Hellenistic mix.

Figures focused on religious (having to do with gods and such) thought and practice were likely attracted to the new currents that scholars describe as the development of dogmatic Platonisms in part because of the broadly shared telos of likeness to God and a broad interest in ancient texts. That goal can stand for a whole attitude of focusing interest and value toward religion and the upper cosmos. We have good evidence that Jewish intellectuals in this period were attracted to the new Platonism in the writings of Wisdom, Philo, Fourth Maccabees and possibly Aristobulus who is difficult to date. I would argue that Paul should be added to this list. Philo uses Platonic, Pythagorean and Stoic doctrines to interpret the world, including human nature and the social order, by interpreting the Judean scriptures. Paul's use of Stoic and Platonic doctrines is much more focused. It serves his intellectually and textually based practical project of recruiting, "educating" and training a select group of non-Jews to become Christ-like beings representing the "nations" who will join their Lord to play some crucial role in bringing about a new cosmic order. He likely adopted teachings about Stoic *pneuma* and Platonic assimilation to God because he thought they were true and helpful explanations of what his project was about, how it worked. Platonic assimilation with a role for a god-connected mind was central to his thought because the goal of his particular project was a form of divinization. But it seems that a noetic and indivisible world above did not fit his understanding of how the world worked. Indeed, his anthropomorphic understanding of God and other divine beings would ironically have better fitted a Stoic-like nominalism. As Engberg-Pedersen has shown, he used "materialist" ideas about types of *pneuma*. But I have argued that he did so partly to make sense of ideas about mind and assimilation drawn from Platonism. If this is correct, then it has great interest for the history of philosophy as an early witness to the doctrine of assimilation along with Eudorus and Philo.

Is there any precedent for Philo's quasi-materialism or Paul's Stoicizing interpretation of Platonic doctrines? There may be an instructive instance. Although the debate is ongoing, in one interpretation of Antiochus he probably held a view that he gave to the Old Academy that mind and the stars are corporeal and consist of fire (Cicero, *Acad.* 1.39).[69] If correct, we have a follower of Plato going even further than Philo in making the mind/soul consist of fire/divine *pneuma* in a Stoic mode. Antiochus also seems to have dispensed

---

[69] Charles Brittain, ed. and trans., *Cicero: On Academic Scepticism* (Indianapolis: Hackett, 2006), xxxii–xxxiii.

with a noetic world. My point is not to return to a discredited exaggeration of Antiochus's influence or to make him the founder of Middle Platonism, but to show that such Stoicizing interpretations of Platonic physics were conceivable, and apparently plausible to some.

I find a Platonic mixture in Paul's thought, along with the clearly Stoic elements that Engberg-Pedersen has so illuminated. The new Platonic-Pythagorean τέλος of assimilation to God could be interpreted with an otherworldly emphasis. Contrast Stoicism. The Stoics interpret living according to nature which is living according to virtue in a radically this worldly way in terms of skillful everyday activity. One ought to imitate God, but this means following the immanent providential rationality seen in nature, where humans perfectly fit. A few Platonic sounding ideas in the Roman Stoics does not change the basic character of Stoicism. The wisdom of the sage manifests itself in the sage's ability to select and perform skillfully the activities that make up everyday life. There is no goal beyond this that motivates the good life, especially not a heavenly afterlife or seeking oneness with a god or God in a way that transcends this wise skillfulness in mundane living. A heavenly life is not a goal of the Stoic ethical system. Paul with other known Judean thinkers, I believe, drew on the new Platonic and Pythagorean (and supposedly Pythagorean) currents for the reasons noted above, but with a Stoic-like role for *pneuma*. This reading should be compared with Engberg-Pedersen's different Paul who in Christ expresses a fully Stoic vision.

CHAPTER SEVEN

What is Pauline Participation in Christ?

Albert Schweitzer made the classic case for the idea that participation in Christ is the central or most basic or most important element in Paul's thought.[1] But it is due to Ed Sanders' incisive critical reassessment of Schweitzer's position in *Paul and Palestinian Judaism* that the centrality of participation has been widely accepted in New Testament scholarship.[2] Among other things, Schweitzer and Sanders showed decisively that in forming arguments for moral advice, Paul draws these arguments from facts about participation in Christ and not justification by the believer's faith.[3] If there has been wide acceptance of the centrality of participation, the agreement has ended on how to characterize the phenomenon indicated in Paul's discourse. From incomprehensible mystery to a form of corporate personality, the proposals have varied greatly and failed to win wide assent. As argued in Chapter Six, I understand participation as assimilation to Christ by way of God's pneuma. Here I want to focus on one aspect that features Gentile paternity.

Schweitzer's answer was clearer than most. He proposed a historical explanation of sorts for the origins of the idea and a broad cultural context. The context was a rather uniform Jewish eschatology, or as New Testament scholars might say today, apocalypticism, that he posited. Jews, including Paul, held to a series of strict and logically interrelated doctrines about their own age, past ages and the world to come. Paul created the idea of participation in Christ as a solution to the dilemma caused by his belief that the Messiah had come and been raised from the dead well ahead of the end time and its general resurrection. Paul had

---

[1] Albert Schweitzer, *The Mysticism of Paul the Apostle*, trans. William Montgomery (London: A&C Black, 1931).
[2] E. P. Sanders, *Paul and Palestinian Judaism* (Philadelphia: Fortress Press, 1977).
[3] Schweitzer, *Mysticism*, 42–43; Sanders, *Paul and Palestinian Judaism*, 439, 456, and throughout 447–74.

to make the elect mystically share in the death and resurrection of the Messiah already in this natural age. He writes:

> Paul's conception is that believers in mysterious fashion share the dying and rising again of Christ, and in this way are swept away out of their ordinary mode of existence, and form a special category of humanity. When the Messianic Kingdom dawns, those of them who are still in life are not natural men like others, but men who have in some way passed through death and resurrection along with Christ, and are capable of becoming partakers of the resurrection mode of existence, while other men pass under the dominion of death.[4]

Schweitzer provides a possible conceptual context for the larger problem that confronted Paul, but not for language and discourse of participation itself. That was Paul's pure creation, in his view, a matter of irresistible reasoning from the system of eschatological doctrines that led Paul to invent the language.[5] Schweitzer assures us that Paul came to the idea that believers are in Christ, Christ is in them and that they participate in his death and resurrection with the logical reasoning of a genius, but he never tells us how the idea of one person being in another person or sharing in the experiences of another would make sense to Paul or to others in his culture.[6] For all of the celebration of Schweitzer's discovery of Paul's apocalyptic context, there has been little recognition that apocalyptic thought did not explain the central idea of participation. We need a discourse or discourses that provide the conditions of intelligibility for the language of participation. Schweitzer's absolute oppositions between Palestinian Judaism and Hellenism and eschatology and Hellenism will not do.[7] What was common sense in the 1920s and 1930s when most Europeans and Americans assumed that supposed racial groups and their fractions had inherently different minds/cultures, and intrinsic and mutually exclusive cultural practices, should no longer make sense. In spite of Schweitzer's often admirable liberal values, the antimonies of his constructions belong to his milieu, even if they still frame much New Testament scholarship.

One of his great contributions was the consistency with which he held, against the common liberal understandings of the apostle, that Paul belonged to a milieu that was quite alien to modernity. Schweitzer was certain that

---

[4] Schweitzer, *Mysticism*, 96–97.
[5] For example, Schweitzer (*Mysticism*, 38) argues that Paul created his mysticism out of inferences from beliefs that the early Christians and Palestinian Jews held in common.
[6] On Paul's unique logical genius see Schweitzer, *Mysticism*, 100, 139–40.
[7] The fantastic amalgam that Schweitzer called Hellenism based on the work of scholars in the mode of Richard Reitzenstein holds no credence among scholars today. For critique of the binary, see Troels Engberg-Pedersen, ed., *Paul Beyond the Judaism/Hellenism Divide* (Louisville: Westminster John Knox, 2001).

Paul's language did require a realistic conception of the supernatural existence that had entered the natural. Participation was a sharing in the corporeality (*Leiblichkeit*) of Christ. He insisted that the language was not symbolic or mere metaphor.[8] Sanders wholeheartedly affirmed this realism even though he did not know how to characterize it. Against Rudolph Bultmann and many others who have proposed that although Paul's language seems to indicate something physical, it has a non-physical reference that is its true meaning, Sanders writes:

> It seems to me best to understand Paul as saying what he meant and meaning what he said: Christians really are one body and Spirit with Christ, the form of this world really is passing away . . . But what does this really mean? How are we to understand it? We seem to lack a category of 'reality' – real participation in Christ, real possession of the Spirit – which lies between naïve cosmological speculation and belief in magical transference on the one hand and a revised self-understanding on the other. I must confess that I do not have a new category of perception to propose here. This does not mean, however, that Paul did not have one. . . . To an appreciable degree, what Paul concretely thought cannot be directly appropriated by Christians today.[9]

Richard Hays has argued on the contrary, both that there is a fitting conception of participation, and that modern Christians can appropriate it. He has recently made a number of proposals about the metaphorical nature and categories of participation, but his most sustained argument has been that participation involves imaginative identification with narratives about Jesus Christ.[10]

---

[8] Schweitzer, *Mysticism*, 15–17, 19, 127–30.
[9] Sanders, *Paul and Palestinian Judaism*, 522–23. Unfortunately, Bultmann brought into the conversation the concepts of magic, transference and cosmological speculation in uncritical, anachronistic and undefined ways that obscure the differences between ancient and modern thought. The legitimate point picked up from the language by Sanders is that Paul's letters depict a real and substantial change in those who are in Christ, but such people are still in the flesh and human. For critique of the category magic, see Randall Styers, *Making Magic: Religion, Magic and Science in the Modern World* (New York: Oxford University Press, 2004).
[10] Hays, *Faith of Jesus Christ*. For recent proposals, Richard B. Hays, "What Is 'Real Participation in Christ?': A Dialogue with E.P. Sanders on Pauline Soteriology," in *Redefining First-century Jewish and Christian Identities*, ed. Fabian E. Udoh, et al. (Notre Dame: University of Notre Dame Press, 2008) 336–51. Hays describes this language as a hermeneutical problem for modern Christian theology and proposes four interpretive categories for the language: familial participation, political/military participation, ecclesial participation, and narrative participation. The first two categories consist of metaphorical language, on this interpretation, and the third seems to be a combination of metaphors and a reference to experiences or practices by Paul. The fourth concerns imaginative identification with the stories of Israel and of Jesus. Unfortunately, Hays picks up the red herrings of whether participation is "magical" and "automatic" instead of showing why Paul's language should not be taken realistically (*Faith of Jesus Christ*, 213–15).

As he puts it in the sermonic Christian we, "we are caught up into the story of Jesus Christ."[11] Hays glosses Gal 2:19–20 where Paul speaks of being crucified with Christ and now living in Christ with: Jesus Christ's "story transforms and absorbs the world."[12] I find it difficult to determine the scope and significance of Hays's claims. Sometimes it sounds like what I would call a "narrative idealism," as when he criticizes realistic readings with the comment that all language is metaphorical.[13]

Hays also chides Bultmann for his demythologizing of this language.[14] I believe that Hays's hermeneutic is just as modernist as Bultmann's. Since, however, it is in part unconscious of its translation from Paul's ancient culture, it lacks the critical reflexivity of Bultmann's approach. Part of the basic structure of modernity, in radical contrast to the ancient world, is the natural/supernatural divide that thinkers like René Descartes created to protect religion from science and science from religion.[15] There is a natural realm of cause and effect in which humans live that is constituted of matter and persistent physical laws that apply equally everywhere. The supernatural, including God and the spiritual, is totally other and constitutes a "realm" to which the principles of the natural realm do not apply. One can only point to this "realm" symbolically and metaphorically. In contrast, ancient and medieval thinking had one unified realm consisting of a hierarchy of being or substances, each of which had its own qualitative properties. Anything including God and God's activity could, in principle, be explained in physical terms. This was a holistically interactive cosmos without a neat separation between the symbolic-spiritual and the instrumental-physical.

Thus, in modernist thought the spiritual is that which is beyond and in contrast to the physical, substantial and merely natural. But in Paul's world *pneuma* (wind, air, breath, spirit), for example, is a refined, qualitatively higher

---

[11] See especially xxix to the second edition of Hays, *Faith of Jesus Christ* and 210–15. One hopes that the contention of the Bultmann school and others that Paul's anthropological language and faith language refers to the twentieth-century category of human existence has been put to rest. See, Macdonald, *History of the Concept of Mind*, esp. 100.

[12] Hays, *Faith of Jesus Christ*, 29.

[13] I find it difficult to understand or accept Hays's philosophical position. If one should agree that all language is metaphorical, does that mean that "Bob's arm" does not also refer to the flesh, bone and blood body part of the person Bob? Schweitzer was not claiming that there might not be metaphor involved in the language of participation, but that the language was not *only* metaphorical or figurative with no central reference to substances and objects. This misleading criticism of Schweitzer is clear also in Hays's discussion of him in *Faith of Jesus Christ*, 44–45.

[14] Hays, *Faith of Jesus Christ*, 47–52 and Bultmann, *Theology of the New Testament* (New York: Scribners, 1951), 1:268–69, 302.

[15] M. R. Wright, *Cosmology in Antiquity* (London: Routledge, 1995). For a more specialized discussion of some key issues, see Norman Kretzmann, ed., *Infinity and Continuity in Ancient and Medieval Thought* (Ithaca, NY: Cornell University Press, 1982). For comparison with modernity, see Alexandre Koyré, *From the Closed World to the Infinite Universe* (Baltimore: Johns Hopkins University Press, 1957).

substance with its own power of movement and intelligence. Paul betrays exactly this kind of physics and cosmology. So, for example in 1 Corinthians 15, the substances of the lower and heavenly cosmos vary qualitatively in a grand hierarchy:

> Not all flesh is the same flesh, humans have one flesh, but animals another, birds another, and fish another. There are heavenly bodies and earthly bodies, but the glory of the heavenly is one thing and the glory of the earthly is different. The sun has one kind of glory, and the moon another glory, and different glory for the stars, in fact star differs from star in glory.[16]

Humans participate in Adam because they share bodies consisting of the same stuff as Adam (15:42–9). Those in Christ participate in him because they share with him the most sublime kind of *pneuma*, divine *pneuma* that he received in being resurrected from the dead. Paul's language here is not metaphorical or at least not only metaphorical in the sense that it does not involve a realistic meaning and reference.

Sanders is right to stress a realist ontology. One reinterprets into the modernist framework by treating the language of participation as fundamentally metaphorical without the referent of a substantial ontology. Both modern largely anthropological and literary conceptions of myth and modern Christian theology have insisted that myth and theology are about something called meaning in opposition to what is out there. The elaborate modern practices of studying myth and scripture have traded on this opposition and on seeing that the meaning of the text could never include significant notions about the stuff and the processes of the world. Meaning is the realm of religion, literature, art and the humanities; stuff belongs to science and has no meaning.

When Hays dismisses Schweitzer's interpretation as "a crudely literal belief in a shared physical substance between the Messiah and his people," he is overwriting Paul's thought with modernity.[17] The move amounts to unconscious demythologizing. Protestants and European and American Roman Catholics, among others, share a non-human world that is largely disenchanted and "mechanical" – without human-like intelligence and teleology – compared to Paul's world. From the thousand thousands and ten thousand ten thousands of heavenly beings who administer the world for God in Daniel (e.g., 9:10), and the qualitatively physical principles of purity, pollution and holiness in the Priestly sources, to the aither, *pneuma* and purposive species essences of

---

[16] On flesh, body, soul and the hierarchy of being see, Dale B. Martin, *The Corinthian Body* (New Haven: Yale University Press, 1995), 105–36.

[17] Hays, *Faith of Jesus Christ*, 451.

Hellenistic and Greco-Roman cultures, the ancient conceptions understood the world to work by the principles of mind (e.g., value, purpose) permeating the cosmos. But New Testament scholars have often assumed that a relative lack of explanation in these terms in some texts meant that Paul, for example, had the scholar's common sense, that is, modern mechanistic understanding of the world as a background for beliefs about God, Christ, angels and how the supernatural, say in the form of Christ's resurrection, could enter the natural world. The fact that ancient writings do not always refer to these ancient ways of understanding the world should no more be taken to imply modern-like assumptions than my failure to mention atoms, electrons and evolutionary selection should be taken to imply that I hold some non-modern understanding of the world.

Some of those who have tried to describe the logic and origins of Paul's participationist language have appealed to Paul's or early Christian experience.[18] But I do not view that as an explanation. The conditions for the experiences themselves must be explained rather than treated as originary mysteries. Moreover, Paul does not use our modern language of experience. He does not have an interest in the individual's inner feel for some special event, but on the event itself and its broader significance.

I want to stress three points. First, a hierarchy of qualities of substances is central to the discourse and should not be treated as symbolic for some supposedly deeper theological meaning or existential posture that Paul really meant. Second, the most basic principle by which this thinking with substances works is according to the logic of contiguity of substances, a matter of extension, identity and contiguousness or lack thereof. Third, these are principles by which Paul reads and constructs narratives about Abraham and his descendants, Adam and his descendants, and Christ and those who are contiguous with him by the logic of patrilineal lineage and physical relatedness. These are components out of which the language of participation comes.

I can illustrate these points with some brief comments on 1 Cor 6:12–20. Paul explains that God will destroy both the stomach and food, but the Lord is for [or with] the body. God raised the Lord, and he will raise those who are members of Christ. This argument makes sense because there is a contrast between the resurrection body and the human fleshly body. The best commentary on 6:13–14 is 15:35–50. Paul follows important strains of Hellenistic thought in treating the human body or bodies in general as like forms that can have various sorts of content.[19] The body that will perish is made of flesh

---

[18] For a critique the notion, see Matthew Bagger, *Religious Experience, Justification and History* (Cambridge: Cambridge University Press, 1999).

[19] Stoic thought regarding bodies was the most influential, but only one among many kinds of thought that treated the concept in this way. In the Stoic view, for anything to exist it had to have extension and qualities that we would attribute to mass (*SVF* 2.359, 381, 525). Matter is

and was probably thought of as concocted out of food grown from the earth. But a better form of the body would consist of divine *pneuma*. It comes as no surprise then, that in 6:18 the current body is a temple of this pure or holy *pneuma*. Paul is clear that a fully pneumatic body will replace the flesh body only at the resurrection (15:44). So far, we have types of stuff, but there is also the contiguity. Those in Christ are members of him. The relation is like the relation of the arm to the rest of the body. The same stuff makes Christ and believers contiguous. Paul means this so realistically that for a believer to be joined to a prostitute in sexual intercourse would be to join her to Christ and create that arm/body relation. On the one hand, Paul explains that the person who is joined to the Lord is one *pneuma* with him. On the other hand, he cites Gen 2:24 to show that in sexual intercourse the partners become one entity: "the two shall become one flesh." Enigmatically, Paul comments that such sexual intercourse is uniquely a sin "against," or more likely, "into" the body.[20] I suggest that he may have in mind the context of the Genesis passage. There, just before the statement about becoming one flesh, Eve is made from one of Adam's bones and she is said to be "bone of his bone and flesh of his flesh." This preceding context makes the "one flesh" statement seem very literal. Man and woman come together so as to share the same substance. Finally, "bone of my bone and flesh of my flesh" is a biblical expression for being a descendant or a relative of someone. This conception of human relatedness by the identity of substance clearly preceded and informed the statement from Genesis. Indeed, I will argue that the basic model for the discourse of participation is that of descendants and relatives sharing the same stuff as ancestors or those to whom they are related.

The reading supposes the subjective genitive construal of *pistis Christou* and related expressions.[21] The reading shows why Paul's focus on what Christ and Abraham did makes sense. In other words, the Pauline letters do no argue that Christ brought a new way to be saved, that is, through the believer's faith,

---

completely indeterminate and passive. In this creation, it always comes in particular forms that are acted upon by God and the kind of action makes the combination corporeal (e. g., *SVF* 2.310; Diogenes Laertius 7.134). On Stoic corporealism see, David Hahm, *The Origins of Stoic Cosmology* (Columbus: Ohio State University Press, 1977), 3–28 which needs to be combined with Stoic discussions of the human body and soul. The point is well made by Martin (*Corinthian Body*, 104–36) who cites all kinds of views from different periods including medical sources.

[20] Martin (*Corinthian Body*, 177–78) makes the highly plausible suggestion that *eis* in this context means into the body rather than against it.

[21] Above all, the subjective genitive is superior to the objective because it allows constructions that read as Greek rather than some bizarre uniquely Pauline language. We can no longer tolerate bloopers like the RSV or NRSV (text) translations of Rom 3:26 and 4:16 (i.e., compare the inconsistent translation of exactly the same construction, *ek pisteos Iesou/Abraam*) and a number of other passages. The subjective genitive also makes Paul's thought much more coherent and less like a modern thinker. See, among others, Hays, *Faith of Jesus Christ*, 249–97.

over against the old way of keeping the law. Rather, salvation in an apocalyptic scenario hinges on Abraham's and Christ's faith or faithfulness and not on the believer's faith. Through their actions, God has founded covenants that descendants inherit merely by being born of the chosen lineage.[22] In reading Paul's texts in this way, I would argue, he does not sound as if he were "spiritualizing," religion, but as if he had a genuine investment in Jewish beliefs about kinship and descent that are central to the Hebrew Bible.[23]

In Gal 3:7–8 Paul writes, "those who come out of faithfulness are sons of Abraham."[24] I take this to be first of all Abraham's faithfulness in this context. In the Genesis stories, because Abraham believed the unlikely promise that he would have an heir and then acted faithfully so as to have a child, Paul can think of the descendants of Isaac as the lineage of Abraham's faith and of God's promise.[25] Then in Gal 3:8–9, "Scripture foreseeing that God would justify the gentiles out of faithfulness, proclaimed the gospel beforehand to Abraham, namely, 'in you (*en soi*) will all the gentiles be blessed.' So that those who come out of [Abraham's] faithfulness are blessed with (*syn*) the faithful Abraham." Paul uses the language of ancient genetics and lineage from the *Septuagint* to say that the gentiles who are in Christ were blessed when Abraham was blessed because Christ was in Abraham as his seed. Christ was in Abraham at that

---

[22] Faith is "required" for getting in and baptism, but, as in many traditional western interpretations, Paul does not make it involve a transaction between God and individual humans that essentially skips over Abraham, Israel and Christ by, for example, making Christ only an object of faith. On this reading, they actually do the work of salvation through God's spirit. Paul certainly does talk about the *pistis* of the believer in several places.

[23] I draw on my work and Caroline Johnson Hodge, *If Sons, Then Heirs: A Study of Kinship and Ethnicity in the Letters of Paul* (New York: Oxford University Press, 2007). The gist of much of the interpretation is summed up in a passage from my *A Rereading of Romans* (246):

> The apostle likes this formulation of the promise because it contains the idea of descendants and heirs being incorporated into the ancestor who founded the lineage. Thus the promise was made to Christ, who was present in Abraham together with his fellow adoptees, sons of God by the Spirit. Christ is both a descendant by blood and an adoptee by the Spirit in the resurrection (1:3–4). Paul's language of "predestination" seems also to come from the logic of patriliny: "Those whom he foreknew he also designated beforehand [cf. *horizein* in 1:4] to be conformed to the image of his son, in order that he might be the first born of among many brothers" (8:29). God gives and knows all of the line's offspring because they are already in the founder's seed. Thus Abraham's gentile heirs "in Christ" were already "designated beforehand" in Abraham. Just as each generation passes on and shares the 'image" of the ancestor, so also those in Christ are brothers sharing with Christ and each other the image of God the father.

See also 225, 229–30, 280, 283.

[24] On ethnic mythmaking, see Johnson Hodge, *If Sons, Then Heirs*, 93-107. On Galatians 3, see Stowers, *Rereading of Romans*, 201, 221, 225, 229–30.

[25] For Paul's and ancient use of *ek* phrases for descent, see Johnson Hodge, *If Sons, Then Heirs*, 79–82.

point and participated in him. He was one with Abraham. I think that the "in Christ" language derives from this logic of descent and genetic participation.[26] Paul may have been just as literal as Hebrews 7, which argues that although he was not yet born, Levi paid tithes to Melchizedek because he was in the loins of Abraham as seed when Abraham paid tithes to Melchizedek. Paul emphasizes the presence of Christ in Abraham when the promises were given. Thus 3:16 says, "the promises were pronounced to Abraham and to his Seed."

In Gal 3:14, one reads that Christ died "so that the blessing of Abraham might come to the gentiles in Christ Jesus so that we might receive the promise of the spirit through faithfulness." I take this to be the faithfulness of Abraham and Christ. Nils Dahl long ago suggested that Paul's allusion to Gen 22:18 in 3:14 might be the basis for Paul's "in Christ," expression, at least in some contexts.[27] In 3:26–7, Paul continues "You are all sons of God in Christ Jesus through [his] faithfulness. For all who have been baptized into Christ have put on Christ." And 3:29: "If you are of Christ [participate in Christ], you are the seed of Abraham and heirs according to promise." The logic is this: Abraham and Jesus as blood relatives share the same stuff and the same characteristic of faithfulness to God's promises and are the crucial beginning and end of the God-chosen lineage bearing the promise of blessing. Paul takes the particular blessing promised to the gentiles as the gift of possessing God's *pneuma*. As Christ participated in Abraham and shared his stuff, so gentiles who come to share the *pneuma* of Christ in baptism share in this contiguity back to Abraham and are thus seed of Abraham and co-heirs as they participate in the stuff of Christ. But Christ's spirit is not any normal human *pneuma*. It is the divine *pneuma* that brought him back to life on a new level of existence after he allowed himself to die in faithfulness to God's promises.

This interpretation of Galatians 3 allows one to understand why it has been so difficult to fit 3:28 together with Paul's other statements about women, men, Judeans, non-Judeans, slave and free and make them cohere with modern liberal and rights-based conceptions of equality. Gal 3:28 is first of all a denial of a set of ontological differences and an affirmation of an ontological unity. Those in Christ are literally of the same stuff. All share the very same *pneuma*, Christ's. It would be a wrong turn, however, to in modern fashion separate substance from quality, the spiritual (in the modern sense) from the material. Epictetus illustrates this unity (*Diss.* 3.3.22), "When someone has a spell of dizziness, it is not the abilities and the virtues that are thrown into confusion, but the *pneuma* of which they exist. When the *pneuma* settles down, the abilities and virtues are settled." Habituated skills and virtues such as courage

---

[26] For Paul's use of *en*, see Johnson Hodge, *If Sons, Then Heirs*, 94–106; Stowers, *Rereading of Romans*, 230.

[27] Nils A. Dahl, *Studies in Paul* (Minneapolis: Augsburg, 1977), 131.

or self-control are conditions of a person's *pneuma*. Epictetus acknowledges that because of the substantial nature of these abilities, an external physical force can cause an interruption of normal consciousness that temporarily incapacitates them. It makes perfect sense for Paul to associate pneuma with moral and mental qualities. He goes on to say (Gal 5:24, 16–23) that "those who are of Christ have crucified the flesh with its passions and desires" and to oppose the virtues (fruit) of the *pneuma*, including self-control, with the vices of the flesh. Substances have their qualities and capabilities. Unlike Epictetus's person, Paul's Christ-person has not only ordinary *pneuma* like all human beings, but also an interpenetration of Christ's *pneuma* that came directly from God.[28]

Those in Christ are not descendants of Christ, but contemporary kin. As Rom 8:29 reveals, Paul thought of them as brothers of Jesus Christ. This perennially vexing passage, which has been treated as consisting of references to God's predestination of each person to salvation or damnation and to the lost image of God, actually uses the language of ancient genetics and descent as argued in Johnson Hodge's *If Sons, Then Heirs*.[29] Ancient biological thought spoke of the image (*eikon*) of the father being passed on through procreation in a seed from the father. It was widely held that *pneuma* of the father concentrated in the seed and was the active and organizing force that shaped the matter supplied by the mother in the womb. Writings of the Hebrew Bible also broadly share in this ancient patrilineal ideology of genetics. Gen 5:3 says that "Adam generated a son according to his likeness and according to his image."[30] The *Septuagint* here uses *eikon* as does Rom 8:29. One of the common ideas of patrilineal thought is that all of the seed of all of the descendants are in the ancestor as Hebrews 7, for example, assumes with Levi in Abraham.

In Romans 9 and elsewhere, Paul emphasizes that God plans ahead of time the chosen lineage through which the promises will be passed, and here he correctly reads Genesis. Romans 9:7–8, for instance, says, "'In Isaac shall your seed be named,' that is, it is not the children of the flesh that are children of God, but the children of promise are counted as seed." This passage is usually taken to mean that Paul is eliminating descent and spiritualizing (in the modern sense) true religion as the religion of faith in God and his promises. On my reading, he is arguing that mere fleshly descent is not enough. Rather the salvific lineage has to be a line of descent chosen by God for promise. So, in Romans 9, he argues that Ishmael and Esau were fleshly descendants of Abraham, but not of the line chosen by God for promise and blessing. God's choosing and empowerment is more important than just flesh. Jeremiah 1:5 is an example of the language of

---

[28] Epictetus' dualism of, for example, the moral will versus the flesh is a purely moral dualism due to his Stoic monism, but Paul's is both a moral and an anthropological dualism.

[29] 79–91, and Stowers, *Rereading of Romans*, 246.

[30] In Gen 1:26, God and his divine helpers create the human in their image and likeness. As many scholars have pointed out, in some early context this meant that humans were divine offspring.

divine foreknowing and shaping of a chosen agent: "before I formed you in the womb, I knew you, and before you came forth from the womb, I set you apart." Thus Rom 8:29–30 is about God shaping the line of salvific participation that would even include gentiles who are grafted in, and not just metaphorically, as a lineage of descendants: "Those whom [God] knew beforehand, he also planned before to be conformed to the image of his son, so that he [Christ] might be the firstborn among many brothers." God has planted the seed of the chosen line in the ancestor from the beginning and this included Christ who carries the image formed by the divine *pneuma* that all of those baptized into Christ share just as sons share the same image of the father. Ancient readers are likely to have understood that Paul likens the resurrection to a birth. Gentile believers share in that birth by "baptism into Christ" and thus become the "seed of Abraham" (Gal 3:26–29; cf. Rom 6:1–11). Paul stresses this key connection between the salvific line of descent ("seed of David") and God's extension of the line to the gentiles by means of the holy *pneuma* given to Christ in the resurrection at the very beginning of Romans (1:1–5). Again, as in Gal 3:8, Paul describes this nexus as the good news preached beforehand in the scriptures.

With this logic, other statements in chapter 8 using the language of participation make sense. Earlier, in 8:9, Paul says, "Anyone who does not have the *pneuma* of Christ, is not of him." He continues, "But if Christ is in you, though the body is dead because of sin, the *pneuma* is life because of righteousness." Paul then speaks of the *pneuma* of him who raised Jesus from the dead dwelling in those who are in Christ. The particular shape of God's *pneuma* that Jesus received in the resurrection is shared by believers so that Christ can be said to be in them. But since they merely share what belongs first of all to Christ, they can also be said to be "of him" or "in him" just as Christ shared the stuff of Abraham and was in him. One simply cannot understand Paul's idea of participation without recognizing that those who are in or of Christ actually possess as part of the stuff of Christ, a portion of his *pneuma*. The chapter goes on to speak of them receiving the *pneuma* of adoption. That *pneuma* cooperates with the individual's own natural *pneuma* to certify this adoption as sons of God. As a result, these people are co-heirs and co-sufferers with Christ. Because they possess part of Christ's vital essence endowed by God, they are not only part of the inheriting lineage, but also experience his suffering as they live temporarily still in a flesh as he did before his resurrection.

How the *pneuma* of Christ and the *pneuma* of the believer relate or intermix is far from clear. Clearly both maintain their substantial natures and identities in some sense. In 1 Cor 2:11–15, the divine *pneuma* communicates between those in Christ and God:

> the *pneuma* searches all things, even the depths of God. For what person knows the things of a person except the person's *pneuma* that is in him. So also no one knows the things of God except the *pneuma* of God.

Now we have not received the *pneuma* of the world, but the *pneuma* out of God so that we can understand the things given to us by God.

Romans 8:16 says that when the readers cry Abba, Father, that "it is the *pneuma* [of God] itself witnessing together with our *pneuma* that we are children of God, and if children also heirs of God . . . and fellow heirs with Christ provided that we suffer with him so that we might be glorified with him." The fact that Paul can easily and without caveat (e. g., "I am speaking in a human way") attribute types of *pneuma* to both God and humans shows that he participates in his ancient culture and Hellenistic thought about *pneuma*.

The divine *pneuma* is clearly not a person, as it becomes in later Christian Trinitarian theology. Paul agreed with the prevailing culture, including philosophers and medical doctors, that *pneuma* was the vital component of the living person and that there were various kinds and qualities of *pneuma* in the workings of the world. Sometimes Paul's language makes it sound as if the divine *pneuma* inhabits the person by a kind of possession so that the natural human *pneuma* and the divine *pneuma* are distinct *homunculi* inside of a person. They are separate but work together. The language of sharing and participation (e.g., *koinonia*), however, may suggest a more "scientific" picture.[31] We learn from the Aristotelian Alexander of Aphrodisias' *de mixtione* (*On the Mixture of Physical Bodies*) about the extremely influential Stoic doctrines regarding the mixing of substances that was their basis for picturing a highly interactive cosmos. Philo, Paul's Jewish contemporary, for example, uses the theory in a quite explicit way in interpreting the Septuagint (e.g., *Conf.* 183–87).[32] In this theory, *krasis* is the type of mixing that occurs in the constitution of the human being as *pneuma* interpenetrates the whole person.[33] It is not the mere juxtaposition of stuff. Nor is it fusion so that the *pneuma* and the other substances lose their identities, but the complete extension of active *pneuma* through passive matter so that each substance retains its identity. Such a theory would facilitate Paul's talk of double identity between Christ and the person in Christ with God's *pneuma* extending through both the passive matter of the body and the active human *pneuma*. The person shares all that Christ has experienced and become, and yet retains her or his own personal identity. Listen to Paul speaking of himself: "I have been crucified together with Christ. I no longer live, but Christ lives in me. And the

---

[31] I owe the idea that the Stoic *krasis* theory might be involved in Paul's thinking to Caroline Johnson Hodge who first proposed the idea in a 1995 graduate seminar at Brown University. See also Johnson Hodge, *If Sons, Then Heirs*, 75.

[32] Tertullian also famously uses this theory of mixing to explain Christ's divinity by the interpenetration of God's pneuma.

[33] A. A. Long, "Body and Soul in Stoicism," in *Stoic Studies* (Berkeley: University of California Press, 1996), 224–49.

life I now live in the flesh, I live in the faithfulness of the son of God who loved me and gave himself up on my behalf" (Gal 2:19–20).

Schweitzer, Sanders and others have very clearly shown that Paul's ethical thought, and his language of freedom from sinning and justification depend on his conception of participation.[34] But how does this connection fit my theory that Paul builds participation on notions of participating in founding ancestors by physical descent? What does all of this have to do with faith or faithfulness? It is in the very texts where Paul has traditionally been taken to argue his supposedly central concept of justification by the believer's faith and Jesus' atoning death by substitution that Abraham becomes a topic (Romans 4 and Galatians 3). This tradition takes Abraham as a model of how the believer can be saved by faith alone. In my reading, Paul is arguing that non-Jews/Judeans do not have to become Jews/Judeans in order to become right with God by getting into Christ. They do not have to keep the Judean law and are free from its just condemnation of their sin. By participating in Christ and his death and new life, Gentiles inherit what Abraham and Christ achieved by their faith or faithfulness so that God promised, and now insures blessings to their descendants. Jews or gentiles born into the line do not earn their status by law-keeping. So, for example, Rom 4:15b–17a says, "where there is no law there is no violation. For this reason, the promise comes out of [Abraham's and Christ's] faithfulness, so that the promise might be secure, by gift [from God], for all of the seed, not only for those who are of the law, but also for those who are out of the faithfulness of Abraham who is father of us all. As it is written (Gen 17:5), 'I have made you the father of many peoples (or Gentiles)'."[35] Thus I believe that William Wrede, Schweitzer, Sanders, Krister Stendahl and others are correct when they see justification as in some sense secondary or dependent on participation. But putting this understanding of justification together with the arguments about gentile contiguity in a line of Abraham through Christ provides a reintegration of the supposedly separate discourses. The believer's faith does not effect salvation, but Abraham's and Jesus' faith, and that faith centrally includes faith in (or faithful action in view of) God's promises about blessed lineages consisting of those whom God actively works to make right with him. God's own *pneuma*, conveyed to the ungodly through the death and resurrection of Jesus Christ, forms the chief instrument of justification. Gentiles "in Christ" are materially improved people who not only have past sins forgiven, but more importantly are empowered and filled with a holy stuff that actively enables obedience to God.

I would like to conclude with a few of many possible reflections on the significance of what I have argued. Ancient Christianity was often eager to

---

[34] Another example is Denys Whiteley, *The Theology of St. Paul*, 2nd ed. (Oxford: Blackwell, 1974).
[35] Johnson Hodge, *If Sons, Then Heirs*, 87–91.

get rid of an interest in lineage and birth in its readings of Paul. These had to be rejected as the carnality of the Jews. But it is modernist interpreters who have been most threatened by the hierarchy of substances and physics of contiguity. Descartes, still using the language of the scholastics, asserted that the medieval cosmos of interactive qualities of substances had to be replaced by an exhaustive dualism of *res extensa* and *res cogitans*. Extension was to be purged of quality, meaning and teleology. Religion had to be limited to mind, culture and the symbolic, and separated from any discourse about the material world, cause and effect. A Paul who asserted that true religion was a matter of faith has been a perfect instrument for modernity. The Bible has nothing to say about science, but concerns pure meaning. Paul's message could be made to be about the discontinuity of the physical and the spiritual, matter and meaning. Furthermore, in my view, it is not just as a result of scholarly progress that twentieth-century scholarship discovered that eschatology is the essence of primitive Christianity. Modernity made the category of time, temporality, triumph over place, space and stuff. Interpretation that focused on narrative has been one means for this triumph in New Testament Studies. The story can be rendered with character, plot and so on in a way that leaves behind the ancient baggage of place and stuff with all of its particularity. For moderns, time (e.g., history) has seemed to have an indeterminacy not possessed by the scientific hardness and law-following behavior of stuff, space, and place – a refuge from traditional Western understandings of the human and the divine. Because of this, we have lost the sense that part of the meaning for Paul was in the concept and reference to stuff and its particularity.

One example of this departicularizing abstraction, I believe, occurs regarding gender. The understanding of participation outlined here would reveal the depth, detail and logic of the patriarchal and patrilineal thought that is the raw material for Paul's creative reworkings of biblical stories and commonplace physics and cosmology. The approach, for example, helps us to understand why Paul usually speaks of "sons of God" rather than "children of God." Or why even though language from this tradition in Paul's letters suggests that becoming a son of God is like the birth of a child, that there is no mother, but only a father and sons. If we produce abstracted narratives that have only God, Christ, Christians and unbelievers, then we leave out rich, but troubling conceptions of men, women, slave, free, Jew and gentile, fleshly bodies, and pneumatic bodies. The great irony of this reading is that the ultimate elimination of flesh bodies for pneumatic bodies would seem to eliminate procreation and gender, but the very logic leading to this conclusion derives from a logic of participation in human procreation and kinship.

CHAPTER EIGHT

Paul's Four Discourses about Sin

The time is right for reassessing what Paul's letters have to say about sin. Modern scholarly treatments of the topic usually assume that Paul had a unified and coherent doctrine of sin that somehow lay behind all of the many things that he says about sin, including the rich and varied metaphorical language. I will call this the "invisible meta-narrative." This habit arises at least partly as a holdover from ancient and medieval Christian thinkers who constructed unifying narratives by synthesizing from all parts of scripture in light of their assumptions about human moral psychology, cosmology, physics, and Christian tradition. I will argue that Paul employed a number of distinct discourses about sin among which he made certain connections, but without condensing these into one theology of fallen human nature as Augustine did. These discourses, known to have been prevalent in Paul's time account for letters' language about sin. Further, I will argue that the eclipse of the discourse about moral psychology in modern scholarship has led to distortions in understanding Paul's thought about sin.

A number of new assumptions and perspectives that are an outgrowth of scholarship in the last forty years motivate my conviction about a need for reassessing Paul on sin. I will list some of these that I consider most important.

1. The persuasive critique of the binary opposition between Jewish and Hellenistic (or Jewish and Persian, Babylonian, "Canaanite," and so on) that rendered anything Jewish or "of the Old Testament" *sui generis*, unique and therefore incomparable, has enabled research into the complex cultural mix of which Paul was heir.[1] Many of the numerous studies claiming to show "the origins of Paul's theology" regarding sin and other matters "in the Old Testament" and in Judaism are ways of reading contemporary theological convictions into Paul's letters.[2]

---
[1] Troels Engberg-Pedersen, ed., *Paul Beyond the Hellenism/Judaism Divide* (Louisville: Westminster John Knox, 2001).
[2] Jonathan Z. Smith, *Drudgery Divine: On the Comparison of Early Christianities and the Religions of Late Antiquity* (Chicago: University of Chicago, 1990).

2. Now a substantial amount of historical work has been done on the various discourses that may have contributed to Paul's thinking about sin. Discourses do not respect boundaries that writers and authorities claim for or seek to impose upon particular populations (such as the thought of Syrians, Greeks, Judeans, Romans, Christians). Such discourses above all circulated among networks of literate experts, and the networks crossed ethnic boundaries.[3]
3. There has been a minor revolution in the broader historical understanding of Western conceptions of human nature and human psychology. Specialists in several disciplinary areas and in the ancient, medieval and modern periods have traced the development of important differences through these periods.[4] This scholarship makes it more difficult to justify finding our contemporary assumptions in Paul's letters.
4. Closely related to the last point is the implausibility of the existentialist interpretation of Paul's thought. This approach dominated scholarship on Paul's conceptions of sin and human nature from the mid-1930s until perhaps the late 1970s and is especially associated with Hans Jonas, Rudolph Bultmann and his Marburg colleague Martin Heidegger.[5] But as Paul Macdonald writes of the claim that Paul's talk of flesh is about not clinging to the ephemeral quality of human existence: It "imputes to Paul and his audience an understanding of *existence* as a primordial dimension of human being, an existential dimension the concept of which was simply not articulable by either the philosophical or religious mentality of that epoch."[6] My sense is that an existentialist understanding of Paul's psychological or

---

[3] See Chapter One in this volume ("The Religion of Plant and Animal Offerings").
[4] There is a large bibliography here. I can only list a few important publications: Stephen Everson, ed., *Psychology*, Companions to Ancient Thought 2 (Cambridge: Cambridge University Press, 1991); Christopher Gill, *Personality in Greek, Epic, Tragedy and Philosophy* (Oxford: Clarendon Press, 1996); idem, *The Structured Self in Hellenistic and Roman Thought* (Oxford: Clarendon Press, 2006); idem, ed., *The Person and the Human Mind: Issues in Ancient and Modern Philosophy* (Oxford: Oxford University Press, 1990); Richard Sorabji, *Emotion and Peace of Mind* (Oxford: Clarendon Press, 2000); idem, *Self: Ancient and Modern Insights about Individuality, Life, and Death* (Chicago: University of Chicago Press, 2006); David Konstan, *Pity Transformed* (London: Duckworth, 2001); *From Soul to Self*, ed. James Crabbe (London: Routledge, 1999); Raymond Martin and John Barresi, *Naturalization of the Soul* (London: Routledge, 2000); J. B. Schneewind, *The Invention of Autonomy* (Cambridge: Cambridge University Press, 1998); Phillip Carey, *Augustine's Invention of the Inner Self: The Legacy of a Christian Platonist* (New York: Oxford University Press, 2000).
[5] Influentially modernizing Paul and declaring him unique, Werner Georg Kümmel, *Das Bild des Menschen im Neuen Testament* (Züruch: Zwingli Verlag, 1948) that was translated into English as *Man in the New Testament* (Philadelphia: Westminster, 1963).
[6] Macdonald, *History of the Concept of Mind: Speculations about the Soul, Spirit and Mind from Homer to Hume*, (Burlington, VT: Ashgate, 2003), 100.

so-called "anthropological language" still dominates Pauline scholarship, even though scholars are often not aware of the fact.[7]

5. A much richer understanding of thinkers in ancient forms of Christianity has made implausible the often-unacknowledged inference that no one in the ancient church truly understood Paul's thought until Augustine, especially regarding sin and grace.[8] I can think of nothing more sobering for a Pauline scholar than to trace what the extant Christian writers from Paul to Augustine wrote about sin. On the one side, writers say shockingly little from the later Western perspective. On the other side, they unify Paul's thought and that of scripture and tradition by creating meta-narratives that are obviously foreign to Paul's thinking. Augustine continues to dominate scholarly understandings of Paul on sin, but there is little awareness of the point that Rowan Greer makes: "What is clear, however, is that Augustine's conclusion that we all sinned in Adam's fall represents both a transformation of the older view he inherited and a radical novelty."[9] Most versions of the sin as power interpretation only make sense on the basis of Augustinian assumptions.

6. Related to all of the above is the implausibility of the "sin as a power" interpretation of Paul's thought that has dominated scholarship from the waning of the existentialist approach until the present.[10] The importance of this interpretation requires some critical comments. But an analysis of this scholarship faces a substantial challenge. The challenge comes from the incoherency of the idea of powers, including sin as a power, as it has been developed in this scholarship. It is extremely difficult to know what claims these interpretations are making. What is a power and how does it affect humans? Scholars claim, among other things, that sin is a sphere, a demonic being, and most vaguely of all "a power" or a "cosmic power." "Cosmic" here must mean worldwide or involving extension across the universe or something similar, but the sense is rarely made explicit. The claim seems to be that describing sin as a power means more than that all sin and that this error against God dominates human life. But what is that

---

[7] An important exception is the Society of Biblical Literature's unit, "Hellenistic Moral Philosophy and Early Christianity" with many important publications.

[8] Famously noted by Krister Stendahl, "The Apostle Paul and the Introspective Conscience of the West," *HTR* 56 (1963), 199–215; repr. *The Writings of St. Paul*, 2nd ed. Wayne A. Meeks and John T. Fitzgerald (New York: W. W. Norton, 2007), 501–10.

[9] Rowan Greer, "Sinned We All in Adam's Fall," in *The Social World of the First Christians: Essays in Honor of Wayne A. Meeks,* ed. L. Michael White and O. Larry Yarbrough (Minneapolis: Augsburg Fortress, 1995), 382–94, at 394.

[10] For scholarship advocating the powers interpretation, see Joseph R. Dodson, *The 'Powers' of Personification: Rhetorical Purpose in the Book of Wisdom and in the Letter to the Romans* (Berlin: Walter de Gruyter, 2008), 20–24.

more? The problem comes not only from the vague idea that sin is some sort of cosmic being or force. This incoherency, I think, comes also from the fact that the writers in question have not supplied a coherent psychology from the letters to explain how these powers work on humans. Thus, the modern talk of powers in Paul's letters stands in sharp contrast to ancient and medieval doctrines of sin and original sin that had coherent moral psychologies, even if they featured humans struggling with the Devil and demons. Now the groundbreaking work of Emma Wasserman has demolished the claim that sin as the powers of evil finds its basis in Jewish apocalyptic writings.[11]

Christian thinkers until Augustine, and after him in the East, assume and even explicitly acknowledge that Paul had a basic psychology common to educated people in the Greco-Roman world and beyond. When he talks about mind (*nous*) and several synonyms, the emotions (*pathē*), appetite (*epithumia*), the flesh, the body and its parts, and so on, these Christian writers recognize a version of this psychology. Christian writers before Augustine who interpret Paul on sin hold that mortal fleshly human nature is the cause of the tendency toward sin, and they explain this claim with the moral psychology that is lucidly presented in Romans 7 and other places.[12] As Theodoret nicely summarizes, "such a nature needs many things . . . and these needs often arouse the passions to disorder. The disorder generates sin."[13] Before his radical turn, Augustine agreed: "Thus here [Rom 6:12] he shows we still have desires but, by not obeying them, that we do not allow sin to reign in us. But these desires arise from the mortality of the flesh, which we bear from the first sin of the first man, whence we are born fleshly" (*Prop. Ad Rom.* 13–18).[14]

Augustine, drawing especially from the thought of the founder of Neo-Platonism, Plotinus, makes a number of quite dramatic changes to this basic psychology. Most radically, he introduces a ruling will that is distinct from and can stand back from and in judgment on its own reasonings, beliefs, and desires, and the idea of a perverted will.[15] When combined with the Neo-Platonic

---

[11] *Apocalypse as Holy War: Divine Politics and Polemics in the Letters of Paul* (New Haven, CT: Yale University Press, 2018).

[12] Lucid, that is, if taken in terms of the ancient conceptions, but highly confused by attempts to read modern conceptions and claims about Jewish uniqueness into the texts.

[13] Translation from Greer, "Sinned We All," 287.

[14] Translation by Paula Fredriksen Landes, *Augustine on Romans: Propositions from the Epistle to the Romans; Unfinished Commentary on the Epistle to the Romans* (Chico, CA: Scholars Press, 1982), 7.

[15] For the idea of the will and Augustine's contribution, see Sorabji, *Peace of Mind*, 319–40, 400–417; Simo Knuuttila, "The Emergence of the Logic of the Will in Medieval Thought," in *The Augustinian Tradition*, ed Gareth B. Matthews (Berkeley: University of California Press, 1999), 206–21. On the bizarre autonomy from oneself, see Tad Brennan, *The Stoic Life: Emotions, Desire and Fate* (New York: Oxford University Press, 2005), 288–305.

notions that this pinpoint true self and God are to be found by introspection, a view of the person emerges that is dramatically different than Paul's. In Paul's letters and in Classical and Hellenistic thought – and I would argue ancient Mediterranean folk thought generally, including Jewish – willing is inseparable from one's beliefs, reasonings, and rational desires. In spite of his innovations, Augustine worked within the framework of ancient psychology, including his famous misreading of the Stoic ideas of assent to impressions and the pre-passions, and its developments in Neo-Platonism.[16] Both the "existentialist" and the "powers" approaches either ignore or deny this ancient psychology, sometimes claiming that Paul is *sui generis* or has some unique Jewish or Old Testament psychology.[17]

The scholarship also comes in two major varieties with different emphases.[18] The conservative variety uses "sin as a power" to stand in for traditional theologies of original sin. This is the personal and inherited sin for which Christ died. "Sin as power" supposedly explains, among other things, why all need Christ and why "humans cannot do good on their own." Instead of focusing on the sinfulness of each individual, the liberal variety speaks more vaguely of existential evils such as death and the law and especially of social and political evils as powers. In viewing the latter as structural and not just a matter of individuals, scholars suggest that these evils are like or are symbolized by demonic powers. The approach enables the construal of Paul's message as liberal and liberatory.

Although this tradition has frequently invoked a supposedly apocalyptic background for the idea of powers, that background does not exist. Apocalyptic literature does speak of Belial, Satan, fallen and evil angels, demons, and so forth, but not personified or metaphorical abstractions such as sin, law and grace.[19] Moreover, in these writings such evil beings do not take over human agency from the outside or control the world as envisaged in the powers interpretation.[20] The very psychology used by Paul in Romans 7 and elsewhere is used by ancient Christian writers before Augustine to argue that although humans can

---

[16] Sorabji, *Peace of Mind*, 372–84; Knuuttila, "Logic of Will," 208–11.

[17] For criticism of these claims, see Robert H. Gundry, *Soma in Biblical Theology, with an Emphasis on Pauline Anthropology* (Cambridge: Cambridge University Press, 1976); David E. Aune, "Human Nature and Ethics in Hellenistic Philosophical Traditions and Paul: Some Issues and Problems," in *Paul in His Hellenistic Context*, ed. Troels Engberg-Pedersen (Edinburgh: T&T Clark, 1994), 291–312, at 298–99.

[18] For one attempt to draw a lineage to debates about sin, death, and law as powers, See Martinus C. de Boer, *The Defeat of Death: Apocalyptic Eschatology in 1 Corinthians 15 and Romans 5* (Sheffield: Sheffield Academic, 1988), 15–37.

[19] Emma Wasserman, *Apocalypse as Holy War*, 6–17. See John Collins's sober assessment – the assessment of an expert on apocalyptic literature – of apocalyptic elements in Paul's letters: John J. Collins, *The Apocalyptic Imagination*, 2nd ed. (Grand Rapids: Eerdmans, 1998), 264–68.

[20] Wasserman, *Apocalypse as Holy War*, 173–210.

be sorely tempted by evil agents, they have the capacity to resist.[21] Second, and most importantly, Paul's language about sin and psychological conceptions in Romans 6–8 can be fully accounted for with elegant economy and coherence of thought without appeal to the thesis of external or internal powers.

Paul's letters give evidence of four major discourses that relate to the theme of sin. These four have histories and cultural settings that sometimes overlapped and were sometimes related to one another by writers before Paul.[22] They are: (1) the sinfulness of the non-Judean peoples; (2) the degeneration of humanity; (3) the time of the apex of sinfulness; (4) the psychology of sin. I will briefly discuss each and then address their usefulness in accounting for Paul's conception of sin.

I begin with "the degeneration of humanity" because it is in many ways the most comprehensive and widespread.[23] Indeed, this way of thinking seems to be endemic to highly traditional cultures. The basic idea is that early humans were better than those of the present day and that at some point wickedness set in and has become more and more prevalent as time moves toward the present. Genesis 1–10 is written from a similar perspective, and there is much evidence that Jews in the Greco-Roman world read it in this way and sometimes harmonized it at various points with Hesiod's decline from a golden age and other myths of degeneration.[24] There is massive evidence for the prevalence of such narratives and their central importance in Ancient Mediterranean and West Asian cultures. Jewish apocalyptic literature centrally draws on this kind of myth. The Watchers myth, the race of giants and the loss of human longevity, for example, are motifs from such narratives.[25] As Gen 3:22–24 and

---

[21] Origen crafts what becomes the standard account when he reinterprets the Stoic pre-passions as bad thoughts that are sent by demons and the Devil. Individuals always have the ability to recognize and reject these. See Sorabji, *Peace of Mind*, 346–71 and 372–84 for Augustine's revolutionary changes (compare 315–40, 400–417).

[22] Key work on Paul and myth is being done by Stephen Young, such as "Mythological Themes in Romans," in *The Oxford Handbook of the Letter to the Romans*, ed. Davina Lopez (New York: Oxford University Press, Forthcoming) and his forthcoming book on Paul as mythmaker.

[23] Arthur O. Lovejoy and George Boas, *Primitivism and Related Ideas in Antiquity* (New York: Octagon Books, 1965). Among other studies are W. K. C. Guthrie, *In the Beginning: Some Greek Views on the Origins of Life and the Early State of Man* (London: Methuen, 1957); Ludwig Edelstein, *The Idea of Progress in Classical Antiquity* (Baltimore: Johns Hopkins University Press, 1967); Bodo Gatz, *Weltalter, goldene Zeit und sinnerwandte Vorstellungen* (Hildersheim: G. Olms, 1967); G. R. Boys-Stones, *Post-Hellenistic Philosophy: A Study of its Development from the Stoics to Origen* (Oxford: Oxford University Press, 2001). For West Asian sources, M. L. West, *Hesiod: Works and Days* (Oxford: Oxford University Press, 1978), 172–78.

[24] Stowers, *Rereading of Romans*, 88–92.

[25] Ronald Hendel, "Nephilim Were on The Earth: Genesis 6:1–4 and its Near Eastern Context," in *The Fall of Angels*, ed. Christoph Auffarth and Loren T. Stuckenbruck (Leiden: Brill, 2004), 11–34, at 30–34, on similar Greek traditions see, Loren T. Stuckenbruck, "The Origins of Evil in Jewish Apocalyptic Traditions: The Interpretation of Genesis 6:1–4 in the Second and Third Centuries B. C. E.," in Auffarth and Stuckenbruck, *The Fall of Angels*, 87–118.

especially 6:3 were sometimes read by Jews and early Christians as an explanation for human mortality, so also the Hesiodic myth of the first sacrifice and the Pandora story were so read. On this basis, both cultures connected the origins of death with sin against the divine. Paul's gentile audiences would not have found his connection of sin and death with primeval humanity either novel or strange.

Such primitivism was important in the thinking of philosophers of different schools. Building on Augustine's misunderstandings and misrepresentations of Greek and Roman philosophy, especially Protestant theological and exegetical traditions have often spoken of the "optimism" of Greek philosophy, but a much more nuanced understanding is needed. Stoicism, for example, taught that all humans, with a handful of possible exceptions, perhaps some of the earliest humans, were so deeply mired in wickedness that no one did anything that was truly good.[26] Stoics explained the universality of wickedness with an account of how innate human tendencies lead to corrupt socialization that mired people in false values and hardened habits.[27] They did allow for much progress toward virtue and actions that were approximations in the direction of the truly good, but insisted nevertheless that all were vicious. Epicureans taught that humans had lived morally good lives in the simple society of a primitive past, but that all of human society had evolved into a deep corruption.[28] Cynics had a similar primitivism. The moral degeneration of humanity was a particularly popular motif in the post-Augustan period in which Paul lived.[29] No one would have been shocked by Paul's statement that "all are under sin." Yet the conventional approach is to suppose that Paul's teachings about sin were novel and shocking.

It is of interest that various writers, and especially philosophers, brought law into their accounts of human degeneration.[30] There appears a common pattern that Paul shares. The first human beings lived well in a state of nature with a good relationship to the gods. Then at some point degeneration began and at another point they invented law to help control the growth of human wickedness. While sources may claim that the ancient laws were wise, even divinely guided, they hold that they could not stem the general development of wickedness. So Paul's contemporary Seneca has law come in to address the growth of human evil (*Ep.* 90.4–6, 37–39). Before the growth of wickedness,

---

[26] On Stoics and the other schools, see n. 23 above and Stowers, *Rereading of Romans*, 98–99, 181–2.

[27] Margaret Graver, *Stoicism and Emotion* (Chicago: University of Chicago Press, 2007), 154–71.

[28] David Konstan, *A Life Worthy of the Gods: The Materialist Psychology of Epicurus* (Las Vegas: Parmenides, 2008), 79–125.

[29] Stowers, *Rereading of Romans*, 52–65.

[30] For Cynic texts on law, see H.W. Hollander and J. Holleman, "The Relationship of Death, Sin and Law in 1 Cor 15:56," *NovT* 35 (1993): 270–91. Hollander and Holleman and my *Rereading of Romans* independently have argued for the importance of the primitivism and degeneration themes for Paul's thought.

Seneca says that people sinned (*peccare*), but since they were ignorant of virtue and vice, they were less blameworthy (*Ep.* 90.46). The Stoic Posidonius had a variation on this scheme. There were earlier effective lawgivers of the golden age that included Moses and Solon, but later laws and law-keepers became corrupt.[31] Some Cynic writing in the name of Diogenes at a date near Paul's career, after excoriating Greeks for vice and lust, says, "Therefore nature takes vengeance on you, for in contriving laws for yourselves you have allotted to yourselves the greatest and most pervasive delusion that issues from them, and you admit them as witnesses to your ingrained evil."[32] Or in a letter of Ps. Heraclitus to the Ephesians, we hear:

> You transgress the laws, you enact illegalities, you perform by force everything which you cannot do by nature. The things which seem to be preeminently the symbols of justice among you, the laws, are evidence of vice. For if they did not exist, you would commit vice freely all the same, but now you are curbed, even if just a little, by fear of punishment you are kept from committing injustice.[33]

Here law restrains evil just enough to be a witness to the wickedness of the Ephesians.

What is missing from Jewish, Hellenistic and Paul's accounts of sin is the pinpointing of Adam's or the primal human act of disobedience and explaining sin or human nature by an analysis of that primal sin. Rather, Jewish and Hellenistic sources, together with Paul's letters, treat sin by giving it a history. In contrast, for Augustine, nothing truly essential was added to the nature of sin after Adam's primal act. This is in part because of Augustine's meta-narrative now invisible to many New Testament exegetes that took the explanation back to the fall of angels (*Gen. imp.* 11.24–5; *Civ.* 14.11). Primal human sin was anticipated by the fall of angels, one of whom sent the serpent to the garden (*Gen. imp.* 11.2–3; *Civ.* 14:11). The perversion of the angelic will is a model for human perversion due to acts of pride and "being pleased with oneself."[34] Behind this narrative lies Plotinus's account of the fall of humans into bodies with an act of pride (*tolma*) that was a turning away from the Good, by a "willing to belong only to themselves" and "being pleased with" their own self-determination (*Enn.* 5.1, alluded to in Augustine, *Civ.* 10.23). As in Origen's meta-narrative of a

---

[31] If indeed Posidonius is the source for Strabo, *Geogr.* 16.2.34–39 as is often thought.

[32] Trans. Benjamin Fiore, in A. J. Malherbe, *The Cynic Epistles* (Missoula, MT: Scholars Press, 1977), 121.

[33] Translation from Harold Attridge, *First Century Cynicism in the Epistles of Heraclitus* (Missoula, MT: Scholars Press, 1976), 6.

[34] For the pride of angels, see *Conf.* 7.3.5 and for the primal human fall, *Civ.* 14.13. There is, of course, much more to be said including about lust as a result and punishment for the act of disobedience in the later Augustine.

grand pre-creation fall of spiritual creatures, the result was embodiment. Modern interpreters have suffered from amnesia about the cosmic and primal dramas of the perverting act, but with the mediation of the Protestant reformers, they have inherited a naturalized "anthropology of sin" from Plotinus and Augustine. But Rom 7 and other key texts betray a robust Hellenistic language, structure and conceptuality that cannot be made to square with a divided, perverted will that makes sin into a universal controlling power.

In spite of the massive amounts of ink that have been spilled on asking how in Rom 5 Adam's sin was causative of human sinfulness, Paul follows extant Jewish sources in showing no interest in that question.[35] Rather, his interest is in epochs in the history of sin and salvation. Paul's mention of sin and death – beginning with Adam, and then sin being in the world before the law, the period from Adam to Moses (5:12–14) and then on to his big point about the universality of Adam and Christ – clearly envisages sin as having the kind of history seen in Jewish and other forms of primitivism. Sin began, it spread, it was not reckoned in the period before the law, Adam sinned in one way, later people in another, and law came in to make the trespass greater. This is not a view of sin from the perspective of a moment in the pre-mundane heavenly realm or in the Garden that changed human nature.

Paul connects the second major discourse about sin, the Gentiles as sinners, with his narrative about the degeneration of humanity. The turning of the nations away from God and to idols forms a central event of that story. Of course, this is a standard reading of Gen 1–11 seen in Jewish sources. Romans 1:18–32 is about the degeneration of the Gentiles into idolatry and therefore moral debasement. As scholars agree, there is indeed much evidence in extant Jewish writings (mostly preserved by Christians) produced by literate elite that characterized non-Jews as sinful peoples who had rejected the true god. Most Jews likely did not hold such views of their non-Jewish neighbors. This rhetoric can only be understood historically if we remember that writers, and moralists more broadly, in the Greco-Roman world had declared that humans had degenerated morally over the course of history. It is even possible for Greek and Roman writers to connect this degeneration with the beginnings of iconic worship. In his *Antiquities*, Varro wrote that the Romans had worshipped without images for 170 years after the founding of Rome: "If this practice had continued to the present . . . the worship of the gods would have been purer . . . Those who first set up the images for the people diminished reverence in their cities and they increased error (frag. 18; Augustine, *Civ.* 4.31)."

As I have argued in detail elsewhere, Rom 1:18–2:16, indicts Gentiles from the perspective of their historic turning away from God and formation of various peoples who replaced the worship of the Judean God with iconic

---

[35] John R. Levinson, *Portraits of Adam in Early Judaism from Sirach to 2 Baruch* (Sheffield: Sheffield Academic Press, 1988).

cults representing different cultures.³⁶ As Joseph Fitzmyer writes about commentators who want to find the narratives about Adam from Gen 2–3 in Rom 1, "this interpretation reads too much into the text." Moreover, it ignores Paul's clear focus on the Gentiles and the way of thinking about sin through narratives of degeneration found in Jewish writings before and contemporary with Paul. Two other important themes from the degeneration discourse also appear in this section of Romans: natural worship without icons and the entry of the law as witness to the decline into vice. I have already discussed the law motif in Greek and Roman writers. Romans 1:32 ("they know God's regulation") anticipates the motif as it rhetorically sets up the appearance of the imaginary Gentile addressee of 2:1–16 and becomes explicit in 14–16. In 1:19–30 Paul reviews the history of Gentile degeneration that he makes relevant to the situation of contemporary Gentiles by speaking to an imaginary individual in 2:1–16. Regardless of how one solves the issue of the Gentiles having the law in 2:14–16 they do at least sometimes know the law and one result is that the law known in their minds will bear witness to the conflicted psyche of the Gentile. The verses anticipate the conflicted person of 7:7–24. The law is not the solution to the moral and religious condition of the Gentiles.

Chapter One indicates an age of natural worship without icons before the turn to idols. Paul clearly agrees with Genesis, Jewish writers, Varro and others when he talks about how the truth about the one God was clear to these people through what could be perceived in the creation, and then says that, "they changed" to worshipping gods "in the form of humans (e.g., Greeks, Romans), birds (e.g., Egyptians), four footed animals (e.g., Egyptians, "Canaanites"), or reptiles (Egyptians)." They changed from something and the something has to be "the eternal power and divinity" said to be clearly manifest in created nature (1:19–20). Paul agrees in supposing a golden age or age of truth and purity before the turn to false gods and the build-up of evil. Commentators habitually and rightly point to Wis 12–15 and sometimes *Sib. Or.* 3.8–45 where God is known in the creation, but this idea is a key feature of golden age primitivism more generally. Wisdom draws on Greek philosophical religious critiques as well as West Asian and Jewish aniconic discourses. Again in Seneca's letter that treats early humans, the onset of degeneration, and the introduction of law, he writes about the early religion: "Such are wisdom's rites of initiation, by means of which is unlocked, not a village shrine, but the vast temple of all the gods – the universe itself, whose true portraits and features she offers to the gaze of minds" (*Ep.* 90.28).³⁷ Before the degeneration, humans did not need images made with

---

³⁶ Stowers, *Rereading of Romans*, 1–150.
³⁷ Translation is from Attridge, *First-Century Cynicism*, 21. I have changed his "apparitions" and his "aspects" to "portraits" and "features" respectively because I read *simulacra* and *facies* as playing on *sacrum*, a human made representation of the god or the gods presence.

hands because they could clearly see God's nature in the created universe.[38] The letter cited above about law in the name of Heraclitus rants,

> You stupid people, teach us first what God is, so that you may be trusted when you speak of committing impiety. Secondly, where is God? Is he shut up in temples? You are a fine sort of pious people, who set up god in darkness! ... You ignorant people, don't you know that God is not wrought by hands, and has not from the beginning had a pedestal, and does not have a single enclosure? Rather the whole world is his temple, decorated with animals, plants and stars (*Ep.* 4.10–15).[39]

The truth about God can be seen in the creation and he was not originally worshipped with images. Images are an abomination. About the time that the building of the second temple in Jerusalem was being finished, the real Heraclitus wrote, "they pray to such statues as if they were idly talking to houses, knowing nothing of the gods or heroes, who they really are" (*Fr.* 5). Xenophanes, who was born seventeen years after the fall of the first temple, was an even harsher critic of iconic religion (*Fr.* 21.B11, 12, 14–16). Judean writings on these topics was not *sui generis* but participated in broader cross-cultural discourses.

Examples could be multiplied, but the point is that in talking about sin, Romans exhibits an approach that dominated important intellectual strains of Greek, Roman and Jewish culture of assuming an age where people naturally worshipped in the right way, then, the onset of some pattern of religious and moral degeneration, sometimes with a discussion of law. This discourse figures the current moral and religious state of the world as a result of this history. The approach also seen in Paul belies explanations of the current state by means of "The Fall," an idea that Christian scholars have intensively, but with little luck, looked for in early Jewish texts.[40] Sin for Paul has a genuine history that is central to the apocalyptic aspects of his thought.

In explaining how humans degenerated into the idolatrous Gentile peoples, three times Paul writes that "God handed them over" to successively greater degrees and amounts of moral evil (1:24, 26, 28). Each repetition and expansion suggests another stage in the history of degeneration in allusion to Paul's way of reading Genesis. Now this is where, on the sin-as-an-evil-power

---

[38] Stoics accommodated popular belief and talk of "gods" as a reference to the many aspects of God's power and manifestations in the world and believed in celestial divinities.

[39] Translation is from Attridge, *First-Century Cynicism*, 59. I have changed his "men" to "people" because the word is *anthropos*. I also think that it would be better to capitalize "god" because the Cynic writer is certain to have had a specific conception of a deity in mind, the one God.

[40] Made clear in Levinson, *Portraits of Adam*; Stowers, *Rereading of Romans*, 86–89.

reading, one would expect such beings to be introduced. The Jewish sources to which the powers reading appeal connect the origins of idolatry with the origins of evil superhuman powers in their reading of Gen 6:4, where the sons of God come down from God's court and mate with women, leading to the flood and its aftermath, and the punishment of the giant offspring. These traditions are extremely complex and cannot occupy us here. But the gist of a likely connection with Paul would be that the origin of fallen angels, evil spirits and demons on the earth was traced to the descent and punishment of these beings. 1 Enoch 19:1 predicts, "They [spirits of the angels] have defiled the people and will lead them into error so that they will offer sacrifices to the demons as unto gods."[41] Paul's thought may be indebted to this tradition. His command for women to wear head coverings "because of the angels" (1 Cor 11:10) may reflect the idea of angels subject to temptation or evil angels. He writes that when Gentiles sacrifice, they sacrifice to demons (1 Cor 10:20–21). Interestingly, at the conclusion of this section, a warning about the temptation to evil, he writes that the story of the golden calf is a lesson for "us upon whom the end of the ages has come." Then he says (10:13), "no temptation has come to you that is not common to humans. God is faithful and he will not allow you to be tempted beyond your power to resist." So not only does Paul not bring in "apocalyptic powers" to explain the turn of the nations toward idolatry and sin, but he holds a view generally found in those apocalyptic writings that humans cannot be taken over by such evil beings against their wills.[42] Of course, Paul thinks that the age is dominated by masses of people who have allowed themselves to serve evil beings.[43] But such cooperation is not what scholars have in mind when they speak of sin as a power.

Even more dramatically at odds with the way that Paul's ideas about sin are usually presented, he writes plainly and pointedly that God has caused the Gentile wickedness. He does not explain how God is the cause, but Jewish and even apocalyptic writings offer an explanation in their assumption that God is in control of the earth and the larger cosmos.[44] God may allow evil

---

[41] Translation is by E. Isaac in *OTP*, 1:23.

[42] Wasserman, *Apocalypse as Holy War*.

[43] So in Gal 4:8 the readers of the letter were formerly enslaved to beings that are not truly gods. In 1:4, "Christ gave himself for our sins to free us from the present evil age according to the will of God." The idea of God's control of history is clear in the passage and fits with my reading of Romans. People and even cultures as a whole can choose allegiance to God or the evil beings, but (1) such allegiance involves choice and culpability and (2) God is ultimately in control of the course of history. An important text is 2 Cor 4:4 where the "god of this world" (likely Belial as in 6:4) is said to have blinded the minds of "the unbelievers" (Paul's competitors) so that they cannot accept Paul's message and legitimacy. The idea here, I think, is that they have participated in their own downfall allowing themselves to come under to influence of Belial.

[44] Wasserman, *Apocalypse as Holy War*.

spirits and evil humans some freedom to cause havoc, but usually with a larger purpose. In Jubilees, for instance, as in the writings in the Enoch corpus, evil spirits and demons are the souls or spirits of the dead giants. When God orders the angels to bind these spirit beings for judgment, their leader, Mastema, begs to allow a portion of the spirits to remain in order to tempt humans to evil and cause sickness (10:8, 12). These evil powers are limited by God (10:13), operate with God's permission and finally will be destroyed (10:8). The two most prominent purposes for causing or allowing moral degeneracy or the operation of evil beings are to punish evil and to allow the righteous to suffer as a test of faithfulness.[45]

We might be able to ignore Paul's talk of God "handing the Gentiles over" were it not for some other key passages. The same metaphor of imprisonment occurs in Gal 3:22–23. Paul has just asked rhetorically, "Is the law against the promises of God?" Note that Paul is thinking "historically" and "apocalyptically" (e.g., *apokalyptein* in 3:23) in talking about the promises of God. He has been talking since 3:6 about the promise given to Abraham as scripture "declared the gospel beforehand," that the Gentiles would be blessed in his seed.[46] In answering the question about the law being against the promises, he writes that this could only be the case if the law could bring about human life. Then he continues, "scripture imprisoned all things under sin in order that the promise through the faithfulness of Jesus Christ might be given to those who are faithful." Only here and in Romans does Paul talk in this programmatic way about sin.[47] Both letters focus on the Abrahamic promise to the Gentiles. Again, it is not sin as a cosmic power or an evil being that is behind "all being under sin," but God as he has recorded it and ordained it in scripture. According to Paul's reading of scripture and its prophetic foretelling of history, "all things" were somehow required by God to be imprisoned under sin so that the promise of Abraham might come to the Gentiles. And I would argue also that other promises might come to the Jews, but Paul only hints at that, although he says a bit more in Romans.

The language about sinfulness, all being under sin and God causing sin also appears in Romans 9–11 where Paul dramatically announces that "all Israel" (the Jews) will be saved according to scripture when "a deliverer will come from Zion" (11:26). This salvation of the Jews will only happen after "the full number of Gentiles has come in" (11:25). The discussion in this whole section

---

[45] Barry D. Smith in *Paul's Seven Explanations of the Suffering of the Righteous*, (New York: Peter Lang, 2002), discusses these motifs in Paul and some of the Jewish literature. I cannot, however, accept his absurd claim that Paul was uninfluenced by "Hellenism" and his highly uncritical Christian theological construction of Judaism.

[46] See Chapter Seven in this volume.

[47] He does of course talk about Christ dying on behalf of sin. A passage outside of Romans and Galatians that might be in the same ballpark is 1 Cor 15:56.

has been an embarrassment to theologians and commentators who have feared apocalyptic forms of Christianity and who have wanted Paul's theology to be neatly about fallen human nature and its restoration. The scandal is that Paul turns out to be a committed Judean of his own time and not a Christian apostate. In a passage that seems to be a conclusion to the long discourse that began in 1:18, he uses the same verb, "to imprison," that he uses in Gal 3:22:

> As regards the gospel, they (the Jews) are enemies on your (Gentiles, the audience) behalf, but as regards God's choosing them (Jews), they are loved because of the patriarchs, for God's gifts and calling cannot be revoked. Just as you (Gentiles, the audience) were once disobedient to God, but now have been shown mercy due to their (Jews) disobedience, so they (Jews) have now become disobedient so that by the mercy shown to you (Gentiles) they (Jews) also may now be shown mercy.

Who caused this disobedience of all? "For God imprisoned all in disobedience so that he might have mercy upon all" (11:32).

Just as chapter 1 explains how God handed the Gentiles over to wickedness, so chapter 9 explains how God has caused the Jews to be disobedient, ending with a quotation from Isaiah, in which God says that he is planning to make his people stumble (Isa 28:16 and 8:14 in 9:33).[48] The chapter stresses that God is not unjust, however, because he only does this for the greater good and in order to be merciful as in the examples of making only some of Abraham's descendants part of the chosen lineage that will save all and as in causing the Pharaoh to hold the Israelites so that he could save them. While the now dominant Western reading of Romans has taken the letter's talk of Gentile sin in chapter 1 as about the Adamic Fall, Chapters 9–11 clearly could not be forced into the pattern and have been therefore treated as historical and prophetic. After all, the focus of these chapters is on recent history. As I read it, God has stalled the expected judgment of the world's peoples in order to allow their turning to God. If the judgment had occurred with Christ's coming, only the Jews would have been saved. God's temporary hardening of the Jews has allowed the decades for Paul's successful mission to the Gentiles. "When the full number of Gentiles come in" God's hardening will come to an end, and all Israel will be saved (11:25). God has imprisoned all in sin (3:9–20; 5:18–21; 11:25–32; Gal 3: 21–29) so that he can have mercy on all. From the idolatrous turning of the peoples after the flood, to the choosing of a someday universally salvific people with Abraham, to Jesus Christ the saving descendant of Abraham, to the temporary unbelief of the Jews, to the mission

---

[48] Stowers, *Rereading of Romans*, 285–316.

to the Gentiles, God has in some sense caused the rising and falling, the sinfulness of peoples so that he can bring about a universal equality in redemption. Whether this is a coherent scenario that makes God just is not my concern, but taking Paul's claims seriously does make his conception of sin more coherent for a historical reading. The reading brings this coherency without an invisible meta-narrative of a pre-mundane fall, a change of human moral nature in the Garden, or sin as a cosmic power that controls humans.

The third discourse, the apex of sin, is important for making sense of my combination of the four passages above that speak of all being under sin.[49] Romans 1:18–3:20 does not attempt to prove that all humans – first the Gentiles and then the Jews – are equally sinful due to the ontological change that occurred in the Adamic Fall. Rather the anger of God that is now manifest in the current historical moment is called forth by human sinfulness having reached epic proportions, the fullness of sin, the apex of sin. The sinfulness of the Jews and the other peoples have different histories that have led to the crisis of the present moment. The germ of the idea can be traced back to Gen 15:16 and the theme of the immoral Canaanites. The Genesis text explains why Abraham's descendants have to wait in exile for the land: The wickedness of the Amorites is not yet complete. In the "table of nations," Gen 10:15–20 explains how the cursed descendants of Canaan settled in the land and included the Amorites. Elsewhere writers identify the wickedness of the Canaanites as both sexual immorality (Lev 18:24–30), already suggested in Canaan's cursing, and idolatry (Ex 23:23–24). The Canaanites become the paradigm of the morally depraved idol-worshipping Gentiles. Add the Sodom story read as about the moral nature of the Canaanites and one has key elements Paul's scriptural background for the degeneration of the Gentiles stimulating much later literature and seen in Romans.

Daniel 8:23 uses the motif when Gabriel interprets Daniel's dream as a vision about the "time of the end" when "transgressions have reached their full measure" and when a king will arise. The king, of course, is Antiochus IV to be punished by God when God vindicates his people. The episode becomes the model for later apocalyptic scenarios. Paul knows and explicitly uses the concept in 1 Thess 2:14–16, a passage often wrongly punctuated and mistranslated in ways that have read traditional Christian anti-Jewish ideas into it.[50] The verses do not say that God's wrath has come upon all of the Jews, but upon just the Jews who killed Jesus and the prophets and who have opposed Paul's mission

---

[49] This discourse includes the sufferings and tribulations of the time before the end well-known from Mark 13 and parallels. See further Stowers, *Rereading of Romans*, 185–193. For a discussion of the Jewish evidence, see Dale C. Allison, *The End of the Ages Has Come* (Philadelphia: Fortress, 1985), 5–25.

[50] Abraham J. Malherbe, *The Letters to the Thessalonians* (New York: Doubleday, 2000), 164–79.

to the Gentiles. These Judeans thus "constantly fill up their sins. [God's] Anger has come upon them [moving] toward its completion (*eis telos*)."⁵¹ As Abraham Malherbe points out, this expresses an apocalyptic conception elsewhere seen in 1 En. 84:4: "and your wrath shall rest upon the flesh of the people until the great day of judgment." The idea that God's anger has in the past punished and is now punishing up until the last judgment is central to Rom 1:18–2:16.

In 1:18, God's anger is now being revealed against the Gentiles.⁵² What is this punishment of idolaters? God has caused or allowed them to be unable to resist the impulses of their appetites and emotions (1:24, 26–27) and, as chapter 7 will explain, to have a mind that does not have the strength to resist the appetites and emotions. In 1:27, he calls the result "a penalty for their error" suffered "in themselves." When Paul's authorial voice addresses an imaginary Gentile in 2:10–16 who does the "same things" as the Gentiles in chapter 1, Paul proclaims (2:5–13) that he will be judged impartially with all evil Jews and Gentiles on the "day of wrath." But Paul also explains that Gentiles somehow have the law in themselves and that the record of their mental awareness will testify to their divided self on the day of judgment. Here I think that Paul is forecasting the divided person of Rom 7:7–25. The person's mind wants to do God's law but cannot because it is enslaved to and overpowered by its appetites of the flesh. God's sentence of enslavement to the appetites and emotions does not eliminate knowledge of God and the good, but results in a terrible inner division as Gentiles have an awareness of their own bondage. God's punishment of the Gentiles lies in the historical past, but also the present and will be finalized on the day of judgment.

"Fullness of sin" makes sense in this context of sin with a history and limited future. Thus, for Jews who killed Christ and hindered the Gentile mission, Paul says that in acting this way they "fill up constantly the measure of their sins."⁵³ Here is the idea that God allows the truly evil who have rejected him to accumulate a record of evil to a level at which a horrible final punishment is just and imminent. The concept involves a distinction between the wicked, on the one hand, and fallible humans as ordinary sinners, on the other. So, an opposing conception usually applies to Israel, the Jews. As 2 Macc 6:14 says:

> For with other peoples (Gentiles), the Lord patiently (*makrothymein*) holds back from punishing them until they have attained the full measure of their sins; but he does not see fit to deal this way with us (Jews), in order that he may not take vengeance on us later when our sins have reached their limit (*telos*).

---

⁵¹ Malherbe has shown it quite unlikely that *eis telos* could mean "forever" or "at last." I am not sure that I understand his translation of "until the end." But the idea is that the divine anger seen now is on a trajectory toward a final or total expression of that anger.

⁵² Paul refers only to the Gentiles in 1:18. God's anger is against the impiety and wickedness of those who suppress the truth, and 1:18–24 explains this as the use of images in worship.

⁵³ Trans. Malherbe, *Thessalonians*, 165.

God punishes the Jews as history goes on so that their sins do not accumulate (also Wis 12:1), but the sins of the Gentiles are filling up toward their destruction.

This concept of the fullness of sin, and not the Adamic nature, is central to the arguments and rhetoric of Rom 1:18–3:26. Insight comes by noticing that in this concept God's patience and his holding back of punishment are negative and have dire consequences for the wicked. Thus, Paul warns the Gentile that his refusal to repent and accept God's mercy means that he is "storing up wrath for the day of wrath" (2:4–5). Sam K. Williams has argued persuasively that 3:25b-26 contains the idea of God through Christ taking care of the accumulated Gentile sins that he had overlooked.[54] I translate it as follows: "This was to demonstrate God's righteousness because he passed over previous [Gentile] sins when he held back punishment; it was to demonstrate his own righteousness at this time in history so as to be righteous himself and to make righteous the person who lives on the basis of Jesus's faithfulness." In my reading, Paul is here specifically giving an account of how the Gentiles are being saved. As 3:9–20 shows, the Jews are also sinners in need of God's mercy, but it is the Gentiles who have had their sin passed over. They have a very long history of unforgiven and unatoned sins. The punishment by bondage to passion does not satisfy God's judgment that they deserve death (1:32) and God has allowed their sins to accumulate. In a discussion with an imaginary Jewish teacher of Gentiles or a Gentile who wants to become a Jew (2:17–3:8), Paul forecasts chapters 9–11 by suggesting that Jews have failed to accept Christ and fulfill their mission of being a light to the Gentiles (3:1–8; 2:19–24).[55] God is therefore just in exercising his wrath against them (3:5–7).

The words that I translate as "the present time in history" (*nun kairo*) indicate that God's act, like the current revelation of his anger (1:18), is a central event in his final plan for the world's peoples. The discussion with the Jewish teacher (2:17–3:8) clearly has the Jewish reaction to Christ and the Gentile mission in view. It makes no sense then to follow the exegetical tradition of treating 3:9–20 as the conclusion of an argument that all humans have a timeless depraved Adamic nature. That section, like those that come before and after, are about God's climactic actions in recent history. The section resembles passages in apocalypses that describe the fullness of sin, the apex of wickedness that prompts God to intervene and to save the righteous. Paul took the chain of scriptural passages (3:10–18) as prophetic of the fullness of sin when all peoples, including Israel, would at the same time stand in sinful rebellion. Because the Jews are included, there is nothing about the sins caused by

---

[54] Sam K. Williams, *Jesus' Death as Saving Event: The Background and Origin of a Concept*, (Missoula, MT: Scholars Press, 1975).

[55] Stowers, *Rereading of Romans*, 143–175: Runar Thorsteinsson, *Paul's Interlocutor in Romans 2: Function and Identity in the Context of Ancient Epistolography*, (Stockholm: Almqvist & Wiksell International, 2003).

appetite and passion. Rather the chain features rejection of God (11–12, 18), hateful and deceiving attitudes (13–14), and violence. I suspect that behind the choice of texts stands the paradigm of the crucifixion and rejection of Jesus and the gospel that Paul sees as signifying the apex of sinfulness. Paul, I think, refers to this apocalyptic mystery in 1 Cor 2:6–8: the rulers of this sinful age who crucified Jesus ironically did not know what their act would bring. Since Romans chapter 2 has already stressed the point that Gentiles are also under the law, 3:19–20 serves as a key claim that in the fullness of sin all peoples have been made equal before God by their rejection of God. Paul will go on to explain how God has made universal sin into a plan for universal salvation in 3:21–5:21 and chapters 9–11. At this time of the fullness of sin, works of the law or knowledge of the law cannot make things right as prophesied in Ps 143:2 (Rom 3:20; Gal 2:16). Indeed, as he has already illustrated, knowledge of the law has only brought condemnation and a conflicted psyche to Gentiles.

In the narrative of Gentile degeneration, Paul adds a key Hellenistic element in writing that God handed them over to passions and appetitive desire. Like the description of the accusing and excusing mind in 2:12–16, the disorder of passion and desire anticipates chapter 7. This fourth major discourse is the moral psychology of sin. I have saved discussion of it for last in order to make a telling point: without the discourse's key text of Rom 6–8, the interpretations of Paul featuring the innate sinful nature of the Adamic fall and the recent "bondage to cosmic powers" reading would not be possible and would likely never have arisen. It is in these chapters that one finds the language taken to be about external power, the evil will and coercion. Yet I have already outlined a rich set of connecting discourses about sin without one of the invisible meta-narratives of a primal act of a perverted will of angels, Eve and Adam or of controlling demonic-like powers. I will first summarize important recent research on the language and conceptions in chapters 6–8 and then discuss its relevance to the Gentiles as sinners.

I will be drawing especially upon important recent research that uses mainstream academic scholarship on ancient philosophy and ancient moral and psychological thought more generally.[56] The moral psychologies of the Hellenistic philosophies and of educated writers of the period employed two limiting cases in thinking about ethics and psychology.[57] On one end of the

---

[56] Especially Emma Wasserman, *The Death of the Soul in Romans 7: Sin, Death, and the Law in Light of Hellenistic Moral Psychology* (Tübingen: Mohr Siebeck, 2008); idem, "The Death of the Soul in Romans 7: Revisiting Paul's Anthropology in Light of Hellenistic Moral Psychology," *JBL* 7 (2007) 793–816; idem, "Paul Among the Philosophers: The Case of Sin in Romans 6–8," *JSNT* 30 (2008) 387–415. For Romans 7 as Platonic and characteristically mixing Platonic and Stoic elements see my, "Paul and Self-Mastery," in *Paul and the Greco-Roman World*, vol 2, 2nd ed. Paul Sampley (New York: Bloomsbury T. & T. Clark, 2016), 270–300.

[57] On this psychology among the educated, see S. M. Braund and Christopher Gill, eds., *The Passions in Roman Thought and Literature* (Cambridge: Cambridge University Press, 1997).

spectrum of human possibility was the sage, someone like Moses in Philo's account or Jesus in the Synoptic gospels.[58] On the other end of the spectrum was the case of complete moral failure.[59] This latter type of person is what 1:24–32 and 7:7–25 depict, using the idiom of later Platonism that was close to popular everyday moral conceptions. The "inner person" is the well-known metaphor for the mind from Book 9 of Plato's *Republic*, often used by Philo and other later Platonists.[60] In this psychology, the person consists first of the element that should rule the other parts of the soul, the mind (*vous*; 7:23, 25), also described as the "I" or the inner person. The parts to be ruled by the mind are appetitive desire (*epithumia*; 1:24; 6:12; 7:7–8) and the emotions (1:26; 7:5). The appetites always want to pursue their objects of sex, food, drink and so on no matter whether the act be right or wrong. This kind of desire must be strongly controlled by mind/the inner person. In Paul's time the words for passions could either mean just the emotions or the whole non-rational or non-mental part (appetites and emotions) of the person. The emotions, unlike the appetites, could be directed by the mind but were prone to run out of control and work against the mind. The appetites are intimately connected with the bodily parts with which they are associated. This makes perfect sense of Paul's language about "passions of sins in our bodily parts" that is also "in the flesh" (7:5). He distinguishes sin that lives in the flesh from the core self, the "I" that is the mind (7:18). The inner person that Paul equates with the mind and the "I" (7:22–23) wants to follow God's law (7:22–23, 25b), but appetitive desire which lives in the flesh wants to follow the law of sin (7:7–8, 17–18, 21–23, 25b). Paul's psychology is Platonic and absolutely typical. Stoics would have strongly disagreed with almost everything in the description that I have given.[61]

What has been more difficult and has been proclaimed distinctive or unique are the metaphors of death, slavery, captivity and sin as an agent. Emma Wasserman, however, has shown that these metaphors are typical of tropes in the Platonic tradition of moral psychology. The speaking "I" in that chapter represents the plight of mind in the case of total moral failure. In such cases, Wasserman shows that Platonists personified vice or wickedness just as Paul does sin. Vice or wickedness could be said to have stimulated passions and

---

[58] On Jesus, see Chapter 11 in this volume ("Jesus as Teacher and Stoic Ethics in the Gospel of Matthew").

[59] Wasserman (*Death of the Soul*) discusses complete moral failure extensively.

[60] Theo Heckel, *Der Innere Mensch: Der paulinische Verarbeitung eines platonischen Motivs* (Tübingen: Mohr Siebeck, 1993); Christoph Markschies, "Innerer Mensch," *Reallexicon für Antike und Christentum* 18 (Stuttgart: Anton Hiersemann, 1997): 266–312. Unfortunately, these works show the influence of existentialist interpretations of Paul and the tendency to make him unique.

[61] Despite Troels Engberg-Pedersen's (*Paul and the Stoics* [Louisville, Kentucky: Westminster John Knox, 2000]) learned and valiant attempt to read Romans 7 in a Stoic way. See Stowers, "Self-Mastery," for a response and Graver, *Stoicism and Emotion*.

desires so as to have killed, imprisoned, ruled, and dominated reason. Paul's contemporary fellow Jew, Philo, in particular develops the metaphors of life and death in connection with either reason dominating the irrational parts or being dominated by wickedness through the passions. So also in Romans, the "I" conquered by sin *via* desire dies and sin comes alive (7:8–11). For reason to dominate the passions and desires in the bodily members is to put them to death (6:3–11). The *pneuma* (poorly trans. as spirit) of God renews the mind.[62] Paul can write, "You will live if you put to death the actions of the body by means of the *pneuma*" (8:13). Philo explains that people who are examples of total moral failure have suffered death of the soul. A wide array of ancient authors personify wickedness, vice, and other words for moral and religious error as Paul does. In the case of total moral failure, such wickedness conquers, enslaves and rules the inner person who is helpless to do what it wants. These metaphors do not work well for Stoic and Epicurean psychologies which stress psychophysical holism, but since Platonists divided the person into three parts, if the cooperation and harmony that they advocated was lost, conflict and even inner warfare and conquest could be the result. As Wasserman shows, the ancient evidence resembles Paul's usage in such complex detail that it simply preempts the need to invent an invisible meta-narrative of controlling cosmic powers.

Complete moral failure comes about when the appetites and emotions become so much stronger than the mind that the mind becomes enslaved to them. It then cannot do what it wants to do. The other parts control actions. The core self, the I, becomes alienated from what ought to rightly be its whole self. The appetites and passions can also cloud and hinder the mind's thinking, but what they cannot do is to take away the mind's desire to do the good, in Paul's case, the law. This is why, when a Gentile comes to know the law, that knowledge does no good at all and makes the situation worse (Rom 1:32; 2:14–16; 3:20; 4:15; 5:13; 7:7–13; Gal 3:19–4:7; 1 Cor 15:56). Now wicked acts become knowing sins against God; the Gentile becomes highly conflicted, and some Platonists said that knowledge of the good only excited the passions and appetites to even greater wickedness in cases of complete moral failure.[63] In Rom 7, the mind repeatedly says that it wills to do the good (7:15–20) and "I delight in the law of God as the inner person" (7:22).

Nothing could be further from Augustine's perverted will, which can never fully desire the good or Luther's adoption of that will and addition of enslavement to demons and the Devil. Luther writes,

---

[62] Also, Rom 12:3 and 2 Cor 3:18; 4:16–5:10. The 2 Corinthians texts are packed with Platonic themes including the inner person again, reflection of a perfect model, inner sight, the body as a tent, the temporal and the eternal, and other motifs.
[63] Wasserman, "Death of the Soul," 815.

And doubtless that ignorance and contempt [of God] are not seated in the flesh, in the sense of the lower and grosser affections, but in the highest and most excellent powers of man, in which righteousness, godliness and knowledge and reverence of God should reign – that is, in reason and will, and so in the very power of freewill . . .[64]

This astounding reversal of the sense of the text required that Augustine and the Reformers make Rom 2:14–16 and Rom 7 as descriptions of the psychology of the Christian.[65] Paul's portrayal of total moral failure became the picture of the Christian who still had the perverted will caused by pride but who now knew that he could only be saved by grace.

Although Paul certainly holds that his fellow Jews as a whole are under sin because of their disbelief in Christ and their failure to be a light to the Gentiles, he never charges them with complete moral failure and the appetitive sins that characterize the condition. The one text that has been pressed into service by exegetes to prove the contrary will not bear that burden for several reasons.[66] Paul apostrophizes either a Jewish teacher of Gentiles, or a Gentile who pretends to be a Jew in Rom 2:17–29 using the second person singular.[67] What Paul suggests about this individual cannot be pressed into a proposition about all Jews even if one takes the first interpretation. The passage suggests that Jews who want to reform Gentiles need to tend instead to their own proclivity to sin, but this is far from the idea of complete moral failure. The assumption that Jews sin but have recourse to repentance and forgiveness is clear in extant Jewish literature. But Paul talks about Gentiles in a different way that contrasts with Jews and those who are "in Christ." In Gal 2:15 he reports saying to Peter, "we ourselves are Jews by birth and not Gentile sinners." He exhorts the Thessalonians (1 Thess 4:4–5) "each to possess [or acquire] his own wife in holiness and honor, not in appetitive passion like the Gentiles who do not know God." Only of the Gentiles does he say that because they worshipped idols "God handed them over to the appetites of their hearts," "dishonorable passions" and "a debased mind" and then attribute a mind-numbing list of evils to them (1:24, 26, 28). Of course, in the Western theological tradition

---

[64] Martin Luther, *The Bondage of the Will*, trans. J. I. Packer and O. R. Johnston (Old Tappan, NJ: Revell, 1957), 280–81.

[65] Augustine took the text to be Paul's post-Christian struggle representing general Christian experience as was common in this tradition. See, for example, *Ep.* 157.2.6; *S.* 151.6.6; 152.2; 154.3.3 and for an excellent account of Augustine on Romans 7, Patout Burns, "Augustine's Changed Interpretation of Romans 7 and His Doctrine of Inherited Sin," *Journal of Religion and Society Suppl. Ser.* 15 (2018): 104-27.

[66] Stowers, *Rereading of Romans*, 143–75. The same point is made by Thomas S. Tobin, SJ, *Paul's Rhetoric in Context: The Argument of Romans* (Peabody, MA: Hendrickson, 2004), 117 n. 36.

[67] Stowers, *Rereading of Romans*, 143–75 and n. 55 above.

such differences of history and culture are swept away as interpreters assume a common underlying Adamic sinfulness that renders Paul's distinctions only illustrations of the universal sinful human nature passed down from Adam.

If I am correct, Rom 7 is not Paul's picture of human nature, but of something that happened in history to people in particular cultures both due to their own and God's actions. Moreover if this holds, then Christian interpreters before Augustine, and afterwards in the East, well understood Paul's moral psychology and its implications about sin, freedom and often even the law.[68] As Robert Wilken writes,

> In the Greek commentators of the fourth and fifth century, Romans did not become, as it did for Augustine, a treatise on the various stages in the life of an individual: prior to the law, under the law, under grace, and finally in peace. Romans was first and foremost a book about God's purpose in the history of the Jews and in the life of the Christian community. It was read in the context of Paul's mission to the Gentiles.[69]

Up to a point, Paul's discourses about the degeneration of humanity, which allowed for talk of whole cultures fundamentally going astray, and his discourse about the apex of sin, could have both worked much as they do now in Paul's letters without the Hellenistic psychology of sin. But apparently Paul was unable to imagine the fulfillment of God's ancient promises to Israel and the other peoples without also imagining a material improvement of the human constitution. Not an improvement that would correct a will perverted by a primal pride, but a physical constitution that would support the inner person that always longed for God and the good. This is why Paul insists that the inner person of the one who is "in Christ" is in a process of renewal due to the divine *pneuma* (e.g., 2 Cor 4:16–5:5; Rom 12:1–3). The mind is strengthened and continues, but the body of dust with its passions and appetitive desires will eventually be replaced with a body made of *pneuma* (e.g., 1 Cor 15:42–53). The kinds and degrees and specific causes of human sinning that had in Paul's understanding characterized most of history could not be ended until the material conditions that had made such evil possible, and even endemic as the world had grown older, had been eliminated.[70]

---

[68] I find much to support this claim in Mark Reasoner, *Romans in Full Circle: A History of Interpretation* (Louisville: Westminster John Knox, 2005).

[69] Robert Wilken, "Free Choice and the Divine Will in Greek Christian Commentaries," in *Paul and the Legacies of Paul*, ed. William S. Babcock (Dallas: Southern Methodist University Press, 1990), 123–40, at 138.

[70] The aging of the world was another common component of Hellenistic primitivism seen also in Judean apocalyptic writings, and also in Rom 8:18–25. See F. Gerald Downing, "Common Strands in Pagan, Jewish and Christian Eschatologies in The First Century," *TZ* 51 (1995): 196–211.

CHAPTER NINE

Are Paul's Moral Teachings Designed for Ordinary Humans?

In this chapter I want to try and answer the question of whether Paul's moral teachings were meant to be fitting for ordinary humans. This may seem a strange question, but perhaps less so when we remember that the concept of the sage loomed as central to Hellenistic ethical thought. And, according to Seneca, the sage was an ideal human (*Ep.* 42.1; also, Alexander, *De Fato* 196.24–197.3)[1] as rare as the Phoenix that appears only once in 500 years, so hardly an ordinary human. Stoics did not even consider as sages the extraordinary founders of Stoicism: Zeno and Chrysippus.[2] The concept of the sage affected moral thought widely well into the Roman Empire and the later Christian idea of the saint.[3]

But I take my start on Paul's moral thought from another characteristic of ancient philosophy and ancient thought more broadly. Unlike the principled rejections of the metaphysical and the ontological that arose in the wake of Kant's self-proclaimed "Copernican Revolution" and which in the middle third of the last century characterized modern philosophy, the ancients held that rigorous moral thinking must be based on some conception of the way the world is, including what it consists of and how it works.[4] Platonists had a cosmos made up of something like thought, the noetic, and its relative absence, matter. Epicureans had a world of colliding and sometimes compounding atoms and

---

[1] A. A. Long and D. N. Sedley, *The Hellenistic Philosophers*. 2 vols. (Cambridge: Cambridge University Press, 1987), 61N.
[2] Stoics came to regard individuals who were making moral progress toward the nearly unreachable ideal under the category of the *prokoptōn* or *proficiens*.
[3] For sage holy men, see Graham Anderson, *Sage, Saint and Sophist: Holy Men and Their Associates in the Early Roman Empire* (New York: Routledge, 1994). On the pervasiveness of the concept, René Brouwer, *The Stoic Sage: The Early Stoics on Wisdom, Sagehood and Socrates* (New York: Cambridge University Press, 2014).
[4] For the Hellenistic philosophies, an indispensable guide with texts and commentary is Long and Sedley, *The Hellenistic Philosophers*.

Stoics a world composed of *pneuma* in various degrees of tension creating a *scala naturae*, a hierarchy of being. This physics in each case plays an indispensable role in how the system brings about achievement of the ethical goal. In some forms of Platonism, by proper use of the mind one acquires a noetic existence and the abilities to exercise that noetic power. In Epicureanism, recognition of the non-teleological nature of a world of colliding atoms allows an untroubled life shared with others. In Stoicism, being in harmony with the divine pneumatic nature of the world allows one to live according to its providential order and unfolding.

This assumption that the question "how should we live and act?" only makes sense on the basis of understanding how the world is, coheres with ancient Mediterranean folk and West Asian scribal traditions. In the Hebrew Bible, for instance, what is right and wrong and how best to live are questions that only make sense in the context of a world governed by the Judean God, his organization of the world of plants and animals with humans at the top, his divine hierarchy of underlings, the histories of peoples, and a history of what we might call ethnic folk traditions such as about "wisdom." There is a way that the world is such as the levels of the cosmos, the place of humans on the earth, the purity and impurity of some foods with respect to divine presence and so forth. Like many educated Jews of his time, Paul was informed both by ethnic folk traditions and, at the minimum, by philosophical ideas that had become koine in the culture for those who were literate and "cosmopolitan." Put in a less accurate, but more traditional, scholarly language, Paul's ethical teachings have a cosmological context. For Paul, I have argued that participating in the pneumatic existence given to Christ in the resurrection allows those who are in Christ to become sons of God, divine beings.[5] At baptism, the transformation into a mind like Christ's begins, but a fully pneumatic existence comes only at the resurrection for the tiny number who have died or, for most, who will still be alive, it will happen at the return of Christ. God's own *pneuma* forms the medium and does the work.[6]

Paul is certainly no philosopher, but like Aristobulus, the author of Wisdom, Philo, 4 Maccabees, and likely numerous others, he used dominant intellectual

---

[5] See Chapter Six in this volume. For recent work on deification in Paul, see George H. van Kooten, *Paul's Anthropology in Context* (Tübingen: Mohr Siebeck, 2008); Michael Gorman *Inhabiting the Cruciform God: Kenosis, Justification and Theosis in Paul's Narrative Soteriology* (Grand Rapids: Eerdmans, 2009); Michael Christensen and Jeffery Wittung, eds., *Partakers of the Divine Nature: The History and Development of Deification in the Christian Traditions* (Grand Rapids: Baker Academic, 2007); and especially, M. David Litwa, *We Are Being Transformed: Deification in Paul's Soteriology* (Berlin: de Gruyter, 2012).

[6] Although I do not agree that Paul's thought is in some sense fully Stoic, Engberg-Pederson (*Cosmology and Self*) provides an excellent account of the role of *pneuma* in the letters. I would add key elements from the Platonic appropriation of *pneuma* doctrines.

resources from his era.[7] Paul in his own way did so to explain the significance of Christ. I have argued elsewhere that like his fellow Judeans, he combined a Platonic moral psychology with the idea of divine *pneuma* as the highest stuff of the cosmos and a Stoic-like *scala naturae* seen clearly in 1 Cor 15.[8] Paul's conviction that Jesus Christ had been remade of God's *pneuma* led him to work out a complex apocalyptic scenario that featured a central role for that *pneuma*.[9] But he also featured the idea that had recently become central to Platonism seen prominently in Philo and Eudorus of Alexandria of assimilation to god, the second god not the transcendent God of all, and thus in Paul's case assimilation to Christ.[10] My claim gives sense to the great mass of language in the letters about being "in Christ," participating in Christ, having Christ within, conforming to Christ (or his image), having the mind of Christ, becoming fellow sons of God with Christ, assimilation to the image of Christ, and so on.

That everything in Paul's thought seems to interconnect makes it difficult to answer this chapter's question without at least outlining that interconnected structure. This chapter is one take on the structure that makes an answer to its question rather obvious. A controversial element now affirmed by numerous scholars finds that in Paul's account God's plan for humankind is ethnically differentiated, with Jews and non-Jews treated differently in some respects, and Paul the apostle to the Gentiles.[11] I agree and will attempt to tease out the kernel of Paul's moral thought in its conceptual context with five theses.

---

[7] Carl Holladay, *Fragments from Hellenistic Jewish Authors. Volume III: Aristobulus*, SBLTT 39 (Atlanta: Scholars Press, 1995), no. 39; Gregory Sterling "The Love of Wisdom: Middle Platonism and Stoicism in the Wisdom of Solomon," in in *From Stoicism to Platonism: The Development of Philosophy 100 BCE-100CE*, ed. Troels Engberg-Pedersen (Cambridge: Cambridge University Press, 2017), 198–213; David A. deSilva, *Fourth Maccabees and the Promotion of the Jewish Philosophy: Language, Intertexture and Reception* (Eugene, OR: Cascade, 2020).

[8] For Platonic traditions in the letters, see Wasserman, *Death of the Soul*; "Paul Beyond,"; van Kooten, *Paul's Anthropology*; Litwa, *We are Being Transformed* and my *Rereading of Romans*, 79–84, 261–64; "Paul and Self-Mastery," 524–50.

[9] Engberg-Pederson, *Cosmology and Self*; Stowers, "Dilemma of Paul's Physics." For the relation of *pneuma* to Paul's thought about kinship, ethnicity, and gentile Christ-people, see Chapter Seven in this volume and Johnson Hodge, *If Sons, Then Heirs*.

[10] On the development of later Platonic assimilation to God, see Gretchen Reydams-Schils, "'Becoming like God' in Platonism and Stoicism," in *From Stoicism to Platonism: The Development of Philosophy 100 BCE-100CE*, ed. Troels Engberg-Pedersen (Cambridge: Cambridge University Press, 2017), 142–58, with bibliography; and for Paul, Stowers, "Dilemma of Paul's Physics"; van Kooten, *Paul's Anthropology*; Stanley K. Stowers, review of *Paul's Anthropology in Context: The Image of God, Assimilation to God, and Tripartite Man in Ancient Judaism, Ancient Philosophy and Early Christianity* by George van Kooten, CBQ 73 (2011): 162–64; Litwa, *We are Being Transformed*. On the resistance of many New Testament scholars to seeing Platonic elements in Paul, see my "Paul and the Terrain of Philosophy," EC 6 (2015): 141–56.

[11] A recent fulfillment of this approach's promise is Paula Fredriksen, *Paul: The Pagans' Apostle* (New Haven: Yale University Press, 2017); and the groundbreaking work of Matthew Thiessen, *Paul and the Gentile Problem* (New York: Oxford University Press, 2016).

Five Theses About Paul's Moral Thought

Thesis one: Paul's moral thought centrally involves the transformation of a normal human mind into a mind of divine *pneuma* through assimilation to Christ's mind. Paul describes this *pneuma* as a down payment or earnest deposit and first fruits toward becoming fully made of divine *pneuma* when Christ returns (2 Cor 1:22; 5:5; Rom 8:23; cf. Rom cf. 8:11). For now, those in Christ must live in fleshly bodies made of dust that possess emotions and appetitive desire and these in Platonic fashion want to act apart from the control of the mind. Three features display the Platonic nature of the mind in Paul's moral psychology. First, the mind in Rom 7 that has been defeated by its own passions and desires of its body, even though enslaved, still desires the good and God's law, something impossible in the Stoic moral psychology (7:14, 16, 25).[12]

This intrinsic orientation of the mind suggests the second feature of both an ontological and moral psychological difference and dualism between mind and body. Numerous texts suggest a Platonic-like mind or true self in that it is distinct from the body and at home in a higher realm. Paul writes (2 Cor 12:2–3) that he once traveled to the third heaven, likely where the court of God is. Whether this trip occurred while he was in his body or outside of his body, he does not know (v. 2). "In the body" suggests a miracle of God such as in some other Jewish writings in which a person is taken up bodily into the heavens.[13] But it also seems easy for Paul to talk of his self as being able to leave his body. He would rather be away from the body and with Christ (2 Cor 5:8; Phil 1:21–23). Christ lives a pneumatic existence in the heavens so being in the body means being away from him (2 Cor 5:6–9). At present, Christ people live in an earthy tent, but they will live in an eternal heavenly tent not made by hands (2 Cor 5:1–2).[14] The current state of mortality weighs them down (2 Cor 5:4), but the pneuma given now is a guarantee of the full pneumatic existence (v. 5). At present, they see only enigmatically in a mirror, but finally they will see face to face (1 Cor 13:12). What can be seen is temporary, but the unseen is eternal (2 Cor 4:18).

---

[12] See Chapter Six in this volume.

[13] Engberg-Pedersen's (*Cosmology and Self*, 89) interpretation of the passage with the idea of types of pneumatic bodily states seems unconvincing. "Out of the body" can only refer to Paul's true self, his mind, to be sure, made of *pneuma*. "In the body," must mean his current flesh body.

[14] I agree with Engberg-Pedersen (*Cosmology and Self*, 48–50) that the heavenly dwelling is the pneumatic body, but the true self in the terrible earthly dwelling must be a Platonic-like mind in a Platonic-like body of a different ontological order. The contrast here is not a Stoic one between one's character and choices that are under one's control and externals such as the body which aren't. The underlying problem for Paul is the weak and decaying nature of the substance(s) that make up the body. Uncontrolled emotions and desires ontologically belong to the fleshly body.

The third feature involves texts that have the mind subsisting and developing by something akin to Platonic contemplation of Christ, which constitutes assimilating to his mind. Paul's faithful Corinthians in 2 Cor 3:18, "all with unveiled faces seeing the Lord's shining splendor as if reflected in a mirror are being transformed into the same image from shining splendor to shining splendor as from the Lord, the *pneuma*."[15] Length precludes arguing the case, but not only as scholars often admit does Paul use the language of Platonism in chapters 3–5, he also uses the idea of assimilation to a god, clear Platonic content.[16] Contemplation is a kind of mental seeing that connects one with the divine, in this case Christ.

This combination of a Platonic-like mind made of Stoic-like *pneuma* might seem bizarre, but later Platonists absorbed Stoic *pneuma* into their cosmic and ontological schemes.[17] Philo, our most important instance, has a higher realm of *pneuma* between the noetic and the material cosmos.[18] For him, this highest *pneuma* substance has some qualities of the material realm and some of the noetic. As with the material, it has extension and can act causally on substances in the created world, but like the noetic is changeless, indestructible and invisible to sensible perception. The pneumatic body in 1 Cor 15 seems to match. Paul's highly anthropomorphic world-involving God cannot fit into a noetic realm, but shorn of the noetic, with divine *pneuma* the highest most perfect substance in the cosmos, Paul's schema resembles Philo's in important ways.[19] With this role for *nous*, the typical Platonic word for the mind, it comes as no surprise that Paul begins his most extensive hortatory moral passage with "be transformed by the renewal of your mind so that you can discern what is the will of God, the good, the acceptable and the perfect," in Rom 12:2. The unhindered mind is inherently able to know what God wants, what is good, and what God finds acceptable and perfect. It makes good sense to treat the detailed moral psychological passages such as Rom 7–8 as explanatory of Rom 12:2–3 and other isolated statements about the *nous* (mind).

Thesis Two: Contrary to the often-bizarre exegetical contortions to make Paul's idea of the Christ groups completely egalitarian, Paul's moral thought hinges on levels of attainment and the idea of moral progress.[20] Those contortions

---

[15] See Chapter Six in this volume and Litwa, *We are Being Transformed*.
[16] For Platonic phraseology in Paul, see Engberg-Pedersen, *Cosmology and Self*, 48–50.
[17] For the development of the relations of the two, see Engberg-Pederson, *From Stoicism to Platonism*; Christoph Helmig and Mauro Bonazzi, *Platonic Stoicism – Stoic Platonism: The Dialogue between Platonism and Stoicism in Antiquity* (Leuven: Leuven University Press, 2008).
[18] John Dillon, "ASŌMATOS: Nuances of Incorporeality in Philo" in *Philon d'Alexandrie et le langage de la philosophie*, ed. Carlos Lévy (Turnhout: Brepols, 1998), 99–110.
[19] On Paul's anthropomorphic understanding of God, see Chapter Six in this volume.
[20] Laura Dingeldein, "'ὅτι πνευματικῶς ἀνακρίνεται': Examining Translations of 1 Corinthians 2:14," *NovT* 55 (2013): 31–44; idem, "Gaining Virtue, Gaining Christ."

are nowhere more evident than in 1 Corinthians 2 and 3 where scholars have claimed that Paul is using the language of his opponents and being ironic. He doesn't truly believe what he writes.[21] In 1 Cor 2:10–13:

> God has revealed [the mysteries] through his *pneuma*. For the *pneuma* searches everything, even the depths of God. For what human knows the things of a human except a human pneuma? So also no one knows the things of God except the *pneuma* of God. But we have not received the *pneuma* of the cosmos, but the *pneuma* out of God so that we might understand the things given to us by God.

Paul then writes that the person with God's *pneuma* is able to understand these mysteries by means of that *pneuma*, but the soulish person who presumably only possesses normal human *pneuma* cannot understand them. Later in the letter he speaks of a "soulish body" (1 Cor 15:44). Both "soulish person" and "soulish body," I think, mean something like the Platonic irrational soul in its attachment to the body. Paul writes (1 Cor 2:15–16): "The pneumatic person critically judges all things but is critically judged by no one. 'For who has known the *nous* (mind) of the Lord so as to instruct him? But we have the *nous* of Christ.'" Those "in Christ" now have the mind of Christ, at least in development, and will soon have the pneumatic body of Christ.

This passage illustrates the impossibility of treating "the *pneuma* of God" as only an objective genitive, the *pneuma* that God gives to people. God has or is a type of *pneuma*. God's *pneuma* has cognitive and communicative powers. Those who have been baptized into Christ and reached a pneumatic level also have this *pneuma* in them and thus share its cognitive and communicative powers. This situation contrasts with the cognitive and communicative limitations of people who have only an ordinary human soul that Paul later in the letter describes as mortal, decaying and made of earthy material (15: 45–49). The analogy between the God of the universe and Christ followers is quite striking and points to the divinization that becoming one with Christ entails.

The attempts to read these texts as ironic with Paul using the language of pneumatic/*pneumatikoi* as if taken from supposed opponents falls foul of both an unforced reading of the language and texts even outside of the Corinthian correspondence. One illuminating passage with an interesting play on words is Gal 6:1: "Brothers if a person is found in some fault, you who are *pneumatikoi* are to restore such a one in *pneuma* of gentleness." This comes after chapter 5 has treated the nature of walking by the *pneuma*. The text assumes

---

[21] Dingeldein, "'ὅτι πνευματικῶς ἀνακρίνεται'."

some individuals who are pneumatic and others who are not. Another text showing how Paul thinks in terms of character types with degrees of progress comes in 1 Thess 5:12–14. After Paul exhorts his audience to recognize those who work among them so as to promote their development, including admonishing them, he writes, "admonish the disorderly, encourage the small souled persons, and bear with the weak." Each of these three were character types in Hellenistic moral literature.[22]

These texts and many more show Paul with a conception of an ideal state expressed in ontological language related to *pneuma* and a range of moral development characterized by specific failings of character that stand in the way of attaining the ideal state. These failings are recognizable in concepts found in the moral writings of the era, both Jewish and non-Jewish.[23] That Paul has an ontological conception of such moral immaturity can be seen in that he at least sometimes characterizes such people as soulish, having only an ordinary human soul made of mortal dust (1 Cor 2:14; 15:44, 46; Gen 2:7 in 15:45). I cannot argue the case here, but as 1 Cor 2:15–16 suggests, I think that the mind of Christ is nothing other than the pneumatic mind, the mind possessed by Christ's *pneuma*. Paul employs birthing metaphors for this process: "My children, with whom I am again in childbirth until Christ is formed in you" (Gal 4:19).

Thesis Three: Paul conceptualizes the subjects of his moral teachings as Gentiles who have been idolaters enslaved to their emotions and appetitive desires. He never describes Judeans as typically controlled by passion and desire. I have argued this case as has Emma Wasserman and now many other scholars.[24] He thinks, I suggest, that, beginning at Sinai, Judeans have embodied a different kind of character through the law. These assumptions help in understanding something of why Paul found a Platonic moral psychology to be so congenial to his purposes. As Emma Wasserman has shown, this psychology dramatically depicts total moral failure, TMF and Platonists employed the kinds of images of attack, enslavement, captivity, and so on seen in Romans 7 that calls mind the *nous* and the "inner person" and is the "I" that speaks about these assaults of the passions and desire of its own body.[25]

The subjects of Paul's exhortations are people who need to progress from TMF to the fully pneumatic mind of Christ. From this Platonic-like point of view, they have one key advantage: Their minds intrinsically belong to a higher

---

[22] Dingeldein, "Gaining Virtue, Gaining Christ."
[23] For a rich trove of Hellenistic moral materials, see Abraham J. Malherbe, *The Letters to the Thessalonians*, AB 32B (New York: Doubleday, 2000).
[24] Stowers, *Rereading of Romans*; Wasserman, *Death of the Soul*; Thiessen, *Gentile Problem*, 47–53; Stephen Young, "Ethnic Ethics: Paul's Eschatological Myth of Jewish Sin," *NTS* (forthcoming).
[25] Wasserman, *Death of the Soul*.

order that is focused on God and on the good, an idea central to Platonism.[26] In Rom 8:1–17, the answer to the enslavement of chapter 7 is a mind directed by the *pneuma* of God, also called the *pneuma* of Christ. Such people are no longer in the flesh. Contrary to the dominant twentieth-century interpretations inspired by Martin Heidegger and Rudolf Bultmann, the change is not existential, an attitude of finitude, but ontological. Indeed, quite to the contrary of their claim that Paul's gospel was about accepting human frailty and limitation, the apostle holds out the goal of a divinized mind and body.[27]

For my purposes here, the key point is that Paul constantly construes the moral life as one of dealing with the emotions and desires arising from the body. These desires and emotions challenge the will of the mind. Famously in Romans 7, the true self, the I, cannot do what it wants to do because the flesh and desires of its bodily parts (aka "members") have become more powerful than the mind (7:14–15, 18–20). Instead of the moral life being a matter of balance between the body with its passions and the mind as is typical of Platonists, Paul in the key passages treats the moral life as a zero sum game. He thinks this way, I suggest, because becoming one with Christ, with his mind, a fully pneumatic one, places one in a different order of existence beyond the ordinary human. This is the mental condition designed to join the body made of God's *pneuma* when Christ returns for those who have mentally become Christ beings and for the few who have died to be resurrected.

Galatians 5, for instance, spells out just what becoming pneumatic entails. In v. 17, "What the flesh desires is opposed to the *pneuma*, and what the *pneuma* desires is opposed to the flesh; for these are opposed to each other, to prevent you from doing what you want." The mind, for instance, wants to do God's law, but the flesh with its desires tries to make the body do something else such as the vices listed in vv. 20–21. Those who do such things cannot inherit the Kingdom of God (v. 21). Flesh and blood are indeed *incapable* of inheriting the Kingdom of God (1 Cor 15:50). The fruit of the *pneuma* are opposing virtues (v. 22). How can those who are of the *pneuma* have such moral character? "Those who are of Christ have crucified the flesh with its emotions and desires (v. 24)." The one who is of Christ and of the *pneuma* of Christ has not balanced, moderated, controlled, or dominated the flesh with its emotions and desires. Rather, the Christ person has crucified the flesh and its emotions and desires. To crucify is to kill, to utterly destroy. Fleshly bodies, and in the Platonic (but not the Stoic) view the emotions and desires

---

[26] A vast literature exists on these topics. Wasserman (*Death of the Soul*) discusses them for Plato, Philo, Paul and near date Platonists. Up to date more technical treatments can be found in *Psychology, Companions to Ancient Thought 2*, ed. Stephen Everson (Cambridge: Cambridge University Press, 1991).

[27] See Chapter Eight in this volume.

that belong to those bodies, will play no part in the existence lived when the Galatians join Christ above the clouds.[28]

Thesis Four: The central moral quality for those in Christ is *pistis* with *pistis* having its normal semantic range centering on faithfulness, loyalty, trustworthiness, obedience and sometimes trust or commitment.[29] Understanding this quality takes one to the heart of Paul's project. One has to understand the goal or telos to understand the Greek and many other moral systems or even informal patterns of moral thought. Classically, for most Stoics it was to live according to divinely ordered nature which means to live according to virtue.[30] Virtue paradoxically meant living an ordinary human life perfectly, becoming a sage. For those who used to be called Middle Platonists, the telos was to become like or assimilated to God in so far as possible and this goal could be interpreted in several this worldly and otherworldly ways.[31] For those to whom Paul writes, the goal, I would argue, is to become assimilated to Christ.[32] As Rom 8:29 and other places tell us, this does not mean losing one's own identity: "Those whom he foreknew, God predestined to be conformed to the image of his son so that he might become firstborn among many brothers." Those in Christ do not become Christ but rather brothers of Christ and pneumatic sons of God like Christ, the same genetic blueprint but with the mind developed by each individual somehow shaped by Christ's.

But why this goal? Was it so Christ could take all of his followers up to heaven to play harps on the clouds? People often assume something like that upon reading 1 Thess 4. But when the archangel blows the trumpet – and that sounds very much like the beginning of a cosmic war – and in a Roman Empire of many millions with a much vaster world population, a pitiful handful of people from Paul's Gentile assemblies meet Christ, they do not have to be going right back to heaven or, if they are, perhaps it is for individual judgment and assignment to work with Christ in some apocalyptic scenario. The letters provide several clues that the latter is the case. Paul's goal cannot be saving the world's population by converting them to Christ, say, one thousand saved and one hundred million eternally lost. Paul's language does not imply such failure.

---

[28] Stoic teachings on the emotions are widely misunderstood in biblical studies. For Stoics wisdom produced "good emotions." See Margaret Graver, *Stoicism and Emotion* (Chicago: University of Chicago Press, 2007).

[29] Jennifer Eyl, *Signs, Wonders and Gifts* (New York: Oxford University Press, 2019), 170–212; "Philo and Josephus on the Fidelity of Judeans," *JAJ* 12 (2021): 94–121.

[30] Dirk Baltzly, "Stoicism," *The Stanford Encyclopedia of Philosophy*, https://plato.stanford.edu/archives/spr2019/entries/stoicism/.

[31] Gretchen Reydams-Schils, "'Becoming like God' in Platonism and Stoicism," in *From Stoicism to Platonism,* 142–58.

[32] Stowers, review of *Paul's Anthropology*; "Paul and the Terrain,"; Litwa, *We are Being Transformed* and Chapter Six in this volume.

A couple of Paul's asides suggest a picture of what this band of Christ people will be doing. In 1 Cor 6:1–2 the Corinthian holy ones will be judging the world and even judging angels.[33] This suggests a new species of being – sons of God and brothers of Christ – refashioned in the image of Christ and made of God's own *pneuma* with the mind of Christ who assist Christ as he sets about to bring every being in the cosmos whether human or divine in heaven or under the earth or on the earth (Phil 2:10; cf. Rom 10:6–7) into subjection to God (1 Cor 15:24–28; cf. Rom 8:34–38). They are ontologically and morally above angels, just like Christ. Paul serves Christ by assembling a band of these holy ones chosen by God to become Christ beings.[34] All will be affected by Christ's work for God's plans, and all are to be subject to his rule, but not all will be cosmic servants as brothers of Christ.[35] God alone has chosen and "predestined" that particular number of newly created holy ones (e.g., Rom 8:29). The letters simply allow no picture of Paul seeking to convert the world to a new religion of personal salvation and his "churches" that we read about in the letters as being the first steps in this worldwide mission. Paul, I believe, implies that lots of things will be going on when Christ returns, rather than some simple uniform universal judgment, salvation and home in heaven, although there will certainly be plenty of judgment and salvation.

A key clue lies in the claim that these Christ beings who are to meet Christ coming very soon from the court of God will be in authority over angels. Angels and the gods of the nations, that for Paul exist and were appointed by God for their tasks, do not come off very well in Paul's letters. Here I draw on the important recent book by Emma Wasserman (*Apocalypse as Holy War*) that demolishes the old dualistic account of Jewish apocalypticism. God has not lost control of any part of the cosmos even if some lower-level divine beings

---

[33] Litwa (*We are Being Transformed*, 182–88) makes this important connection.

[34] "Holy ones," "assembly" and "chosen" are key concepts related to Paul's ideas about the creation of this new species, but their discussion is beyond the scope of this piece.

[35] The textual evidence leaves a cloudy and difficult picture regarding the extent and varied effects of "Christ's work." The evidence makes one uniform scheme of salvation for humans from unlikely to impossible. Christ's work and effects looks more like the messy and often complex scenarios seen in Jewish apocalyptic writings (Wasserman, *Apocalypse as Holy War*). Even in 1 Cor 15, some statements about life, resurrection and salvation seem universal and others seem to imply a distinction between the saved and unsaved sinners or some other disjunction. I cannot treat these issues here, but two considerations must be kept in mind. First, passages like Rom 5 and 1 Cor 15 ought to be read in the context of Paul's arguments and not in the context of later Christian schemes of salvation. Second, the scholar has no right to ignore passages that describe the future punishment or destruction of – and this is unclear – sinners, the unsaved, opponents, or those not chosen (e.g., Rom 2:6–10, 9:22–23; Gal 1:8–9, 6:8; 2 Thess 1:8–9). Clearly some undifferentiated scheme of sin/salvation including the elimination of the distinction between Jews and non-Jews will not work.

have been overly zealous or done their jobs poorly or do not fully realize who they work for or have joined some local temporary rebellion. From divine beings, including some angels, to peoples of the nations, lack of faithfulness to the sovereign God and lack of fully genuine obedience is endemic, but God has all of this working for his own purposes. To this picture, I would add that what God's empire needs is a perfectly obedient and faithful species of subordinate governors to perfect God's rule and correct the flawed work of the current ones. God remade the perfectly obedient Judean teacher Jesus Christ of the most perfect material in the cosmos to be the archetype (Rom 8:29) of a perfectly obedient species. Such character, which we tend to call Paul's ethical teachings for his gentile assemblies, is what these predestined, chosen and baptized holy ones get when they become "conformed to the image of his [God's] son so that he [Christ] might be the firstborn among many brothers" (cf. Gal 2:19–20).[36] No wonder that faithfulness and obedience play such important roles in the letters. We do not know the full story, but Paul himself was uniquely chosen to midwife a band of Gentiles to play some role in the events leading to Christ's subjection of the cosmos to God, and perhaps including the end of the age events in Jerusalem where they would represent the obedience of the nations.[37]

With this scenario the so-called Christ hymn (Phil 2:5–11) and other texts resonate with their full meaning.[38] The supposed hymn appears in the midst of exhortations to social cohesion and solidarity based on obedience to Christ by having the mind of Christ: "have the thinking among you that was also in Christ." We are back to the centrality of mind again. Unlike the gods of the peoples and the angels, Christ did not exploit his divine status but humbled himself and was obedient to God even to the point of crucifixion. Therefore, God exalted him to take charge of governing the cosmos so that every knee will bow; those in heaven, those on the earth, and those under the earth (Phil 2:9). The subjugating, organizing and governing work requires interacting with a cosmos full of lower gods and non-evident beings. No wonder Paul thought that these new sons of God both needed to be constructed of God's own *pneuma* and modelled on the perfectly faithful Jesus Christ. But why do these people who are in Christ need such cohesion and solidarity? Because, as Paul emphasizes in various places (1 Thes 4:17; 5:10; Rom 8:38–39), the new Christ people will be with him and with Paul serving Christ in his cosmic work forever. In Philo's cosmos, one has the noetic world of the supreme and unknowable God, and

---

[36] Thus, the subjective genitive understanding of *pistis Christou*, Christ's faithfulness (not faith in Christ) is on this account central to Paul's message. See Stowers, *Rereading of Romans*, 194–226; Chapter Seven in this volume.

[37] Fredriksen, *Paul*, 163–65.

[38] Wasserman, *Apocalypse as Holy War*, 108–40.

the corruptible material world, but in addition, closest to God in the ontological hierarchy, angels, souls and the divine heavenly bodies.[39] These are made of the pure form of divine *pneuma*. Paul's cosmos is not the same, but insofar as it is also made of that *pneuma* it gives one the ability to know what God wants and to move about the cosmos with power. But in addition to being made of such perfect stuff, in order to be a species of Christ beings who will be fully obedient to God, unlike the gods and angels, those in Christ must have the moral quality of *pistis*, of complete faithfulness to God's plans, a *pistis* like Christ had when he went to his death in fidelity to God's plans.[40] Mind of Christ, *pneuma* of Christ and faithfulness of Christ belong together.

Thesis Five: I can only suggest in the briefest way. Because those in Christ are humans in the process of acquiring the mind of Christ and have died from the normal human fleshly life in baptism so as to follow God's will directly under Christ, they cannot live according to the law designed by God for a portion of the human population. No matter whether woman or man, Jew or Gentile, slave or free, to be in Christ means becoming sons of God who are under a new regime, the immediate regime of those who will be cosmic servants and ministers of Christ forever.[41] The risen and remade Christ sits at the right hand of God in God's heavenly court. Christ is not a human being living in Jerusalem or in another city or on a farm somewhere. And his species of pneumatic sons of God live by a regime that fits their conditions and their cosmic roles. "Flesh and blood cannot inherit the kingdom of God" (1 Cor 15:50). Paul's great challenge with this kind of thinking, of course, was that the people in his assemblies were human beings and often acted as such. But he believed that God was transforming the minds of those whom he had selected. As is a commonplace in scholarship, Paul frequently writes as if this should be a sudden complete process, but in fact, Paul and his people have to believe that it is only happening gradually even if some decisive change has already occurred. So as many accounts of Pauline ethics have stressed, the moral thought has to treat its subjects as having one foot in this world and the other in the next or as I would put it, they are partly of an ordinary human

---

[39] Dillon, "ASŌMATOS," 104–6.
[40] See Eyl, *Signs, Wonders, and Gifts*, 170–212; "Philo and Josephus." I would like to thank Jennifer Eyl for her comments on this article.
[41] This provides a clue as to how I read Galatians. Galatians 2:15–21, for instance, has Paul as a model for those of the new species. Paul will be together forever with Christ and this band of Gentile holy ones who are conformed to Christ. In his thinking, by definition he and they cannot live by the law such as being circumcised on the eighth day, offering first fruits in the temple, following the temple's festivals and on and on. As for "male and female," I suspect that in addition to his culturally typical subordination of women, Paul believes that sex and gender will be irrelevant to these pneumatic sons of God.

constitution and partly of a divinized human construction.[42] Such people live as ordinary and extraordinary at the same time, but the goal is to crucify the emotions and desires of the body so they can do what they want to do, that is, to be totally faithful to God just as Christ was and is, and thus unlike the gods and angels who have drifted into less than perfect fidelity.

The standard cannot be the holy and just law that treats ordinary human life, but rather righteousness before God means embodying Christ's own faithfulness in a perfected pneumatic existence. Such people know God's will for them and do it as Paul explains in 1 Cor 2:10–16. But alas by their behavior these Corinthians show themselves to still be fleshly (3:1–4), "still human beings (3:3)." And that humanness is the problem for Paul. In Albert Schweitzer's scheme, he thought it a Jewish doctrine adapted by Paul that the law could only be in force until the beginning of the Messianic Age when this natural world ended.[43] I do not think that the natural world ends in Paul's thought or that Jews would cease to live by it during the rectifications brought by Christ's rule.[44] But Paul was not like the writer of Jubilees who claimed that angels were circumcised (15:27–28). In Paul's thought, angels would not have needed that kind of body. Paul's was by the standards of his day a more sophisticated more hierarchical ontology and cosmology in which angels, the heavenly bodies and so on consisted of qualitatively higher stuff with, as he puts it, increasing degrees of *doxa*, weakly translated as glory (1 Cor 15:40–4). Those in Christ, Paul's now justified Gentile sinners, are becoming beings who will move around all levels of the cosmos, including being with Christ when he sits on his throne at the right hand of God (Rom 8:34). Laws about bodily pollution, birth and death, farming, eating food, temple offerings from one's fields and flocks, days for work, rest and celebration and on and on can hardly apply. The law is about the descendants of Abraham, Isaac and Jacob living in the Land, birth and death, flocks and crops, gifts to God in the temple, and so on. Little to none of the legislation about these things bears relevance to beings who will be moving around the cosmos taking charge over angels and likely aiding Christ in the scenario laid out in 1 Cor 15:23–28. Why then would non-Jews want to work on observance of the law when their true

---

[42] Mid-twentieth century New Testament theology was dominated by an existentialist and especially Lutheran interpretation of Paul that read a message about human finitude into the letters so that Paul is constantly urging his followers to resist thinking that they are already "divine" or advanced people. But the writers of ancient Christianity – excepting in some regards Augustine – got it right. For Paul, God is in the process of making those people divine, sons of God with human finitude as the problem not the solution.

[43] Schweitzer, *Mysticism*.

[44] Paul lacks the modern and even the later medieval ideas of two realms, the natural and the supernatural. Paul's was the continuous hierarchical cosmos of antiquity.

work should be conforming to the image of Christ and solidifying into cohesive unit of Christ's holy ones?

So to answer the paper's question, Paul's moral teachings do envision both ordinary human life and the life of those truly conformed to Christ, but the ordinary is set against the background of the process and goal of assimilation to the mind of Christ in the present and then endowment with a body like Christ's at his return from the court of God in heaven.[45] The crucifying of the flesh with its emotions and desires is not an ethical program for ordinary human life.

---

[45] One might analyze the moral teachings of the letters by breaking them down into rough overlapping categories; some envision and treat issues regarding ordinary human getting along together including with outsiders while others imagine a super human purity, holiness and social cohesion fitting for sons of God. Perhaps a third category has its focus on the mind of Christ that has crucified the impulses of a normal human bodily life so as to have a perfectly faithful mind.

PART IV

Historians and Critical Historiography

CHAPTER TEN

The Concept of Community and the History of Early Christianity

The way the concept of "communities" and "community" is deployed in scholarship hinders historical work on early Christianity, especially if early Christianity is to be treated as a normal human social phenomenon studied in the non-sectarian university.[1] In contemporary English, "community" has a number of senses connected to uses developed in nineteenth and twentieth century Europe and North America. One sense of the word is territorial or features place as in "rural communities" and "flooding affected many households in the community." A neighborhood in this sense can be called a community even if its inhabitants have almost no social interaction with one another. We also speak of a "linguistic community," although there may be enormous cultural and political differences among those speakers. The range of meanings that has been important for scholarship on ancient Christianity, however, has a different history not only in Christian thought, but also in European and American social and political thought. This is the idea of community as a deep social and mental coherence, a commonality in mind and practice. Although Enlightenment traditions sometimes approached the idea, as in the French Revolution's fraternity in "liberty, equality and fraternity," it has been the anti-Enlightenment and Romantic traditions that have featured community in this sense. Most famously, the sense was central to Fascism, National Socialism, many other twentieth century pre-World War Two conservative movements, and both Christian and non-Christian forms of communitarianism. A now much criticized, but influential, sociological approach to the concept is found in the work of Ferdinand Tönnies with his dualism between *Gemeinschaft* (community) and *Gesellschaft* (society), the former

---

[1] Stanley Stowers, "The History of Ancient Christianity as the Study of Religion," paper presented at the North American Association for the Study of Religion section at the Annual National Meeting of the Society of Biblical Literature, New Orleans, LA, 2009.

supposedly based upon the essential will (*Wesenwille*) of the participant.² The idea of an essential and totalizing identity and commitment is very much like the idea of early Christian conversion. Factors within Christian traditions, together with broader European culture, have contributed to the pervasive appeal of communities and community, which have made the study of early Christian history oddly different from other ancient histories. The uses of the concepts in the study of early Christianity are far from descriptive and analytical.³ They instead carry strongly normative freight from both of these historical sources.⁴ It would certainly be wrong to imply that the liabilities of "community" discussed here appear whenever a scholar uses the word, but the promiscuous use of the term in the field, on the whole, does manifest the problems.

One among several routes for Romantic influence is a link to the interpretation of the canonical Gospels. Johann Gottfried Herder contrasted the author/audience kind of literary prose against a more primitive and authentic kind of literature exemplified by ancient poetry and the Hebrew Bible.⁵ Because the Hebrew literature derived from the original, pure and primitive roots of the nation, the Bible escaped the decadence of literature from Greco-Roman times of the New Testament. The more authentic and *Geist*-filled literature came therefore not from the rational manufacture of authors, but grew organically from peoples, cultures and communities. Herder's account of the Gospels provided the basis for later Form Criticism and standard assertions about oral tradition, a fact well recognized in standard New Testament scholarship.⁶ Form critics and many of their heirs have continued to deny that the early Christian writings are properly literature. Letters and Gospels are rather deposits of folk speech or so-called oral tradition. The Gospels contained the *Geist* of the preaching, teaching and primitive churches because they are residues of oral speech such as parables, stories, testimonies and "the gospel message itself." Thus, the essential core of New Testament writings is both an expression of an authentic non-literary individual-social experience and Hebrew-Jewish in its essence, in spite of some external Greek forms.

---

² Ferdinand Tönnies, *Gemeinschaft und Gesellschaft* (Leipzig: Fues Verlag, 1887).
³ I am, of course, not claiming that more descriptive and analytical concepts are somehow free from normative implications.
⁴ I am not invoking types of historicism entailing that a word/concept's history somehow intrinsically inheres in later uses of the word or the related idea that words accumulate masses of historical implications from their histories that inhere in words as individuals use them. I am simply claiming that "community" belongs to a larger discourse about early Christianity that shapes the meanings that readers attribute to the word.
⁵ Johann Gottfried Herder, *Vom Geist der ebräischen Poesie: Eine Anleitung für die Liebhaber derselben und der ältesten Geschichte des menschlichen Geistes*, 2 vols. (Dessau: Herder, 1782–83); idem, *The Spirit of Hebrew Poetry*, trans. James Marsh (Burlington, VT: Edward Smith, 1833).
⁶ Werner Georg Kümmel, *The New Testament: The History of the Investigation of its Problems* (Nashville: Abingdon, 1970), 79–83; William H. Baird, *History of New Testament Research: Volume One: From Deism to Tübingen* (Minneapolis: Fortress, 1992), 177–83.

Herder's work had a profound influence on Hermann Gunkel, usually seen as the founder of Form Criticism, and the History of Religions School. Another member of that school was Johannes Weiss, the teacher of Rudolf Bultmann. Bultmann also studied with Gunkel himself and was the most important exponent of Form Criticism of the Gospels.

The Form Critics did not emphasize the experience of discrete local communities expressed in the Gospels, because following certain German Romantic strains, they instead thought of them as collections of small oral texts that had been composed and circulated among folk communities over time in ways too complex to identify the mark of particular communities. Central to their approach were the Romantic ideas of communal creativity and communal authorship. The Redaction Criticism that developed from the work of the Form Critics kept their assumptions but complained that the Form Critics had neglected the editors who had collected this material and composed it in ways that reflected social settings (*Sitze im Leben*) that were more than the Form Critics' sorting of materials into those that had come from Palestinian Jewish Christian, Hellenistic Jewish Christian or Gentile Christian communities. This move fleshed out the German Romantic equation of unique historical experience, language, tradition and *Volk* in terms of unique Christian communities. Increasingly, Redaction Critics treated the Gospels not only as originating in the experience of particular Christian communities, but also as being stories about Jesus that were also stories and lessons about the communities of authorship. It has therefore become standard to speak of the Markan community, the Matthean community, the Johannine community and finally, the Lukan community.[7] With Luke and Acts there was some hesitation, because Luke was thought to be more like a normal Hellenistic author and thus the idea of something that suggested communal authorship was exposed for its oddness.

The idea that the Gospels reveal communities has been approached in two ways, which are often combined. First, the author's "theology" might be seen as the thought that was created or developed in a particular community, the theology that defined and differentiated the community from other communities. Here the writer is the voice of the group. Second, the writer might be seen as composing a story about Jesus that in almost every detail addresses the issues and needs of a particular community. The Gospels are almost like allegories about communities or sermons for particular communities.[8] Scholars have even attempted to outline the history of these communities on the basis of reading the gospels in this way. Books with titles such as *Matthew's*

---

[7] Coming to full expression in Philip F. Esler, *Community and Gospel in Luke-Acts* (Cambridge: Cambridge University Press, 1987).

[8] This is a point made by Richard Bauckham (*The Gospels for All Christians: Rethinking the Gospel Audiences* [Grand Rapids: Eerdmans, 1998]) and others in the volume that I discuss below edited by Bauckham. The volume also does a good job of documenting the tendency from Form Criticism onward, of attributing authorship to communities.

Community and *The Social History of the Matthean Community* and extensive scholarly discussions about the history of the Johannine community signal the centrality of this consensus that sees the Gospels as community products and as about particular communities.[9]

The 1970s and 1980s saw an important and salutary turn toward the social sciences and social history in the study of early Christianity.[10] The trend, however, exacerbated the tendency to read communities behind early Christian writings. Although the scholarly trend was helpful in bringing into the discussion other social formations such as households and schools, the assumption that from the beginning the basic social formation in the movement that would become Christianity was communities was rarely questioned. The question was usually one of the social organization of these communities. Were they egalitarian, hierarchical, patriarchal, sectarian and so on?[11] Against my strong expectations, scholarship on the Corinthian letters, with all of the evidence for social disunity did not turn out to be an exception to this tendency. It has certainly been a gain to bring in thought about issues such as social strata, gender and patron/client relations, but such scholarship usually works with the idea of an existing coherent congregation as a social norm against which other social considerations and occasionally other social formations are then viewed.[12] In spite of talk about social stratification, scholarship with a social bent still suffers from a pervasive confusion of solidarity with equality.[13] My admittedly untested intuition is that in addition to the desire for liberal values, this confusion suggests romantic and communitarian conceptions of community on the part of scholars. Indeed, it has been often and powerfully argued that this confusion and conflation lies at the heart of communitarian thinking.[14] The clash of communitarian conceptions and liberal values meanwhile goes unnoticed.[15]

---

[9] Thomas L. Brodie, *The Quest for the Origins of John's Gospel* (New York: Oxford University Press, 1993), 15–21.

[10] For bibliography on the heyday of the movement (about 1980–1995), see K. C. Hanson, "Greco-Roman Studies and the Social-Scientific Study of the Bible: A Classified Periodical Bibliography (1970–1994)," *Forum* 9.1–2 (1994): 63–119.

[11] One example is the debate over "love patriarchalism" with its heavily normative Christian theological agenda: e.g., David G. Horrell, *The Social Ethos of the Corinthian Correspondence: Interests and Ideology from 1 Corinthians to 1 Clement* (Edinburgh: T&T Clark, 1996).

[12] For an overview, see *Christianity at Corinth: The Quest for the Pauline Church* ed. Edward Adams and David G. Horrell (Louisville: Westminster John Knox, 2004).

[13] E.g., Richard A. Horsley, "1 Corinthians: A Case Study of Paul's Alternative Society," in Adams and Horrell, *Christianity at Corinth* (Louisville: Westminster John Knox, 2004), 227–37.

[14] William R. Lund, "Communitarian Politics and the Problem of Equality," *Political Research Quarterly* 46 (1993): 577–600; idem, "Politics, Virtue, and the Right to Do Wrong: Assessing the Communitarian Critique of Rights," *JSPh* 28.3 (1997): 101–22; Elizabeth Frazer, *The Problem of Communitarian Politics: Unity and Conflict* (Oxford: Oxford University Press, 1999).

[15] From a normative Christian perspective, David Horrell (*Solidarity and Difference: A Contemporary Reading of Paul's Ethics* [London: T&T Clark, 2005]) explicitly brings Paul's letters into

One feature of the trend that clearly contributed to the strengthening of communities and community as explanatory assumptions was the Durkheimian inspiration behind many of these studies.[16] For Durkheim and most functionalist forms of social explanation, religious beliefs, symbols and rituals represent the group that produces them. Society worships itself. Furthermore, that tradition placed an enormous emphasis on social cohesion as the inherent goal of religious activities and all culture. The normative social formation for Durkheimians has been groups with a deep social and mental coherence, a commonality in mind and practice. In other words, what scholars of ancient Christianity call "communities." This kind of deeply criticized social theory works with the idea of social wholes such as society conceived as organic unities or like machines with every part contributing to the functioning of the whole.

The theological or ideological origins of the totalizing role of community in the Christian imagination about early Christianity can be pinned on Paul and his letters. Paul did not merely try to persuade those whom he wanted as followers that they ought to become a very special kind of community. He in fact told them that they had in their essence already become such a community. This was a brilliant strategy. Instead of putting an impossible ideal before them and saying, "try to reach this goal," he said, "you are this community of transformed people so live up to what you are." As the sociologist Rogers Brubaker writes, "ethnopolitical [or religious] entrepreneurs . . . by invoking groups, they seek to evoke them, summon them, call them into being."[17] Paul told them that no matter what their ethnic-religious identity, gender, or social status, they were all ontologically one (Gal 3:27–28). They all shared the same ontological status of being "in Christ."[18] They all shared the very same divine *pneuma* (intelligent self-powered airy substance) given to Christ by God. Paul told his audiences in his letters that they had come out of mind-boggling levels of moral and religious degeneracy (e.g., 1 Thess 4:3–8; 1 Cor 6:9–11; Rom 1:18–32) to achieve moral perfection in Christ. "Those who are of Christ have crucified (killed, destroyed!) the flesh with its emotions and appetitive desires (Gal 5:24; cf. Rom 6:1–6)." They shared Christ's mind and traits of character.[19]

---

the "communitarian/liberal debate" and rightly concludes that Paul's thought better fits communitarian conceptions. Unfortunately, he assumes that that the differences Paul sometimes defends on certain issues indicate liberal values.

[16] For a critique of functionalist inspired scholarship, see Richard A. Horsley, *Sociology and the Jesus Movement*, 2nd ed. (New York: Continuum, 1994).

[17] Rogers Brubaker, *Ethnicity without Groups* (Cambridge: Harvard University Press, 2004), 10.

[18] Stanley Stowers, "The Ontology of Religion," in *Introducing Religion: Essays in Honor of Jonathan Z. Smith*, ed. Willi Braun and Russell T. McCutcheon (London: Equinox, 2008), 434–49.

[19] Paul's basic idea here is assimilation to Christ (e. g., 2 Cor 3:18; Rom 8:29) that Paul describes as a process that has substantially taken hold of those who are in Christ.

Such ideas are pervasive in the letters. For scholars, these ideas and often the idea of "the Pauline communities" are correlates of an equally miraculous idea of conversion. Paul came to Corinth, preached the gospel and the Corinthians in question converted and became a Christian community. Paul, then, long before Acts turned the idea into a narrative, created a central idea of the Christian myth of origins that the new movement grew in a miraculous way.

What Paul himself proclaimed as a miraculous creation by God, scholarship has often taken as sociological data. When Paul does talk about, so to speak, actual life on the ground, the picture is quite different. This disparity is most well known in the Corinthian letters but shows up in most of letters. Interpreters know 1 Corinthians as the poster child for the danger of division in the community. The problem is not that interpreters have missed the disparity between Paul's ideal and the actuality. Rather, it is the failure to bring to bear normal academic social analysis and instead hold to Paul's mystified and miraculous social rhetoric. As a contemporary sociologist writes, "We must, of course, take vernacular categories and participant's understandings seriously, for they are partly constitutive of our objects of study. But we should not uncritically adopt *categories of ethnopolitical practice* as our *categories of social analysis.*"[20]

The way that "conversion" and "community" govern so much thinking about the formation of Christianity also implies the concepts of orthodoxy and heresy. If Paul and other apostles preached the gospel and that led to conversion and the formation of communities, then deviation from the unity of belief and sentiment implied in the concept of community must be like heresy. It was a departure from an original state of purity in thought and action. Thus instead of scholars thinking that, as one might expect, Paul was never able to get the Corinthians, or Galatians or Philippians to accept or fully accept his ideas, practices and demands, they instead often ask, "what false teacher came in from the outside or what set of ideas from the cultural context seduced some of those in the community so as to produce false belief or immoral behavior or division in the community?"

Paul writes in 1 Corinthians that those whom he addresses as the assembly or congregation of God (1:2) are one body with one *pneuma* (spirit) no matter what their ethnic background or social level (12:13), they have been made holy (1:2, 30; 6:11; 7:14), they are God's temple with God's *pneuma* in them (3:16–17: 6:18–19), they are rich in all speech and knowledge (1:4–5), they lack no pneumatic endowment (1:7) and they are "of Christ and God" (3:23). And yet they are deeply divided around different teachers or teachings (1:10–17, 3:4), they are immature and lack pneumatic endowment (2:14–3:4), they are arrogant toward one another (1:6–7), they tolerate incest (5:1–2), they are taking one another to court (6:1–7), they consort with prostitutes

---

[20] Brubaker, *Ethnicity without Groups*, 10; emphasis original.

(6:12–20), they are ungrateful for God's gifts (4:7), and so on of this very familiar litany. But the interpreter should not get caught up in the oppositions. There never was a social body, a congregation, a community, on the one hand, nor were there defilements of a social purity, rifts and defections from such a non-existent social miracle of harmony and unity of mind, on the other hand, except in Paul's imagination and rhetoric. To conclude that Corinth was indeed a problematic case of communal failure, but that the Thessalonian or Philippian churches were communal successes is to miss the point. Scholarship needs to think about the social formations associated with Paul in terms of what are known to be ordinary human social processes. Paul's categories and those of traditional scholarship are not only ideal and rhetorical, but they are also too holistic. One of the motivations for the turn to theories of practice in social theory has been to break down these traditional social wholes such as society, community and identity into knowable patterns of human activity.[21] The move gives individuals agency without in any way diminishing the social character of activity and social formations can be analyzed from their smallest constituents of linked practices.

I have illustrated problems with the pervasive scholarly use of the concept of community and communities with the letters of Paul and the canonical Gospels, but I could have used other later literature. My impression is that this usage shows itself by far most prominently in the era of Christian origins that, depending on the particular scholar, may extend well into the second century or later. A historian or anthropologist of religion might immediately recognize concepts such as early Christian community, conversion and deviation from the original state as typical elements of the myths of origin.[22] They are features of a fabulous and singular time of origins when things happened in a very special way. The writer of Acts, who in my view was heavily dependent on his reading of Paul's letters, certainly featured such community in his myth of origins. Thousands, for example, convert and form a community in Jerusalem at the hearing of one sermon. The author writes, "the great number of those who believed were of one heart and one mind and no one said that any of his possessions were his own, but everything was common to all of them" (4:32). They all submit themselves to the apostles (4:35), listen to the amazing teachings of the apostles and spend their time together (2:44–47). Unsurprisingly, many scholars have been captured by this picture, even if they have added

---

[21] Joseph Rouse, "Practice Theory," in *Philosophy of Sociology and Anthropology*, ed. Stephen P. Turner and Mark W. Risjord (Oxford: Elsevier, 2007), 639–82.

[22] The notable exception to ignoring the mythic nature of early Christian writings is Burton L. Mack, *The Christian Myth: Origins, Logic and Legacy* (New York: Continuum, 2001). See also the work of the Society of Biblical Literature Seminar, Ancient Myths and Modern Theories of Christian Origins, in Ron Cameron and Merrill P. Miller, *Redescribing Christian Origins* (Leiden: Brill, 2004).

critical caveats around its edges and expand the story to explain traditions discovered by modern scholars.[23] Ulrich Luz can confidently write,

> Historically, the Matthean community is part of the post-history of the saying source Q. It is a Jewish Christian community originating in the activity of the Jesus messengers who were among the bearers of the Q tradition. Later, after the failure of the mission to Israel and the Jewish War, the community settled in Syria, where it received significant inspiration from the Gospel of Mark.[24]

I have certainly used the concept of early Christian community and communities uncritically myself. Many scholars, of course, have intuited or explicitly seen problems in these concepts and have made good efforts at corrections. I will discuss some of these below.

In what follows, I will list and briefly discuss major reasons why the concepts should be used only in the most sparing way and the implied picture of mythic origins abandoned.

1. Use of the "community" and "communities" is almost always unjustified. By unjustified, I mean that writers do not give evidence and arguments for taking the social formations in question to be highly cohesive with commonality in belief and practice. The claim that an early Christian group or social formation was a community ought to require as much evidence and argument as any other historical claim. Appeal to what Paul and other writers thought some population had miraculously become and ideally ought to be is not good evidence for an actual community.
2. The claims about communities are usually unreflective and almost always untheorized. In other words, the concepts are not used as analytical concepts that can do work in some project of historical inquiry that employs social theory. They are often normative theological concepts parading as descriptive and explanatory social concepts. For Paul and other early Christian writers, Christian community is a normative idea. So also, for modern Christians. This may be quite fine, but holding to this normative status is not a practice that contributes to the normalization of the study of ancient Christianity in the non-sectarian academy.

---

[23] Typical is Helmut Koester's (*History and Literature of Early Christianity* [Philadelphia: Fortress, 1982]) widely used account in which he cautions that Acts's episodes about the Jerusalem church are "dominated by legendary and idealizing tendencies" (86) but then accepts Acts basic picture of its community as an agent for the origins of the new religion (86–91).
[24] Ulrich Luz, *Studies in Matthew* (Grand Rapids: Eerdmans, 2005), 7.

3. The approach treats "pagans," Greeks, Romans and others, as passive dupes instead of socially and humanly plausible persons. It may seem plausible to some that the message of the early Christian teachers was simply so wonderful that it inevitably totally captured those with good hearts, but the scenario is not plausible in light of the massive work of modern history, ethnography and the social sciences. For those at all attracted to someone like Paul, the reaction is mostly partial and selective acceptance of the message and practices, and assimilation of the teachings to the person's own interests and frame of reference rather than unqualified understanding, acceptance, and submission, as a very large body of ethnography and history makes clear.[25] Certainly some individuals submit, but such unqualified acceptance is unusual. Accepting baptism, even if it was freely chosen and not because a master, patron, parent or husband wanted it, might be done for many reasons and with many of the would-be initiate's own explicit and implicit understandings. Studies of modern missionaries describe typical reactions of negotiation and resistance for those with any interest at all. The missionized often appropriate what they want selectively and assimilate what they appropriate to their own beliefs, practices and interests.

The idea of Greeks and Romans as horrifically evil and immoral people before their conversion to Judaism or Christianity still informs much scholarship on ancient Christianity, with a few notable exceptions.[26] In this way, community is taken not only to mean high social cohesion with commonality in belief and practice, but also moral goodness. But the one idea does not necessarily entail the other idea. After all, the Nazi Party arguably had a high level of social cohesion with commonality in belief and practice. The traditional concept of an early Christian community has implied both a social cohesion and a moral goodness that was in contrast to unconverted Greeks and Romans. The idea of such a wondrous community, in such an evil world, made pagan willingness to fully convert seem plausible. The scenario, however, belongs to the realm of myth, not critical history.

---

[25] E.g., Eytan Bercovitch, "The Altar of Sin: Social Multiplicity and Christian Conversion among a New Guinea People," in *Religion and Cultural Studies*, ed. Susan L. Mizruchi (Princeton: Princeton University Press, 2001), 211–35; Smith, *Relating Religion*, 340–61; Jean Comaroff, *Body of Power, Spirit of Resistance: The Culture and History of a South African People* (Chicago: University of Chicago Press, 1985); Jean Comaroff and John Comaroff, *Of Revelation and Revolution: Vol I: Christianity, Colonialism, and Consciousness in South Africa* (Chicago: University of Chicago Press, 1991); Elizabeth Furness, "Resistance, Coercion, and Revitalization: The Shuswap Encounter with Roman Catholic Missionaries, 1860–1900," *Ethnohistory* 42.2 (1995): 231–63; James A. Sandos, *Converting California: Indians and Franciscans in the Missions* (New Haven: Yale University Press, 2004).

[26] E.g., Jennifer Wright Knust, *Abandoned to Lust: Sexual Slander and Ancient Christianity* (New York: Columbia University Press, 2006).

One antidote to mythic and magical ideas of conversion is a plausible theory of mind. It should now be beyond dispute that the human mind is not a unified and all-purpose reasoning or central planning machine.[27] There are two major points to be made from the brain/mind sciences and areas such as cognitive anthropology. First, the modularity or evolved systems (without following the massive modularity thesis[28]) of the human brain/mind makes the idea of totalizing domination by ideas and commitments and consistency in thought and action across the domains of life unlikely, to say the least. Second, some mental representations are more easily gotten, held, and transmitted than others. Unfortunately, humanistic and especially post-structuralist scholarship has operated with untheorized and implicit conceptions of mind as a blank slate and a culture sponge,[29] even though they have often helpfully criticized the integrated Cartesian subject. One simply cannot write and think about human beings without some implicit theory of how minds operate. In the sponge conception, people indiscriminately soak up whatever representations come their way. Thus, one often sees the claim that individuals are socially constructed in their entirety by culture. But cognitive psychology and other fields have shown that some cultural items are easily acquired, held and transmitted while others are only obtained, held or transmitted through a great and ongoing socio-cultural labor.[30] I see little likelihood that early Christian thought belonged to the easily acquired, remembered and transmitted variety. I make these passing comments on a large and complex area of scholarship only to suggest some of what I mean by "humanly plausible." Humanly plausible need not mean only our common sense or scholarly

---

[27] E.g., Laurence Hirschfeld and Susan A. Gelman, *Mapping the Mind: Domain Specificity in Cognition and Culture* (Cambridge: Cambridge University Press, 1994); Antonio Damasio, *Descartes' Error: Emotion, Reason and the Human Brain* (New York: G. P. Putnam's Sons, 1994); Gerd Gigerenzer, *Adaptive Thinking: Rationality in the Real World* (Oxford: Oxford University Press, 2000); Michael Gazzaniga, "Forty-five Years of Split Brain Research and Still Going Strong," *Nature Reviews Neuroscience* 6 (2006): 653–59; Robert Kurzban and Athena Aktipis, "Modularity and the Social Mind: Are Psychologists too Selfish?" *Personality and Social Psychology Review* 11.2 (2007): 131–49.

[28] Jerry A. Fodor, *Modularity of Mind* (Cambridge: MIT Press, 1983).

[29] Janet McIntosh, "Cognition and Power" (paper presented at the Society for Literature and Science Meetings, Pittsburgh, PA, Oct 31–Nov 2, 1997), http://cogweb.ucla.edu/Culture/McIntosh.html.

[30] Scott Atran and Douglas Medin, *The Native Mind and the Cultural Construction of Nature* (Cambridge: MIT Press, 2008); Harvey Whitehouse, *Modes of Religiosity: A Cognitive Theory of Religious Transmission* (Walnut Creek, CA: AltaMira, 2004): *Theorizing Religions Past: Archeology, History and Cognition* ed. Harvey Whitehouse and Luther H. Martin (Walnut Creek, CA: AltaMira, 2004); Petri Luomanen, Ilkka Pyysiäinen, and Risto Uro, ed., *Explaining Christian Origins and Early Judaism: Contributions from Cognitive and Social Science* (Leiden: Brill, 2008).

intuitions. History, anthropology and psychology ought to also inform our sense of what is plausible.

4. The relationship between early Christian literature and early Christian communities posited in much scholarship makes early Christian literature unique and incommensurable with other ancient literature and writing practices. In all other areas that study ancient Mediterranean and West Asian literature, a writing is studied as the product of an individual writer working in a particular social and historical context, not as the product of a community. Classicists do not approach Vergil's or Philodemus's writings as the products and mirrors of Vergil's and Philodemus's communities. Indeed, the most important social formations for these individuals as writers may have been other writers and associated networks that taught high literacy, interpreted and circulated writings, mostly people whom they had never known. The approach to early Christian literature posits a tight fit between a writer and a face to face social group with commonality in belief and practice.

As noted above, this has been especially the case for the canonical Gospels, but also affects the way that scholars read Paul's letters. Interpreters, often but not always, read the letters as responding in intricate detail to particular communities that – except perhaps for Romans – Paul supposedly knew very well.[31] A perceived note of sarcasm, the use of a particular word and always allusive language that rarely spells out particular and concrete details about the supposed community are taken as corresponding to a social reality. There are at least three problems here. First, the audiences who potentially could have or actually did hear Paul's letters may have never consisted of anything nearly so coherent as a community. Second, Paul's knowledge of and understanding of his potential audience may not have been so perfect. At Corinth, he may have known Crispus and Gaius (1:14) well, but not the slaves and women in another household who had been present for some of Paul's meetings. Paul says that he baptized the whole household of Stephanas (1:16). Did he understand the dynamics and individuals in what could have been a large, complex and highly disunited household well? Third, this approach robs Paul of the creativity and known tendencies of writers and speakers to produce writings that have a rhetorical and artistic semi-autonomy and that respond to imagined audiences in broadly creative rather than narrowly specific ways. Admittedly, with letters the correspondence between writing and actual audience is one of more and less. But the model of letter-writing that envisions two

---

[31] Romans has been increasingly read in this way with the "weak" and "strong" of 14:1–15:13 connected with the supposed expulsion of Jews from Rome and then the letter treated as Paul's detailed intervention and expression of religious ecumenism.

friends exchanging letters can be misleading when used to imagine Paul and those whom he describes as the assembly of God at Galatia, Corinth or Thessalonica. A friend is likely to be less complex, more coherent and knowable than a socially diverse group of people from different households. While the scholar of the New Testament or the Apostolic Fathers typically constrains herself by this tight writer–community relation, the classicist can study the way that writers and writing culture produces literary-rhetorical dynamics that tend to give writing a semi-autonomy in relation to the wider social context and a special relation to networks of writers and highly literate readers. At the same time, the normal academic approach to literature followed by the classicist allows the scholar to place the writer in a vastly more complex social (including political, economic, religious) context than the writer–community model allows, since the bounded and sealed idea of a community inhibits thought about social formations that cut across the groups or populations covered by the idea of community. The social spaces, for example, consisting of the specialized practices of highly literate writers, interpreters and consumers of writings held together and cut through many other social formations, including the populations known as Pauline churches. Similarly, if Paul had been a leather worker, his associations with a network of others connected with the trade would have touched on those church populations in the person of Paul, but without those people being parts of the social formation(s) of which the trade consisted.

5. The uncritical assumption that early Christianity exclusively consisted of communities precludes and occludes the possibility of finding other social formations in the history of early Christianity. The task of the historian ought to be one of inquiry into which of the vast number of possible social formations were involved in the beginnings of what came to be known as Christianity and the roles of those formations in those historical processes. The interest of the last forty years in insights from the social sciences and in social history has led to the study of households, ancient associations, schools and so forth. The results have been good, but in my estimation, limited. One cause of the limited success has been the tendency to keep the enchanted idea of early Christian communities and then to ask how the study of households, schools and so on might enhance our understanding of these communities. Did the social hierarchy of ancient households affect the organization of Christian communities? Community often becomes one of those holisms of thought with quasi-metaphysical properties like society, culture, tradition, identity, a system of differences, the symbolic order, discourses or the *Volk*. A social formation that cannot be broken down into smaller units such as actions and practices that explain the larger formation is ultimately a mystery, often a comfortably useful holism. These concepts need to be critically disaggregated. Are they truly holisms? Do these entities not consist of complexly linked actions and social practices of

people? The social complexity hidden by community needs to be described and explained.

Why should community or even households-plus-communities be the only social formations that can be used in the explanation of early Christianity? Why should formations such as neighborhoods, merchant networks, patterns of social connection based on religious places, artisan networks, religious entrepreneurial–consumer relations and networks, circles of slave friends, linked levels of social domination, coalitions of friendship and enmity, age and gender sets (e. g., elderly men, early teenage girls), many sorts of markets, patterns and practices of ethnic identification and non-identification and many other social formations not be important for the social explanation of early Christianity? Although I am sure that there was some early Christian community, I would argue that another social formation was more important: Fields or networks of literate cultural producers with various types of expertise.[32] A social formation that produced, circulated and consumed writings, speeches, divine messages and learned interpretations came before and was causative of anything like the communities envisioned in scholarship and Christian myth. In antiquity, where only a tiny fraction of the population was literate at all and a much smaller fraction was literate enough to write and interpret literature, networks or fields of writers, interpreters of writings and readers educated into particular niches of the fields formed highly specialized social arenas that produced and contested their own norms, forms of power, practices and products of literacy. Banishing individual persons as writers from the account of Christian beginnings both mystifies interests and power relations. If the writings that constitute virtually all of our evidence and could have been the most powerful force in the movement, simply swell up from vague communities, then these writings do not clearly have interests and are not the results of explainable social processes.

It would be misleading to not stress that some scholars have implicitly intuited problems with the pervasive appeal to communities and others have explicitly criticized uses of the concept. I can only mention a few of these here. Attention to these criticisms can be an aid in developing a broader assessment of the field's approaches to Christian beginnings. In 1977 Abraham Malherbe wrote,

> We must, for instance, resist the temptation to see so much of early Christian literature either as a community product or as reflecting the actual circumstances of the communities with which the writings are associated. We too frequently read of communities that virtually produced one or another of the Gospels or for which they were produced.[33]

---

[32] See the Introduction and Chapter One in this volume.
[33] Abraham J. Malherbe, *Social Aspects of Early Christianity* (Baton Rouge: Louisiana State University Press, 1977), 13. To be sure, Malherbe does not critique the idea of communities themselves and contrasts the social to individuals and leaders in a way that is theoretically inadequate.

Then Malherbe points to examples of movements that never formed anything like communities and yet nevertheless produced literature. He also draws attention to the Roman Pythagoreans who came about as a group because of literature from the Hellenistic age written by intellectuals writing in the name of famous Pythagoreans and imagining the continued existence of the long extinct Pythagorean groups. Literature can be causative of social formations. The literary movement created a myth of origins of Pythagoreanism as the primal philosophy. As far as I have been able to determine, Malherbe's cautions went unheeded and his examples unnoticed.

Some scholars have not so much critiqued the use of the ideas of community and communities as they have ignored, or side stepped, the issue because of particular interests and theoretical commitments. Several approaches inspired by literary criticism focus on the text or reader as autonomous, either with little interest or overt denial of the role of author and the assertion of the autonomy of the reader.[34] In certain cases, literary approaches have led to treating the gospels as ordinary literature directed toward a more general audience of readers.[35] This is a large, complex and theoretically and philosophically troubled area that is beyond the scope of this chapter, although the arena's influence needs to be noted. Most important for the issue of community, many of these approaches operate with a naïve or implicit idealism that undermines inquiry into the socio-historical materiality of writings.[36]

From the direction of conservative Christian scholarship, another challenge to "Gospel's communities" has come in a debate stirred by a book of essays, *The Gospels for All Christians*. In the lead essay for the volume, the editor, Richard Bauckham, argues

> not merely the implied audience of a Gospel is larger than the current consensus allows, but that it is *indefinite rather than specific*. This is a difference of kind, not just of degree, from the current consensus. The evangelists, I have argued, did not write for specific churches they knew or knew about, not even for a very large number of such churches. Rather, drawing on their experience or knowledge of several or many specific churches, they wrote *for any and every church* to which their Gospels might circulate.[37]

---

[34] Sean Burke, *The Death and Return of the Author: Criticism and Subjectivity in Barthes, Foucault and Derrida* (Edinburgh: Edinburgh University Press, 1998); Stephen Moore, *Literary Criticism and the Gospels: The Theoretical Challenge* (New Haven: Yale University Press, 1989).

[35] May Ann Tolbert, *Sowing the Gospel: Mark's World in Literary-Historical Perspective* (Minneapolis: Fortress, 1989).

[36] See my, "The Ontology of Religion," in *Introducing Religion: Essays in honor of Jonathan Z. Smith*, ed. Willi Braun and Russell T. McCutcheon (London: Equinox, 2008), 434–49.

[37] Richard Bauckham, "For Whom Were Gospels Written?" in Bauckham, *Gospels for All Christians* (Grand Rapids: Eerdmans, 1998), 9–48, at 46. Emphasis is original.

This position, affirmed by other authors in the volume, would indeed make the Gospels more like other ancient literature in some ways. While this is a gain, and many of the volume's arguments against the consensus position are sound, I believe that Bauckham's and the book's revised position moves even further from a non-mythic and normal academic historical approach to early Christianity.

To begin with, the approach keeps the same enchanted communities and merely changes the relationship between the canonical Gospels and the communities. Now instead of a Gospel being created by or mirroring, say, the community in Antioch, Baukham envisions that an author/evangelist wrote that Gospel and addressed all Christians everywhere. In this familiar model, the possibility for this universal address and communication occurred because the writer and the audience shared the same Empire-wide community, the Christian church, created by the same gospel message. On the basis of the preaching of this gospel, churches/communities were brought into existence across a wide swath of the Roman Empire that had a commonality of belief and practice. Without eliminating a certain degree of diversity, the scenario seems to imply a universal Christian subject that allowed mutual recognition, again the miracle of conversion.

The writers of the volume dwell on the well-known conditions of high mobility and good communication in the Roman Empire and evidence especially in the letters of Paul and from the second century for communication between "churches." Bauckham emphasizes that Christians had a sense of being part of a worldwide movement. "Gentile converts were inculturated into a new social identity that was certainly not purely local."[38] In all of this, appeal to Acts plays a central role, and for the first century, the letters of Paul. Bauckham would have a difficult time mounting his case if he did not take the letters of Paul to be depicting this scenario. But what we know for sure is that Paul did not envision the kind of institution that became "the church," as Bauckham supposes. Whatever his "assemblies of God" or "of Christ" are, when he wrote 1 Thessalonians, he assumed that this movement consisting of a paltry handful of followers in the Northeast quadrant of the Mediterranean and a few other places would have reached its missionary end during his lifetime when Christ returned from heaven. When he writes Romans, he says that he has fully preached the good news to the Gentiles all the way from Jerusalem to Illyricum and that he will soon be ready to go on to Spain by way of Rome in order to finish the mission by going to the West. He clearly does not have the later idea of either an enduring worldwide church or of a mission to convert the whole world. His assemblies are likely to represent those Gentiles that God has assembled to meet Christ upon his return and take

---

[38] Bauckham, "For Whom," 33.

eschatological offerings to the temple in Jerusalem.[39] Bauckham is not following Paul here, but rather Acts' and Eusebius' reinterpretations of Paul. The empire-wide miracle of the Spirit-driven mission in Acts and Eusebius that creates a universal church is a myth of the origins of a worldwide community. This is historically less plausible than the varied and often isolated communities of the consensus. The scholarly consensus from the Form Critics to Walter Bauer and the present was created because of the vast evidence that the Acts-Eusebian story was historically implausible. Differing isolated communities each producing their own theologies and literature better fit the evidence of the second and third centuries indicating that there never was a coherent and unified orthodox Christianity from the beginning. The consensus also seems more plausible in that it envisions less institutional development and a gradual socially embedded development of "theology." But the consensus picture created its own improbabilities. Abandoning the working premise that there were Christian communities everywhere that there is evidence for some activity – e.g., teaching and writing about Jesus Christ – holds promise for opening a space to imagine more historically explanatory social formations.

After Paul's letters, we have the Gospel of Mark, but Mark tells us nothing of communities or an expansive church or even of a religion called Christianity. It is an odd story about an executed god-empowered teacher of mysteries. Next, we likely have Matthew, probably in the 90s or later. The author of Matthew, like Paul, has clear ideas that he advocates about an ideal Israel and about a social and ethical order for the coming Kingdom of Heaven.[40] He also knows of assemblies, possibly from Paul, and has Jesus announce a worldwide mission to the Gentiles. But none of this, even at the end of the First Century, is evidence for the myth of origins seen in Acts and the volume edited by Bauckham, much less a historically and socially plausible explanation for how Christianity came about.

The problem that most challenges the group of scholars in the volume edited by Bauckham is that their scenario has no account of how Christianity or the church formed in terms of ordinary social processes. "The church" as a coherent trans-empire entity just appears when a handful of individuals make speeches. Even if this scenario might seem to have some plausibility, and I do not think that it does, one would have to explain how the hearers of these speeches could even understand this alien message, how they gave enough legitimacy to the messengers for things to get off the ground and indeed why the message would have had any appeal. Even more important, one would

---

[39] Brent Nongbri, "Paul without Religion: The Creation of a Category and the Search for an Apostle Beyond the New Perspective" (PhD diss., Yale University, 2008), 161–203.
[40] See Chapter Twelve in this volume.

have to explain how speeches and teachings, should they be understood and accepted, could have caused such a far-flung, but socially and ideologically uniform and cohesive social institution in such a short time. All four of these questions would need to be answered in terms of understandings, beliefs, practices and social formations that made sense in Greco-Roman culture and not in terms of the self-obviousness projected by the Christian myths of origin. Any such account must show both how the historical phenomenon emerged from the cultures of Mediterranean antiquity and how it is humanly plausible.

CHAPTER ELEVEN

Jesus the Teacher and Stoic Ethics in the Gospel of Matthew

I do not think that the author of the Gospel of Matthew was a Stoic, but I do think that the writer freely adapted elements of Stoic thought in creating his picture of Jesus the moral teacher. I arrived at my conclusions by asking what is distinctive about Matthew's depiction of Jesus as a teacher of ethics. This holds especially for the so-called Sermon on the Mount, but recent scholarship has shown that Stoicism was also a component of the gospel's thought more generally.[1]

Recognizing the importance of Stoic thought for Matthew should entail a revolution in our scholarly thinking. We have all been captured by the narrative world created by the writer that both informed and coincided with our romantic and theological stereotypes of what was genuinely Jewish, an imagined "Palestinian Judaism." But Matthew was not written in archaizing Hebrew or in Aramaic and discovered in some Judean cave. It was written in Greek and directed toward that cosmopolitan world eager for exotic foreign wisdom. We should have long ago guessed the imaginative construction at play from the fact that Matthew makes its Markan source more Jewish in its exoticizing and ethnicizing way.[2] Now current scholarship has rightly shifted the cultural locations of the gospels from the ghetto of our imaginations to the known vigorous cultural landscapes of the early Roman empire.[3]

---

[1] Especially here see, Runar Thorsteinsson, *Jesus as Philosopher: The Moral Sage in the Synoptic Gospels* (New York: Oxford University Press, 2018) with bibliography. Erin Roberts in papers delivered at several venues and forthcoming publication is working on Matthew's idea of *palingenesia* (Mt. 19:28) and related issues.

[2] Anne M. O'Leary, *Matthew's Judaization of Mark: Examined in the Context of the Use of Sources in Graeco-Roman Antiquity* (London: T&T Clark, 2006).

[3] Especially, Robyn Faith Walsh, *The Origins of Early Christian Literature: Contextualizing the New Testament within Greco-Roman Literary Culture* (Cambridge: Cambridge University Press, 2021) and O'Leary, *Matthew's Judaization*.

It will be helpful to review what are taken as basic facts in gospel studies and studies of the earliest traditions about Jesus. In the earliest sources, the only sources that precede and are not definitively shaped by the Roman destruction of the Judean temple in Jerusalem, one cannot even determine that Jesus was a teacher of ethics.[4] If Paul knew that Jesus was such a teacher, he does not appeal to the teachings or the idea that Jesus was a teacher, even though the teachings from the later Matthew and Luke would be very relevant and overlap with his own teachings. In the Gospel of John, Jesus teaches, but those teachings are about himself (such as "I am the light of the world" in 8:12) and there are no teachings that might be considered broadly moral teachings beyond the saying that his disciples should love one another (John 15:12). This brings us to Matthew's primary source, the Gospel of Mark, which Matthew almost entirely reproduces as a basis for his own major additions and transformations. Mark presents Jesus as a teacher of mysteries about the coming kingdom of God, mysteries so obscure that none of Jesus' disciples are able to understand them. Jesus in Mark is about as remote from a guide about how one ought to live day to day as one can imagine. Luke's, and above all, Matthew's idea that Jesus was centrally a great ethical teacher, offering definitive interpretation of Jewish scripture, owes something, perhaps much, to their use of the sayings source Q. The question of what Q was and whether it preserves quite early materials is a set of issues that is best to bracket here. But the author of Matthew clearly exploited Q in the process of developing the gospel's distinctive portrait of Jesus' moral teachings. Even with the debt to Q however, what is distinctive about the ethical teachings of Jesus in Matthew clearly belongs to that writer and appears in additions to and reinterpretations of Q and Mark.

I will limit this chapter to a few of the most notable Matthean ideas: the idea of a universal ethic for individuals based on divine law; the demand for perfection; the so-called criterion of interiority or intention, universal love and not returning evil for evil. If the logic of these notions does indeed have a Stoic inspiration, however, it will be difficult to isolate these from other moral concepts. Stoicism is and was famous for its systematic coherency, even if many critics charged that its central notions were counterintuitive and its demands impractical. These themes express the central tenets of the highly distinctive Stoic ethical system.

Jesus' teachings in Matthew present themselves as an interpretation of Judean law that authoritatively reveals its true meaning. Stoic thought presented its

---

[4] Paul's letters have two "commands of the Lord" (1 Cor 7:10; 9:14), but 1 Thess 4:15 and other considerations make it likely that these were prophetic commands of the risen Lord. Even if Paul is referring to the historical Jesus, they do not provide enough of a picture to determine that Jesus was a great teacher rather than one who had given a few pronouncements. One cannot rule out that Jesus' teachings about divorce in the synoptic gospels came from Paul's comment.

ethical theory as the universal law of Zeus or God. I suggest that this conjunction of ethics and law in Stoic thought made it congenial for the writer of this gospel to attribute his Stoically-inflected teachings to Jesus the Judean sage. Although New Testament scholarship describes Stoicism as pantheistic, it was in fact a combination of theism and pantheism.[5] God is both the active organizing principle of the universe and the mind that is the author and administrator of each cycle of the universe. It denied that God had a human-like form, but accommodated traditional Greek thought about Zeus and the gods as symbolic. My point is not that Matthew adopted Stoic conceptions of the divine, but only that there was enough similarity between Stoic and Judean conceptions – the latter being extremely diverse and untheorized – that a Judean thinker could find it possible and indeed congenial to adapt some Stoic thought to his own purposes. And this is exactly what we find other Jewish writers such as Philo, Paul and the author of the Wisdom of Solomon doing. The Stoic interpretation of divine law as ethics and ethics as the will of Zeus aids in understanding a feature of Matthew and the other Jewish writers: Although moral teachings occupy only a small amount of the legal material in the "Books of Moses," and much more is cultic, or about genealogical and royal history and so-on, these writers treat scriptural law as virtually the equivalent of ethics.

Cleanthes' famous Hymn to Zeus, which a number of scholars have compared to the Lord's Prayer, spoke of Zeus as "first cause and ruler of nature, governing everything with your law."[6] Moreover, "it is right for all mortals to address you: for we have our origin in you, bearing a likeness to God." After praising God's kingly rational rule of the universe, the hymn turns to human rebellion: "This all mortals that are bad flee and avoid, the wretched, who though always desiring to acquire good things, neither see nor hear God's universal law, obeying which they could have a good life with understanding." Instead, these people pursue glory, wealth and indulgence in pleasure (24–29). Cleanthes prays for Zeus to "deliver human beings from their destructive ignorance" (33). Replace "Zeus" with "the God of Abraham, Isaac, and Jacob" and Mathew agrees with all of this, including the emphasis on understanding. The law is a manifestation of divine wisdom and Jesus an embodiment.[7]

---

[5] For a good recent discussion of Stoic theology with bibliography, see Anthony Long, *Epictetus: A Stoic and Socratic Guide to Life* (Oxford: Clarendon, 2002), 142–79; Johan C. Thom, *Cleanthes' Hymn to Zeus: Text, Translation and Commentary* (Tübingen: Mohr Siebeck, 2005).

[6] Translation is from Thom, *Cleanthes' Hymn to Zeus*. On the hymn and the Lord's Prayer, see Johan C. Thom, "Cleanthes' Hymn to Zeus and Early Christian Literature," in *Antiquity and Humanity: Essays on Ancient Religion and Philosophy Presented to Hans Dieter Betz on His 70th Birthday*, ed. Adela Yarbro Collins and Margaret M. Mitchell (Tübingen: Mohr Siebeck, 2001), 493–95.

[7] Jack M. Suggs, *Wisdom, Christology and Law in Matthew's Gospel* (Cambridge: Harvard University Press, 1970).

The law that humans ought to follow in their actions and that the sage always obeys are not laws of a set code like those of the laws of cities and peoples. Rather, obeying this law is following right reason in each circumstance of life as willed by Zeus.[8] So how might a Jewish writer relate Judean law to Stoic thought about divine law? One could do this by borrowing from Stoicism a structure that distinguished and related the common ordinary human law and morality manifested in particular societies from the conditions of character required for obeying those laws correctly. This distinction appears in the concepts of the *kathekonta*, variously translated as proper or natural functions, appropriate actions, the befitting, and so on, and the *katorthomata*, right or perfect actions.[9] Everything that a sage does is an appropriate action and a perfect action, but non-sages who are all wicked sinners and fools perform appropriate actions depending upon their degree of progress toward virtue (= wisdom). They never perform a perfect action. So, for example, the ordinary person and the sage might both perform exactly the same external act in honoring parents, but the action of non-sage will be vicious and the action of the sage virtuous. The difference is that the sage performs the act from a virtuous or wise character. The act is thus qualitatively different. Merely performing the right action does not suffice for moral goodness and for obeying the commands of God. The right action must be performed in the right way, meaning with the right disposition of character.

Especially later Stoics and those of the Roman period emphasized that the *kathekonta* corresponded to what was commonly agreed upon across the laws and moral codes of human cultures. All the things that cultures agreed upon as actions and habits of good people were appropriate acts because that agreement reflected natural human moral development. Thus, Cicero's *De Officiis* – *officiis* being his translation for *kathekonta* – is based on the Stoic Panaetius' *Concerning Appropriate Acts*, but highly adapted to Roman moral sensibilities and featuring *praecepta*, moral rules. Both Philo and Paul know the term *ta kathekonta* and use the concept for moral teachings from the law such as indicated in the Ten Commandments.[10]

This, however, is not the whole story, as ultimately there is only one way to know what is the right thing to do in a particular circumstance or what Zeus requires: consult a sage. According to circumstances, the sage might even go against what convention and local law deemed to be appropriate actions in order to perform an appropriate and perfect action. The sage's action, obedient

---

[8] A now classic discussion of this Stoic theory is Brad Inwood, *Ethics and Human Action in Early Stoicism* (Oxford: Oxford University Press, 1985).
[9] An appropriate action or proper function is a condition or behavior that is natural to a plant or animal and is rational in that sense, even if only the perfected human follows right reason.
[10] E.g., Philo, *Cherubim*, 14–15; Rom 1:28.

to reason/God, ultimately defines what constitutes a perfectly appropriate action in any particular circumstance.[11] Moral authority on this view requires a perfect moral expert. Only the sage, then, stands as an authoritative interpreter of these common norms, codes and local laws. This made the sage into a rather formal concept for ethical thinking, since Stoics doubted that a sage had ever lived or thought that perhaps one or two had existed, perhaps Socrates, Heracles, or the earliest humans before sin set in. Philo of Alexandria makes Moses into such an authority, a sage who embodies the law. I suggest that Matthew's Jesus who unlike the traditional Judean experts on the law interprets the law with total authority and embodies God's own wisdom is a figure shaped by the Stoic idea of the sage. Of course, there are also many non-Stoic elements in Matthew's Jesus including the Jesus of Mark that Matthew had inherited and had to accommodate.[12]

Because Stoic ethics began with the idea of common ordinary morals natural to humans as a foundation for complete human development, Stoics used the language of "the perfect" and "perfection" when they talked about that full potential for humans. Archedemus from the second century BCE even formulated the human end as "to perfect all appropriate actions in one's life."[13] Stoics defined the kind of action that a sage performed, a *katorthoma*, as a perfectly appropriate action (*teleion kathekon*).[14] Discussion of Matthew's use of perfection will also, I believe, clarify the Stoic conception.

Matthew 5:48 makes a good place to begin: "Therefore you be perfect (*teleioi*) as your heavenly father is perfect (*teleios*)."[15] The idea that humans ought to be morally perfect and have a kind of perfection that they share with the divine is odd and at odds with Jewish traditions that posit a great difference between God and humans and that insist on human goodness and obedience not perfection.[16] The contradiction to normal Jewish, and I would argue, normal human moral thought more generally, has often been seen as a puzzle. That this counterintuitiveness comes from Stoic theory is suggested by the structure of thought in much of the Sermon on the Mount.

What God requires for righteousness is not simply the performance of actions that in themselves are generally accepted as morally good, but rather

---

[11] Tad Brennan, *The Stoic Life: Emotions, Duties, and Fate* (Oxford: Clarendon, 2005), 191–94.
[12] Some caution is due here. Stoicism and the figure of the sage were so pervasive in the Eastern Mediterranean that in a more general way than for which I am arguing regarding Matthew this thought may have or was even likely to have already shaped the picture of Jesus in Q and Mark.
[13] Diogenes Laertius 7.88.
[14] Diogenes Laertius 7.107; Arius Didymus in Stobaeus 2.85.
[15] I see no good reason for construing *esesthe* as a future rather than an imperative.
[16] The image of God motif in Jewish traditions though, could conceivably be interpreted in a Stoic fashion with humans sharing God's ability to reason.

that such actions be done with the right moral disposition that is the equivalent of doing God's will.[17] That in having the right disposition (based on wisdom), the sage was like God and imitating God was basic to Stoic thought. Stoicism had only two categories of people: sages who were perfect and non-sages who were all wicked and foolish. Those who do what Jesus teaches will become like a wise man, a sage, whose good is indestructible (7:24).[18] Matthew adds this statement as an explanation of the story of the builder taken from Q so that Luke (6:46–49) tells it without the reference to the wise man. Jesus as depicted in the Sermon on the Mount not only calls for perfection but treats those whom he addresses with his teachings as wicked (7:11): "If you then who are wicked (*poneroi*) know how to give good gifts to your children, how much more will your heavenly father give good things to those who ask him." The next verse connects this perfection to the law: "Whatever you want people to do to you, do also to them; for this is the law and the prophets." But there are few who are virtuous: The wide road leads to destruction and few make it on the hard road through the narrow gate (7:13). Earlier Jesus had said that he had not come to do away with the law, but to fulfill it (5:17–20). Every bit of it must be done. A person cannot enter the kingdom from heaven unless he or she possess righteousness that "excessively exceeds" that of the recognized moral and religious exemplars, the scribes and the Pharisees (5:20). The pleonasm, I suggest, indicates that the righteousness of which Matthew speaks is to be understood qualitatively and, in a way, similar to virtue or wisdom in Stoicism. The scribes and the Pharisees can do everything that the law requires and not be righteous. Righteousness is a particular qualitative state of the soul.

At first, the story of the rich young man in 19:16–22 might seem to belie this conclusion: If the man just keeps one more commandment, he will be perfect. Acquiring perfection seems to be incremental:

> "Teacher, what good should I do so that I might have eternal life." He said to him, "Why do you ask me about the good? The good is one. If you want to enter into life, keep the commandments." He said to him, "Which ones?" Jesus said, "You shall not kill; you shall not commit adultery; you shall not steal; you shall not witness falsely; honor

---

[17] So, for instance, Matthew adds 7:21–23 to the following material (24–27) that it shares with Luke. What they share teaches the lesson that one must actually do what Jesus teaches, but 21–23 adds a different and more radical notion that even seemingly good actions, including miracles of the kingdom of God are wicked unless they are a result of doing the will of God. But what could that be if not doing things that clearly are a result of God's power? They must also be done righteously, a matter of a particular quality of character. Not even the ability to perform a miracle guarantees righteousness.

[18] The word is *phronimos*, a word used by Stoic writers as a synonym for *sophos* (*SVF* 3.157–58) and Long, *Epictetus*, 37.

your father and mother; and you shall love your neighbor as yourself." The young man said to him, "I have kept all of these things. What do I still lack?" Jesus said to him, "If you want to be perfect, go sell your possessions and give them to the poor, and you will have a treasure in the heavens, and come follow me." When the young man heard the reasoning (or word/speech), he went away grieving because he had many possessions.

Matthew bases the story on Mark 10:17–31, but shapes it according to his own agenda including the addition of Jesus' words about becoming perfect and appending the commandment to love the neighbor (Lev 19:18). In Mark, instead of asking what the good is that he must do, the man (not a "young man") runs up, kneels before Jesus, and calls him "good teacher."[19] Jesus rebukes him and says that only God is good. The verse, together with the versions in Matthew and Luke, caused fits for theologians in the fourth and fifth centuries who were inventing the orthodox Christological and Trinitarian doctrines. But Matthew is unaware of any of these issues.

Rather, he has reshaped Mark in a way that echoes the structure of Stoic thought about value and moral development. A fragment preserved in Stobaeus (5.906,18–907, 5; *SVF* 3.510) makes a good point of departure for analysis:

> Chrysippus says, 'The man who progresses to the greatest limit performs all appropriate acts without exception and omits none. Still his life,' he says, 'is not yet happy, but happiness supervenes on it when these intermediate actions (or indifferents) acquire the additional qualities of firmness and tenor and their particular fixity.'

The person who has made the furthest progress toward wisdom/happiness/virtue will be doing all of the appropriate actions, exactly the things and kinds of things that Jesus lists, and still not be wise, happy, or good. Jesus' call for the young man to give up his possessions is not a call to keep yet another commandment. There is no such commandment. Rather, it is like a Socratic bit of questioning. The challenge reveals that the young man does not possess the good/wisdom/happiness that Matthew calls righteousness even if he does all of the expected righteous acts.

A Stoic would analyze the situation like this. Outwardly the young man does all of the things that a wise or righteous person does, but his system of values does not cohere into the qualitative whole (i.e., Chrysippus' firmness, tenor and fixity). The man's constitution is so structured that he thinks that wealth is a good rather than an indifferent that the sage will skillfully deploy depending upon circumstances with virtues such as justice and love of others.

[19] Matthew's "young man" clearly seems also to be a play of contrast on "perfect" as in mature.

The young man does not understand that if he loses or gives away the wealth it will not affect his goodness, happiness, or wisdom.

Attention to Matthew's use of Mark shows the moral structure of the former's reshaping. Commentators assimilate Matthew's "the good is one" to Mark's (and Luke's who follows Mark) "No one is good except God." But why would Matthew, who is notorious for trying to explain and make Mark clear, change the unambiguous reference to God into "the good is one" or even "the good is One" ("one" is *eis*, a masculine)? Furthermore, Matthew changes the issue from one about Jesus being good, to a question about the nature of good in a moral and legal sense. I tentatively suggest that Matthew's changes refer to the Stoic doctrine of the unity of virtue.[20] The virtues entail each other, and one must have them all as a unity to have virtue at all. For Stoics there is no such thing as possessing some of the virtues and not others. Matthew's version of the story goes on to show that the young man does appropriate acts but not perfectly appropriate acts due to his lack of wisdom indicated by false values regarding the good.

But why did Matthew add the love command? For his Stoically-shaped interpretation to work he must make clear reference to virtue or a virtue appropriate to the context. Matthew has made it clear in his larger narrative that for him love is the master virtue. In Stoic thought the virtues add the adverbial element that is central to their ethic. Virtues are the moral skills of the sage. Honoring parents, being a monogamous husband and having wealth are for the Stoics in the category of "indifferents." Such things as constitute the appropriate acts have value and are to be sought, but do not involve virtue (and the good) until the adverbial aspect is added. Acting as a child toward one's parents, a husband or using possessions involve virtue and perfectly appropriate acts when these things are done justly, courageously, wisely, lovingly, and so on. The addition of the love command makes it clear that giving to the poor would entail the perfection of the young man's appropriate acts/keeping of the commandments if it were done lovingly. Then he would be a follower of Jesus.

This Stoically-inflected reading of Matthew helps to explain the gospel's so-called emphasis on intention or interiority, which has puzzled and distinctively shaped Christian ethics throughout history. This tendency is clear and well-known in the beatitudes. Broad scholarly agreement holds that Luke follows Q and that Matthew's dramatic changes and additions reflect its own preoccupations. So, Luke makes it clear that the blessing to come in the kingdom of God is pronounced on actual poor, hungry and oppressed people (Luke 6:20–26). Matthew changes "blessed are you poor" to "blessed are the

---

[20] Perhaps the best discussion of the topic is Malcolm Schofield, "Ariston of Chios and the Unity of Virtue," *Ancient Philosophy* 4 (1984): 83–96.

poor in spirit (*pneumati*)" meaning something like those who know that they lack strength of pneumatic stuff.[21] *Pneuma*, of course, plays a central role in Stoic thought.[22] Among other things it is the active material of one's mind, soul and character. Whether Matthew's *pneuma* has a Stoic shaping or not it is clear that the writer has shifted the blessing's meaning from referring to a class of people to a quality of character. Instead of blessing people who lack food, Matthew pronounces happiness in the kingdom on "those who hunger and thirst after righteousness." I have already suggested that righteousness for Matthew is something like virtue for Stoics. The writer also adds blessings for mercifulness, purity of heart and the peacemakers (5:7–9).[23] Luke's Jesus announces a mission directed at the poor and the oppressed. Matthew's Jesus teaches about a rigorous quality of character that is the goal of his ethic and that will characterize the winners in the future kingdom.

Even more important for the moral thought of Christendom are teachings in negative formulation that have been taken on one extreme as indicating a radical asceticism and on the other as implying that the law is impossible to keep and that Jesus is cleverly abrogating it.[24] To be angry at someone is as morally evil as murder (5:21–22) and to desire someone's wife sexually is as bad as, and equivalent to, the act of adultery (5:27–28). Thus, Jimmy Carter confessed that he had committed adultery thousands of times. But the teachings are better understood through the lens of Stoicism. Cato representing the Stoic position in Cicero's *De finibus* (3.32), says:

> Whatever takes its start from wisdom must be immediately perfect in all of its parts. For in it is situated what we call "desirable." Just as it is wrong to betray one's country, to show violence to one's parents, to steal from temples, actions which consist in bringing about certain results, so even without any result it is wrong to fear, to show grief, or to be in a state of lust. As the latter are wrong not in their after-effects and consequences but immediately in their first steps, so those things which take their start from virtue are to be judged right from their first [moral psychological] undertaking and not by their accomplishment.[25]

---

[21] Spirit here is typically given what I take to be an anachronistic modern understanding as a reference to one's subjective interiority or essential self.

[22] Troels Engberg-Pedersen, "A Stoic Understanding of *Pneuma* in Paul," in *Philosophy at the Roots of Christianity*, ed. Troels Engberg-Pedersen, et al. (Copenhagen: Faculty of Theology, University of Copenhagen, 2006), 101–23.

[23] Concepts for which there is arguably something similar in Stoicism.

[24] Dale C. Allison, *The Sermon on the Mount: Inspiring the Moral Imagination* (New York: Crossroad, 1999), 1–5.

[25] Trans. from *The Hellenistic Philosophers* vol 1 ed. A. A. Long and D. N. Sedley (Cambridge: Cambridge University Press, 1987), 363. I have changed "concupiscence" to "lust" and added the words in the brackets.

This ethic derives from a highly technical Stoic theory of action that resulted in making people morally responsible for their emotions and not just their actions motivated by emotion (e.g., anger leading to murder). What matters ethically about any action – and Stoics treated emotions like actions – is the mental event that initiates the action. The mental event is a kind of assent that something is appropriate. For walking to be an action, and not just an accidental stumbling forward, it must involve assent to the impression that walking is appropriate at this moment.[26] Unlike in much thought in the Cartesian tradition, the mental event need not be and was usually not thought to be conscious. Stoics emphasized that the things to which people assented involved values such as in beliefs and that most of the time these reflected one's habits of thought and dispositions, that is, character. Stoics analyzed anger as an assent to the false belief that someone has caused you harm and the desire for revenge with an accompanying psychophysical upheaval. If one held to the correct value that only one's virtue/character/righteousness was a good and that it could not be harmed by others, then one could not assent as in the case above and have anger. A Stoic inspiration makes good sense of Matthew's Jesus teaching that the moral error in anger and sexual desire are matters of initiating mental events and not simply the final actions. In a similar way, 5:33–37 forbids oaths. Oath-taking was one of the most important mercantile/economic, political and religious practices in antiquity. The reason given for the prohibition is that what will happen in the future is beyond a person's control. One only has control over one's own character – whether it is truthful and trustworthy or not – a fundamental Stoic tenet.[27]

It is important to understand Stoic thinking here in order to distinguish it from modern, often Kantian, ethical theories that make morality depend upon the agent's intentions, and the appeal to good intentions sometimes in instances of ancient moral thinking. The point is not that the sage did not have the right intentions, but that the more restricted modern focus misses the larger point that the Stoics wanted to make. It is not that the sage needs to have thoughts about virtue or acting virtuously or altruistically or to will that the principle guiding her action apply to all humans. Both a sage and a wicked person can borrow money from a friend with exactly the same intention to pay it back, but the sage acts virtuously while the regular guy acts with moral error. The sage will, of course, characteristically have altruistic and generally virtuous thoughts and motivations, but the integration and consistency of her character organized around the good and not correct thoughts as an ethical subject are what make

---

[26] I borrow the example from Margaret R. Graver, *Stoicism and Emotion* (Chicago: Chicago University Press, 2007), 27.

[27] Nathaniel DesRosiers, "The Establishment of Proper Mental Disposition and Practice: The Origin, Meaning, and Social Purpose of the Prohibition of Oaths in Matthew" (Brown University, PhD diss., 2007).

the difference. For Matthew, I suspect that righteousness involves a character that is constituted by total commitment and obedience to God and his law in a way that is similar to the Stoic conception.

The other side of righteousness as a matter of character is the hard polemic against the hypocrisy of those who are outwardly doing the right things but lack the right inner formation. Immediately after the exhortation to be perfect like God, comes a series of warnings against seeming to be altruistic and pious in order to win honor and good reputation when one is not truly altruistic and pious (6:1–17). God is able to see one's true inward character and will reward and punish (6:18).[28] The theme is prominent outside of the Sermon in Matthew and focuses on the scribes and Pharisees. Chapter 23 is an extremely harsh and extensive polemic against them. Matthew borrows a much less extensive hypocrisy theme from Mark and Q, but develops the theme that the scribes and Pharisees only seem to be righteous because they possess vices such as vanity, greed, and lack of self-mastery (23:5–6, 25) and do not have virtues such as justice, mercy and trustworthiness (23:23).

Returning to Matt 5:48, it is important to note that although scholars widely agree that the call to perfection is a general moral principle for Matthew, the immediate context is the call to love one's enemies:

> Love your enemies and pray for those who are persecuting you, so that you may be sons of your father in the heavens. For he makes his sun rise on the evil and the good and makes it rain on the righteous and the unrighteous. For if you love those who love you, what reward do you have? Even the tax collectors do the same do they not?" . . . be perfect as . . .

The command to imitate God in this respect is central to the thought of the sermon as a whole. God's love is for all. It is perfect, complete. There has been persistent inconclusive debate about the role of Lev 19:8 in 5:43, but when one looks for both the idea of love or benevolence toward enemies and the kind of reasoning that supports the idea here, the evidence for this odd idea strongly points to Stoicism.

Epictetus (according to Arrian, *Diss.* 3.22.54) says that true philosophers if flogged "must love the one who flogs them." And Seneca urges, "Someone gets angry with you? Challenge him with kindness in return" (*Ira* 2.34) and "We shall never cease working for the common good, helping everyone and even our enemies, until our helping hand is feeble with age" (*De Otio* 1.4). For Stoics, the idea of following or imitating God (Seneca, *Vit. Beat.* 15; *Ep.*, 16:5; Epictetus, *Diss.*, 1:30; Marcus, 7:31) means caring for the creation, and above all fellow

---

[28] The first part of this is also Stoic. Epictetus, for example, says that Stoics hold that God not only cares for the world, but "sees and not only what person does, but also what one intends and thinks" (*Diss.* 2.14.11).

rational animals, in the way that divine Providence administers the common good.[29] Matthew 5:45 almost sounds like an echo of Seneca, *De Ben.* 4:26: "If you are imitating the gods, you say, 'then bestow benefits also upon the ungrateful, for the sun rises also upon the wicked, and the sea lies open to pirates . . .'" Matthew 7:25–34 (also 10:29–31) develops the theme of God's providential care for the universe, teaching that God takes care of birds and flowers and humans alike in service of an exhortation to refrain from being anxious. What people are to do instead of worrying is to strive to have "God's righteousness" (6:33). A Stoic would say that instead of treating the necessities of food and clothing as genuine goods and their lack as evils, those who are progressing toward virtue ought to realize that they share what is truly good with God, and that they ought to pursue that reason/wisdom/virtue. Foremost of the eupathic emotions (good emotions) of the sage was joy and sources give one of the sub-species of joy that would characterize the sage as *euthumia*, defined in one source as "joy at the administration of the universe."[30]

Again, there is detailed technical Stoic theory behind their distinctive attitude toward enemies and love of humanity.[31] In their theory of human moral development (*oikeiosis*), the morally mature human will extend the kind of affection and concern that "good people" have for family and close kin to all humans when called upon to do so by fitting circumstances. Recent scholarship has shown how especially Stoics of the Roman period developed and extended these ideas.[32] But again I want to emphasize the point that Matthew does not have to detail or explicitly appeal to this technical theory in order to use Stoic thought to construe Jesus and create an ethic for him, especially since he is unlikely to want the connection to be specific and since the form is that of narrative.

I am convinced that the Stoic explanation works well in explaining the materials that I have treated thus far. There is a major problem that challenges my whole enterprise, however.[33] In the Sermon on the Mount, Jesus teaches that any anger at all is wrong, but later in the narrative Jesus seems to attack the moneychangers in anger (Matt 21:12–13). One scholar has described the episode as Jesus' "temple tantrum."[34] There is indeed a problem of Jesus

---

[29] Gretchen Reydam-Shils, *The Roman Stoics: Self, Responsibility, and Affection* (Chicago: University of Chicago Press, 2005), 73.

[30] Ps. Andronicus, *On Emotions* (*SVF* 3.432).

[31] On grounds for philanthropia in late Stoicism and especially theology, see Gaëlle Fiasse, "Les fondements de la philanthropie dans le nouveau stoïcisme, deux cas concrets: l'esclavage et la gladiature," *EPh* 63 (2002): 527–47.

[32] Reydam-Shils, *Roman Stoics*, 53–82; Anne Banateanu, *La théorie stoïcienne de l'amitié*, Vestigia 27 (Fribourg: Éditions Universitaires; Paris: Du Cerf, 2001).

[33] This problem was first pointed out to me by Erin Roberts.

[34] E.g., see the Introduction of Paula Fredriksen, *From Jesus to Christ: The Origins of the New Testament Images of Jesus*, 2nd ed. (New Haven: Yale University Press, 2000).

seeming to blatantly contradict his own teachings. On a broader level this has long been recognized, so that Hans Dieter Betz, for instance, in his monumental commentary has argued that the Sermon on the Mount was a pre-existing moral treatise that Matthew placed in his narrative without fully integrating it by making the whole consistent.[35] Betz' creative idea has not won assent.[36] To continue with examples of contradictions, in 5:22, Jesus teaches that someone who calls another person a fool will be liable to burn in Hell. But in 23:17 he calls the scribes and Pharisees "fools" – using exactly the same word. If Matthew had adapted the Stoic position that emotions of the unwise were moral errors, then we would expect this to apply not only to anger, but also to other emotions such as grief. But Jesus is said to have "grieved and been agitated" and says, "I am extremely grief-stricken even to the point of death" (26:37–8). Would a Stoic sage act like that?

Is Matthew's Jesus radically inconsistent or is there another explanation? Any answer must come to terms with that gospel's use of sources. It closely follows Mark's passion narrative that is tightly constructed around allusions to and quotations from the Greek translation of the Hebrew scripture. Mark's brilliant creation may have had too much authority by the time that Matthew wrote to allow for major changes or changes in key features of the story. So, for example, Mark's "I am extremely grief-stricken even to the point of death" followed by Matthew is a quotation from Ps 42:6 (41:6 LXX)

But I want to suggest that there is a Stoic way to interpret Jesus' behavior. This argument involves two general claims. First the sage's action although always following the will of God, the universal law and reason, might *in particular circumstances* be contrary to what the accepted moral norms of non-sages indicated was right, even for sages. This would go along with the theme that Matthew borrows from Mark of Jesus's ability to teach and act with unique authority. Thus, Matthew's narrative gives the sense that only Jesus was rightly able to teach what he taught and act in the often dramatic and unorthodox ways that he acted. Of course, this is because he is God's son and the messiah, and the son of man. But to put it in these terms is to be anachronistic and to fail to imagine the possibilities that readers contemporary with the author could have brought to its reading. As is well-known and widely accepted in contemporary scholarship, "son of god," for example, was a common expression for individuals thought to have a special relationship with the divine from Roman emperors to King David and on. The gospels are in the process of inventing the Christian idea that the Jews were looking for "the messiah." In

---

[35] Hans Dieter Betz, *The Sermon on the Mount: A Commentary on the Sermon on the Mount, Including the Sermon on the Plain (Matthew 5:3-7:27 and Luke 6:20-49)* (Minneapolis: Fortress, 1995), 70–88.
[36] Graham N. Stanton, *A Gospel for a New People: Studies in Matthew* (Edinburgh: T&T Clark, 1992), 307–25.

order to avoid anachronism, the historian has to ask what culturally available components Matthew drew upon to construct this strikingly new, yet conventional, figure. My claim is that the Stoic sage and aspects of Stoic ethics should be added to the mix.

Second, contrary to popular conceptions of the Stoic, the sage was to be a highly passionate person who had and expressed strong feelings.[37] Scholars of early Christianity consistently treat Stoic *apatheia* as a total lack of emotion like that exhibited by Spock on *Star Trek*. But the Stoic teaching was that the sage would have a set of good emotions (*eupatheiai*) instead of the diseased emotional states of the non-sage. The sage was certainly wired in a different way, but he was not without feeling, even intense feeling. In Stoic theory, all impressions involve an act of assent that involves a judgment usually based upon one's preexisting values and therefore entailing moral responsibility for the ensuing mental states. The Stoics taught that in the present cultures deeply corrupted by false values (such as that wealth is a good, others can truly harm me, prestige and repute are goods) emotions as shaped by these values were moral diseases. The sage, however, would have "emotions" based solely on true values, virtue is the only good and vice the only evil. The evidence, I believe, following recent scholarship, shows that these good emotions might involve intense feeling such as in joy, religious reverence and even erotic love.[38] A sage would never experience ordinary grief, anger or fear.

Matthew seems to present Jesus as sinless, as the only living righteous one in the story and the embodiment of God's wisdom.[39] So Jesus can without hypocrisy call the Pharisees "fools" because he knows with certainty that they are fools and that he himself is consistently wise. It is just and righteous censure. The unrighteous and the imperfect, on the other hand, cannot justly censure others in this way. But grief and anger are more difficult. My hypothesis is that the author of Matthew may have conceived of Jesus in a consistent way encouraged by contemporary treatments of God's frequent displays of anger in the Hebrew scriptures. It is well-known that Philo and other Jewish writers denied that God had this emotion and claimed that the texts were an accommodating way to express God's just indignation. The temple episode does not use the word "anger." A sage does not have anger because she knows that no other person can truly cause unjust harm to the sage's good. Stoic theory might make it seem that the good emotions would only concern the sage's own good – and for the most part they do. But sources for the sub-species of the good emotions also have good emotions that express concern for the

---

[37] For what follows, see above all Graver, *Stoicism and Emotion*.
[38] See Graver, *Stoicism and Emotion*, with relevant bibliography.
[39] For some specific statements regarding Jesus' righteousness, see Matt 3:15 and 27:4, 19.

good of others. Ps. Andronicus, *On Emotions* (*SVF* 6.342), for instance, defines good intent (*eunoia*) as "a wish for good things for another for that person's sake." One might then conceive of Jesus's action as an expression of his just indignation that the moneychangers were causing harm to their good and the good of others by devaluing a place where only the model of God's perfection ought to be exhibited. Instead of fear, the sage was to have an emotion usually translated as caution. Andronicus defines one subspecies, reverence (*hagneia*), as "caution against misdeeds concerning the gods." These considerations, I think, show that the hypothesis of a consistent Jesus shaped by the Stoic idea of the sage deserves further study.

Matthew could not do much with an inherited episode of Jesus fulfilling scripture by grieving deeply. Origen, who along with many ancient Christian writers, assumed like the Stoics that grieving was morally wrong, had an interpretation that may deserve consideration.[40] Origen claims that Matthew writes "Jesus began to grieve" and uses the Stoic concept of a pre-emotion to explain that text.[41] Jesus did not have an emotion – that requires assent – but only the initial reaction that the Stoics said were involuntary and natural. Matthew gets "began" from Mark but changes Mark's word *ekthambeisthai*, which usually (at least without the prefix) means to "be amazed" in Mark and elsewhere. But translators assimilate it to Matthew and the Psalm and usually render it as to "be distressed." Matthew changes this to the common word for grief that the Stoics used, a word that connects verse 37 to the word for grief in the quotation from Ps 42. Matthew can then be read in this Stoic way: Jesus had the initial "biting contraction" of grief that is natural to all humans, including sages, accompanied with his proclamation of the scripture that predicted it, but never allowed the natural pre-emotion to develop into an evil and unnatural emotion that construed his impending death as an evil. In Stoic thought, death is a preferred indifferent. Life ought to be desired, pursued and preserved, but one is not to think that who one truly is and what is truly valuable will be harmed by that natural and universal state that is another part of God's plan. The prayers of Jesus that follow can be read as expressing this attitude. At the end of the scene (26:42) that starts with the "pre-grief," he calmly says to God, if my death cannot be avoided, then your will be done.

If this reading is correct, then Philo employs the same strategy in treating Abraham's grieving over Sarah (*QG* 1.79). Even though Gen 23:2 says that "Abraham came to mourn for Sarah and to weep," Philo strongly denies that Abraham had the emotion of grief. Margaret Graver shows that Philo's argument uses the Stoic concepts of impression, assent and pre-emotion.[42] Abraham

---

[40] Graver, *Stoicism and Emotion*, 102–6; idem, "Philo of Alexandria and the Stoic *propatheiai*." *Phron.* 44 (1999): 300–25.
[41] Graver, "Philo of Alexandria."
[42] Following Graver, *Stoicism and Emotion*, 103.

had the initial natural pangs of loss, but did not allow this to develop into the emotion that expresses the judgment that God taking Sarah was a genuine evil. From the surviving Stoic writers, Seneca seems to go the furthest when he grants that the sage will involuntarily weep and shake with sobs at a funeral (*Ep.* 99). The sage will also voluntarily (i.e., in a manner that is constructed with reason) and therefore eupathically weep in a way that involves joy when remembering the goodness and companionship of the loved one. That a major Stoic figure can go this far shows that Matthew's author and ancient readers could quite easily construe Jesus's grieving in a way that would be consistent with the Stoically inflected teachings in the Sermon on the Mount.

The reasons why the author of Matthew drew upon Stoic ethics seem clear. That writer inherited a Jesus who was known as a teacher but had no clear and elaborated ethical teachings that would make him like, or rather superior to, the other great teachers of the culture. Stoicism was the most prominent and widely respected philosophy of the day. Furthermore, it had a reputation for being both rigorous and popular. It was popular in the sense that it was directed at everyone and focused upon those who were sinners and those who were trying to make moral progress. But it also held up the nearly impossible ideal of the sage and urged people to measure themselves against this model of human perfection. The rigor fit well with Matthew's harsh apocalyptic ideas about an exacting and vengeful god who would consign all but a faithful few to eternal torment.[43]

The Matthean gospel's adaptation of the ethic also helped to solve a huge problem that it had inherited from Mark and Q. How is it that people of God, the Jews, had been so blind and so evil that God had to destroy the nation and the religion as it had been known? How is it that they could have rejected and killed God's chosen messiah and been allowed to bear such evil guilt that even their descendants would share it? With resources adapted from Stoicism, Matthew could "argue" that they were evil because in spite of all outward appearance of being good people, they lacked the essential qualitative aspect of character that God had always required and taught through his law: righteousness. The problem that Matthew left for future generations of Christian thinkers was that the rigorous ethical side wedded

---

[43] Matthew substantially intensifies Mark's apocalyptic severity. For example, Matt 7:13–14 is harsher than the parallel in Luke 13: 23–24. The standards for escaping destruction are extremely strenuous (e.g., Matt 7:21–23; 5:20–22). Future judgment pervades the Sermon on the Mount. Gehenna occurs seven times in Matthew but only three in Mark and once in Luke, and Matthew emphasizes the horrible suffering (outer darkness, fire, burning, weeping and gnashing of teeth and so on). Note also the many references to judgment such as 8:13–29; 10:15: 26–28; 11:20–24; 12:41; 13:42, 50; 18:3, 10; 22:13; 24:51; 25:30. Note also Matthew's redactional additions about the judging of the Son on Man in 3:12 and 16:27. In addition Matthew stresses fear of destruction as a central motivating force of his ethic (e.g., 10:26-28).

to an apocalyptic framework with a vengeful god possessed an ill fit with the love of enemies and the universal providential care of God that the writer also borrowed from Stoicism. This dilemma is, I think, one reason why later Christian thinkers from Origen to Augustine had to add another story about an originary or pre-mundane fall that would provide an explanation in terms of a deep general human recalcitrance that was then read as the backdrop for the stories of scripture.

CHAPTER TWELVE

The Secrets of the Gods and the End of Interpretation

In a volume, *Secrecy in Religions*, Kees Bolle, as editor responsible for the introduction and author of the lead essay, excoriates scholars for attempting to explain mystery that he counts as the essence of religion.[1] He writes as if secrecy and mystery are *sui generis* givens and neglects the role of human agency in producing secrecy. The concepts of secrecy and of concealment differ from the concept of the unknown in that the former entails the idea of agency and mind. They are activities involving intentionality. I am one of those who believe that religion is most usefully treated in the academy as the study of human practices that involve imagining interaction with certain classes of agents, that is, gods, ancestors, saints, spirits, the world as mind and many other types of non-obvious beings. Most study of secrecy in religion has treated esoteric traditions, mysticism and social formations that feature secret knowledge. Instead, I want to think about the way that various kinds of practices involve different modes of imagining the secrets of and about these non-obvious agents.

I begin with a central characteristic of conceiving these agents across cultures that ensures a large role for secrecy in religion. Normally humans do not have full and direct access to gods, ancestors and so on, but recognize their activity in traces that the gods have left.[2] A trace could be a strike of lightening, an illness, a bountiful crop, a healing, a heightened mood, a possessed individual, divine embodiments in plants, animals or natural features, or a deposit of divine words that needs an interpreter. One usually sees not the god but the

---

[1] Kees W. Bolle, "Secrecy in Religions," in *Secrecy in Religions*, ed. Kees W. Bolle (Leiden: Brill, 1987), 1–24.
[2] The account of traces is particularly important in Justin L. Barrett, *Why Would Anyone Believe in God?* (Lanham, MD: AltaMira, 2004), 36–39. On gods knowing what people do not, see Pascal Boyer, *Religion Explained: The Evolutionary Origins of Religious Development* (New York: Basic Books, 2001), 256–67.

results of divine activity as in Ps 77:19; "The rumble of your thunder was in the whirlwind; your lightening flashed light at the world; the earth trembled and shook. Your way was through the sea, your path through the great waters; yet your footprints were not seen." Traces are partial, mysterious and require interpretation such as the writer of the Psalm and other authors are eager to supply. Most of all, traces often raise the question of divine intentions. Thus, religion has involved enormous investment in human interpretive practices.

I hope to illuminate issues of imagined agency, secrets, interpretation and kinds of practices in types of social environments with two kinds of examples. The first I call the religion of everyday social exchange.[3] In such religiosity, non-obvious beings typically relate to people as co-inhabitants of the physical and social landscape rather than as legislators, moral exemplars, or possessors of the big secret, but as interested parties open to interaction with humans.[4] Such beings know everything that humans do or at least know more than humans do. Contrary to our Western thinking, non-obvious beings are often local, relatively inconsequential and sometimes even thought to be dim-witted, but they seem always to know some things that humans do not know. People in these cultures may not think of the gods as omniscient and might think the question of omniscience a strange bit of speculation. Humans have quite incomplete knowledge of what other people do, but gods and ancestors know what people do and think. Living with gods and ancestors adds a level of epistemological play and complexity to human social interaction.

So, for example, this understanding of what gods and people know is the basis for one of the most important practices in Greek and Roman culture, across the Mediterranean and in West Asia, oath-taking. Oaths were the basis for almost all business and legal transactions, as well as for crediting political and military offices and professional statuses.[5] They took the place of contracts. Oaths were so important in business that markets were equipped with altars for oath-taking rituals. Greeks and Romans did not represent the relevant gods and non-obvious beings as agents who wanted to establish and oversee human morality and behavior with laws or in other ways that are often represented as totalizing in other types of religiosity. But the gods were nevertheless present, could potentially see everything that people did, and could be asked by humans to act as interested parties willing to guarantee promises. Oaths called on particular deities or general categories of non-evident beings ("non-evident being" is often an excellent translation for the Greek word, *daemon*) to punish either of the parties who cheated and broke the oath. The gods know what

---

[3] See Chapter One in this volume ("The Religion of Plant and Animal Offerings").
[4] I borrow "interested parties" from Boyer, *Religion Explained*, 172–74.
[5] Nicholas Rauh, *Sacred Bonds of Commerce: Religion, Economy, and Trade Society in Hellenistic Roman Delos 166-87 B. C.*, (J.C. Gieben: Amsterdam 1993).

is secret between humans, but the divine watching is hidden from humans, a dynamic of secrecy and knowledge.

Among the Kwaio of the Solomon Islands, *adalo* is a word that means both ancestors and the rather mysterious wild spirits. Individuals usually have a special interest in and closeness to near kin who have died. Roger Keesing describes how the Kwaio constantly interact with these *adalo* including offerings of food to them, meeting them in dreams, and talking to them.[6] Traditional Kwaio religious beliefs and activities are entirely focused on everyday life.[7] Keesing elicited a response that is familiar to numerous ethnographers when he asked big questions like, "How and why do the ancestors control events?"; "What are wild spirits?" People either said that they did not know, or they gave differing, hesitant, vague speculations. Above all, knowing such big general things about the ancestors was of little or no interest to them. No role exists in traditional Kwaio culture for the revelation of such big secrets about non-obvious beings. Similarly, myths of creation exist widely throughout sub-Saharan Africa in traditional cultures, but these creator deities play almost no role in religious life. Among the Fang, Mebeghe created the whole natural world and was followed by Nzame, who invented all cultural objects.[8] Although the Fang assume that the two are still around, they have no cults to them, and they play no role in their ritual activities. These gods of grand myth have little or no relation to practical concerns.

One might think that with Homer and with Hesiod's *Theogony* that the situation would be different for the ancient Greeks. There is no doubt that the systematizing and rationalizing representations of these writings had more and more influence on Greek culture as the centuries passed, but there was always an enormous gap between the thought worlds of those writings and much of traditional Greek religion. From Homer and Hesiod, one would think that Greeks simply conceived of Zeus as the majestic high king of the gods who was rather distant from the mundane minutiae of everyday life. Instead, the non-literary Zeus ubiquitous in everyday life was not one Zeus, but numerous localized Zeuses treated as distinct deities in cult and daily life. No evidence exists that Greeks had a way to rationalize the distance between the great Olympian Zeus and Zeus of the household storeroom represented by a jar or a pendant on a jar or Zeus of the of Household Fence and Zeus of Boundary Markers. Numerous epithets indicate the local and socially specialized nature of

---

[6] Roger Keesing, *Kwaio Religion: The Living and the Dead in a Solomon Island Society* (New York: Columbia University Press, 1982).
[7] Boyer, *Religion Explained*, 138–40, 155–60, uses the Kwaio to illustrate god concepts as persons and the role of strategic information. I draw on his discussion here and below but have shifted the emphasis from cognition to types of practices.
[8] Boyer, *Religion Explained*, 160.

Greek religion: Zeus of the City Council, Zeus of the City, Zeus the Kindly, Zeus the Overseer, Zeus the Deliverer, Zeus of the Brotherhood, Zeus Teleios associated with marriage, and many others. Nor do we have evidence that these Zeuses or numerous other everyday deities had myths or theology that answered questions about who they were, their natures and their histories (see Chapter One). There might be foundation myths for particular cult sites and related mythic fragments, but like most knowledge of the divine this was related to the practical know-how of social and socio-economic exchange that implicated the gods, heroes and other kinds of beings in that exchange. The Gods gave the fruit of the earth, animal and human offspring, and aided human excellence. In return, humans offered sacrifices, first fruit offerings and gave many types of honors in order to thank and maintain the good will of the gods.

From our western perspective, the uncertainty and humility about knowledge of divine nature, divine activity and divine history is striking in the religion of mundane social exchange. Not only were most of these things unknown, but there was little sense of either the right or the need to turn these unknowns into valued secrets that might be hidden or revealed.[9] Divination and healing are two practices typical of such cultures across time and the globe that fit this epistemological minimalism. In divination, practitioners want to discover the intentions of the unseen beings toward particular individuals and particular undertakings. The information gathered from divinatory practices is aimed at either pre-emptive actions or remediation of problems and misfortunes. Practitioners ask which god, spirit, demon or ancestor caused a misfortune and why? Answers to the "which" and "why" questions afford the inquirers enough information to undertake some action that would conciliate the unseen agent or otherwise rectify the situation.

Traditional Kwaio divination often involves problem-solving.[10] When someone is sick, for example, they consult a diviner who tries to determine which *adalo* is angry and why. The diviner will ask particular yes and no questions and pull knotted leaves until one side or the other breaks, indicating an answer. The sick person may have broken a rule like urinating in an improper place. Although unseen by humans, the *adalo* knows about the polluting act. If they sacrifice a pig to the wrong *adalo*, and not the specific one who is angry, the person will not get well. It is not unusual to have several rounds of divination and sacrifice until the right *adalo* has been found. The Kwaio are always looking for traces, signs of the *adalo*, but they maintain good relations with them by regularly offering pigs and in return get healthy taro crops.

---

[9] A partial exception is the Eleusinian mysteries at Athens. The mysteries, however, were not very big secrets, sometimes unspoken open secrets and were much like secret ritual revelations in initiation and even healing cults in many cultures.

[10] Keesing, *Kwaio Religion*, 113–17.

No particular revelation of their intentions is needed. But when the crops fail, divination becomes necessary. Praying, that is talking to the *adalo*, looking for signs, giving gifts to the *adalo*, divining and healing, are all practices of a socio-economic exchange in which the gods participate from their mostly concealed, but mundane, vantage.

Greeks and Romans had many means of divination that were woven into the fabric of life.[11] For Greeks, these means of finding traces of gods and other non-obvious beings included oracular gods and their shrines, the interpretation of dreams, unusual celestial phenomena such as thunder without rain, dice oracles, reading the behavior of birds and sneezing. Another designated by the word *symbolon*, from which our word "symbol" comes, was overhearing pregnant words in a conversation, especially of children. Ubiquitous animal sacrifices were always divinatory with practices such as reading the entrails and watching the way that the tail and organs moved and burned on the altar. Like the Kwaio, Greeks often wanted to know which god, hero, or other *daimon* was angry and why – in order to find a remedy. Had sacrifices been neglected, or a sacred precinct been polluted? Greeks often dealt with the problem of knowing which deity was angry, by directing inquiries, prayers or sacrifices to "the god" or "the *daimon*" in an indefinite form that meant whichever agent was appropriate. In some circumstances one could address the gods in general, covering all bases. When trying to decide what to do in some situation, Greeks would often ask a question in the form of "Is it more beneficial and advantageous to do X?" Again, we find the pursuit of traces and little revelations that serve everyday ends woven into socio-economic exchange. There is little room for the big secret and its revelation.

I now shift away from the religion of social exchange, its conceptions of non-evident beings, its treatment of what is secret and concealed about these beings, and the relevant practices. I shift to a couple of examples of what I will call the "religion of literate mythmaking," which I view as particularly dramatic instances of the ways that this kind of religion has dealt with secrets about non-evident beings. This use of secrecy is one of several discursive strategies that has characterized the religion of literate religious experts. I will focus on the Gospel of Mark, but also say some things about the Gospel of John. In John, Jesus is unambiguously a god, a non-evident being, who came from heaven, can disappear, walk through walls and so on. Mark's Jesus is more ambiguous, but is probably best described as a possessed human being. He has been taken over by the Judean god's own spirit or *pneuma*, the ultimate vital intelligent stuff. But this is no ordinary case of possession from the religion of social exchange. Rather it is the case of possession to end all possession.

---

[11] Sarah Isles Johnston, *Ancient Greek Divination* (Oxford: Wiley Blackwell, 2008).

Importantly, the two writings know the religion of mundane social exchange and pose their main character against the background of this pervasive ancient religiosity. The beginning of the episode with the blind man in John (9:1–41) might be seen as symbolic for this opposition. The disciples ask, "Teacher, who sinned, this man or his parents so that he was born blind?" Jesus's answer is "neither." The man was "born blind so that God's activities might be made manifest in him." Jesus rejects the kind of "why?" question that allowed just enough concealed information about the relevant non-obvious beings to maintain relations of social exchange. There is no everyday social exchange with this strange new representative of the Judean god. Rather, God allowed the man's blindness so that Jesus could heal him and provide evidence of his own divine origins. Jesus rejects the normal religion of exchange and instead offers himself as the revelation of the great secret about the divine order of history and the cosmos. The Jesus that the people in the narrative world of John perceive is a trace that points to a mystery.

The writer's next move makes this revelation mysterious and unfathomable for the characters in the narrative. In seeming explanation of the healing as a display of God's actions, Jesus says, "I must perform the actions of him who sent me while it is day; night is coming when no man can act." Here we see a chief characteristic of both Mark's and John's methods; the teachings, actions and healings of Jesus as well as these gospels as wholes simultaneously proclaim the revelation of a great secret and conceal the revelation.[12] They give with one hand and take away with the other. The characters in the narratives are blind, stupid, duped and simply do not possess the capacity to grasp the meanings of the divine secrets. Readers are lured into the sense that they are privileged observers who know the truth. After all, John begins by telling the reader that Jesus was with God at creation and Mark makes the reader present and understanding at Jesus's baptism with God's spirit. The reader is made to marvel at the dullness of the disciples and the other characters. But both writings seek to leave the reader in a situation of unknowing about the big secret.

The big secret concerns who Jesus is and what he is about. In these narratives, knowledge of the divine still appears in traces – healings, exorcisms, wonders, actions and sayings that must be divined – but the writers have welded these into a global and totalizing set of references to one big secret. All of the little puzzles point to one big secret. But doesn't Jesus explain the nature of the kingdom of God in Mark and then reveal himself as the suffering messiah? On one level yes, but this interpretation is also a domestication of Mark's mystery and fails to grasp the deeper sense, as Mark would have it.

Take the well-known difficulty of the parables in Mark. Jesus tells the parable of the seed and the types of soil to a large crowd, ending with the challenge, "let

---

[12] Frank Kermode, *The Genesis of Secrecy* (Cambridge: Harvard University Press, 1979), 47. My reading below draws broadly on Kermode.

anyone who has ears to hear listen!" Then he takes the disciples aside alone and says (4:11), "To you is given the secret of the kingdom of God, but for those outside, everything is in parables so that 'they may indeed look, but not see, and may indeed listen, but not understand; so that they may not reform and be forgiven." Jesus teaches the masses in parables so that those outside of his inner circle will not understand. But even after chastising his students for not understanding and then explaining the parable with a pedantic allegory, the disciples still fail to understand. Next (4:22–23), just as he challenged the crowd, Jesus repeats to his inner circle, "there is nothing hidden except to be revealed, nor is anything secret except to come to light. Let anyone with ears to hear, listen!" A number of parables, mostly (pedantic or profound?) similes, follow such as "the kingdom of God is like a mustard seed." The section on parables ends with the narrator telling us that Jesus explained all of his teachings in private to his students (4:33). Then comes the story of Jesus stilling the storm (4:35–41), which is meant to show that the disciples have no understanding of who Jesus is even though they have seen his miracles and the testimony of demons (3:11) who as non-evident beings from the world of everyday social exchange know what humans do not: Jesus is the Son of God. As Frank Kermode has emphasized, the disciples are in a situation similar to the one that the gospel writer wants to construct for the reader.[13] The disciples do know the facts, but they are utterly unable to grasp their ultimate import.

Rejecting the idea that Mark could foist such a tease, many literal minded scholars find the answer in the scene with Peter's confession in chapter 8. Surely this is a revelation scene that breaks the secret. Jesus is the messiah who must suffer. When Peter does not understand that Jesus is the messiah who must suffer, Jesus rebukes him and explains the idea to him (8:31–33). Of course, Peter's later denial before Jesus's crucifixion seems to imply that he never understood. In the scene that follows, the confession episode, the transfiguration, with all of its apocalyptic imagery focused on Jesus, Peter shows that he completely misunderstands another dimension of who Jesus is. God has to speak out of a cloud to set things straight. From the gospel's beginning to its ending, with the women running in fright from the empty tomb, no human truly understands.

The tease, I think, is that many characters and especially the reader do understand a lot of things about Jesus that Mark has given to them: Jesus is the Son of God, the mysterious Son of Man, the suffering messiah and more. Mark is trying to suggest that one can know all of that and still not understand the big secret. Wayne Meeks, though writing about the Gospel of John, makes a central point that also applies to Mark:

> The dialogue with Nicodemus and its postscript connected with John the Baptist constitute a virtual *parody* of a revelation discourse. What is

[13] Kermode, *Genesis of Secrecy*, 143.

'revealed' is that Jesus is *incomprehensible* . . . The forms of speech which would ordinarily provide warrants for a particular body of information or instruction are here used in such a way that they serve solely to emphasize Jesus' strangeness. Yet it is not quite right with Bultmann to say that Jesus reveals only that he is the revealer. He reveals rather that he is the enigma . . .[14]

Jesus is in a class of his own. If interpretation is translation from a lesser-known idiom into a better-known idiom, then according to Mark's sleight of hand interpretation comes to an end with Jesus. Jesus cannot be translated into even the completely correct knowns such as son of God and suffering messiah. Just when the big secret seems right in one's grasp – it vanishes, but in that vanishing it has become a rarer, more desirable, and more enticing mystery.

Many a scholar of religion would stop the paper here, a good ending for a sermon. But the topic rightly calls for a different sort of translation, that is, a translation into the idiom of explaining human sociality designated by the expression "social practice." Can we understand what I have styled as two types of religion in terms of different social practices? The case of the religion of social exchange is obvious and the explanation is imminent in the overt description. This is no accident. This type of religion does not seek to hide or euphemize its relation to economic practices, power, social exchange, and the mundane. The gods and ancestors are interested unseen observers and participants in human life who reliably leave traces of their intentions. There is no specialized religious domain of life or required guild of experts. Religious practices are distributed and embedded among all of the practices that make up the society, but especially in practices of socio-economic exchange. There are religious specialists who have particular practical skills, but there is no mechanism for the massive accumulation and concentration of religious knowledge by a few specialists. The secrets of religion are little secrets.

The religion of literate mythmaking is more difficult. That difficulty partly results from our closeness to its social and cultural mechanisms. If the religion of social exchange involves a dispersal of practices and of cultural power, literate mythmaking is a concentration of these. Literate practices cause that concentration and the fact that probably less than 2% of the population of the Roman Empire were literate enough to skillfully read much less write works like Mark and John is the other side of the coin of cultural power. The practices of reading, writing and skillful interpretation by individuals who formed networks of literate exchange constitute the basis for this kind of mythmaking and religiosity. I can only comment briefly on key characteristics of these practices that

---

[14] Wayne A. Meeks, "The Man from Heaven in Johannine Sectarianism," *JBL* 91 (1972): 57.

tend to be atopic, translocal, intertextual, competitive and totalizing. While the religion of exchange is socially embedded and largely face to face, the literate practices float free of place and time. A writing can go anywhere and remain a text as long as there are people with the literate skills to read and interpret it. Loss of attachment to an author or place of composition is normal but can be made into a tool of literary and ideological power over readers. So, for instance, Mark and John are anonymous, and indeed they gain in their mythic power for that. They come from nowhere and take a universalizing and omniscient perspective on their narration as if written by an unseen god. The stance aids myth and ideology presented as givens. At most, the author in such instances is a secret, mystery, or *aporia*.

The interpretive context for such writing is not a place or author, but other writings to which it links. In our case, for instance, "Mark" has narrated his story of Jesus in a way that connects Jesus with apocalyptic writings. Such writings compete to give totalizing cosmic-historical accounts that claim to be revelations of heavenly secrets. The tradition displays contestation over defining the boundaries between the representation of knowledge and divine secrets. Newer strategies sought to outdo older strategies in representing mystery and setting the limits of interpretation. John and Mark have drawn the boundary of religious incomprehensibility with Jesus. The author, the human element in writing that ought to be subject to social and historical particularity, can become like a god, leaving only traces in the artifact of the writing, but being invisible, without place and omniscient, always looking knowingly over the characters in the story and the struggles of the reader through the traces of narration.

I have presented these types of religiosities to aid in thinking about ways of constituting the secrets of the gods. The religion of literate mythmaking frequently strives to overcome the religion of social exchange, but I would not want to leave the impression that the two are always pure and unmixed, even if consisting of distinct kinds and clusters of practices. The story of how, for example, traditional religions of social exchange both incorporate and resist when subject to the processes of Christianization and Islamic conversion is well-known.[15] The studies of the psychologist, Justin Barrett, have shown that contemporary Roman Catholics and Protestants often operate religiously with practices and conceptions that depart markedly from official theology and that resemble patterns from the religion of everyday social exchange.[16] Even one of the most prolific and brilliant literate mythmakers of them all, Augustine, fell prey to the lure of an ancient Greek divinatory practice. He was directed to

---

[15] For some modern examples of such melding, see Brain Morris, *Religion and Anthropology: A Critical Introduction* (Cambridge: Cambridge University Press, 2006), 77–111, 147–87.

[16] Justin Barrett, "Theological Correctness," *MTSR* 11 (1999): 325–39.

the reading that prompted his conversion when he overheard a child outside the garden say, "pick it up and read it." This is the ancient Greek *symbolon*. But Augustine incorporates the practice into his religion of the grand revelation. The voice does not reveal to him what to do today or whether to begin a business venture or a new relationship or how to find healing but prompts him to make the dramatic change in his life that he renders as an autobiographical narrative set inside a cosmic myth in his *Confessions*.

The fate of John and Mark was a form of institutional domestication that had already begun when Mathew and Luke wrote to correct Mark. Jesus was not an incomprehensible mystery even if there is a proper sense of mystery and God's secrets are on the horizon. Another act of domestication occurred with the four gospels coming into a larger canon of authoritative writings. Institutions, especially dominant orthodox ones, know that contestation over the representation and construction of divine secrets is dangerous. So, they seek to control reading and bring an end to certain types of interpretation. Such institutions do not appreciate the kinds of tease and play about the limits of the knowable indulged in by Mark and John. Christians were thus trained to read with a harmonizing and rationalizing master story to control the wiles of the earlier mythmakers. This meant that readers were to read with the sense that the secrets God had revealed were clear and knowable teachings, but what remained secret was not to be entertained. New mythmaking must come to an end. Curiosity is a sin.

I return to the idea that comparing two ways of imagining the gods and non-evident beings belongs to different kinds of social practices. The beings in the religion of social exchange exist in some secret state normally unseen by humans and often they are immortal or at least live for a very long time. Then there is also their ability to see what people are doing even though the people cannot see them watching. So, these beings clearly have advantages over humans. But they are also not beyond necessity or at least choose to limit themselves. These gods, heroes, ancestors and spirits either desire to live in contact with humans or somehow must live with them. They desire the flesh of sheep, offerings of grain and libations of wine. They enjoy actions of respect and honor from humans, and they are repelled and even driven away by polluting filth. These are the kinds of beings whom philosophers and theologians like to mock for their limitations. But it is precisely these necessities that allow for a good fit between these gods and the everyday life of human societies. Transcendent gods who share nothing of human existence must have sacred books interpreted by a skilled class of experts in order to relate to humans.

The practices of the literate producer of cultural goods are only possible in a condition that frees the scholar from many of the normal constraints of everyday life: farming, fishing, hunting, competing for a mate, raising children to work in the fields and all of the complex social and economic exchange that goes along with these. The literate mythmaker must have many years of schooling with books and must become intimately acquainted with some particular tradition of writings such as apocalyptic writing, and must have the leisure to write and publish the writings. These practices remove the highly literate from everyday human life in important ways and from its imminent necessity. Is it only an accident that the gods of the literate mythmakers are defined above all by their freedom from necessity, distance from everyday human life and by their need for mediating revealer-writers in order to connect with that life?

Could it be that even so modern a scholar as Kees Bolle could be unconsciously universalizing the conditions of his scholastic existence?[17] He warns against the accounts of ethnographers. They get lost in the minutiae and the particularities and therefore miss what is important. He cites Karl Preuss writing about the Kagaba people and the chants, dance, magic rocks, demons and secret knowledge of their priests. Bolle faults Preuss for thinking that the little secrets of these practices mean anything in themselves. Preuss misses that what stands behind all of, as Bolle puts it, "secretive kaboodle," is secrecy itself. Bolle goes on to write,

> Scholarly considerations of this type are beneficial, but they should not carry us away. Whether a religion embraces one tiny village or a third of mankind is irrelevant to the structure of religion. . . . Any religion is universal and exists only by virtue of the fact. Hence its central secret has bearing on the one thing that counts in the world.[18]

The writers of Mark and John and Franz Kafka would be impressed by Bolle, if perhaps for different reasons. Religion, which is the source of all value, is mystery itself. This approach to religion is so totalizing that the myriads of cultures with the religion of mundane social exchange and their tedious details of everyday necessity disappear as so many reflections of the One. Bolle is eager to prescribe the limits of scholarly interpretation. I am one of the explainers whom Bolle casts into the darkness of eternal blindness to what is real and good. I have suggested that religion is not one thing.

It is common for those writing about parables, the Gospel of Mark and about mystery to cite Franz Kafka. They use his parables to make the point that the mystery of meaning is sought as what is most valuable, but that the quest must always result in frustration. I suppose that I cannot resist the Kafka temptation. But in concluding, I want to suggest that we can hear Kafka's famous parable about parables in a different way, as a complaint about the struggle of the everyday to resist being swallowed up by the big secret.

---

[17] On the scholastic point-of-view, see Pierre Bourdieu, *Practical Reason* (Stanford, CA: Stanford University Press, 1998), 127–40.
[18] Bolle, "Secrecy in Religion," 5.

Bibliography

Algra, Keimpe, 'Stoic Theology Keimpe Algra', in Brad Inwood (ed.), *The Cambridge Companion to the Stoics* (Cambridge: Cambridge University Press, 2003), pp. 153–78.
Allison, Dale C., *The End of the Ages Has Come* (Philadelphia, PA: Fortress, 1985).
Allison, Dale C., *The Sermon on the Mount: Inspiring the Moral Imagination* (New York: Crossroad, 1999).
Anderson, Graham, *Sage, Saint and Sophist: Holy Men and Their Associates in the Early Roman Empire* (London: Routledge, 1994).
Arafat, Karim, *Classical Zeus: A Study in Art and Literature* (Oxford: Oxford University Press, 1990).
Aretsinger, Kathryn, 'Birthday Rituals: Friends and Patrons in Roman Poetry and Cult', *Classical Antiquity*, 11: 2, 1992, pp. 175–93.
Arnal, William, 'The Collection and Synthesis of "Tradition and the Second Century Invention of Christianity', *Method and Theory in the Study of Religion*, 23, 2011, pp. 193–215.
Arnim, Hans von, *Leben und Werke des Dio von Prusa, mit einer Einleitung: Sophistik, Rhetorik, Philosophie in ihrem Kampf um die Jugendbildung* (Berlin: Weidmann, 1898).
Finkelstein, Aryay Bennett, *Julian Among Jews, Christians and "Hellenes" in Antioch: Jewish Practice as a Guide to "Hellenes" and a Goad to Christians* (Doctoral dissertation: Harvard University, 2011).
Ascough, Richard S., Philip A. Harland, and John S. Kloppenborg (eds), *Associations in the Greco-Roman World: A Sourcebook* (Waco, TX: Baylor University Press, 2012).
Atran, Scott, 'The Trouble with Memes: Inference Versus Imitation in Cultural Creation', *Human Nature*, 12, 2001, pp. 351–81.
Atran, Scott and Douglas Medin, *The Native Mind and the Cultural Construction of Nature* (Cambridge: MIT Press, 2008).
Attridge, Harold, *First Century Cynicism in the Epistles of Heraclitus*, (Missoula. MT: Scholars Press, 1976).
Attridge, Harold, '*The Philosophical Critique of Religion under the Early Empire*', *Aufstieg und Niedergang der römischen Welt*, II.16.1, 1978, pp. 45–78.
Aune, David E, 'Human Nature and Ethics in Hellenistic Philosophical Traditions and Paul: Some Issues and Problems', in Troels Engberg-Pedersen (ed.), *Paul in His Hellenistic Context* (Edinburgh: T&T Clark, 1994), pp. 291–312.

Baal, Jan van, 'Offering, Sacrifice and Gift', *Numen*, 23, 1976, pp. 161–78.
Bagger, Matthew, *Religious Experience, Justification and History* (Cambridge: Cambridge University Press, 1999).
Bagnani, Gilbert, 'Peregrinus Proteus and the Christians', *Historia: Zeitschrift für Alte Geschichte*, 4, 1955, pp. 107–112.
Baird, William H, *History of New Testament Research: Volume One: From Deism to Tübingen* (Minneapolis, MN: Fortress, 1992), pp. 177–83.
Baker, Alan, 'Simplicity', *Stanford Encyclopedia of Philosophy* (Berkeley: University of California Press, 2010).
Bakker, Jan Theo, *Living and Working with the Gods: Studies of the Evidence for Private Religion and its Material Environment in the City of Ostia (100–500 AD)* (Amsterdam: Gieben, 1994).
Baltzly, Dirk, Marion Durand, and Simon Shogry, 'Stoicism', in Edward N. Zalta and Uri Nodelman (eds), *The Stanford Encyclopedia of Philosophy*, <https://plato.stanford.edu/archives/spr2019/entries/stoicism/> (last accessed 24 July 2023).
Banateanu, Anne, *La théorie stoïcienne de l'amitié* (Fribourg: Éditions Universitaires; Paris: Du Cerf, 2001).
Barrett, Justin L. and Frank C. Keil, 'Conceptualizing a Non-Natural Entity: Anthropomorphism in God Concepts', *Cognitive Psychology*, 31, 1996, pp. 219–47.
Barrett, Justin L., 'Theological Correctness: Cognitive Constraints and the Study of Religion', *Method and Theory in the Study of Religion*, 11, 1999, pp. 325–39.
Barrett, Justin L., *Why Would Anyone Believe in God?* (Lanham, MD: AltaMira, 2004).
Barton, S. C. and G. H. R. Horsley, 'A Hellenistic Cult Group and the New Testament Churches', *Jahrbuch für Antike und Christentum*, 24, 1981, pp. 7–41.
Bauckham, Richard, 'For Whom Were Gospels Written?' in Richard Baukham (ed.), *Gospels for All Christians* (Grand Rapids, MI: Eerdmans, 1998), pp. 9–48.
Bauckham, Richard, *The Gospels for All Christians: Rethinking the Gospel Audiences* (Grand Rapids, MI: Eerdmans, 1998).
Beard, Mary, 'Writing and Religion: Ancient Literacy and the Function of the Written Word in Roman Religion', in Mary Beard (ed.), *Literacy in the Roman World* (Ann Arbor, MI: Journal of Archaeology, 1991), pp. 35–58.
Bendlin, Andreas, 'Gemeinschaft, Öffentlichkeit und Identität: Forschungsgeschichtliche Anmerkungen zu den Mustern sozialer Ordnung in Rom', in Ulrike Egelhaaf-Gaiser and Alfred Schäfer (eds), *Vereine in der römischen Antike: Untersuchungen zu Organisation, Ritual und Raumordnung* (Tübingen: Mohr Siebeck, 2002) pp. 9–40.
Bénatouïl, Thomas, 'How Industrious can Zeus be? The Extent and Objects of Divine Activity in Stoicism', in Ricardo Salles (ed.), *God and Cosmos in Stoicism* (Oxford: Oxford University Press, 2009), pp. 23–45.
Bercovitch, Eytan, 'The Altar of Sin: Social Multiplicity and Christian Conversion among a New Guinea People', in Susan L. Mizruchi (ed.), *Religion and Cultural Studies* (Princeton: Princeton University Press, 2001), pp. 211–35.
Bernard, Wolfgang, *Spaetantike Diktungstheorien: Untersuchungen zu Proklos, Herakleitos und Plutarch* (Stuttgart: Teubner, 1990).

Betz, Hans Dieter, *The Sermon on the Mount: A Commentary on the Sermon on the Mount, Including the Sermon on the Plain (Matthew 5:3-7:27 and Luke 6:20-49)* (Minneapolis: Fortress, 1995).

Bittini, Maurio, *Women and Weasels: Mythologies of Birth in Ancient Greece and Rome* (Chicago: University of Chicago Press, 2013).

Boer, Martinus C. de, *The Defeat of Death: Apocalyptic Eschatology in 1 Corinthians 15 and Romans 5* (Sheffield: Sheffield Academic, 1988).

Bohak, Gideon, *Ancient Jewish Magic: A History* (Tel-Aviv: Tel-Aviv University Press, 2011).

Bolle, Kees W., 'Secrecy in Religions', in Kees. W. Bolle (ed.), *Secrecy in Religions* (Leiden: Brill, 1987), pp. 1–24.

Bosman, Philip R., 'Traces of Cynic Monotheism in The Early Roman Empire', *Acta Classica*, 51, 2008, pp. 1–20.

Bonner, Stanley, *Education in Ancient Rome* (Berkeley: University of California Press, 1977).

Bourdieu, Pierre, 'Genesis and Structure of the Religious Field', *Comparative Social Research*, 13, 1991, pp. 1–44.

Bourdieu, Pierre, 'Legitimation and Structured Interests in Weber's Sociology of Religion', in Scott Lash and Sam Whimster (eds), *Max Weber: Rationality and Modernity* (London: Allen and Unwin, 1987) pp. 119–36.

Bourdieu, Pierre, *The Field of Cultural Production* (New York: Columbia University Press, 1993).

Bourdieu, Pierre, 'Genesis and Structure of the Religious Field', *Comparative Social Research*, 13, 1991, pp. 1–44.

Bourdieu, Pierre, *The Rules of Art: Genesis and Structure of the Literary Field* (Cambridge: Polity Press, 1996).

Bourdieu, Pierre, *The Field of Cultural Production* (New York: Columbia University Press, 1993).

Bourdieu, Pierre, *Practical Reason* (Stanford: Stanford University Press, 1998).

Boyer, Pascal, *Religion Explained: The Evolutionary Origins of Religious Development* (New York: Basic Books, 2001).

Boyer, Pascal, 'Why Do Gods and Spirits Matter at All?', in Ilkka Pyysiänen and Veikko Anttonen (eds), *Current Approaches in the Cognitive Science of Religion* (London: Contiuum, 2002), pp. 68–92.

Boys-Stones, G. R., *Post-Hellenistic Philosophy: A Study of its Development from the Stoics to Origen* (Oxford: Oxford University Press, 2001).

Boys-Stones, G. R., *Metaphor, Allegory, and the Classical Tradition* (Oxford: Oxford University Press, 2003).

Braun, Willi and Russell T. McCutcheon (eds), *Introducing Religion: Essays in Honor of Jonathan Z. Smith* (London: Equinox, 2008).

Braund, Susanna M. and Christopher Gill (eds), *The Passions in Roman Thought and Literature* (Cambridge: Cambridge University Press, 1997).

Bremmer, Jan N., *The Rise of Christianity Through the Eyes of Gibbon, Harnack and Rodney Stark* (Groningen: Barkhuis, 2010).

Brennan, Tad, *The Stoic Life: Emotions, Duties, and Fate* (Oxford: Clarendon, 2005).

Brittain, Charles (ed. and trans.), *Cicero: On Academic Scepticism* (Indianapolis: Hackett, 2006).

Brodie, Thomas L. *The Quest for the Origins of John's Gospel* (New York: Oxford University Press, 1993), pp. 15–21.
Brouwer, René, *The Stoic Sage: The Early Stoics on Wisdom, Sagehood and Socrates* (New York: Cambridge University Press, 2014).
Brubaker, Rogers, *Ethnicity Without Groups* (Cambridge, MA: Harvard University Press, 2004).
Bruneau, Philippe and Jean Ducat, *Guide de Délos*, 4th edn (Paris: Boccard, 2005).
Bruneau, Philippe, *Recherches sur les cultes de Délos à l'époque hellenistique et à l'époque impériale* (Paris: Boccard, 1970).
Buell, Denise Kimber, *Why This New Race: Ethnic Reasoning in Early Christianity* (Columbia: Columbia University Press, 2005).
Bultmann, Rudolf, *Theology of the New Testament* (New York: Scribner, 1951).
Burke, Sean, *The Death and Return of the Author: Criticism and Subjectivity in Barthes, Foucault and Derrida* (Edinburgh: Edinburgh University Press, 1998).
Cameron, Ron and Merrill P. Miller, 'Ancient Myths and Modern Theories of Christian Origins', in Ron Cameron and Merrill P. Miller (eds), *Redescribing Christian Origins* (Leiden: Brill, 2004), pp. 1–32.
Carrier, Richard, 'The Prospect of a Christian Interpolation in Tacitus, Annals 15:44', *Vigiliae Christianae*, 68, 2014, pp. 264–83.
Carter, Jeffrey (ed.), *Understanding Religious Sacrifice: A Reader* (New York: Continuum, 2003).
Chadwick, Henry, *Early Christian Thought and the Classical Tradition* (Oxford: Oxford University Press, 1966).
Chaniotis, Angelos, 'Reinheit der Körper – Reinheit der Seele in den griechischen Kultgesetzen', in Jan Assmann and Theo Sundermeier (eds), *Schuld, Gewissen, und Person: Studien zur Geschichte des inneren Menschen* (Gütersloh: Gütersloher, 1997), pp. 142–79.
Carey, Phillip, *Augustine's Invention of the Inner Self: The Legacy of a Christian Platonist* (New York: Oxford University Press, 2000).
Christensen, Michael and Jeffery Wittung (eds), *Partakers of the Divine Nature: The History and Development of Deification in the Christian Traditions*, (Grand Rapids, MI: Baker Academic, 2007).
Christes, Johannes, *Sklaven und Freigelassene als Grammatiker und Philologen im Antiken Rom* (Wiesbaden: Steiner, 1979).
Cole, Susan Guettel, *Landscapes, Gender, and Ritual Space: The Ancient Greek Experience* (Berkeley: University of California Press, 2004).
Cole, Susan Guettel, *Placing the Gods: Sanctuaries and Sacred Space in Ancient Greece* (Oxford: Clarendon, 1994).
Collins, John J., *The Apocalyptic Imagination*, 2nd edn (Grand Rapids, MI: Eerdmans, 1998).
Comaroff, Jean, *Body of Power, Spirit of Resistance: The Culture and History of a South African People* (Chicago: University of Chicago Press, 1985).
Comaroff, Jean and John Comaroff, *Of Revelation and Revolution: Vol I: Christianity, Colonialism, and Consciousness in South Africa* (Chicago: University of Chicago Press, 1991).
Conte, Gian Biagio, *The Hidden Author: An Interpretation of Petronius' Satyricon* (Berkeley: University of California Press, 1996).

Corley, Kathleen E., *Private Women, Public Meals* (Peabody, MA: Hendrickson, 1993).
Courtney, Edward, *A Companion to Petronius* (Oxford: Oxford University Press, 2001).
Crabbe, James (ed.), *From Soul to Self* (London: Routledge, 1999).
Dahl, Nils A., *Studies in Paul* (Minneapolis, MN: Augsburg, 1977).
Damasio, Antonio, *Descartes' Error: Emotion, Reason and the Human Brain* (New York: G. P. Putnam's Sons, 1994).
Dennett, Daniel, *Darwin's Dangerous Idea: Evolution and the Meaning of Life* (New York: Simon & Schuster, 1995).
deSilva, David A., *Fourth Maccabees and the Promotion of the Jewish Philosophy: Language, Intertexture and Reception* (Eugene, OR: Cascade, 2020).
Desmond, William Desmond, *The Greek Praise of Poverty: Origins of Ancient Cynicism* (Notre Dame, IN: University of Notre Dame, 2006).
DesRosiers, Nathaniel, *The Establishment of Proper Mental Disposition and Practice: The Origin, Meaning, and Social Purpose of the Prohibition of Oaths in Matthew* (Doctoral dissertation, Brown University, 2007).
Dillon, John, 'ASŌMATOS: Nuances of Incorporeality in Philo', in Carlos Lévy (ed.) *Philon d'Alexandrie et le langage de la philosophie* (Turnhout: Brepols, 1998), pp. 99–110.
Dingeldein, Laura, '"ὅτι πνευματικῶς ἀνακρίνεται": Examining Translations of 1 Corinthians 2:14', *Novum Testamentum*, 55, 2013, pp. 31–44.
Dingeldein, Laura, *Gaining Virtue, Gaining Christ: Moral Development in the Letters of Paul* (Doctoral dissertation, Brown University, 2014).
Dodds, E. R., *Pagan and Christian in an Age of Anxiety* (New York: Norton, 1970).
Dodson, Joseph R., *The 'Powers' of Personification: Rhetorical Purpose in the Book of Wisdom and in the Letter to the Romans* (Berlin: Walter de Gruyter, 2008).
Donaldson, Terence L., *Judaism and the Gentiles: Jewish Patterns of Universalism (to 135 CE)* (Waco, TX: Baylor University Press, 2007).
Downing, F. Gerald, 'Common Strands in Pagan, Jewish and Christian Eschatologies in The First Century', *Theologische Zeitschrift*, 51, 1995, pp. 196–211.
Dunn, James D. G., *Christology in the Making: A New Testament Inquiry into the Origins of the Doctrine of the Incarnation*, 2nd edn (Grand Rapids, MI: Eerdmans, 1996).
Edelstein, Ludwig, *The Idea of Progress in Classical Antiquity* (Baltimore, MD: Johns Hopkins University Press, 1967).
Ehrman, Bart, *The New Testament: A Historical Introduction*, 2nd edn (Oxford: Oxford University Press, 2000).
Eilberg-Schwartz, Howard, *The Savage in Judaism* (Bloomington, IN: Indiana University Press, 1990).
Eisenbaum, Pamela, 'Paul as the New Abraham', in Richard Horsley (ed.), *Paul and Politics: Ekklesia, Israel, Imperium, Interpretation* (Philadelphia, PA: Trinity Press International, 2000), pp. 130–45.
Eisenbaum, Pamela, 'A Remedy for Having Been Born of Woman: Jesus, Gentiles, and Genealogy in Romans', *Journal of Biblical Literature*, 123, 2004, pp. 671–702.
Elliott, John H., *Beware the Evil Eye: The Evil Eye in the Bible and the Ancient World* (Eugene, OR: Cascade, 2016).
Engberg-Pedersen, Troels, *Paul and the Stoics* (Edinburgh: T&T Clark, 2000).

Engberg-Pedersen, Troels (ed.), *Paul Beyond the Judaism/Hellenism Divide* (Louisville: Westminster John Knox, 2001).
Engberg-Pedersen, Troels, 'A Stoic Understanding of *Pneuma* in Paul', in Troels Engberg-Pedersen et al. (eds), *Philosophy at the Roots of Christianity* (Copenhagen: Faculty of Theology, University of Copenhagen, 2006), pp. 101–23.
Engberg-Pedersen, Troels, *Cosmology and Self in the Apostle Paul: The Material Spirit* (Oxford: Oxford University Press, 2010).
Eshleman, Kendra, *The Social World of Intellectuals in the Roman Empire: Sophists, Philosophers and Christians* (Cambridge: Cambridge University Press, 2012).
Esler, Philip F., *Community and Gospel in Luke-Acts* (Cambridge: Cambridge University Press, 1987).
Esler, Philip F., 'Community and Gospels in Early Christianity: A Response to Richard Bauckham's *Gospels for All Christians*', *Scottish Journal of Theology*, 51, 1998, pp. 235–48.
Everson, Stephen (ed.), *Psychology (Companions to Ancient Thought 2)* (Cambridge: Cambridge University Press, 1991).
Eyl, Jennifer, *Signs, Wonders, and Gifts: Divination in the Letters of Paul* (New York: Oxford University Press, 2019).
Eyl, Jennifer, 'Philo and Josephus on the Fidelity of Judeans', *Journal of Ancient Judaism*, 12, 2021, pp. 94–121.
Faraone, Christopher A. and Dirk Obbink (eds), *Magika Hiera: Ancient Greek Magic and Religion* (New York: Oxford University Press, 1991).
Fiasse, Gaëlle, 'Les fondements de la philanthropie dans le nouveau stoïcisme, deux cas concrets: l'esclavage et la gladiature', *Ephemenedies Philologische*, 62, 2002, pp. 527–47.
Fitzgerald, John T., *Cracks in an Earthen Vessel: An Examination of Catalogues of Hardships in the Corinthian Correspondence* (Atlanta, GA: Scholars Press, 1988).
Fitzmyer, Joseph A., *Romans: A New Translation with Introduction Commentary* (New York: Doubleday, 1993).
Flohr, Miko, *The World of the Fullo: Work, Economy, and Society in Roman Italy* (Oxford: Oxford University Press, 2013).
Flower, Harriet I., *The Dancing Lares and the Serpent in the Garden: Religion at the Roman Street Corner* (Princeton: Princeton University Press, 2017).
Fodor, Jerry A., *Modularity of Mind* (Cambridge: MIT Press, 1983).
Frazer, Elizabeth, *The Problem of Communitarian Politics: Unity and Conflict* (Oxford: Oxford University Press, 1999).
Fredriksen Landes, Paula, *Augustine on Romans: Propositions from the Epistle to the Romans; Unfinished Commentary on the Epistle to the Romans* (Chico, CA: Scholars Press, 1982).
Fredriksen, Paula, 'Judaism, the Circumcision of Gentiles, and Apocalyptic Hope: Another Look at Galatians 1 and 2', *Journal of Theological Studies*, 42, 1991, pp. 532–64.
Fredriksen, Paula, *From Jesus to Christ: The Origins of the New Testament Images of Jesus*, 2nd edn (New Haven, CT: Yale University Press, 2000).
Fredriksen, Paula, *Paul: The Pagan's Apostle* (New Haven, CT: Yale University Press, 2017).

Frier, Bruce W., 'Demography', in Alan K. Bowman, Peter Garnsey, and Dominic Rathbone (eds), *The Cambridge Ancient History XI: The High Empire, A.D. 70–192* (Cambridge: Cambridge University Press, 2000), pp. 827–54.

Furness, Elizabeth, 'Resistance, Coercion, and Revitalization: The Shuswap Encounter with Roman Catholic Missionaries, 1860–1900', *Ethnohistory*, 42.2, 1995, pp. 231–63.

Gager, John, *Curse Tablets and Binding Spells from the Ancient World* (New York: Oxford University Press, 1992).

Gatz, Bodo, *Weltalter, goldene Zeit und sinnerwandte Vorstellungen* (Hildersheim: G. Olms, 1967).

Gazzaniga, Michael, 'Forty-five Years of Split Brain Research and Still Going Strong', *Nature Reviews Neuroscience*, 6, 2006, pp. 653–59.

Ghiselin, Michael, 'Categories, Life and Thinking', *Behavioral and Brain Sciences*, 4,1981, pp. 269–313.

Giacobello, Federica, *Larari Pompeiani: Iconografia e culto dei Lari in ambito domestic* (Milan: University of Milan, 2008).

Gigerenzer, Gerd, *Adaptive Thinking: Rationality in the Real World* (Oxford: Oxford University Press, 2000).

Gill, Christopher (ed.), *The Person and the Human Mind: Issues in Ancient and Modern Philosophy* (Oxford: Oxford University Press, 1990).

Gill, Christopher, *Personality in Greek, Epic, Tragedy and Philosophy* (Oxford: Clarendon Press, 1996).

Gill, Christopher, *The Structured Self in Hellenistic and Roman Thought* (Oxford: Oxford University Press, 2006).

Glaim, Aaron, *Reciprocity, Sacrifice, and Salvation in Judean Religion at The Turn of The Era* (Doctoral dissertation: Brown University, 2014).

Goody, Jack, *The Logic of Writing and the Organization of Society* (Cambridge: Cambridge University Press, 1986).

Gorman, Michael, *Inhabiting the Cruciform God: Kenosis, Justification and Theosis in Paul's Narrative Soteriology* (Grand Rapids, MI: Eerdmans, 2009).

Gourinat, Jean-Baptiste, 'The Stoics on Matter and Prime Matter: Corporealism and the Imprint of Plato's Timaeus', in Ricardo Salles (ed.), *God and Cosmos in Stoicism* (Oxford: Oxford University Press, 2009), pp. 46–70.

Graf, Fritz, *Magic in the Ancient World* (Cambridge, MA: Harvard University Press, 1997).

Graf, Fritz and Sarah Iles Johnston, *Ritual Texts for the Afterlife: Orpheus and the Bacchic Gold Tablets* (London: Routledge, 2007).

Graver, Margaret, 'Philo of Alexandria and the Stoic *propatheiai*', *Phronesis*, 44, 1999, pp. 300–325.

Graver, Margaret, *Stoicism and Emotion* (Chicago: University of Chicago Press, 2007).

Greer, Rowan, 'Sinned We All in Adam's Fall' in L. Michael White and O. Larry Yarbrough (eds), *The Social World of the First Christians: Essays in Honor of Wayne A. Meeks* (Minneapolis, MN: Augsburg Fortress, 1995), pp. 382–94.

Gudme, Anne Katrine de Hemmer, *Before the God in this Place for Good Remembrance: A Comparative Analysis of the Aramaic Votive Inscriptions from Mount Gerizim* (Berlin: Walter de Gruyter, 2013).

Gundry, Robert H., *Soma in Biblical Theology, with an Emphasis on Pauline Anthropology* (Cambridge: Cambridge University Press, 1976).
Guthrie, W. K. C., *In the Beginning: Some Greek Views on the Origins of Life and the Early State of Man* (London: Methuen, 1957).
Hahm, David, *The Origins of Stoic Cosmology* (Columbus, OH: Ohio State University Press, 1977).
Hanges, James C., *Paul, Founder of Churches: A Study in Light of the Evidence for the Role of 'Founder-Figures' in the Hellenistic-Roman Period* (Tübingen: Mohr Siebeck, 2012).
Hanson, Kenneth C., 'Greco-Roman Studies and the Social-Scientific Study of the Bible: A Classified Periodical Bibliography (1970–1994)', *Forum*, 9.1–2, 1994, pp. 63–119.
Harland, Philip A., *Associations, Synagogues and Congregations: Claiming a Place in Ancient Mediterranean Society* (Minneapolis, MN: Fortress, 2003).
Harland, Philip A., 'The Declining Polis? Religious Rivalries in Ancient Civic Context', in Leif Vaage (ed.), *Religious Rivalries in the Early Roman Empire and the Rise of Christianity* (Waterloo, ON: Wilfred Laurier University Press, 2006), pp. 21–50.
Harrison, Peter, *"Religion" and the Religions in the English Enlightenment* (Cambridge: Cambridge University Press, 1990).
Hays, Richard, *The Faith of Jesus Christ: The Narrative Substructure of Galatians 3:1–4:11* (Chico, CA: Scholars Press, 1983. 2nd ed. Grand Rapids, MI: Eerdmans, 2002.
Hays, Richard, '"What Is 'Real Participation in Christ?": A Dialogue with E.P. Sanders on Pauline Soteriology', in Fabian E. Udoh, et al. (eds), *Redefining First-century Jewish and Christian Identities* (Notre Dame: University of Notre Dame Press, 2008), pp. 336–52.
Heckel, Theo, *Der Innere Mensch: Der paulinische Verarbeitung eines platonischen Motivs* (Tübingen: Mohr Siebeck, 1993).
Helmig, Christoph and Mauro Bonazzi, *Platonic Stoicism – Stoic Platonism: The Dialogue between Platonism and Stoicism in Antiquity* (Leuven: Leuven University Press, 2008).
Hendel, Ronald, 'Nephilim Were on The Earth: Genesis 6:1–4 and its Near Eastern Context' in Christoph Auffarth and Loren T. Stuckenbruck (eds), *The Fall of Angels* (Leiden: Brill, 2004), pp. 11–34.
Herder, Johann Gottfried, *Vom Geist der ebräischen Poesie: Eine Anleitung für die Liebhaber derselben und der ältesten Geschichte des menschlichen Geistes*, 2 vols. Dessau: Herder, 1782–83); *The Spirit of Hebrew Poetry*, translated by James Marsh (Burlington, VT: Edward Smith, 1833).
Hersch, Karen K., *The Roman Wedding: Ritual and Meaning in Antiquity* (Cambridge: Cambridge University Press 2010).
Hasenohr, Claire, 'Les Compitalia à Delos', *Bulletin de correspondance hellénique*, 127, 2003, pp. 167–249.
Hezer, Catherine, *Jewish Literacy in Roman Palestine* (Tübingen: Mohr Siebeck, 2001).
Hirschfeld, Laurence and Susan A. Gelman, *Mapping the Mind: Domain Specificity in Cognition and Culture* (Cambridge: Cambridge University Press, 1994).
Hock, Ronald F., 'Heracles and Christ: Heracles Imagery in the Christology of Early Christianity' in David L. Balch, Everett Ferguson, and Wayne A. Meeks

(eds), *Greeks, Romans and Christians: Essays in Honor of Abraham J. Malherbe* (Minneapolis, MN: Fortress, 1990), pp. 3–19.

Hodge, Caroline Johnson and Denise Kimber Buell, 'The Politics of Interpretation: The Rhetoric of Race and Ethnicity in Paul', *Journal of Biblical Literature*, 123, 2003, pp. 235–51.

Hodge, Caroline Johnson, *If Sons, Then Heirs: A Study of Kinship and Ethnicity in the Letters of Paul* (New York, Oxford University Press, 2007).

Johnson Hodge, Caroline, *"My God and the God of This House": Christian Household Cult Before Constantine* (University Park: Pennsylvania State University Press, forthcoming).

Hoffman, Joseph R., *Celsus: On the True Doctrine: A Discourse Against the Christians* (Oxford: Oxford University Press, 1987).

Holladay, Carl, *Fragments from Hellenistic Jewish Authors. Volume III: Aristobulus* (Atlanta: Scholars Press, 1995).

Hollander, H. W. and J. Holleman, 'The Relationship of Death, Sin and Law in 1 Cor 15:56', *Novum Testamentum*, 35, 1993, pp. 270–91.

Holleran, Clare, *Shopping in Ancient Rome: The Retail Trade in the Late Republic and the Principate* (Oxford: Oxford University Press, 2012).

Horrell, David G., *The Social Ethos of the Corinthian Correspondence: Interests and Ideology from 1 Corinthians to 1 Clement* (Edinburgh: T&T Clark, 1996).

Horrell, David G. (ed.), *Christianity at Corinth: The Quest for the Pauline Church* (Louisville, KY: Westminster John Knox, 2004).

Horrell, David G., *Solidarity and Difference: A Contemporary Reading of Paul's Ethics* (London: T&T Clark, 2005).

Horsley, G. H. R. and John A. L. Lee, 'A Preliminary Checklist of Abbreviations of Greek Epigraphic Volumes', *Epigraphica*, 56, 1994, pp. 129–69.

Horsley, Richard A., *Sociology and the Jesus Movement*, 2nd edn (New York: Continuum, 1994).

Horsley, Richard A., '1 Corinthians: A Case Study of Paul's Alternative Society' in Edward Adams and David G. Horrell (eds.), *Christianity at Corinth: The Quest for the Pauline Church* (Louisville: Westminster John Knox, 2004), pp. 227–37.

Horst, Pieter Willem van der, *Japheth in the Tents of Shem: Studies in Jewish Hellenism in Antiquity* (Leuven: Peeters, 2002).

Hutchinson, Sharon. *Nuer Dilemmas: Coping with Money, War and the State* (Berkeley: University of California, 1995).

Inwood, Brad, *Ethics and Human Action in Early Stoicism* (Oxford: Oxford University Press, 1985).

Inwood, Brad, *Seneca: Selected Philosophical Letters* (Oxford: Clarendon, 2007).

Inwood, Brad, 'Antiochus on Physics' in David Sedley (ed.), *The Philosophy of Antiochus* (Cambridge: Cambridge University Press, 2012), pp. 188–219.

Jervis, Robert, 'International History and International Politics: Why Are They Studied Differently?' in Colin Elman and Miriam Fendius Elman (eds), *Bridges and Boundaries: Historians, Political Scientists and the Study of International Relations* (Cambridge, MA: MIT Press, 2001), pp. 385–402.

Jewett, Robert, *Romans: A Commentary* (Minneapolis, MN: Fortress, 2007).

Johnston, Sarah Iles, *The Restless Dead: Encounters Between the Living and the Dead in Ancient Greece* (Berkeley: University of California Press, 1999).

Johnston, Sarah Iles, *Ancient Greek Divination* (Oxford: Wiley-Blackwell, 2008).

Jones, Christopher P., *Culture and Society in Lucian* (Cambridge, MA: Harvard University Press, 1986).
Jones, Christopher P., 'The Historicity of the Neronian Persecution: A Response to Brent Shaw', *New Testament Studies*, 63, 2017, pp. 146–52.
Kadushin, Charles, *Understanding Social Networks: Theories, Concepts and Findings* (New York: Oxford University Press, 2012).
Kahneman, Daniel, *Thinking, Fast and Slow* (New York: Farrar, Straus and Giroux, 2011).
Keesing, Roger, *Kwaio Religion: The Living and the Dead in a Solomon Island Society* (New York: Columbia University Press, 1982).
Kennedy, George, 'Encolpius and Agamemnon in Petronius', *American Journal of Philology*, 99, 1978, pp. 171–78.
Kermode, Frank, *The Genesis of Secrecy* (Cambridge, MA: Harvard University Press, 1979).
Kindt, Julia, *Rethinking Greek Religion* (Cambridge: Cambridge University Press, 2012).
Kingsley, Peter, *Ancient Philosophy, Mystery, and Magic: Empedocles and the Pythagorean Tradition* (Oxford: Clarendon Press, 1995).
Klauck, Hans-Joseph, *Herrenmahl und Hellenistischer Kult: Eine religionsgeschichtliche Untersuchung zum ersten Korintherbrief*, 2nd edn (Münster: Aschendorff, 1986).
Klauck, Hans-Joseph, *The Religious Context of Early Christianity* (Minneapolis, MN: Fortress Press, 2003).
Kloppenborg, John S., 'Collegia and Thiasoi: Issues in Function, Taxonomy and Membership' in John S. Kloppenborg and Stephen G. Wilson (eds), *Voluntary Associations in the Graeco-Roman World* (Oxford: Routledge, 1996), pp. 16–30.
Kloppenborg, John S., 'The Moralizing Discourse in Greco-Roman Associations' in Caroline Johnson Hodge, Saul M. Olyan, Daniel Ullucci, and Emma Wasserman (eds), *"The One Who Sows Bountifully": Essays in Honor of Stanley K. Stowers* (Providence, RI: Brown Judaic Studies, 2013), pp. 215 –28.
Kloppenborg, John S., *Christ's Associations: Connecting and Belonging in the Ancient City* (New Haven, CT: Yale University Press, 2019).
Knust, Jennifer Wright, *Abandoned to Lust: Sexual Slander and Ancient Christianity* (New York: Columbia University Press, 2006).
Knuuttila, Simo, 'The Emergencee of the Logic of the Will in Medieval Thought', in Gareth B. Matthews (ed.), *The Augustinian Tradition* (Berkeley: University of California Press, 1999), pp. 206–21.
Koester, Helmut, *History and Literature of Early Christianity* (Philadelphia, PA: Fortress, 1982).
Konstan, David, *Pity Transformed* (London: Duckworth, 2001).
Konstan, David, 'The Active Reader in Classical Antiquity', *Argos*, 30, 2006, pp. 5–16.
Konstan, David, *A Life Worthy of the Gods: The Materialist Psychology of Epicurus* (Las Vegas, NV: Parmenides, 2008).
Kooten, George H. van, *Paul's Anthropology in Context: The Image of God, Assimilation to God, and Tripartite Man in Ancient Judaism, Ancient Philosophy and Early Christianity* (Tübingen: Mohr Siebeck, 2008).
Koyré, Alexandre, *From the Closed World to the Infinite Universe* (Baltimore, MD: Johns Hopkins University Press, 1957).

Kretzmann, Norman ed. *Infinity and Continuity in Ancient and Medieval Thought* (Ithaca, NY: Cornell University Press, 1982).
Kümmel, Werner Georg, *Man in the New Testament* (Philadelphia, PA: Westminster, 1963).
Kümmel, Werner Georg, *The New Testament: The History of the Investigation of its Problems* (Nashville, TN: Abingdon Press, 1972).
Kurzban, Robert and Athena Aktipis, 'Modularity and the Social Mind: Are Psychologists too Selfish?', *Personality and Social Psychology Review*, 11, 2007, pp. 131–49.
Laks, André and Glenn Most, *Studies in the Derveni Papyrus* (New York: Oxford University Press, 1997).
Larson, Jennifer, *Understanding Greek Religion* (London: Routledge, 2016).
Last, Richard, 'The Neighborhood (*vicus*) of the Corinthian *Ekklesia*: Beyond Family-Based Descriptions of the First Urban Christ-Believers', *Journal for the Study of the New Testament*, 38, 2016, pp. 399–425.
Lave, Jean and Etienne Wenger, *Situated Learning* (New York: Cambridge University Press, 1991).
Levinson, John R., *Portraits of Adam in Early Judaism from Sirach to 2 Baruch* (Sheffield: Sheffield Academic Press, 1988).
Lightstone, Jack N., *The Commerce of the Sacred: Mediation of the Divine among Jews of the Greco-Roman World* (New York: Columbia University Press, 2006).
Litwa, M. David, *We Are Being Transformed: Deification in Paul's Soteriology* (Berlin: Walter de Gruyter, 2012).
Long, Anthony A. and D. N. Sedley, *The Hellenistic Philosophers*, 2 vols. (Cambridge: Cambridge University Press, 1987).
Long, Anthony A., 'Body and Soul in Stoicism', *Stoic Studies* (Berkeley: University of California Press, 1996), pp. 224–49.
Long, Anthony A., *Epictetus: A Stoic and Socratic Guide to Life* (Oxford: Clarendon, 2002).
Lovejoy, Arthur O. and George Boas, *Primitivism and Related Ideas in Antiquity* (New York: Octagon Books, 1965).
Lund, William R., 'Communitarian Politics and the Problem of Equality', *Political Research Quarterly*, 46, 1993, pp. 577–600.
Lund, William R., 'Politics, Virtue, and the Right to Do Wrong: Assessing the Communitarian Critique of Rights', *Journal of Social Philosophy*, 28.3, 1997, pp. 101–22.
Luomanen, Petri, Ilkka Pyysiäinen, and Risto Uro (eds), *Explaining Christian Origins and Early Judaism: Contributions from Cognitive and Social Science* (Leiden: Brill, 2008).
Luther, Martin, *The Bondage of the Will*, translated by J. I. Packer and O. R. Johnston (Old Tappan, NJ: Revell, 1957).
Luz, Ulrich, *Studies in Matthew* (Grand Rapids, MI: Eerdmans, 2005).
Macdonald, Paul S., *History of the Concept of Mind: Speculations about Soul, Mind and Spirit from Homer to Hume*, (Aldershot: Ashgate, 2003).
Mack, Burton L., *The Christian Myth: Origins, Logic and Legacy* (New York: Continuum, 2001).

MacMullen, Ramsay, *The Second Church: Popular Christianity: A. D. 200–400* (Atlanta, GA: Society of Biblical Literature, 2009).
McIntosh, Janet, 'Cognition and Power', a paper presented at the Society for Literature and Science Meetings, Pittsburgh, PA, Oct 31–Nov 2. 1997. http://cogweb.ucla.edu/Culture/McIntosh.html.
McCready, Wayne O. and Adele Reinhartz (eds), *Common Judaism: Explorations in Second-Temple Judaism* (Minneapolis, MN: Fortress, 2008).
Maier, Franz G., *Griechische Mauerbauinschriften* (Heidelberg: Quelle & Meyer 1959).
Malherbe, Abraham J., '"Gentle as a Nurse": The Cynic Background of 1 Thess ii', *Novum Testamentum*, 12, 1970, pp. 203–17.
Malherbe, Abraham J., *Social Aspects of Early Christianity* (Baton Rouge: Louisiana State University Press, 1977).
Malherbe, Abraham J., *The Cynic Epistles* (Missoula, MT: Scholars Press, 1977).
Malherbe, Abraham J., *Paul and the Popular Philosophers* (Minneapolis, MN: Fortress, 1989).
Malherbe, Abraham J., *The Letters to the Thessalonians* (New York: Doubleday, 2000).
Malinowski, Bronislaw, *Argonauts of the Western Pacific* (New York: Dutton, 1922).
Mannzmann, Anneliese, *Griechische Stiftungsurkunden* (Münster: Aschendorff, 1962).
Markschies, Christoph, 'Innerer Mensch', *Reallexicon für Antike und Christentum, vol. 18* (Stuttgart: Anton Hiersemann, 1997).
Martin, Dale B., *The Corinthian Body* (New Haven, CT: Yale University Press, 1995).
Martin, Raymond and John Barresi, *Naturalization of the Soul* (London: Routledge, 2000).
Meeks, Wayne A., 'The Man from Heaven in Johannine Sectarianism', *Journal of Biblical Literature*, 91, 1972, pp. 44–72.
Meeks, Wayne A., *The First Urban Christians: The Social World of the Apostle Paul* (New Haven, CT: Yale University Press, 1983).
Miller, Merrill P., 'The Social Logic of the Gospel of Mark: Cultural Persistence and Social Escape in a Postwar Time', in Barry S. Crawford and Merrill P. Miller (eds), *Redescribing the Gospel of Mark* (Atlanta, GA: Society of Biblical Literature, 2017), pp. 207–399.
Mikalson, Jon D., *Honor Thy Gods: Popular Religion in Greek Tragedy* (Chapel Hill: University of North Carolina Press, 1991).
Mitchell, Margaret M., *Paul and the Rhetoric of Reconciliation* (Louisville: Westminster John Knox, 1991).
Moles, John L., 'Cynic Influence Upon First-Century Judaism and Early Christianity?' in B. McGing and J. Mossman (eds), *The Limits of Biography* (Swansea: Classical Press of Wales, 2006), pp. 89–116.
Moore, Stephen, *Literary Criticism and the Gospels: The Theoretical Challenge* (New Haven, CT: Yale University Press, 1989).
Morris, Brian, *Religion and Anthropology: A Critical Introduction* (Cambridge: Cambridge University Press, 2006).
Moss, Candida, *The Myth of Persecution: How Early Christians Invented a Story of Martyrdom* (New York: HarperOne, 2013).

Mullins, Terence Y., 'Greeting as a New Testament Form', *Journal of Biblical Literature*, 87, 1968, pp. 418–26.
Nagy, Gregory, *The Best of the Achaeans: Concepts of the Hero in Archaic Greek Poetry* (Baltimore: Johns Hopkins University Press, 1999).
Naiden, Fred S., 'Rejected Sacrifice in Greek and Hebrew Religion', *Journal of Ancient Near Eastern Religions*, 6, 2006, pp. 186–223.
Naiden, Fred S., *Smoke Signals for the Gods: Ancient Greek Sacrifice from the Archaic through Roman Periods* (New York: Oxford University Press, 2013).
Newman, Carey, *Paul's Glory-Christology: Tradition and Rhetoric* (Leiden: Brill, 1991).
Nijf, Onno van, *The Civic World of Professional Associations in the Roman East* (Amsterdam: Gieben, 1997).
Nongbri, Brent, *Paul without Religion: The Creation of a Category and the Search for an Apostle Beyond the New Perspective* (Doctoral dissertation, Yale University, 2008).
Oakley, John and Rebecca Sinos, *The Wedding in Ancient Athens* (Madison: University of Wisconsin Press, 1993).
Oates, J. F. et al. (eds), *Checklist of Editions of Greek Papyri and Ostraca*, 5th edn (Oakville, CT: American Society of Papyrologists, 2001).
O'Leary, Anne M., *Matthew's Judaization of Mark: Examined in the Context of the Use of Sources in Graeco-Roman Antiquity* (London: T&T Clark, 2006).
O'Neill, Eugene, *The Complete Greek Dramas* (New York: Random House, 1938).
Padel, Ruth, *In and Out of Mind: Greek Images of the Tragic Self* (Princeton: Princeton University Press, 1992).
Parker, Robert, *Miasma: Pollution and Purification in Early Greek Religion* (Oxford: Clarendon, 1983).
Parker, Robert, *Polytheism and Society at Athens* (Oxford: Oxford University Press, 2005).
Parker, Robert, *On Greek Religion* (Ithaca, NY: Cornell University Press, 2011).
Patzelt, Maik, *Über das Beten der Römer: Gebete im spätrepublikanischen und frühkaiserzeitlichen Rom als Ausdruck gelebter Religion* (Berlin: Walter de Gruyter, 2018).
Perry, Jonathan S. 'L'État intervint peu à peu': State Intervention in the Ephesian "Baker's Strike"' in Vincent Gabrielsen and Christian A. Thomsen (eds), *Private Associations and the Public Sphere: Proceedings of a Symposium Held at the Royal Danish Academy of Sciences and Letters, 9-11 September 2010* (Copenhagen: Det Kongelige Danske Videnskabernes Selskab, 2015), pp. 183–205.
Pervo, Richard I., *Dating Acts: Between the Evangelists and the Apologists* (Santa Rosa, CA: Polebridge, 2006).
Petropoulou, Maria-Zoe, *Animal Sacrifice in Ancient Greek Religion, Judaism and Christianity, 100 BC–AD 200* (Oxford: Oxford University Press, 2008).
Rauh, Nicholas, *The Sacred Bonds of Commerce: Religion, Economy, and Trade Society at Hellenistic Roman Delos, 166–87 B.C.* (Amsterdam: Gieben, 1993).
Jonathan L. Ready, 'Zeus, Ancient Near Eastern Notions of Divine Incomparability, and Similes in the Homeric Epics', *Classical Antiquity*, 31, 2012, pp. 56–91.
Reasoner, Mark, *Romans in Full Circle: A History of Interpretation* (Louisville: Westminster John Knox, 2005).

Rebillard, Éric, *Christians and Their Many Identities in Late Antiquity* (Ithaca, NY: Cornell University Press, 2012).
Reydams-Shils, Gretchen, *The Roman Stoics: Self, Responsibility, and Affection* (Chicago: University of Chicago Press, 2005).
Reydams-Shils, Gretchen, '"Becoming like God" in Platonism and Stoicism' in Troels Engberg-Pederson (ed.), *From Stoicism to Platonism: The Development of Philosophy 100 BCE-100CE* (Cambridge: Cambridge University Press, 2017), pp. 142–58.
Richardson, Peter, 'Early Synagogues as Collegia in the Diaspora and in Palestine,' in John S. Kloppenborg and Stephen G. Wilson (eds), *Voluntary Associations in the Graeco-Roman World* (London: Routledge, 1996), pp. 90–109.
Richardson, Peter, 'Augustan Era Synagogues in Rome', in Karl P. Donfried and Peter Richardson (eds), *Judaism and Christianity in First-Century Rome* (Grand Rapids, MI: Eerdmans, 1998), pp. 17–29.
Ripat, Pauline, 'Expelling Misconceptions: Astrologers at Rome', *Classical Philology*, 106, 2011, pp. 115–54.
Rosenblum, Jordan, 'Home Is Where the Hearth Is? A Consideration of Jewish Household Sacrifice in Antiquity', in Caroline Johnson Hodge, Saul M. Olyan, Daniel Ullucci, and Emma Wasserman (eds), *The One Who Sows Bountifully* (Providence, RI: Brown Judaic Studies, 2013), pp. 153–63.
Rouse, Joseph, 'Practice Theory', in Stephen P. Turner and Mark W. Risjord (eds), *Philosophy of Sociology and Anthropology* (Oxford: Elsevier, 2007), pp. 639–82.
Runesson, Anders, Donald D. Binder, and Birger Olsson (eds), *The Ancient Synagogue from its Origins to 200 C. E.: A Source Book* (Leiden: Brill, 2008).
Runia, David T., *Philo of Alexandria and the "Timaeus" of Plato* (Leiden: Brill, 1986).
Runia, David T., *Philo of Alexandria, On the Creation of the Cosmos according to Moses: Introduction, Translation and Commentary* (Leiden: Brill, 2001).
Rüpke, Jörg, *Religion of the Romans*, translated and edited by Richard Gordon. (Cambridge: Polity, 2007).
Rüpke, Jörg, 'Theorizing Religion for the Individual', in Valentino Gasparini and Richard Veymiers (eds), *The Greco-Roman Cults of Isis: Agents, Images and Practices* (Leiden: Brill, 2016), pp. 61–72.
Russell, Donald A. and David Konstan (eds), *Heraclitus: Homeric Problems* (Atlanta: SBL Press, 2005).
Sambursky, Samuel, *The Physical World of Late Antiquity* (Princeton: Princeton University Press, 1962).
Sanders, Ed P., *Paul and Palestinian Judaism* (Philadelphia, PA: Fortress Press, 1977).
Sanders, Ed P., *Judaism: Practice and Belief 63 BCE-66 CE* (Philadelphia, PA: Trinity Press International, 1992).
Sanders, Ed P., *Paul: The Apostle's Life, Letters, and Thought* (Minneapolis, MN: Fortress, 2015).
Sandos, James A., *Converting California: Indians and Franciscans in the Missions* (New Haven, CT: Yale University Press, 2004).
Satlow, Michael, 'Giving for a Return: Jewish Votive Offerings in Late Antiquity', in David Brakke and Steven Weitzman (eds), *Religion and the Self in Antiquity* (Bloomington: Indiana University Press, 2005), pp. 91–108.

Schatzki, Theodore, *Social Practices: A Wittgensteinian Approach to Human Activity and the Social* (New York: Cambridge University Press, 1996).
Schatzki, Theodore, *The Site of the Social: A Philosophical Account of the Constitution of Social Life and Change* (University Park: University of Pennsylvania Press, 2002).
Schilbrack, Kevin, *Philosophy and the Study of Religions: A Manifesto* (Oxford: Wiley Blackwell, 2014).
Schilbrack, Kevin, 'A Realist Social Ontology of Religion', *Religion*, 47, 2017, pp. 161–78.
Schneewind, Jerome B., *The Invention of Autonomy* (Cambridge: Cambridge University Press, 1998).
Schofield, Malcolm, 'Ariston of Chios and the Unity of Virtue', *Ancient Philosophy*, 4, 1984, pp. 83–96.
Schroeder, Paul W., 'International History: Why Historians Do It Differently than Political Scientists', in Colin Elman and Miriam Fendius Elman (eds), *Bridges and Boundaries: Historians, Political Scientists, and the Study of International Relations* (Cambridge, MA: MIT Press, 2001), pp. 403–16.
Schweitzer, Albert, *The Mysticism of Paul the Apostle* (London: A&C Black, 1931).
Scott, James M., *Paul and the Nations* (Tübingen: Mohr Siebeck, 1995).
Sedley, David, 'The Origins of Stoic God', in Dorothea Frede and André Laks (eds), *Traditions of Theology* (Leiden: Brill, 2002), pp. 41–83.
Simon, 'Zeus', *PW/ Realencyclopädie der Classischen Altertumswissenschaft*, 2/19:253–376; with PWSup 15:993–1481.
Seaford, Richard, *Reciprocity and Ritual: Homer and Tragedy in the Developing City State* (New York: Oxford University Press, 1994).
Slingerland, Edward, *What Science Offers the Humanities: Integrating Body and Culture* (Cambridge: Cambridge University Press, 2008).
Slingerland, H. Dixon, *Claudian Policymaking and the Early Imperial Repression of Judaism at Rome* (Atlanta: Scholars Press, 1997).
Sloman, Steven and Philip Fernback, *The Knowledge Illusion: Why We Never Think Alone* (New York: Riverhead Books, 2017).
Slone, David, *Theological Incorrectness: Why Religious People Believe What They Shouldn't* (New York: Oxford University Press, 2004).
Smith, Barry D., *Paul's Seven Explanations of the Suffering of the Righteous* (New York: Peter Lang, 2002).
Smith, Dennis E., *Social Obligation in the Context of Communal Meals: A Study of the Christian Meal in 1 Corinthians in Comparison with Greco-Roman Communal Meals* (Doctoral dissertation, Harvard Divinity School, 1980).
Smith, Jonathan Z., 'Birth Upside Down or Right Side Up', *History of Religions*, 9, 1969–70, pp. 281–303. Reprinted in Jonathan Z. Smith, *Map is Not Territory: Studies in the History of Religions* (Leiden: E. J. Brill, 1978,) pp. 147–71.
Smith, Jonathan Z., 'The Wobbling Pivot', *Journal of Religion*, 52, 1972, pp. 134–49. Reprinted in Jonathan Z. Smith, *Map Is Not Territory: Studies in the History of Religions* (Leiden: E. J. Brill, 1978), pp. 88–103.
Smith, Jonathan Z., *Drudgery Divine: On the Comparison of Early Christianities and the Religions of Late Antiquity* (Chicago: University of Chicago Press, 1990).

Smith, Jonathan Z., *Relating Religion: Essays on the Study of Religion* (Chicago: University of Chicago Press, 2004).
Smith, Jonathan Z., 'Re: Corinthians', *Relating Religion: Essays in the Study of Religion* (Chicago: University of Chicago Press, 2004), pp. 340–61.
Smith, Mark S., *The Origins of Biblical Monotheism: Israel's Polytheistic Background and the Ugaritic Texts* (Oxford: Oxford University Press, 2008).
Smith, Mark S., *God in Translation: Deities in Cross-Cultural Discourse in the Biblical World* (Tübingen: Mohr Siebeck, 2008).
Sommer, Benjamin D., *The Bodies of God and the World of Ancient Israel* (Cambridge: Cambridge University Press, 2009).
Son, Sang Won (Aaron), *Corporate Elements in Pauline Anthropology* (Rome: Pontifical Biblical Institute, 2001).
Sonia, Kerry M., *Caring for the Dead in Ancient Israel* (Atlanta, GA: Society of Biblical Literature Press, 2020).
Sorabji, Richard, *Emotion and Peace of Mind* (Oxford: Clarendon Press, 2000).
Sorabji, Richard, *Self: Ancient and Modern Insights about Individuality, Life, and Death* (Chicago: University of Chicago Press, 2006).
Sourvinou-Inwood, Christine, 'Further Aspects of Polis Religion', *Annali Instituto Orientale di Napoli: Archaeologia e Storia*,10, 1988, pp. 259–74.
Sourvinou-Inwood, Christine, 'What is Polis Religion?' in Oswyn Murray and S. R. F. Price (eds), *The Greek City from Homer to Alexander* (Oxford: Clarendon Press, 1990), pp. 295–322.
Sourvinou-Inwood, Christine, 'Tragedy and Religion: Constructs and Readings', in Christopher Pelling (ed.), *Greek Tragedy and the Historian* (Oxford: Clarendon Press, 1997), pp. 161–85.
Sourvinou-Inwood, Christine, *Tragedy and Athenian Religion* (Lanham, MD: Lexington Books, 2003).
Sperber, Dan, *Rethinking Symbolism* (Cambridge: Cambridge University Press, 1975).
Sperber, Dan, *Explaining Culture: A Naturalistic Approach* (Oxford: Blackwell, 1996).
Stanton, Graham N., *A Gospel for a New People: Studies in Matthew* (Edinburgh: T&T Clark, 1992).
Stark, Rodney, *The Rise of Christianity* (Princeton, NJ: Princeton University Press, 1996).
Stendahl, Krister, 'The Apostle Paul and the Introspective Conscience of the West', *Harvard Theological Review* 56, 1963, pp. 199–215. Reprinted in Wayne A. Meeks and John T. Fitzgerald (eds), *The Writings of St. Paul*, 2nd edn (New York: W. W. Norton, 2007), pp. 501–10.
Sterling, Gregory, 'The Love of Wisdom: Middle Platonism and Stoicism in the Wisdom of Solomon' in Troels Engberg-Pedersen (ed.), *From Stoicism to Platonism: The Development of Philosophy 100 BCE-100CE* (Cambridge: Cambridge University Press, 2017), pp. 198–213.
Stern, Karen B., 'Vandals or Pilgrims? Jews, Travel Culture, and Devotional Practice in the Pan Temple of Egyptian El-Kanais', in Caroline Johnson Hodge, Saul M. Olyan, Daniel Ullucci, and Emma Wasserman (eds.) *The One Who Sows Bountifully": Essays in Honor of Stanley K. Stowers* (Providence, RI: Brown Judaic Studies), pp. 177–88.

Sthulman, Andrew, *Scienceblind: Why Our Intuitive Theories About the World Are So Often Wrong* (New York: Basic Books, 2017).
Stowers, Stanley, 'Social Status, Public Speaking, and Private Teaching: The Circumstances of Paul's Preaching Activity', *Novum Testamentum*, 26, 1984, pp. 59–82.
Stowers, Stanley, *A Rereading of Romans: Justice, Jews and Gentiles* (New Haven, CT: Yale University Press, 1994).
Stowers, Stanley, 'Greeks Who Sacrifice and Those Who Do Not: Toward an Anthropology of Greek Religion', in L. Michael White and O. Larry Yarbrough (eds), *The Social World of the First Christians: Essays in Honor of Wayne A. Meeks* (Philadelphia, PA: Fortress, 1995), pp. 293–333.
Stowers, Stanley, 'Elusive Coherence: Ritual and Rhetoric in 1 Corinthians 10–11', in Elizabeth Castelli and Hal Taussig (eds), *Reimagining Christian Origins: A Colloquium Honoring Burton L. Mack* (Valley Forge, PA: Trinity Press International, 1996), pp. 68–83.
Stowers, Stanley, 'Truth, Identity and Sacrifice in Classical Athens', a paper presented at the Ancient History Documentary Research Centre, Macquarie University, June 1996.
Stowers, Stanley, 'A Cult from Philadelphia: *Oikos* Religion or Cultic Association?' in Abraham J. Malherbe, Frederick Norris and James W. Thompson (eds), *The Early Church in Its Context: Essays in Honor of Everett Ferguson* (Leiden: Brill, 1998), pp. 287–301.
Stowers, Stanley, 'Does Pauline Christianity Resemble a Hellenistic Philosophy?' in Troels Engberg-Pedersen (ed.), *Paul Beyond the Hellenism-Judaism Dualism* (Louisville: Westminster John Knox, 2001), pp. 81–102. Reprinted in Ron Cameron and Merrill P. Miller (eds), *Redescribing Paul and the Corinthians* (Atlanta, GA: Society of Biblical Literature, 2011), pp. 219–243.
Stowers, Stanley, 'Apostrophe, ΠΡΟΣΩΠΟΠΟΙΙΑ and Paul's Rhetorical Education', in John T. Fitzgerald, Thomas H. Olbricht, and L. Michael White (eds), *Early Christianity and Classical Culture: Comparative Studies in Honor of Abraham J. Malherbe* (Leiden: Brill, 2003), pp. 351–69.
Stowers, Stanley, 'The Concepts of "Religion", and "Political Religion" in the Study of Nazism', *Journal of Contemporary History*, 42, 2007, pp. 9–24.
Stowers, Stanley, 'The Ontology of Religion', in Willi Braun and Russell T. McCutcheon (eds), *Introducing Religion: Essays in Honor of Jonathan Z. Smith* (London: Equinox, 2008), pp. 434–49.
Stowers, Stanley, 'Two Kinds of Self: A Response to Ekkehard W. Stegemann', in Kathy Ehrensperger and R. Ward Holder (eds), *Reformation Readings of Romans* (London: T&T Clark, 2008), pp. 50–56.
Stowers, Stanley, 'What is Pauline Participation in Christ?' in M. Chancey, S. Heschel and F. Udoh (eds), *New Views of Jewish and Christian Self-Definition: Essays in Honor of E. P. Sanders* (Notre Dame, IN: Notre Dame University Press, 2008), pp. 352–71. Reprinted in Eugene Rogers (ed.), *The Holy Spirit: Classic and Contemporary Readings* (Oxford: Wiley-Blackwell, 2009), pp. 91–105.
Stowers, Stanley, 'Theorizing the Religion of Ancient Households and Families', in John Bodel and Saul Olyan (eds), *Household and Family Religion in Mediterranean and West Asian Perspectives* (Oxford: Blackwell, 2008), pp. 5–19.

Stowers, Stanley, 'The Apostle Paul', in Graham Oppy and N. N. Trakakis (eds), *The History of the Western Philosophy of Religion, Vol. 1.* (Oxford: Routledge, 2009), pp. 145–57.

Stowers, Stanley, 'The History of Ancient Christianity as the Study of Religion', a paper presented at the North American Association for the Study of Religion section at the Annual National Meeting of the Society of Biblical Literature, New Orleans, LA, 2009.

Stowers, Stanley, 'Jesus as Teacher and Stoic Ethics in the Gospel of Matthew', in Ismo Dundenberg, Troels Engberg-Pedersen, Tuomas Rasimus (eds), *Stoicism in Early Christianity* (Grand Rapids, MI: Baker Academic, 2010), pp. 59–76.

Stowers, Stanley, 'The Religion of Plant and Animal Offerings Versus the Religion of Meanings, Essences and Textual Mysteries', in Jennifer Knust and Zsuzsanna Varhelyi (eds), *Ancient Mediterranean Sacrifice: Images, Acts, Meanings* (New York: Oxford University Press, 2011), pp. 35–56.

Stowers, Stanley, 'Kinds of Myth, Meals and Power: Paul and the Corinthians', in Ron Cameron and Merrill P. Miller (eds), *Redescribing Paul and the Corinthians* (Atlanta, GA: Society of Biblical Literature, 2011), pp. 105–49.

Stowers, Stanley, 'Gods, Monotheism and Ancient Mediterranean Religion', a paper presented at the Brown Seminar for Culture and Religion of the Ancient Mediterranean (2012) and the Columbia University New Testament Seminar (2012).

Stowers, Stanley, 'Paul as Hero of Subjectivity' in Ward Blanton and Hent de Vries (eds), *Paul and the Philosophers* (New York: Fordham University Press, 2013), pp. 150–74.

Stowers, Stanley, 'Paul and the Terrain of Philosophy', *Early Christianity*, 6, 2015, pp. 141–56.

Stowers, Stanley, 'Self-Mastery', in J. Paul Sampley (ed.), *Paul in the Greco-Roman World, Vol. 2*, 2nd edn (Bloomsbury: T&T Clark, 2016).

Stowers, Stanley, 'Why Expert Versus Non-Expert is Not Elite Versus Popular Religion: The Case of the Third Century', in Nathaniel DesRosiers and Lilly C. Vuong (eds), *Religious Competition in Late Antiquity* (Atlanta, GA: Society of Biblical Literature, 2016), pp. 139–53.

Stowers, Stanley, 'The Dilemma of Paul's Physics: Features Stoic-Platonist or Platonist-Stoic?', in Troels Engberg Pedersen (ed.), *From Stoicism to Platonism: The Development of Philosophy 100 BCE-100CE* (Cambridge: Cambridge University Press, 2017), pp. 231–53.

Stowers, Stanley, 'Why "Common Judaism" Does not Look like Mediterranean Religion', in Michael L. Satlow (ed.), *Strength to Strength: Essays in Honor of Shaye J. D. Cohen* (Providence, RI: Brown Judaic Studies, 2018), pp. 235–55.

Stowers, Stanley, 'Locating the Religion of Associations', in Taylor G. Petrey (ed.), *Re-Making the World: Christianity and Categories: Essays in Honor of Karen L. King* (Tübingen: Mohr Siebeck, 2019), pp. 301–24.

Stowers, Stanley, 'Religion as a Social Kind', a paper presented in the Seminar Redescribing Christian Origins, Annual National Meeting of the Society of Biblical Literature, 2020.

Stowers, Stanley, 'What is the Relation of God to the Ghost that Saul Did Not See?', in Tracy M. Lemos, Jordan D. Rosenblum, Debra Scoggins Ballentine, Karen B. Stern (eds), *With the Loyal You Show Yourself Loyal: Essays on Relationships in the Hebrew*

Bible in Honor of Saul M. Olyan (Atlanta: Society of Biblical Literature Press, 2021), pp. 385–400.

Stowers, Stanley, *History and the Study of Religion: The Ancient Mediterranean as a Test Case* (New York: Oxford University Press, forthcoming).

Struck, Peter T., *Birth of the Symbol: Ancient Readers at the Limits of Their Texts* (Princeton: Princeton University Press, 2004).

Stuckenbruck, Loren T. 'The Origins of Evil in Jewish Apocalyptic Traditions: The Interpretation of Genesis 6:1–4 in the Second and Third Centuries B. C. E.', in C. Auffarth and L. Stuckenbruck (eds.), *The Fall of Angels* (Leiden: Brill, 2003), pp. 87–118.

Styers, Randall, *Making Magic: Religion, Magic and Science in the Modern World* (New York: Oxford University Press, 2004).

Suggs, Jack M., *Wisdom, Christology and Law in Matthew's Gospel* (Cambridge: Harvard University Press, 1970).

Sullivan, J. P., *Petronius, The Satyricon: Seneca, The Apocolocyntosis* (New York: Penguin Books, 1986).

Swain, Simon, *Hellenism and Empire: Language, Classicism, and Power in the Greek World AD 50–250* (Oxford: Clarendon, 1996).

Tarrant, Harold, *Thrasyllan Platonism* (Ithaca: Cornell University Press, 1993).

Thiessen, Matthew, *Contesting Conversion: Genealogy, Circumcision, and Identity in Ancient Judaism and Christianity* (New York: Oxford University Press, 2011).

Thom, Johan C., 'Cleanthes' Hymn to Zeus and Early Christian Literature' in Adela Yarbro Collins and Margaret M. Mitchell (eds), *Antiquity and Humanity: Essays on Ancient Religion and Philosophy Presented to Hans Dieter Betz on His 70th Birthday* (Tübingen: Mohr Siebeck, 2001), pp. 477–500.

Thom, Johan C., *Cleanthes' Hymn to Zeus: Text, Translation and Commentary* (Tübingen: Mohr Siebeck, 2005).

Thorsteinsson, Runar M., *Paul's Interlocutor in Romans 2. Function and Identity in the Context of Ancient Epistolography* (Stockholm: Almqvist & Wiksell, 2003).

Thorsteinsson, Runar M., *Jesus as Philosopher: The Moral Sage in the Synoptic Gospels* (Oxford: Oxford University Press, 2018).

Tilly, Charles, *Trust and Rule* (Cambridge: Cambridge University Press, 2005).

Monson, Andrew, 'The Ethics and Economics of Ptolemaic Religious Associations', *Ancient Society*, 36, 2006, pp. 221–238.

Tobin, Thomas, *The Creation of Man: Philo and the History of Interpretation* (Washington, DC: Catholic Biblical Association of America, 1983).

Tobin, Thomas, *Paul's Rhetoric in Its Contexts: The Argument of Romans* (Peabody, MA: Hendrickson, 2004).

Tolbert, Mary Ann, *Sowing the Gospel: Mark's World in Literary-Historical Perspective* (Minneapolis, MN: Fortress, 1989).

Tönnies, Ferdinand, *Gemeinschaft und Gesellschaft* (Leipzig: Fues Verlag, 1887).

Tremlin, Todd, *Minds and Gods: The Cognitive Foundations of Religion* (New York: Oxford University Press, 2006).

Ullucci, Daniel, 'Contesting the Meaning of Animal Sacrifice', in Jennifer Wright Knust and Zsuzsanna Várhelyi (eds), *Ancient Mediterranean Sacrifice* (New York. Oxford University Press, 2011), pp. 57–74.

Ullucci, Daniel, *The Christian Rejection of Animal Sacrifice* (New York: Oxford University Press, 2012).
Ullucci, Daniel, 'Towards a Typology of Religious Experts in the Ancient Mediterranean', in Caroline Johnson Hodge, S. Olyan, D. Ullucci, and E. Wasserman (eds), *The One Who Sows Bountifully"*: *Essays in Honor of Stanley K. Stowers* (Providence, RI: Brown Judaic Studies, 2013).
Ullucci, Daniel, 'What Did He Say? The Ideas of Religious Experts and the 99%', in N. DesRosiers, J. Rosenblum, and L. Vuong (eds), *Religious Competition in the Third Century C.E.: Jews, Christians, and the Greco-Roman World* (Vandenhoeck and Ruprecht, 2014).
Ullucci, Daniel, 'Competition between Experts and Non-Experts', pp. 133–38 in Nathaniel DesRosiers and Lily C. Vuong (eds), *Religious Competition in the Greco-Roman World* (Atlanta, GA: SBL Press, 2016).
Urbano, Arthur, *The Philosophical Life: Biography and the Crafting of Intellectual Identity in Late Antiquity* (Washington, DC: Catholic University Press of America, 2013).
Van Andringa, William, *La vie religieuse dans la cites de Vésuve à l'époque romaine* (Rome: École française de Rome, 2009).
Van Straten, Folker T., *Hiera Kala: Images of Animal Sacrifice in Archaic and Classical Greece* (Leiden: Brill, 1995).
Van Wees, Hans, 'The Law of Gratitude: Reciprocity in Anthropological Theory', in Christopher Gill, Norman Postlethwaite, and Richard Seaford (eds), *Reciprocity in Ancient Greece* (New York: Oxford University Press, 1998), pp. 13–50.
Vegge, Ivar, *2 Corinthians—a Letter about Reconciliation* (Tübingen: Mohr Siebeck, 2008).
Venticinque, Philip F., 'Family Affairs: Guild Regulations and Family Relationships in Roman Egypt', *Greek, Roman and Byzantine Studies*, 50, 2010, pp. 273–94.
Vernant, Jean-Pierre, *Mortals and Immortals: Collected Essays*, Froma I. Zeitlin (ed.) (Princeton: Princeton University Press, 1991).
Wallace-Hadrill, Andrew, *Houses and Society in Pompeii and Herculaneum* (Princeton, NJ: Princeton University Press, 1994).
Wallace-Hadrill, Andrew, *'Mutatio morum*: The Idea of a Cultural Revolution', in Thomas Habinek and Alessandro Schiesaro (eds), *The Roman Cultural Revolution* (Cambridge: Cambridge University Press, 1997), pp. 1–22.
Wallace-Hadrill, Andrew, *Rome's Cultural Revolution* (Cambridge: Cambridge University Press, 2008).
Wallace-Hadrill, Andrew, *The Origins of Early Christian Literature: Contextualizing the New Testament Within Graeco-Roman Literary Culture* (Cambridge: Cambridge University Press, 2021).
Walsh, Robyn Faith. 'Q and the 'Big Bang' Theory of Christian Origins', in Barry S. Crawford and Merrill P. Miller (eds), *Redescribing the Gospel of Mark* (Atlanta, GA: Society of Biblical Literature, 2017), pp. 483–533.
Waltzing, Jean-Pierre, *Étude historique sur les corporations professionelles chez les Romains depuis les origenes jusqu' à la chute de l'empire d'Occident*, 4 vols (Louvain: l'Academie Royal de Sciences, des Lettres et les Beaux-Arts Belgique, 1895–1900).
Wasserman, Emma, 'The Death of the Soul in Romans 7: Revisiting Paul's Anthropology in Light of Hellenistic Moral Psychology', *Journal of Biblical Literature*, 7, 2007, pp. 793–816.

Wasserman, Emma, *The Death of the Soul in Romans 7* (Tübingen: Mohr Siebeck, 2008).
Wasserman, Emma, 'Paul Among the Philosophers: The Case of Sin in Romans 6–8', *Journal for the Study of the New Testament*, 30, 2008, pp. 387–415.
Wasserman, Emma, 'Paul beyond the Judaism/Hellenism Divide? The Case of Pauline Anthropology in Romans 7 and 2 Corinthians 4–5', in Stanley E. Porter and Andrew Pitts (eds), *Christian Origins and Hellenistic Judaism: Social and Literary Contexts for the New Testament* (Leiden: Brill, 2012), pp. 259–279.
Wasserman, Emma, 'Beyond Apocalyptic Dualism: Ranks of Divinities in *1 Enoch* and Daniel', in *The One Who Sows Bountifully: Essays in Honor of Stanley K. Stowers*, ed. by Caroline Johnson Hodge, Saul M. Olyan, Daniel Ullucci, and Emma Wasserman. (Atlanta: Society of Biblical Literature, 2013), pp. 189–99.
Wasserman, Emma, *Apocalypse as Holy War: Divine Politics and Polemics in the Letters of Paul* (New Haven, CT: Yale University Press, 2018).
Wasserman, Emma, 'Philosophical Cosmology and Religious Polemic: The "Worship of Creation" in the Writings of Philo of Alexandria and the Wisdom of Solomon', *Journal for the Study of the Pseudepigrapha*, 31, 2021, pp. 6–28.
Wendt, Heidi, '*Iudaica Romana*: A Re-Reading of the Evidence for Judean Expulsions from Rome', *Journal for the Study of Judaism*, 6, 2015, pp. 97–126.
Wendt, Heidi, *At the Temple Gates: The Religion of Freelance Experts in the Roman Empire* (New York: Oxford University Press, 2016).
Wendt, Heidi, 'Marcion the Shipmaster: Unlikely Religious Experts of the Roman World', *Studia Patristica*, 99, 2018, pp. 55–74.
West, Martin L., *Hesiod: Works and Days* (Oxford: Oxford University Press, 1978).
White, L. Michael, *The Social Origins of Christian Architecture: Building God's House in the Roman World: Architectural Adaptation among Pagans, Jews, and Christians* (Valley Forge, PA: Trinity Press, 1996).
Whitehouse, Harvey, *Modes of Religiosity: A Cognitive Theory of Religious Transmission* (Walnut Creek, CA: AltaMira, 2004).
Whitehouse, Harvey and Luther H. Martin, *Theorizing Religions Past: Archeology, History and Cognition* (Walnut Creek, CA: AltaMira, 2004).
Whiteley, Denys, *The Theology of St. Paul*, 2nd edn (Oxford: Blackwell, 1974).
Wick, Peter, *Die urchristlichen Gottesdienste: Entstehung und Entwicklung im Rahmen der früjüdischen Tempel, Synagogen und Hausfrömmigkeit* (Stuttgart: Kohlhammer, 2002).
Wilken, Robert, 'Free Choice and the Divine Will in Greek Christian Commentaries', in William S. Babcock (ed.), *Paul and the Legacies of Paul* (Dallas: Southern Methodist University Press, 1990), pp. 123–40.
Wilken, Robert, *The Christians as the Romans Saw Them*, 2nd edn (New Haven, CT: Yale University Press, 2003).
Williams, Sam K., *Jesus' Death as Saving Event: The Background and Origin of a Concept* (Missoula, MT: Scholars Press, 1975).
Wilson, Andrew and Miko Flohr (eds), *Urban Craftsmen and Traders in the Roman World* (Oxford: Oxford University Press, 2016).
Winter, Bruce, *Philo and Paul among the Sophists*, 2nd edn (Grand Rapids, MI: Eerdmans, 2002).
Wittenburg, Andreas, *Il Testamento di Epikteta* (Trieste: Bernardi, 1990).
Wright, M. R., *Cosmology in Antiquity* (London: Routledge, 1995).

Young, Stephen, 'Mythological Themes in Romans', in Davina Lopez (ed.), *The Oxford Handbook of the Letter to the Romans* (New York: Oxford University Press, forthcoming).
Young, Stephen, 'Ethnic Ethics: Paul's Eschatological Myth of Jewish Sin', *New Testament Studies*, forthcoming.
Zamfir, Korinna, 'The Community of the Pastoral Epistles: A Religious Association?' in Vincent Gabrielsen and Christian A. Thomsen (eds), *Private Associations and the Public Sphere: Proceedings of a Symposium Held at the Royal Danish Academy of Sciences and Letters, 9-11 September 2010* (Copenhagen: Det Kongelige Danske Videnskabernes Selskab, 2015), pp. 206–40.
Zetterholm, Magnus, *Approaches to Paul: A Student's Guide to Recent Scholarship* (Minneapolis, MN: Fortress, 2009).
Zwierlein, Otto, 'Petrus in Rom? Die literarischen Zeugnisse' in S. Heid et al. (eds), *Petrus und Paulus in Rom: Eine Interdisziplinäre Debatte* (Freiburg-Basel, 2009), pp. 468–91.

Ancient Sources Index

Page numbers with the suffix 'n' indicate notes (e.g. *188n*)

HEBREW BIBLE

Genesis
1–10 *200*
1–11 *203*
1:26 *190n*
2–3 *204*
2:7 *171, 223*
2:24 *127, 187*
3:22–24 *200*
5:3 *190*
6:3 *201*
6:4 *206*
10:15–20 *209*
15:16 *209*
17:5 *193*
22:18 *189*
23:2 *264*

Exodus
23:23–24 *209*

Leviticus
18:24–30 *209*
19:18 *256, 260*

Deuteronomy
32:8 *176*

Psalms
42:6 (41:6 LXX) *262, 264*
77:19 *268*
82 *176*
104 *160n*
143:2 *212*

Isaiah
8:14 *208*
28:16 *208*
40–50 *94*

Jeremiah
1:5 *190*

Ezekiel
1:4 *172*
1:13–14 *172*
1:27 *172*

Daniel
8:23 *209*
9:10 *185*

DEUTEROCANONICAL WORKS

Wisdom of Solomon
12–15 *204*
12:1 *211*

2 Maccabees
6:14 *210*

PSEUDEPIGRAPHA

1 Enoch
19:1 *206*
84:4 *210*

Jubilees
10:8 *207*

10:12–13 *207*
15:27–28 *229*

Sibylline Oracles
3.8–45 *204*

ANCIENT JEWISH WRITERS

Josephus
Jewish War
4.629 *93*
6.300 *94*
The Life 2 *90*

Philo
Allegorical Interpretation (Leg.)
  3.161 *170n*
On the Cherubim 14–15
  253n
On the Confusion of Tongues
  (Conf.) 183–187 *192*
On the Eternity of the World
  (Aet.)
28 *172*
33 *172*
On Flight and Finding (Fug.)
  133 *170–1*
Questions and Answers on
  Genesis (QG)
1.79 *264*
1.92 *170*
On the Special Laws (Spec.)

1.13–15 *94*
4.123 *171*

That the Worse Attacks the Better (Det.) 83 *172*

Tobit
4.17 *64, 96*

NEW TESTAMENT
Matthew
1:18–20 *146*
3:12 *265n*
3:15 *263n*
5:7–9 *258*
5:17–20 *255*
5:20–22 *265n*
5:21–22 *258*
5:22 *262*
5:27–28 *258*
5:33–37 *259*
5:43 *260*
5:45 *261*
5:48 *254, 260*
6:1–18 *260*
6:33 *261*
7:11 *255*
7:13 *255*
7:13–14 *265n*
7:21–23 *265n*
7:21–27 *255n*
7:24 *255*
7:25–34 *261*
8:13–29 *265n*
10:15 *265n*
10:26–28 *265n*
10:29–31 *261*
11:20–24 *265n*
12:41 *265n*
13:42 *265n*
13:50 *265n*
16:27 *265n*
18:3 *265n*
18:10 *265n*
19:16–22 *255*
19:28 *250n*
21:12–13 *260*
22:13 *265n*
23:5–6 *260*
23:17 *262*
23:23 *260*
23:25 *260*
24:51 *265n*
25:30 *265n*
26:37 *264*
26:37–38 *262*
26:42 *264*
27:4 *262n*
27:19 *262n*

Mark
3:11 *273*
4:11 *273*
4:22–23 *273*
4:33 *273*
4:35–41 *273*
8:31–33 *273*
10:17–31 *256*
13 *209n*

Luke
6:20–26 *257*
6:46–49 *255*
13:23–24 *265n*
14:26 *77*

John
8:12 *251*
9:1–41 *272*
15:12 *251*

Acts
2:25–47 *146*
2:44–47 *237*
4:5 *146*
4:32 *239*
4:32–35 *146*
4:35 *239*
6:1–7 *147*
19:10 *147*
21:20 *147*

Romans
1 *204*
1:1–5 *191*
1:3–4 *188n*
1:4 *163n*
1:5 *147*
1:8 *149n*
1:9 *163n*
1:18–32 *24, 25, 203, 237*
1:18–2:16 *203, 210*
1:18–3:20 *209*
1:18–3:26 *211*
1:19–30 *204*
1:21–25 *49*
1:24 *205, 210, 215*
1:24–32 *213*
1:26 *205, 213, 215*
1:26–27 *210*
1:28 *205, 215, 253n*
1:32 *204, 210, 214*
2:1–16 *204*
2:4–5 *210*
2:6–10 *226n*
2:10–16 *210*
2:12–16 *212*
2:14–16 *214*
2:14–29 *215*
2:17–3:8 *211*
2:19–24 *211*
3:1–20 *211*
3:9–20 *208, 211*
3:11–14 *212*
3:18–20 *212*
3:20 *214*
3:21–5:21 *212*
3:25b–26 *211*
3:26 *187n*
4 *193*
4:15 *214*
4:15b–17a *193*
4:16 *187n*
5 *203, 222, 226n*
5:12–14 *203*
5:13 *214*
5:18–21 *208*
5:19 *175n*
6–8 *165, 200, 212*
6:1–6 *237*
6:1–11 *190*
6:3–11 *214*
6:6 *165*
6:12 *198, 213*
7 *13, 198, 199, 203, 212, 215, 216, 220, 223, 224*
7–8 *221*
7:5 *213*
7:7–13 *214*
7:7–24 *204*

7:7–25 210, 213
7:8–11 214
7:14 220
7:14–15 225
7:14–20 165, 166
7:15–20 214
7:16 220
7:18–20 224
7:22 166, 214
7:23 166
7:25 166, 220
7:54 166
8 167
8:1–17 224
8:9 191
8:13 214
8:16 163n, 192
8:17 175
8:18–25 216n
8:23 175
8:29 169, 188n, 190, 225, 226, 227, 237
8:29–30 175, 191
8:34 229
8:34–38 226
8:34–39 175
8:38–39 227
8.23 220
9 190
9–11 207–8, 211, 212
9:7–8 190
9:22–23 226n
9:33 208
10:6–7 226
11:13–16 174
11:25 208
11:25–26 174, 207
11:25–32 175n, 208
11:32 208
12.1–2 49
12:1–3 25, 130, 167, 216
12:2–3 221
12:2–21 167
12:3 214n
12:3–8 131
14:1–15:6 146
15 155
15:7–13 175n
15:19 147
16 150, 154

16:1–11 151

1 Corinthians
1:2 238
1:4–5 238
1:6–7 238
1:10–16 112, 116
1:10–17 27, 238
1:14 243
1:16 243
1:17 112
1:18 175n
1:18–2:5 27
1:18–2:16 24
1:26 120
1:30 238
2–3 222
2:6–8 212
2:7–10 175
2:10–13 163, 222
2:10–16 165, 175, 229
2:11–15 191
2:11–16 167
2:14 223
2:14–3:4 238
2:15–16 164, 222
2:17 27
3:1–4 229
3:3 173n
3:16–17 238
3:23 238
4:7 239
5:1 26, 118
5:1–2 238
5:1–5 26
5:6 26
6:1–2 226
6:1–7 238
6:2 176
6:3 176
6:9–11 237
6:11 238
6:12–20 164, 186, 239
6:15–19 127
6:18 187
6:18–19 238
7:10 251n
7:14 238
8–11 120, 126
9:14 251n

10:1 118, 119
10:1–22 129
10:13 206
10:16 127
10:17–18 130
10:20–21 206
11–14 133
11:7 173
11:10 206
11:17–18 132
11:17–23 129n
11:18–22 128
11:19 126
11:21–22 129, 133
11:27 126
11:28–29 127
11:29 126
11:30 127
11:30–32 127
11:33–34 129
12 133
12:1 119
12:2 118
12:13 238
12:14–27 133
13:12 167, 220
15 116, 185, 219, 221
15:12 138
15:16–24 175
15:22 175n
15:23–28 174, 175, 229
15:24–28 226
15:29 26, 119
15:35–50 186
15:38–49 163n
15:40–44 229
15:40–49 172
15:41 163
15:42–49 185
15:42–53 216
15:43 163
15:44 187
15:44–46 223
15:44–47 127
15:44–49 164, 222
15:50 130, 173, 225, 228
15:51–52 175
15:56 207n, 214
16:15–17 116
16:15–18 112

2 Corinthians
1:22 220
2:16–17 *175n*
2:17–3:3 *166n*
3–5 *221*
3:1–3 *168*
3:18 *168, 214n, 221, 237*
4:4 *163, 206n*
4:4–6 *169*
4:16–18 *167*
4:16–5:5 *216*
4:16–5:10 *214n*
4:17 *163*
4:18 *167, 220*
5:1–2 *167, 220*
5:1–5 *168*
5:4–9 *167, 220*
6:4 *206n*
11:4–5 *168n*
11:13 *168n*
11:22–23 *168n*
11:22–29 *27*
12:2 *167*
12:2–3 *166, 220*

Galatians
1:4 *206n*
1:8–9 *226n*
1:11–2:10 *24*
1:15–16 *147*
2:7–8 *147*
2:15 *215*
2:15–21 *228*
2:16 *212*
2:19–20 *184, 193, 227*
3 *193*
3:6 *140*
3:7–9 *188*
3:8 *191*
3:14 *189*
3:16 *189*
3:19–4:7 *214*
3:21–29 *208*
3:22 *208*
3:22–23 *207*
3:26–29 *189, 191*
3:27–28 *237*
3:27–29 *140*
4:8 *206n*
4:19 *223*

5:16–23 *190*
5:17 *224*
5:20–22 *224*
5:24 *190, 224, 237*
6:1 *222*
6:8 *226n*

Philippians
1:14–18 *26*
1:21–23 *220*
2:5–11 *174, 227*
2:9 *227*
2:10 *226*
3:20–21 *163*
3:21 *169*

1 Thessalonians
1:2–7 *23*
1:9–10 *22*
1:10 *23*
2 *21–2, 27*
2:1–12 *22, 24*
2:2–3 *27*
2:14–16 *209*
4 *225*
4:3–8 *237*
4:4–5 *215*
4:13–5:11 *147*
4:15 *175, 251n*
4:16–17 *176*
4:17 *175, 227*
5:10 *227*
5:12–14 *223*
5:23 *163n*

2 Thessalonians
1:8–9 *226n*

Hebrews
7 *189, 190*

1 Peter
4:16 *150*

RABBINIC WORKS
Mishnah
Pesachim 10.5 *51*

EARLY CHRISTIAN WRITERS
1 Clement *146*

Augustine
The City of God (Civ.)
4.31 *203*
10.23 *202*
14.11 *202*
Epistles 157.2.6 *215n*
On the Literal Interpretation of Genesis (Gen.imp.)
11.2–3 *202*
11.24–25 *202*
Propositions from the Epistle to the Romans 13–18
198
Sermons
151.6.6 *215n*
152.2 *215n*
154.3.3 *215n*

Eusebius
Ecclesiastical History
2.2.7–24 *148*
2.2.11 *148*
2.3.6–7 *148*
4.3.1–3 *27*

Justin Martyr
First Apology 65–67 *129n*

Origen
Against Celsus 3.12 *23*
Tertullian
Apology 21 *148*
To Scapula 2:10 *148*

GREEK AND ROMAN SOURCES
Alexander of Aphrodisias
De Fato 196.24–197.3
217

Aristophanes
Birds 959–999 *48*
Peace 38–49 *47*
Arius Didymus
Stobaeus *Anthology* 2.85
254

Arrian
Epicteti dissertationes 3.22.54
260

Cicero
Academicae quaestiones 1.39
    179
De finibus 3.32 *258*

Cleanthes
Hymn to Zeus
24–29 *252*
33 *252*

Demosthenes
Against Neaera *127*

Derveni Papyrus
col. II *51*
col. IV *51*
col.V *51*
col.VI *51*
col. XI *51*
col. XX *51*

Dio Chrysostom
Oration 12 (Man's First Conception of God / Olympic Discourse)
    18
Oration 32 (To the People of Alexandria)
32.8 *18*
32.11–18 *18*
Oration 33 (First Tarsic Discourse) *18*
Oration 35 (At Celaenae in Phrygia) *18*
Oration 77/78 (Envy)
    77/78.42 *18–19*

Diogenes Laertius
Lives and Opinions of Eminent Philosophers
7.33 *16*
7.88 *254*
7.107 *254*

Epictetus
Dissertationes
1:30 *260*
2.14.11 *260n*
3.3.22 *189*

Heraclitus
Fragments
5 *205*
12 *205*
14–16 *205*
21.B11 *205*

Inscriptions
Corpus Inscriptionum Latinarum (CIL) 1.2
    1003 *74*
Inscriptiones Graecae (IG)
X 2.1 291 *74*
XII 3.330 *61*
XII 3.330, 7–15 *62*
XII 3.330, 177–194 *62*
Inscriptiones Judaicae Orientis
    I Ach45 *94*
Laum 1914 II no. 43
    61
Lois sacrées de l'Asie Mineure (LSAM) 20 *65*
Lois sacrées des cités grecques (LSCG) 135 *61*
Mitteilungen des deutschen archäologischen Instituts (A) (MDAI A) 228
    68
Sylloge Inscriptionum Graecarum (SIG) 985
    65

Isaeus
8 *(Kiron)* 8.16 *123–4*

Livy
History of Rome 39.16.8–9
    152

Lucian
Ignorant Book Collector
    110
On Salaried Posts *110*

Marcus Aurelius
Meditations 7.31 *260*

Michigan Papyri *(P.Mich)*
V 243 *70*

Petronius
Satyricon
1–2 *113*
5 *114*
48.4 *115*
57.4 *115*
85 *113*

Philostratus
Life of Apollonius *178*
Lives of the Sophists *16*

Pindar
Nemean Odes 3.22 *139*
Olympian Odes 12.7–12
    40

Plato
Laws 909e–910b *48*
Republic
9 *213*
9.588c–591b *166*
909e–910b *35n*
Statesman (Politicus) 287C
    125

Plautus
Rudens 1205–1207 *71*

Plotinus
Enneades 5.1 *202*

Plutarch
Quaestionum convivialum libri IX 727b–728d
    178

Porphyry
Vita Pythagorae 53 *178*

Seneca
De beneficiis 4:26 *261*
De ira 2.34 *260*
De otio 1.4 *260*
De vita beata 15 *260*
Epistulae morales
16.5 *260*
42.1 *217*
64.2 *178*

90.4–6 *201*
90.28 *204*
90.37–39 *201*
90.46 *202*
99 *265*
Heracles Furens 889
    139

Stobaeus
Anthology
2.85 *254*
5.906, 18–907, 5 *256*

Stoicorum Veterum
    Fragmenta (SVF)
2.359 *186n*
2.381 *186n*
2.525 *186n*
3.157–158 *255n*
3.432 *261n*
3.510 *256*
6.342 *264*

Suetonius
Tiberius 36 *152*

Tacitus
Annales
2.85.11–17 *152*
15.44 *148–9*

Xenophon
De equitum magistro
    9.7–9 *40*
Memorabilia 1.1.19
    40
Symposium 4.47–49
    40

Subject Index

Note: Page numbers with the suffix 'n' indicate notes (e.g. 167n).

Abraham
   God's covenant with, 117, 188, 207–8
   grief for Sarah, 264–5
   Jesus as descendant of, 117, 134, 188–90, 193
   lineage of, 8, 115, 117–19, 134, 140, 188–91, 193, 229
Acts, 145–7, 148–9, 156, 239, 247–8
Adam
   body/corporeal existence, 169n, 173, 185, 187, 198
   lineage of, 186, 190
Adamic fall, 197–8, 202–4, 208–9, 211–12, 216
Agdistis, 67
agricultural economy, 13–14, 17, 21–2, 40, 59, 68–9, 88–9
allegory, 17, 46, 51, 273
altars, 67, 69, 73, 88, 124–7, 268
ancestry
   Kwaio people, 269
   non-ethnic identity, 139–41
   Paul/Corinthians, 106, 111, 115–20, 128, 139
   place, 38
   sacrificial meal practices, 124, 128, 131
   substance and relatedness, 187–90
   see also Abraham, lineage of
ancient Mediterranean religion, 9, 24, 33–4, 59, 86–7, 162, 200
ancient psychology, 198–200
angels, 97, 170–1, 175–6, 202, 206, 212, 226–9
anger, 259, 261–2, 263

animal offerings
   domestic sacrifice, 97, 122n
   introduction, 6
   Kwaio people, 270
   problem of sacrifice, 33–4, 42, 53–4, 55
   religion of associations, 63, 68, 71
   sacrificial meal practices, 122–8, 130–1
   social kind sub-kinds of religion, 13, 40–3, 48–54, 89, 270–1
anthropomorphism, 17, 21, 162, 165, 179, 221
Antiochus, 177, 179–80
apocalyptic thought
   assimilation to Christ, 175, 176, 225–6
   Gospels, 248, 266–7, 275
   participation in Christ, 180–2, 188
   Paul's physics, 160, 173–6
   sin discourses, 198, 199, 200, 205–12
Apollo, 72, 77
Apollonius of Tyana, 17, 178
Archedemus, 254
Aristides, 28
aristocracy/elites
   civic religion, 13, 53, 58–9, 88, 91
   Corinthians, 105, 112–13, 115–16, 132–3
   priests, 24, 88, 91–2
Aristophanes, 46–8
assimilation to Christ
   definition, 8–9, 181
   Paul's audience, new human state, 220–1, 225–6, 230
   Paul's physics, 168, 173, 175, 176, 179–80
associations *see* religion of associations
Atbalmin, 101, 105–6, 107, 110, 116

Athens, 44–5
Atran, Scott, 81, 84, 85–6
Attica, 41, 123
attraction
　definition, 102
　response to Paul, 106, 110–11, 113, 115,
　　116–17, 134, 153
Augustine, 195, 197, 198–9, 201, 202, 214–16,
　275–6
authority, 254, 262; *see also* self-authorization
autonomy
　in Corinth, 107, 108
　degrees of, 16, 28–9
　idealized, 17, 114–15, 135–7
　institutional power, 24, 55, 92
　poetry and drama, 44, 46
　in Rome, 92, 150, 151–2, 155
　writer–community relation, 234–7, 243–4
　further mentions, 84, 90, 246

baptism
　for the dead, 111–12, 119–20
　and faith, 188n
　Paul's Platonic explanation of, 9
　pneuma connection to Christ, 111–12,
　　117–19, 127–8, 164, 165, 189, 191
　Stephanas, 112, 243
Barrett, Justin, 275
Bauckham, Richard, 246–8
Bercovitch, Eytan, 105–6
Betz, Hans Dieter, 262
binary operators, 85; *see also* dualisms
body/corporeal existence
　Adam, 169n, 173, 185, 187, 198
　mind/body dualism, 165–8, 173, 213–14,
　　216, 220, 223–5
　participation in Christ, 127–8, 175–6, 183,
　　186–7, 216
　Paul's sin discourses, 198, 202–3, 213–14, 216
　pneuma, 127–8, 130, 132, 136, 139, 166–8,
　　175, 214
　resurrection bodies, 163, 165, 186–7
Bolle, Kees, 267, 277
Bourdieu, Pierre, 101n, 136, 137
Brown University, 5
Brubaker, Rogers, 140, 237
Bultmann, Rudolph, 183, 184–5, 224, 235

Celsus, 19–20
Chadwick, Henry, 26

Christian theological modernism, 102–5, 116,
　117, 135–6
Christianity
　"Christian," emergence as a term, 148–50
　Corinthians, 118
　introduction, 24, 25–8
　origin myths, 143, 146–9, 156, 238, 239–40,
　　248–9
　religion of associations, 66, 74–9
　religion of literate experts, 55, 75, 77, 78
　Rome, 143, 144, 145–9, 151
　universal Christian subject, 247
Chrysippus, 49, 256
churches, Rome, 143–8, 150–1, 155
civic religion
　aristocracy/elites, 13, 53, 59, 88, 89
　description, 12, 53–4, 58, 59, 88–9
　religion of associations, 72, 73, 74–5
　religion of literate experts, interactions, 16,
　　43, 44–6, 50
　temples, 13, 59, 64, 88, 91–3
　further mentions, 20, 21, 24, 41
Claudius, 144, 145, 151, 152
cognitive psychology
　community, 242
　folk biological knowledge, 84, 85–6
　intuitive thinking, 39, 42, 81–3, 87, 93, 98
cognitive science of religion, 6, 7–8, 9, 11–12
Cohen, Shaye, 80
Colophon, 38n
"common Judaism" theory, 80, 83–6, 90, 97–8
communitarianism, 233, 236
community
　conceptions of, 103–5, 233–4
　Corinthians, 104–5, 107, 130, 141, 238–9
　critique of concept usage, 240–7
　empire-wide, 246–8
　ideal, 76, 103–4, 107, 239
　sacrificial meal practices, 128, 130
　writer–community relation, 234–7, 243–4,
　　245
Compitalia, 73
Corinthians
　ancestry, 106, 111, 115–20, 128, 139
　aristocracy/elites, 105, 112–13, 115–16,
　　132–3
　community, 104–5, 107, 130, 141, 238–9
　households, 104–5, 106, 116, 132, 243
　pneuma, 109, 111–12, 115–19, 122, 127–8,
　　130, 132–4, 136, 138–40, 164–5, 238–9

corporeal existence *see* body/corporeal
    existence
Courtney, Edward, 114–15
crucifixion
    of the flesh (emotions/desires), 224, 229,
        230, 237
    of Jesus, 174, 184, 212, 227
cultural economy (writings, interpretations,
    teachings), 13–15, 17, 20–2, 24, 42–4, 60;
    see also allegory; drama; interpretation;
    mythmakers; myths; poetry and poets;
    symbolism and metaphor
Cynic philosophers, 16, 18, 28, 29, 50, 115,
    201–2

Dahl, Nils, 3, 189
dead people, practices for
    baptism for the dead, 111–12, 119–20
    funerary practices, 63, 64, 65, 69, 71–2
    heroes and heroines, 61, 62–5
    Judaism, 95–6
    meals for the dead, 122, 129, 133, 134
Dead Sea Scrolls, 1, 89, 91, 92, 94
degeneration of humanity (discourse), 200–5,
    216
Delos, 73
Demosthenes, 127, 128
Dennett, Daniel, 132
Derrida, Jacques, 4
Derveni Papyrus, 46, 51
Descartes, René, 184, 194
Dillon, John, 171
Diogenes the Cynic, 137, 202
Dionysius, 66–8, 126
divinatory practices
    Augustine, 275–6
    Derveni papyrus, 51
    Gospels, 272
    Josephus, 93
    religion of associations, 68
    Rome, 152, 154
    social kind sub-kinds of religion, 13, 38,
        39–40, 52–3, 270–1
Dodds, E. R., 76
doxa, 101, 108–9, 116, 134, 229
drama, 45–8, 50
dreams, 64, 66, 68, 94, 96, 152, 271
dualisms, 95, 176, 226, 233, 242; *see also* binary
    operators; Descartes, René; Judaism/
    Hellenism dualism; material/spiritual
    dualism; mind/body dualism; natural/
    supernatural dualism; orthodox/
    heretical dualism; sensible/noetic
    dualism
Durkheim, Émile, 237

eating practices *see* meal practices
economics *see* agricultural economy; cultural
    economy (writings, interpretations,
    teachings); modes of production
Egypt, 68, 152, 204
Eliade, Mircea, 136
elites *see* aristocracy/elites
emotions
    fleshly bodies, 220, 224, 229, 230, 237
    moral failure as enslavement to, 210, 214,
        223–4
    Platonism, 162, 165, 166, 212, 224
    Stoicism, 162, 166, 225n, 258–9, 261–65
Engberg-Pedersen, Troels
    pneuma, 163, 165, 167n, 168, 179, 220n
    Stoic-like features in Paul's letters, 159,
        160, 161, 168, 180
enigmas, 46, 48, 50, 274
environments, 12, 14, 37, 38, 53, 59
Epictetus, 116, 166, 260
Epicureanism, 177–8, 201, 214, 215–18
Epikteta of Thera, 61–4
equality, 66, 189, 209, 212, 236
Eshleman, Kendra, 14–15, 18, 22, 29
essentialism, 81–2, 87, 140
ethnicity, 72, 139–41, 144; *see also* Gentiles
Eusebius, 25, 28, 148, 150, 156, 248
existentialism, 196, 199, 224

faith, justification by, 8, 180, 193
faithfulness
    of Abraham, 188–9, 193
    of believers, 187–8, 193, 207, 227–9
    of Christ, 137, 139, 187–9, 193, 207, 211,
        225, 227–9
    of Corinthians, 168, 221
    of Gentiles, 176
    of God, 206
fall
    Adamic fall, 197–8, 202–4, 208–9, 211–12,
        216
    of angels, 202, 206, 212
families, 61–8, 70–2, 77, 97, 104, 106, 124
Fang people, 269

INDEX   309

Fascism, 9, 233, 241
festivals, 73, 88, 91
fields of knowledge
   Corinthians, 107–11, 115, 132, 134
   definition, 153, 245
   religion of literate experts, 14–23, 27–28
   Romans, 153–5
   utopian elements as field effects, 136–8
Fitzmyer, Joseph, 145, 204
folk beliefs, 160
folk biological knowledge, 84, 85–6
folk oral tradition, 26, 52, 234–5
food offerings, 63–4, 68, 96, 269, 270; *see also* animal offerings; plant offerings
Form Criticism, 2, 234–5
freedmen, 66, 73, 114–15, 120
freelance experts *see* religion of literate experts
funerary practices, 63, 64, 65, 69, 71–2

Gaius, 112, 243
gender
   meal practices, 123, 125, 128, 133
   network theory and analysis, 84, 154
   participation in Christ, 194, 228n
   religion of associations, 66, 68, 70
Gentiles
   Abrahamic covenant, 117, 188, 207–8
   Abraham's lineage, 8, 117–19, 134, 140, 188–9, 191, 193
   Gospels, 140, 248
   Paul's audience, new human state, 223–4, 226–7
   Paul's mission to, 147, 173, 174–6, 208, 211, 216, 226–7
   Paul's sin discourses, 201, 203–4, 205–12, 214, 215
   Rome/Romans, 144–6, 147, 151, 155
gift-giving, 13, 17, 21–2, 40–2, 91, 175; *see also* animal offerings; food offerings; plant offerings; sacrifice
Glaim, Aaron, 91
God, conceptions of, 17, 49, 93–5, 161–4
gods, conceptions of, 12, 21, 37–41, 52, 59, 93–5, 161–2
Goldberg, Rube, 142, 143
Gospels, 28–9, 234–7, 246–8; *see also* John, Gospel of; Luke, Gospel of; Mark, Gospel of; Matthew, Gospel of
Graver, Margaret, 264
Greer, Rowan, 197

grief, 258, 262, 263–5
Gunkel, Hermann, 235

Hays, Richard, 183–4, 185
Hellenism/Judaism dualism, 1–2, 29, 195
Hera, 48
Heracles, 138–9
Heraclitus, 205
Herder, Johann Gottfried, 234–5
heretical/orthodox dualism, 103, 238
Hermes, 72
heroes and heroines
   heroic martyr myth, 111, 117, 126–7, 129–31
   local, 138–9
   religious associations, 59, 61–5
Hesiod, 200, 201, 269
Hestia, 67
Hodge, Caroline Johnson, 117, 118, 188n, 190, 192n
Homer, 46, 48, 50, 139, 269
Horst, Pieter W. van der, 96
house churches, Rome, 144, 148, 150
households
   Corinthians, 104–5, 104, 116, 132, 243
   family associations, 61–68, 70–3, 77
   literate exchange relating to, 92–3
   occupational associations, 68–9, 70, 73–4
   Rome, 20, 145, 153–5
   sacrificial meal practices, 124
   site of economic/religious production, 59
Hua people, 119
Hutchinson, Sharon, 140

icons, 21, 35, 48, 176, 203–5
identity formation
   literate exchange, 14–15
   network theory, 85
   non-ethnic, 139–41
   religion of associations, 60, 72, 74
   sacrificial meal practices, 123–4, 126, 130
idolatry, 18, 76, 203–6, 208–10, 215, 223
Ignatius, 150
inscriptions, 61–2, 65–7, 74, 94, 96, 126
interests
   Corinthians, 104, 106, 116, 120, 122, 134
   definition, 59, 101–2
interpretation
   end of, 267–8, 271, 274, 275
   religion of literate experts, 13, 46–7, 60, 90, 111

intuitive thinking
    cognitive psychology, 39, 42, 81–3, 87, 93, 98
    meal practices, 121
    religion of associations, 78–9
    see also doxa
Itza' Maya, 84, 86

Jerusalem temple, 71, 94, 96
Jesus Christ
    Abraham's lineage, 117, 134, 188–90, 193
    crucifixion, 174, 184, 212, 227
    death as sacrifice, 32, 41, 42
    faithfulness of, 137, 139, 187–9, 193, 207, 211, 225, 227–9
    resurrection of, 117, 138–9, 160, 163, 165, 173, 181–2, 185, 191, 193
    secrecy and revelation, 271–4, 275, 276
    as Stoic sage figure in Matthew, 254–65
    as teacher, 29, 250–1
    see also assimilation to Christ; participation in Christ
John, Gospel of, 251, 271–2, 273, 275
John the Baptist, 90
Josephus, 83, 89, 92, 93, 94–5
Judaism
    "common Judaism" theory, 80, 83–6, 90, 97–8
    Corinthians, 118–19
    dead people, practices for, 95–6
    locative/non-locative, 50, 90, 93–4
    religion of literate experts, 55, 75
    Rome, 143–6, 151–2
    temples, 89, 91–4
Judaism/Hellenism dualism, 1–2, 29, 195
Judean apocalyptic thought *see* apocalyptic thought
Judean religion
    ethnicity, 144
    religion of associations, 63, 75
    Rome, freelance experts in, 92, 150, 151–2, 155
    social kind sub-kinds of religion, 53–4, 88, 91
judgment day, 210–11, 225–6

Kafka, Franz, 277
Kagaba people, 277
Kant, Immanuel, 217, 259
Keesing, Roger, 269

Kermode, Frank, 273
kinship, 106–7, 124, 140–1, 188, 190, 269
Kloppenborg, John, 57
knowledge, 81, 267–71; *see also* fields of knowledge; folk biological knowledge; testing practices; truth/true knowledge
Konstan, David, 51
Kuhn, Thomas, 2
Kwaio people, 269, 270–1

Ladinos, 84, 86
Lares, 20, 21, 53, 71, 73
law
    Judaism, 92
    Matthew, 251–2, 255–6, 258
    Moses, 168
    participation in Christ, 188, 193
    Paul's audience, new human state, 223, 228–9
    Paul's sin discourses, 201–5, 207, 210, 212, 214
    Stoic ethics–law conjunction, 252–4
Lévi-Strauss, Claude, 8, 85
linguistics, 4, 7, 81
literacy, 14, 80, 96, 114–16, 245, 274
literary studies, 4, 242
literature, writer–community relation, 232–7, 243–4, 245
locative religion
    Corinthians, 106–7, 132, 133, 134–6, 138–9
    Judaism, 90, 93–4
    religion of associations, 72, 73, 78
    social kind sub-kinds of religion, 36, 50–1, 53, 268, 269
Lord's Supper, 75, 121–3, 126, 128–30, 133, 252
Lucian of Samosata, 18, 49, 110, 111, 115
Luke, Gospel of, 250, 255, 257–8
Luther, Martin, 214–15
Luz, Ulrich, 240

Macdonald, Paul, 196
Mack, Burton, 134–5
Malherbe, Abraham, 1, 3, 4, 7, 17–19, 210, 245–6
Malinowski, Bronislaw, 82
Marcion of Sinope, 28
Mark, Gospel of
    community, 240, 248

Matthew's use of, 251, 256–7, 260, 262, 264, 265
secrecy and revelation, 271–3, 275
martyrs
   Christians in Rome, 148
   heroic martyr myth, 111, 117, 126–7, 129–31
   religion of associations, 78–9
material/spiritual dualism, 102, 170–1
matter, 161, 176n, 184, 186n, 190, 192
Matthew, Gospel of
   apocalyptic thought, 248, 266–7
   Jesus as sage, 252, 254–65
   Jesus as teacher of ethics, 250–1
   law, 250–2, 255–6, 258
   Mark as primary source, 250, 256–7, 260, 262, 264, 265
   perfection, 254–6, 260
   righteousness, 254–6, 258–1, 263, 265
   Stoicism, 250–65
meal practices
   memorials for the dead, 122, 129, 133, 134
   sacrificial (animal offerings), 122–8, 130–1
   see also Lord's Supper
Medin, Douglas, 81, 84, 85–6
Meeks, Wayne, 5, 6, 271
Mercury, 72
metaphor *see* symbolism and metaphor
Mikalson, Jon D., 36n
Miller, Merrill, 29
mind
   of Christ, 9, 165, 167, 173, 219, 222–3, 237
   Paul's audience, new human state, 220–4, 228
   Plato's "inner person," 131–2, 134, 166, 213–14, 216, 221–3
   theory of mind, 242
mind/body dualism, 165–8, 173, 213–14, 216, 220, 223–5
mind goods *see* cultural economy (writings, interpretations, teachings)
Mithraism, 76
Moderatus of Gades, 178
modernism
   concepts of religion, 42, 85, 144–5
   symbolism and metaphor, 38, 60, 184–5, 186, 194
   theological, 102–5, 116, 119, 135–6
modernity
   distorted view of ancient world, 76, 259
   distorted view of Paul's texts, 102, 182, 184, 185–6, 194
   exceptionalist view of Judaism, 90–1, 98
   in New Guinea, 107
modes of production, 59, 91; *see also* agricultural economy; cultural economy (writings, interpretations, teachings)
monotheistic religion, 34, 90–1, 93–4, 144, 161n
moral psychology, 9, 165–6, 198, 212–16, 219–21, 223
morality
   community, 241
   emotions, 203, 205, 209–10, 214
   non-obvious beings, 268
   Paul's audience, new human state, 217–18, 221–4
   pneuma, 190
   religion of associations, 77
   see also sage, Stoic concept of
Moschos, 94
Moses, 50, 168–9, 172, 178, 202, 254
Moss, Candida, 149
Mullins, Terence, 151
Muses, 61, 62, 63
mysteries, 67, 267–8, 277
mythmakers, 105, 112, 120, 133, 138
myths
   of Christian origins, 143, 142–9, 156, 238, 239–40, 248–9
   degeneration, 200–1
   Heracles, 138–9
   heroic martyr, 111, 117, 126–7, 129–31
   kinship, 140–1
   modern scholarship practices, 185
   mythmaking as practice, 105, 121
   religion of literate mythmaking, 271, 274–7

Nagy, Gregory, 46
natural/supernatural dualism, 184, 185–6
Nazism (National Socialism), 9, 233, 241
neighborhood associations, 73–4
Neo-Darwinism, 81, 132
Neo-Platonism, 198–9
Nero, 148
network theory, 57, 81, 84–5, 153–5
Neusner, Jacob, 5

New Testament Studies
　description of Stoicism, 252
　Gospel as oral tradition, 234
　introduction to, 1–3, 7, 101
　participation in Christ, 181–2, 186, 194
　view of Paul, 135
noetic realm *see* sensible/noetic dualism
non-evident beings (NEBS), 41–2, 59, 62–5, 68, 95, 268
non-locative religion
　Judaism, 50, 90
　religion of literate experts, 52, 76, 78, 109, 275
　utopian religion, 2, 135–6, 137–8
non-obvious beings, 267–9, 271

oaths, 67, 68, 72, 125, 127, 259, 268
obedience
　humans and other beings, 176, 227, 254
　of Jesus, 174, 175, 227
　see also Adamic fall
occupational associations, 70–1, 72, 75–6
offerings *see* gift-giving
omniscience, 40, 93, 268, 275
oral tradition, 26, 52, 234–5
Origen, 200n, 202, 264
original sin, definition, 199
orthodox/heretical dualism, 102, 103, 238

paganism, 76
paideia, 107–8, 110–11, 113, 115, 116, 134
Pan, 94
Panaetius, 253
Papua New Guinea, 101; *see also* Atbalmin
parables, 272–3, 277
Parker, Robert, 46
participation in Christ
　apocalyptic thought, 181–2, 188
　body/corporeal existence, 127–8, 175–6, 183, 186–7, 216
　community, 237
　contiguity, 117, 164, 186–7, 189, 194
　Corinthians, 104, 107, 117–19, 127–8, 133–4
　Paul's audience, new human state, 219, 222
　Paul's physics, 164, 169, 175–6
　Paul's sin discourses, 215, 216
　pneuma, 8–9, 117, 119, 127–8, 133, 134, 168–9, 184–5, 187, 189–94, 219, 222, 237
　salvation, 104, 187–8, 190–1, 193

Paul
　audience of, new human state, 217–30
　death of, 25–6, 147
　mission to Gentiles, 147, 173, 174–6, 208, 211, 216, 226–7
　physics, 159–80
　sin discourses, 198–216
　as teacher, 17–19, 20–1, 23
　see also Corinthians; Romans, Paul's letter to
Peregrinus of Parium, 28
perfection, Stoic conception of, 254–7, 260
personhood, of gods, 37, 38–9, 40, 192
Pervo, Richard, 150
Pew Research Center, 98
Pherekydes of Syron, 50
Philadelphia, religious association, 65–6, 68
Philo of Alexandria
　emotions, 263, 264
　Judaism, 83, 93, 94
　participation in Christ, 192
　Paul's audience, new human state, 219, 221, 227–8
　Paul's sin discourses, 214
　Platonism, 170–1, 178–9
　pneuma, 170–3
　Stoicism, 170, 171, 179, 253, 254
Philostratus, 16–17
Phrastor, 127, 128
Pindar, 40, 139
place, 37–8, 40, 45, 64, 194, 196; *see also* locative religion
plant offerings, 33, 40, 43, 50, 53, 54
Platonism
　"inner person," 131–2, 134, 166, 213–14, 216, 221–3
　moral psychology, 9, 165–6, 213–15, 219–21, 223
　Paul's audience, new human state, 217–22, 224
　Paul's physics, 159, 161–70, 172, 173, 177–80
　of Philo, 170–1, 178–9
　further mentions, 49, 125
Plautus, 71
Pliny, 149–50
Plotinus, 198, 202
Plutarch, 49

pneuma
    assimilation to Christ, 8–9, 168, 179–80
    community/social body, 127–8, 130, 132, 133, 237–9
    Corinthians, 109, 111–12, 115–19, 122, 127–8, 130, 132–4, 136, 164–5, 238–9, 138–40
    Gospels, 258, 271
    participation in Christ, 8–9, 117, 119, 127–8, 133, 134, 168–9, 184–5, 187, 189–94, 219, 222, 237
    Paul's audience, new state, 219, 220–4, 228
    Paul's physics, 160, 163–73, 174, 175–6, 179–80
    Philo, 170–3
    resurrection, 117, 127, 163, 165, 173, 191
    further mentions, 26, 46, 214
poetry and poets, 44–5, 46, 113, 114; *see also* Muses
pollution, 13, 64–5, 88, 135, 270, 271
Pompeii, 69, 73
Poseidon, 72
Posidonius, 202
postmodernism, 10–11, 82, 132
post-structuralism, 6, 10–11, 82, 85, 242
practice theory *see* social theory of practice
prayer, 13, 53–4, 63, 88, 271
Preuss, Karl, 277
priesthood, 24, 64, 77, 79, 88, 91–2
primitivism, 201, 203, 204
Protestant Reformation, 26, 102, 215
Protestantism, 98, 185, 201, 203, 275
Pseudo-Heraclitus, 202, 205
psychology, 80–1, 196, 198–200; *see also* cognitive psychology; moral psychology
purity practices, 26, 64, 66–7, 88, 135
Pythagoras, 177, 178, 180
Pythagoreans, 178–80, 246

Q source, 240, 251, 257, 260, 266
Q'eqchi' Maya, 84, 86
Quintus Sextius, 178

rationality, 166, 172, 180, 234, 269, 276
reciprocity
    inscriptions, 65, 67–8, 74
    Judean religion, 91
    religion of associations, 63, 71–2, 75, 77, 79
    social kind sub-kinds of religion, 13–14, 37–9, 42, 59, 90, 137

recognition
    definition, 102
    response to Paul, 104, 110–11, 113, 122, 134, 153
Redaction Criticism, 235
religion
    definitions, 11–12, 35, 60, 144
    theory of, 4–10
religion of associations
    Christianity, 66, 74–9
    Corinthians, 104n
    families, 61–68, 70–3, 77
    Judean religion/Judaism, 63, 75, 92, 97
    occupational, 68–9, 70, 73–4
    overview of scholarship on, 57–8, 60–1, 69–70, 74, 76, 78
religion of everyday social exchange (RESE)
    description, 12–13, 58, 87–8
    religion of literate experts, interactions, 16, 43, 44–6, 48–52
    secrecy/knowledge dynamic, 267–72
    see also divinatory practices; families; gift-giving; households; prayer
religion of literate experts, 14–23, 27–8, 58, 60, 89–90; *see also* cultural economy (writings, interpretations, teachings); fields of knowledge
religion of literate experts and political power, 24, 55, 59, 75
religion of literate mythmaking, 271, 274–7
resurrection
    Corinthians, 117, 127, 135, 138, 139, 185, 186–7
    participation in Christ, 181–2, 185, 186–7, 191, 193
    Paul's physics, 160, 163, 165, 173
    pneuma, 117, 127, 163, 165, 173, 191
revelation, 65, 267, 269–71, 273–5
righteousness
    Abrahamic covenant, 117
    Matthew, 254–6, 258–61, 263, 265
    Paul's sin discourses, 211
    pneuma, 191, 229
    resurrection, 160
sacrifice, 51
suffering, 207
Ripat, Pauline, 152
Roman Catholicism, 26, 83, 98, 185, 275
Romans, Paul's letter to

righteousness (*cont.*)
  overview of scholarship on, 143–5, 150–1
  social formations approach, 142, 143, 151, 152–3, 155–6
Romanticism, 233, 234–5, 236
Rome
  Christianity, 143, 144, 145–9, 151
  civic religion, 88
  freelance Judean experts, 92, 150, 151–2, 155
  Gentiles, 144–6, 147, 151, 155
  households, 20, 145, 153–5
  Judaism, 143–6, 151–2
  religion of associations, 72–3, 74, 77
Rüpke, Jörg, 34n

Sabbath, 81, 84, 95–6, 143
sacrifice
  Jesus' death as, 32, 40, 41
  social kind sub-kinds of religion, 35, 39, 45, 66, 72, 91
  see also animal offerings
sage, Stoic concept of
  definition, 217, 225, 253–4
  Jesus, depicted by Matthew as, 252, 254–65
salvation
  participation in Christ, 104, 187–8, 190–1, 193
  Paul's audience, new human state, 226
  Paul's physics, 160, 173–4
  Paul's sin discourses, 212
  religion of literate experts, 79, 153
  utopian religion, 135
Sanders, Ed, 8, 80, 83, 181, 183, 185
Schweitzer, Albert, 181–2, 185, 229
Second Sophistic, 15, 16, 19, 43, 90, 108, 110
secrecy, 267–77
Sedley, David, 177
self, 130, 134, 165–6, 199, 213–14, 220, 224
self-authorization, 20–1, 23, 119, 134, 137
sensible/noetic dualism
  Paul's worldview, 162, 168, 172, 179–80, 221
  Philo's space between, 170–1, 221
  Platonism, 217–18
Sermon on the Mount, 250, 254–5, 261–2, 265
Shaw, Brent, 149
shrines, 61, 62, 64, 73, 109, 271

sin
  apex of sinfulness discourse, 209–12, 216
  degeneration of humanity discourse, 200–5, 216
  Gentile sinfulness discourse, 203–4, 205–12, 214, 215
  overview of scholarship on, 195–200
  psychology of sin discourse, 212–16
  sinlessness of Jesus, 263
slaves
  in Corinth, 107, 116, 120, 123
  literacy, 114–16
  religion of associations, 59n, 66, 73
Smith, Jonathan Z.
  Drudgery Divine, 26, 135, 136, 138, 195
  essentialism, 82
  locative/non-locative religion, 2, 50, 106–7, 134–6, 138, 139
  "Re: Corinthians," 101, 105–6, 107, 111–12, 119–20
  theory of religion, 4, 7–8
social body
  body metaphor (Rom.), 130–1
  pneumatic body of Christ (1 Cor.), 127–8, 130, 132, 133, 238–9
  see also community
social formations
  approach to studying Romans, 142, 143, 151, 152–3, 155
  types, 105, 244–5
  see also community; fields of knowledge; households
social hierarchy
  households, 66
  literate slaves, 114–16
  priests, 88, 91
  sacrificial practices, 52, 124–5, 128
  see also aristocracy/elites
social kind
  religion as, 2, 10–11, 14, 21, 27, 34
  sub-kinds, 11, 29, 34, 35, 86–90
  see also civic religion; religion of everyday social exchange (RESE); religion of literate experts; religion of literate experts and political power
social networks *see* network theory
social theory of practice
  Corinthians, 102, 120–1, 239
  Judaism, 82, 86
  overview, 6–10, 274, 277

society, conceptions of, 233–4
Society of Biblical Literature, 2–3, 6, 7
Solomon Islands, 269
sophists, 16–19, 20, 21, 23, 29, 45, 110; *see also* Second Sophistic
Sperber, Dan, 8
spiritual/material dualism, 102, 170–1
Stephanas, 112, 116, 243
Stern, Karen, 94
Stoicism
    Paul's audience, new human state, 218–19, 221, 224–5
    Paul's physics, 159, 160, 161–70, 171, 179–80
    Paul's sin discourses, 199, 200n, 201–2, 213–14
    of Philo, 170, 171, 179, 253, 254
    further mentions, 16, 186n–7n, 192, 250–1
    see also sage, Stoic concept of
Stowers, Stanley
    "Greeks Who Sacrifice and Those Who Do Not," 6
    A Rereading of Romans, 4, 6, 8–9, 188n
Struck, Peter, 47
structuralism, 6, 7, 85
substances
    contiguity, 186–7, 189, 194
    hierarchy, 160, 165, 176, 184–6, 189–90, 194
    interactivity, 192–3
    Philo, 170–3
    pneuma, 117
Suetonius, 149, 152
supernatural/natural dualism, 184, 185–6
symbolism and metaphor
    kinship, 140–1
    modernist view of religion, 38, 60, 184–5, 186, 194
    parables, 272–3
    Pauline participation in Christ, 183–6, 191, 194
    Paul's physics, 161–2, 163, 164, 165
    Paul's sin discourses, 199, 213–14
    pneuma, 26
    social kind sub-kinds of religion, 46–50, 52, 271
synagogues, 62, 75, 97, 143–6

teachers
    ideal, 29, 90, 114, 137
    Jesus as, 29, 250–1

    Paul as, 17–19, 20–1, 23
    religion of literate experts, 15
    see also sage, Stoic concept of
Tebtunis, religious association, 65
temples
    civic religion, 13, 59, 64, 88, 91–3
    Corinthians, 106
    Judaism, 89, 91–4
    offerings, 33–4, 50–1, 54, 91, 175
    religion of associations, 64, 75, 76, 77
Tertullian, 148, 192n
testing practices, 125, 126–8, 130–1, 133
Theodoret, 198
theological modernism, 102–5, 116, 119, 135–6
theory of religion, introduction, 4–10
Thessalonike, 74
Thiessen, Matthew, 144
Thrasyllus, 178
Tiberius, 148
Tilly, Charles, 70
time/temporality, 13, 37–8, 45, 59, 194; *see also* universalization
Tobit, 64, 96, 97
tombs, 62, 63, 64, 65, 96
Tönnies, Ferdinand, 233
traces, 267–8, 270, 272, 274
truth/true knowledge, 20–2, 24, 44, 90, 132; *see also* testing practices

universalization
    Christian subject, 247
    Gospels, 251–2, 264, 275
    Paul, 174–5, 203, 212, 216, 226
    social kind sub-kinds of religion, 49–50, 52, 109, 275, 277
    universal church, 248
utopian religion, 2, 135–6, 137–8

virtue, 225, 253, 255–60

Wallace-Hadrill, Andrew, 74
Walsh, Robyn, 29
Wasserman, Emma, 165–6, 198, 213–14, 223, 226
Wendt, Heidi, 92, 151

West Asian religion, 59, 87, 161–2, 200
Wilken, Robert, 31–2, 216
will
   and community, 234
   perversion of, 202–3, 206, 212, 214–15
   ruling vs. perverted, 198–9
Wittgenstein, Ludwig, 24

Xenophanes, 205

Yale University, 1–2, 3–4

Zeno of Citium (Zeno the Stoic), 16, 45, 49, 137
Zeus, versions of, 36, 44–6, 66–8, 124, 161, 252, 269